THE WILD WOODS

THE
WILD WOODS

A regional guide to Britain's ancient woodland

PETER MARREN

ESSO

NATURE
CONSERVANCY
COUNCIL

David & Charles

*To the all-weather, all-terrain field workers of the old
Nature Conservancy Council*

British Library Cataloguing in Publication Data

A catalogue record for this book is available from the
British Library

Copyright © Peter Marren and
The Nature Conservancy Council 1992

The right of Peter Marren to be identified as author of
this work has been asserted by him in accordance with
the Copyright, Designs and Patents Act 1988.

Typeset by John Youé
and printed in Italy
by Milanostampa SpA
for David & Charles plc
Brunel House   Newton Abbot Devon

CONTENTS

FOREWORD

With few, scattered and small exceptions, the British natural woodlands have been diminished and degraded to open heaths with scattered trees ... or else to coppiced scrub on the hillsides, or quaint pollards like the beeches of Burnham or the hornbeams of Epping. Our tall, unblemished woodlands are nearly all the outcome of planting by private landowners on lands enclosed during the past three hundred years. (H. L. Edlin)

The words are those of the late Herbert Edlin, the leading authority on Britain's trees in the 1950s and 1960s, and they reflect the then prevalent view of Britain's native woodland when 'modern forestry' had all but replaced traditional woodmanship in Britain. At that time the future of natural woodland in Britain looked bleak. The individuality of old woods, with their innate quirkiness and capacity to surprise and excite wonder, seemed destined for replacement by 'unblemished' high forest except on the few woodland nature reserves. The use of heavy machinery and herbicides was obliterating the detail of old woods, and the trees planted in their place grew up looking much the same whether one was in Cornwall, Kent or Caithness. Some species of wildlife adapted to the changes, some did not.

Since then, ancient woods have become better understood and more valued. They have been debated by politicians, have received special consideration in the national forestry policy, continue to be the subject of successful appeals by the Woodland Trust and by county wildlife trusts, and have been explored by major research programmes in ecology, history and forestry. It is scarcely possible now to say where human activity stops and nature begins in ancient woodland, so entangled is the relationship between them. What is important is that traditional ways of managing woodland have been good for wildlife, and that the abandonment of management has lessened the conservation value. The cessation of coppicing, for example, has led to a drastic reduction in woodland butterflies and much lower numbers of dormice and nightingales. Fortunately the renewed appreciation of ancient woodland has led to a remarkable revival of coppicing and pollarding during the 1980s, which has done much to revitalise the woods and restore a continuity stretching back to the mists of antiquity.

This book continues the themes of its predecessors, *Woodland Heritage* by Peter Marren and *Woodland Management and Conservation* by Charles Watkins, but this time the context is individual woods. In a sense it is an exploration of the 'blemishes' that make each ancient wood an individual and unique place, whether it is a Devon cleave, a Hereford dingle, a Hampshire hanger or a Kentish copse. In the following pages we explore the ancient and natural woods of each county of England, followed by a brisker tour of Wales and Scotland, in order to portray their regional character and to explain where ancient woods are found and why they are so different from one another. We pause at particular woods along the way to look at aspects of their history, wildlife and local culture and traditions. This book uses the term 'ancient woodland' in its broadest sense to include medieval wood-pastures such as Windsor Great Park and old wooded commons such as The Mens in Sussex, because it is mainly in such places that the oldest trees survive and on which many woodland plants and insects depend.

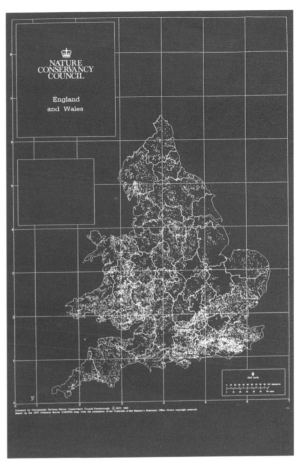

⇧*The distribution of ancient woodland in England and Wales. Each dot indicates one wood, irrespective of size and degree of modification by planting. It exaggerates the extent of ancient woodland in Wales and much of northern England where woods are generally small, but the general pattern is accurate, and shows the scarcity of old woods in former floodland (Humberside, Lindsey, Somerset Levels, The Fens, West Lancashire), in the agricultural heartlands (Norfolk, the east Midlands) and on thin soils (the Wiltshire chalk, west Cornwall, upland England).*
Note the importance of the south-east for ancient woodland – a landscape more like northern France than the rest of Britain

ACKNOWLEDGEMENTS

This book has been made possible through the generous sponsorship of Esso UK plc and has benefitted from the author's access to the vast body of unpublished woodland survey and research carried out by the Nature Conservancy Council between 1973 and 1991. I am grateful in particular to Drs George Peterken and Keith Kirby who were always ready to share their deep knowledge and experience of woodland matters. John Peters of Esso UK has been interested, patient and supportive throughout.

The majority of photographs in this book were taken specially by Peter Wakely and are, I feel, a tribute to his skill and patience (as anyone will know who has tried to photograph the inside of a wood, atmosphere and light are fickle, fleeting and elusive). In effect Peter did the whole job twice; the first set of illustrations were destroyed when the van carrying them to the printer caught fire and exploded, leaving us with the difficult task of finding a replacement set at short notice. I owe my deepest thanks to Peter for coming to the rescue with no loss of quality and also to Ted Green (Windsor pictures), Keith Kirby (Castle Eden Dene), Phil Page (Wistman's Wood), John Robinson (bark-stripping) and Paul Waring (Bernwood Forest) who also took pity and lent slides.

My thanks are also due to those who helped to compile the NCC's inventories of ancient woodland over the past decade, and whose dedication and hard work is now seeing fruit in the beneficial changes to national and local policies for native woodland. The inventories were primarily the work of the following:

Leonie Alexander	Dave Hutton
Jill Barton	Janet Lister
Jamie Bevan	Janet Millington
Ian Bolt	Mike Oxford
Lesley Bond	Stephanie Peay
Philip Bowsher	Andrew Pinches
Karen Buckley	Janice Rate
Rosie Carmichael	Celia Richardson
Alison Carter	Alison Roberts
Rob Cooke	Patrick Robinson
Caroline Eccles	Carol Russell
Sue Everett	David Shackleton
Sarah Garnett	Eileen Sothern
Alison Henchoz	Jonathan Spencer
Kathy Henderson	Rachel Thomas
Amanda Horsfall	Graham Walker
Damien Hughes	Tony Whitbread

I also thank the many members of the NCC's regional staff who read and commented on parts of the text, namely:

Brian Banks
Tim Barfield
John Barrett
Jill Barton
Johnny Birks
John Box
Richard Bradford
Andrew Brown
David Clayben
Bob Corns
John Cox
Hazel Drewitt
Douglas Gilbert
Amanda Giles
Richard Hall
David Harvey
Colin Hayes
Andrew Hearle
Jon Hickling
Dick Hornby
Gareth Howells
Anton Irving
Richard Jefferson
Mark July
Peter Kelly
Sarah Lambert
Maurice Massey
Shona Matheson

Roger Meade
Phil Page
Rosemary Parslow
Jeanette Plumridge
Keith Porter
Joanna Robertson
John Robinson
Keith Selmes
Chris Shaw
Peter Singleton
Ian Slater
Ted Smith
Tony Smith
Jonathan Spencer
Helen Stace
Jan Sylvester
Peter Tinning
Colin Tubbs
Chris Walker
Steven Warman
Janet Welsh
Jim White
Martin Wigginton
Rob Williams
Mike Williamson
Robert Wilkinson
Rob Wolton
Ray Woods
Sarah Woolven

My thanks too to Norman Lewis of the Nottinghamshire Wildlife Trust, Charles Watkins of the Royal Agricultural College, Mark Frater and Helen Read of the City of London Corporation and Professor Donald Pigott of the University of Cambridge for their valuable advice.

Particular thanks are owed to Maureen Symons who typed the whole manuscript so efficiently, to John Riggall, Stuart Wallace, Libby Gluyas and Janet Bateson who produced the county maps, to Shirley Penny, Malcolm Rush and the other NCC library staff for their help in obtaining publications, and to Stefa Kaznowska for her help in editing the text.

It is a pleasure to thank the many scholars whose published work I have referred to and the Woodland Trust and the county wildlife trusts of the Royal Society for Nature Conservation, of whose publications I have made free use. The responsibility for all errors and inconsistencies remains of course my own.

Peter Marren
Easton-on-the-Hill,
Northamptonshire

1
ANCIENT WOODS IN THE LANDSCAPE

One of the marvels of the British countryside is how no more than a dozen kinds of common native trees can produce so endless a variety of woods. Between the chestnut coppices of Kent and the wind-blasted scrub birches of Caithness lie muddy woods on East Anglian hilltops, full of ancient earthworks, moats and ponds; deep-shaded hornbeam woods that once supplied London's firewood; chalky beech hangers celebrated in the writings of Gilbert White and W. H. Hudson; the mellow ashwoods of the White Peak contrasting with the austere oak cloughs of the Dark; the embossed, crab-limbed 'tree-men' of medieval deer parks that 'look as if they had been at the beginning and making of the world, and will probably see its end'; the stately Highland pinewoods, with their light-flecked billowing of blue-green needles and red-plated bark, and many more. There are also woods in unexpected places: the creek woods of the Solent and the Cornish rivers with their feet in salt water; dwarf woods of twisting trees whose mossy boughs straggle over bare boulders, such as Wistman's Wood on Dartmoor and Keskadale Wood in Cumbria; and woods on sea-cliffs in Dyfed, pruned by brine-laden winds into chest-high mats of foliage. In parts of the country there are woods called dingles or dumbles, grips or shaws, hursts or groves. There are woods on clay thick enough for the potter's wheel; or on sand almost as loose as a beach; or projecting from clefts in bare rock.

Each ancient wood expresses not only the natural landscape in which it is rooted and the trees and shrubs of which it is composed, but also the use that mankind has made of it, often over countless generations. Each has been to varying degrees hard-worked, loved, misunderstood, exploited, protected. They have seen the coming and going of boars and wolves, slaves, huntsmen, outlaws, charcoal burners, men with picks and shovels and axes, women with barking irons, men with chainsaws and defoliants, naturalists with binoculars, scientists with tape measures and surveying instruments. Woods have always been highly valued, whether as a source of building material and firewood, as the preserve of deer or pheasants, or simply for their beauty and sense of wonder.

WHAT IS ANCIENT WOODLAND?
For a couple of centuries agriculturalists and foresters have distinguished between woods consisting of planted trees and those which seemed to be natural in origin and were generally managed as coppices. In general, the former are recent and the latter long-established. Although there can be no

Ancient and natural woodland: neglected coppice ⇨ at Thorpe Wood, Peterborough (PETER WAKELY)

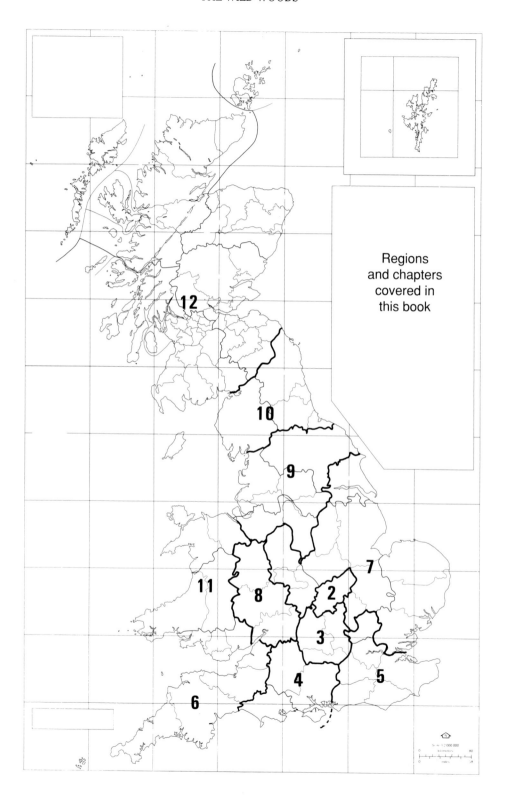

Regions
and chapters
covered in
this book

hard-and-fast distinction between ancient and not-so-ancient woods, for practical purposes it is convenient to draw a line at the year 1600. It was at around this time that the first reasonably accurate maps were being produced. Then, and for some time afterwards, tree planting took place on a limited scale and mostly in orchards, parks and the grounds of large houses, and only rarely in woods. We can assume, therefore, that virtually all woods in existence in 1600 were of natural, and not planted, origin.

In some cases, particularly in East Anglia, it is possible to trace the history of a wood back into the Middle Ages. Hayley Wood in Cambridgeshire, for example, is the Haly Wood of a survey of 1650 and the *Boscus de Heyle* belonging to the Bishop of Ely in 1251. If we could travel back to 1650 or even 1251, we would probably find little change in Hayley Wood, although its surroundings would be very different. Where such documentation does not exist, it is still possible to identify ancient woodland from physical and biological clues such as the presence of undisturbed soil profiles (which indicate that the land has never been ploughed) or of plants known to be poor colonisers, such as small-leaved lime or wild service tree. In some woods there are large coppice stools and pollarded trees that were probably alive in 1600 (although it is seldom possible to age them accurately by annual rings because their interiors have usually rotted away).

Scientific and historical detective work apart, there is usually a *feel* to ancient woodland compounded of a network of mysterious banks and lanes, irregularities in the twist and bend of the trunks and boughs, a layer of *underwood* beneath the canopy trees, and spreading carpets of spring flowers such as primroses, bluebells and wood anemones. In short, there is an intimacy, a density of warp and weft, that is lacking in more recent woodland where such a complexity of detail has not had time to evolve. It is well known that many kinds of plants and animals are found mainly in places that combine stability with variety of natural habitat. Mature bark plastered with large li-chens, boulders and streambanks bearing lush growths of mosses, liverworts and ferns, and large, partly decaying trunks with sticky runnels of sap and holes part-filled by rainwater and rotting plant material are among the features almost confined, over much of Britain, to ancient woodland.

Ten years ago, the then Nature Conservancy Council (NCC) embarked on an ambitious project aimed at finding out how much ancient woodland survives in Britain and to plot its distribution accurately[1]. It was based on a comparison of eighteenth- and nineteenth-century maps with recent aerial photographs, and was backed up by information gathered in the field and, in some cases, by historical material. The completed maps, many of which are reproduced for the first time in this book, reveal intriguing patterns in the distribution of our ancient woodland. In some areas the woodland follows river valleys, representing leafy ribbons through treeless hill country. In others, woods are clumped together, sometimes within former Royal Forests, sometimes in former iron-working areas such as Furness in the Lake District or the Weald in Sussex and Kent. Fertile, intensively farmed countryside and upland grazings have relatively few ancient woods, but no mainland county or district is wholly devoid of them. Even large towns and cities have their share.

In 1984, the Forestry Commission estimated that Britain had 2,000,000ha (4.9 million acres) of woodland. The NCC estimated that, of this, just over one quarter – about 575,000ha (1.4 million acres) – is of probable ancient origin.

Most well-preserved ancient woods are rather small; the majority are farm woods of less than 20 ha (50 acres), surrounded by open fields or moors. Very few are larger than 400ha (988 acres). In the lowlands, woods are nearly always found on soils that are too wet or too infertile to grow crops. In the uplands, they usually occupy land too steep or too inaccessible to be worth clearing for pasture. In some upland moors, they are confined to inaccessible places such as gorges and 'cloughs', where saplings and shoots can find refuge from sheep and deer.

WHATEVER HAPPENED
TO THE WILDWOODS?

For the past two thousand years and, we are beginning to discover, for long before that, England has been a country in which a large rural population could only be fed, clothed and housed by putting most of the available land to work. Even in the Royal Forests, commoners held a variety of rights that included the freedom to graze cattle and pigs, cut underwood and lop dead boughs. For that reason, almost all long-established woodland in Britain shows signs of past use, and has been considerably modified from the tall, dense forests that are assumed to have been their prehistoric ancestors. Scotland and Wales are more thinly populated, but since much of the land is treeless moor or mountain, the pressures on fertile land were possibly even greater than in England (in Wales one hears of farmers growing crops *in* woods!). There was probably little real wilderness even in medieval Scotland.

From at least Norman times onwards, all land has been owned by someone, the boundaries marked by fences, banks and hedges, and the rights attached to each property carefully documented. Ownership implies management, and it is possible that many ancient woods were managed in much the same way from the Bronze Age down to the nineteenth century. The main need of the rural population was for small-bore wood, not large timber. Most houses were built of wattles within timber frames. Everyone needed firewood. Farmers wanted pole-sized wood for tool handles and spokes. Forgemasters needed small wood to make charcoal, tanners the bark from young 'black poles' of oak. Such wood was obtained from the *underwood*, maintained as young, bushy growth by a system of regular cutting known as *coppicing* (see below). In some woods there were evidently no canopy trees at all, but more often timber trees were also grown as *standards*, generally at about a dozen to the acre. Even these were seldom allowed to reach maturity. The absence of big tall trees in British woods is often blamed on wartime emergency fellings in the twentieth century, but such

trees were traditionally the exception rather than the rule. Until the invention of power sawmills, large trunks were needed only occasionally for special uses, such as beams for halls and cathedrals or windmill posts. In Britain, we have no forests of large trees like the famous Bialowieza National Park in Poland (which incidentally was preserved not for timber but for hunting). We had too many farmers and not enough land.

WHAT IS SPECIAL
ABOUT BRITISH WOODLAND?

It is easy (almost instinctive) to take an over-modest view of our native woods and to assume that there are better examples of everything on the opposite sides of the English Channel or the North Sea. Norway certainly contains bigger, wilder woods than any comparable wood in Scotland. At Compiègne, in France, there are mighty four-hundred-year-old trees with sound timber of a kind that has not been seen here since the thirteenth century. Continental woods generally contain more kinds of mammals, amphibians, butterflies or flowers than British woods. We no longer have big fierce animals such as boars and wolves. Over the centuries, our landscape has evolved as a small-scale patchwork of small woods set in farmland or moorland, and today ancient woodland covers only 2 per cent of the land. France, although another country of intensive agriculture, has ten times as much; nearly one-third of Czechoslovakia is ancient woodland. Moreover, both of these countries contain a much greater area of mature forest than Britain and a greater range of methods of managing them.

On the other hand, the varied climate and geology of Britain combine to produce woods of great complexity and botanical variation that quite belie their diminutive size. The number of types of

You could wring the wet from this Atlantic wood ⇨
at Inverfarigaig by Loch Ness: the boughs drip with
mosses and lichens; moss cushions cover every
stump, boulder and fallen bough.
And this is the dry season: June (PETER WAKELEY)

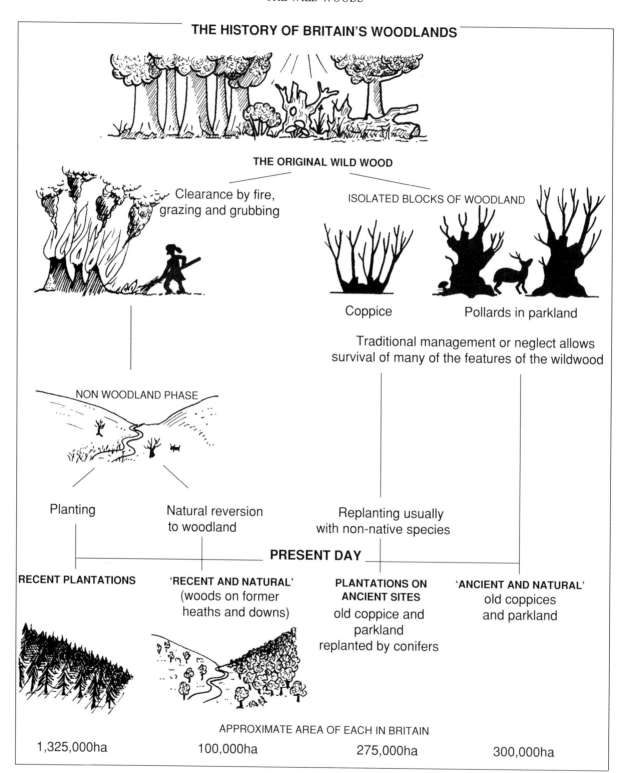

THE HISTORY OF BRITAIN'S WOODLANDS

THE ORIGINAL WILD WOOD

Clearance by fire, grazing and grubbing

ISOLATED BLOCKS OF WOODLAND

Coppice

Pollards in parkland

Traditional management or neglect allows survival of many of the features of the wildwood

NON WOODLAND PHASE

Planting

Natural reversion to woodland

Replanting usually with non-native species

PRESENT DAY

RECENT PLANTATIONS

'RECENT AND NATURAL' (woods on former heaths and downs)

PLANTATIONS ON ANCIENT SITES old coppice and parkland replanted by conifers

'ANCIENT AND NATURAL' old coppices and parkland

APPROXIMATE AREA OF EACH IN BRITAIN

1,325,000ha   100,000ha   275,000ha   300,000ha

natural woodland present in Britain is about the same as those of Belgium and Switzerland, where comparable studies have been made. Moreover our ancient woods are important historical monuments precisely *because* they have been used intensively for a long time. They bear the hallmark of time as visibly as a rustic village or a parish church.

A fundamental difference between Britain's woods and those on the European mainland is that we have only three native conifers: Scots pine, juniper and yew. Silver fir, Norway spruce and

larch, native across the sea, evidently failed to colonise Britain before the land bridge was severed about seven thousand years ago. Most of our woods are therefore composed of broadleaved trees. Among the most widespread are ash, hazel and elm, which do well in our mild, humid climate. Beech and hornbeam, which need hot summers and freezing winters, are confined as native trees to the most 'continental' parts of Britain.

Britain belongs to the Atlantic fringe of Europe, where the rainfall is high and where warm coastal currents keep much of the western coast free of ice. Our conditions are particularly favourable for plants that need moist, humid conditions all year round and we have an outstanding range of them. Bluebells, with their need for places that are neither too dry nor too wet, do particularly well in Britain. The group of plants which benefit most from our climate, however, are the mosses, liverworts and lichens, many of which are confined to the western shores and offshore islands of Europe. Because they are so small and overlooked

◁ *How Britain's woods have developed*

⬇ *The proportion of different types of woodland in Britain (based on the Forestry Commission census 1979-82 and on the NCC's inventories of ancient woodlands)*

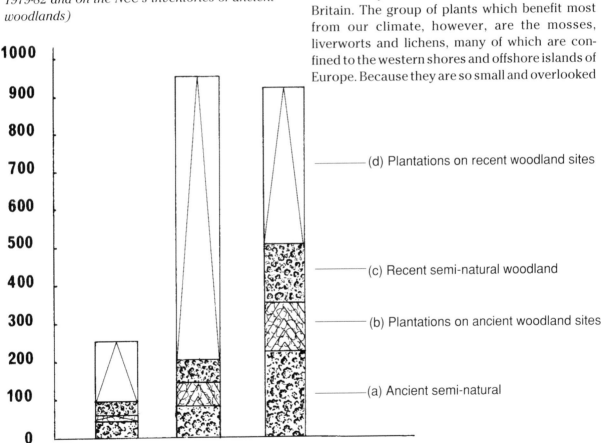

(d) Plantations on recent woodland sites

(c) Recent semi-natural woodland

(b) Plantations on ancient woodland sites

(a) Ancient semi-natural

WALES   SCOTLAND   ENGLAND

by the layman, we tend to underestimate their value. For these plants, however, Britain is of world importance.

The other aspect of ancient woodland that sets Britain apart is the survival here of an ancient system of combining grazing and wood cutting on the same patch of land and known as wood-pasture. Wood-pasture survives, though sometimes swallowed up in recent woodland, on commons, in the native Highland pinewoods and in long-established parkland throughout Britain. It is characterised by wide-spaced, often very old, trees set in grass. Large old trees are normally rare in woods except along ownership boundaries, but in former wood-pasture we have more trees aged over five hundred years than almost any other European nation. Apart from their often dramatic appearance, such trees are very important for wildlife, especially for plants and animals that are associated with mature bark and dead wood. One reason for their survival is Britain's remarkably stable land tenure. A surprisingly large number of woods and parks have been owned by the same family or institution since Tudor times (some were sold off after 1945). The rarity of invasions, civil wars or social revolutions was a force for woodland conservation in England and Wales (Scotland was less fortunate). Collections of mighty trees such as those in Windsor Great Park or the New Forest would probably have fared ill during the French Revolution or the continental wars – for in times of social upheaval such trees often met the same fate as their owners.

EXPLANATION OF TERMS USED IN THIS BOOK

Throughout this book I have used the word 'natural' in the sense of being primarily to do with nature, not man. Thus a wood is described as natural when it is of unplanted origin and regenerates spontaneously, even though it has provided underwood and timber to generations of farmers. Our ancient woods, and particularly their underwood, are much less the creation of man than was once believed, and their soils and some of their plant communities are probably descended

little changed from the prehistoric virgin forest. The *structure* has changed; the *composition* much less so. So, by 'ancient and natural' I mean a wood at least four hundred years old that is still composed mostly of unplanted vegetation. In the Middle Ages most woods were ancient and natural.

Ancient woods originated in two ways. *Primary woods* have been wooded continuously since the original virgin forest (called here by the term coined by Oliver Rackham, *The Wildwood*). They have never been cleared completely. Scientists now believe that a large number of ancient woods have at least a core of primary woodland on steep banks or wet places that were impossible to farm. The Wye Valley, Borrowdale in Cumbria, the Weald and the East Anglian boulder clay are among the places where these oldest of woods are found. *Secondary* woods developed over open ground formerly used for some other purpose. Some secondary woods are ancient; many ancient woods show signs of medieval ridge and furrow that subsequently reverted to woodland. At times of upheaval or plague, during the Saxon invasions, say, or after the Black Death, the abandonment of farmland led to the widespread formation of secondary woods. More recent secondary woods can be found in a variety of places where previous uses have lapsed: on disused railway cuttings, former grouse moors and ungrazed commons, for example. Woods continue to develop before our eyes: conservationists battle hard to prevent lowland heaths and downs from turning into woodland.

Today, just over half of Britain's ancient woodland is believed to be 'natural'. The rest has been clear-felled and replaced by planted trees, most of them conifers. In most instances, this fundamental change was made recently, especially during the 1950s and 1960s, and these woods therefore retain some of their original wildlife along the rides and in places where the original vegetation survives. In the drier parts of Britain especially, plantation forestry in ancient woodland has often failed and the native underwood has grown up again. In many cases the conifers are gradually being cleared and natural, or at least broadleaved, woodland re-

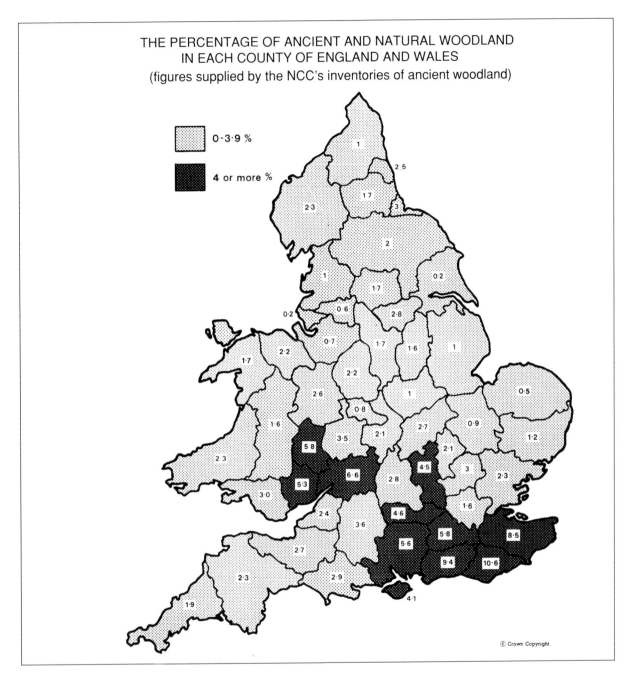

THE PERCENTAGE OF ANCIENT AND NATURAL WOODLAND
IN EACH COUNTY OF ENGLAND AND WALES
(figures supplied by the NCC's inventories of ancient woodland)

0-3.9 %

4 or more %

© Crown Copyright.

stored. If these trends continue, the proportion of 'natural' woods compared to replanted woods should rise.

Traditional woodland management systems were the subject of another book in this series, called *Woodland Management and Conservation*. In the present book I refer to four basic systems: coppice, coppice-with-standards, high forest and wood-pasture. *Coppice* is a system that takes advantage of the ability of most trees to grow up

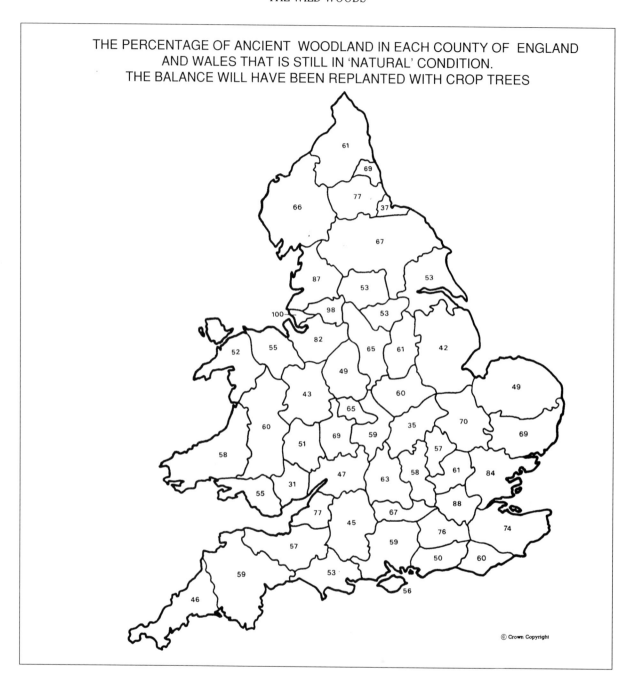

THE PERCENTAGE OF ANCIENT WOODLAND IN EACH COUNTY OF ENGLAND
AND WALES THAT IS STILL IN 'NATURAL' CONDITION.
THE BALANCE WILL HAVE BEEN REPLANTED WITH CROP TREES

© Crown Copyright

again as a thicket of shoots from the cut stump; it seems to have been invented in the Stone Age. The shoots are produced from dormant buds situated on the side of the stump or *stool,* or from buds arising from living tissue around the edge of the cut surface. Coppice shoots are self-thinning, with some of the smaller shoots dying each year until between two and about fifteen remain, producing a characteristic clump or ring of slender trunks. Coppice is usually cut close to the ground, but on

20

land liable to waterlogging a taller stump is left. Coppicing was a useful system for producing firewood and small-to-medium-sized wood up to pole size. Major uses included bark for tanning (oak), charcoal (oak, alder), cleft pale fencing (oak, sweet chestnut) and hop poles (oak, ash).

In order to provide a steady supply of wood, some large coppices were, from the fifteenth century onwards, organised into compartments of roughly equal area, one of which was felled every year so that the entire wood was cut over every twenty years or so. Other woods were probably cut over on a more irregular basis. Coppicing requires a good system of tracks to extract the wood and an exacting standard of woodmanship. Dead coppice stools were generally replaced not by planting but by *layering* or 'plashing', especially for hazel, lime, ash and sweet chestnut. This involves cutting shoots about halfway through, bending them over like a croquet hoop and pegging them down. Root and shoot production is stimulated by making short cuts through the bark. If successful, the layered stool is cut from its parent plant after two or three years. In woods managed as *coppice-with-standards*, taller trees grown for timber were grown along with the coppiced underwood. The favourite standard tree was oak, followed by beech and ash.

High forest consists of tall trees grown for timber and felled when mature. Woods of this kind are often plantations. The oak plantations of Alice Holt, Dean, Delamere and elsewhere were early examples, grown on Crown-owned land as a source of cheap timber for the Royal Navy. Ancient coppices can be converted to high forest by 'storing' or 'singling' the coppice, that is, by selecting healthy stems to grow up and mature. In some woods this conversion has been deliberate policy, in others the consequence of the abandonment of systematic management. High forests are cooler and shadier than coppices, and big, shade-bearing trees such as beech do better than small, light-demanding ones like hazel. On the whole, they are poorer in wildlife because they lack the open glades and varied structure of managed coppices. The birch-

woods of the Scottish Highlands and young woods that have sprung up on recently abandoned land are also, in effect, high forest.

TYPES OF ANCIENT WOODLAND

Ancient and natural woods have been classified by Dr George Peterken into a series of basic types known as *stands*, named after the main communities of trees and underwood. Although there are other ways of classifying woodland, I have chosen the Peterken method because it is easy to use[2]. Bear in mind, however, that most ancient woods contain more than one stand type, and some trees, such as coppiced maples or wych elms, may not be as conspicuous as big oaks and beeches but are equally significant.

1 *Ash-wych elm woodland*
Throughout Britain, but most widespread in the west. Mostly on valley sides on base-rich soil and managed formerly as coppice. On free-draining soils the floor is often awash with dog's mercury or, particularly in western districts, wild garlic.
2 *Ash-maple woodland*
England and South Wales. Woods containing maple, usually with ash, hazel and oak, and typical of heavy soils in the Midlands and drier soils in east and south-west England. Traditionally managed as coppice. Complex, beautiful woods, often rich in wild flowers.
3 *Hazel-ash woodland*
Widespread except in north-east Scotland. Usually contains oak (often planted) as well as hazel and ash. Mainly on acid soils in the lowlands, but more often on alkaline loams in the north and west. Also rich in wild flowers.
4 *Ash-lime woodland*
Local concentrations in England and Wales, especially the Welsh borders, Lincolnshire, East Anglia and north-west England. Mainly on acid loams in east England but on alkaline soils in north-west England and Wales.
5 *Oak-lime woodland*
Local concentrations in England and Wales, but rare in the south. These are woods that contain

lime but not ash, lie on acid soils and are managed as coppice.

6 Birch-oak woodland
Throughout Britain. Woods on acid, mostly free-draining soils, dominated by pedunculate and/or sessile oak. Traditionally managed as coppice or wood-pasture.

7 Alder woodland
Throughout Britain. Always on wet soil, usually in valley bottoms and streamsides, but sometimes on flushed slopes and flat plateaux. Alders are often accompanied by pedunculate oak, hazel, ash and bird cherry.

8 Beech woodland
South England and South Wales. Beech-dominated woods on acid and calcareous soil, and generally managed as high forest or wood-pasture.

9 Hornbeam woodland
Mainly south-east England with a few outliers. Woods containing hornbeam, often with oak, on a variety of soil types. Usually former coppice or wood-pasture.

10 Suckering elm woodland
Throughout Britain as patches of common or small-leaved elm in woodland. Occasionally elm dominates the wood.

11 Chestnut woodland
Mainly south-east England, but locally in East Anglia and south-west England. Woods dominated by sweet chestnut, often on acid, light soils, usually planted but sometimes long-established. Managed as coppice.

12 Pine woodland
The native pinewoods of Scotland, which usually contain birch and, sometimes, oak.

13 Birch woodland
Widespread throughout Britain on a variety of soils, but normally a temporary stage except in parts of upland Scotland. A local variant is birch-hazel woodland that characterises north-west Scotland.

Most of these types of woodland have been further subdivided, according to soil type and degree of wetness, and according to the presence or absence of particular trees.

⇦The delicate stars of the wood anemone, Anemone nemorosa, are among the most familiar woodland flowers; but large carpets of anemone are confined to ancient woodland over much of Britain
(PETER WAKELY)

2
ANCIENT WOODLAND IN ONE COUNTY:
Northamptonshire

INTRODUCTION

Professor W. G. Hoskins ended his best-known book, *The Making of the English Landscape* (1955), by describing the view from the window of his study at Eynsham in Oxfordshire, a landscape that had absorbed the impact of more than ten centuries of rural life. In barely more than half a mile he could pick out ancient fishponds and hedgebanks, a Victorian park, a medieval church and the soft mounds in the field where a village had stood before its inhabitants were wiped out by the Black Death. The window of my own study in Easton-on-the-Hill, Northamptonshire, overlooks no more than a garden and a splendid roofscape of Collyweston slates, but from my village pub, The Oak, you can see the ancient woods of the parish. The Oak itself is not named after any particular oak, and ours is not in fact an oaky neighbourhood: our hedgerows bristle with ash poles and elm suckers and wind-battered ash trees. At the turn of the century many hybrid limes were planted in the village to celebrate Queen Victoria's diamond jubilee. There is a fine square of them in the churchyard accompanying small round yews, and a row of pollard limes graces the street beside the Manor House. In certain gardens there are strangely shaped high-cut limes that have been lopped and trimmed many times to prevent overshading, and have developed into top-heavy trees with notched trunks, like giant rustic broomsticks. Planting

fashions change, and today the craze is for horse chestnuts.

The Oak Inn faces a plateau of oolitic limestone in a loop of the River Welland. Hoskins knew this area well, and after visiting the parish churches of Rutland, just across the river, would, if the weather was fine, sometimes eat a picnic lunch in the hedgebanks of our neighbouring village, Tixover. The plateau was fated to become a wartime aerodrome, later lengthened to accommodate jets. The airfield severed the old wide-verged lane that used to run across the plateau to the Rockingham Forest village of King's Cliffe. Until the 1950s, there was an ancient wood at one end of it called Vigo Wood. Only a shrunken scrap now remains, but at the place where the wood once abutted the lane stands a fine pollarded small-leaved elm, a distinctive tree that probably served as a boundary mark. What is now the busy A47 is lined on both sides by hedgerows in which there are more elms, beautiful trees bearing a delicate tracery of crisp oval leaves. There is also a row of battered, windblown oaks, survivors of the airfield clearance. These are 'ghost hedges' descended from woodland – oak is almost never found in planted hedgerows in this area.

Easton and its neighbours, Collyweston and Wittering, are elongated parishes whose boundaries meet in woodland, visible from The Oak as a line of trees on the horizon. The woodland is divided into three by banks and ditches with old

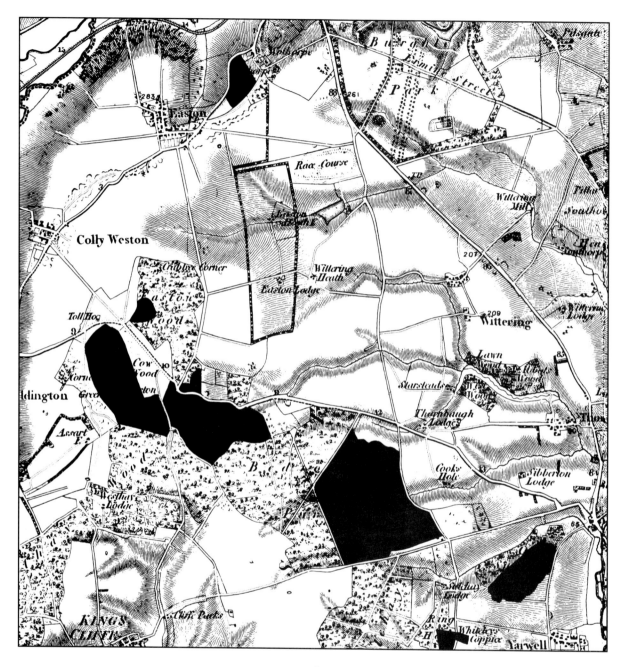

⇧ *The landscape near Easton, Collyweston and Wittering as it was 150 years ago. Ten years after this map was made, about half of the woodland was grubbed up. The centre of the map around Easton Lodge is now an airfield. The woods that remain are shown in solid black*

24

lanes running between them. The woods are, from west to east, Collyweston Great Wood (145ha) [358 acres], Easton Hornstocks (50ha) [123 acres] and Wittering Coppice (15ha) [37 acres]. They have been part of the Burghley Estate since the late sixteenth century when they formed part of a gift of land made by Queen Elizabeth I to her loyal chancellor William Cecil, the first Lord Burghley. They are divided by a network of old lanes connecting the villages with their woods, and their boundaries are marked by banks and pollarded trees. The older trees are nearly all coppice stools, showing evidence of many cycles of cutting and regeneration. The woods were probably used by commoners exercising their age-old rights to harvest underwood and lop dead boughs. Except for some mature beech trees that were planted by the estate, these woods have few large trees. Their appearance is one of dense, even-aged young growth from stools last cut about forty years ago. Now that markets for coppice products are so few, the estate is thinning the stools to promote a potentially more profitable high forest of oak and ash. The woods have also been put to non-woodland uses. The middle of Collyweston Wood is used by RAF Wittering to store bombs while part of Easton Hornstocks has been dug out by quarrymen.

These woods are rich in wildlife. They lie on a natural mosaic of sandy hillocks and clay dells which has apparently never been turned over and mixed by the plough. In May, the sandy areas support beautiful drifts of bluebells and open glades filled with bracken. Before the quarrymen got at it, lily-of-the-valley used to be common under the bracken at Easton Hornstocks. On the clay, dog's mercury and wild garlic or ramsons carpet the ground with their broad green leaves in early summer. Nightingales are often heard in May and June, and tree pipits launch into their cheerful, twittery song flight over the glades.

There is sufficient documentary and map information and field evidence for us to be certain that these are ancient woods [3]. It is possible that their coppiced underwood, consisting entirely of self-sown trees, may even preserve their original primeval composition. Parts are dominated by the small-leaved lime, which no longer regenerates well in England and is rarely found outside old woodland. Lime is commercially almost worthless and is never planted, except recently as a novelty tree. Most of the limes are small or medium-sized coppice stools, but there are also a few large ones 2m (6.5ft) across, that were probably contemporaries of the first Lord Burghley. The name 'hornstocks' probably reflects the smooth, horn-like regrowth of coppiced lime. In places, lime grows with sessile oak and ash in an unusual combination again confined to woods known from other evidence to be ancient. The sum total of plant species in these woods is also impressive. They are particularly rich in flowers such as wood anemone, wood spurge, yellow archangel, lily-of-the-valley and sweet woodruff which are, in this area at least, considered reasonably faithful indicators of ancient woodland. Collyweston Wood and its neighbours, therefore, retain much of their original beauty and variety, despite having been replanted here, cleared there, and generally knocked about or excavated.

WOODLAND SIZE AND DISTRIBUTION

Our map, prepared from the NCC's ancient woodland inventory for Northamptonshire (1988), shows dense concentrations of woodland in the north and south, a scatter of woods elsewhere and large areas in the centre, around Kettering, Northampton and Wellingborough, which have no old woods at all. This pattern is mostly the product of geology and soils. Historically, woodland has nearly always occupied the least fertile ground: sour, hungry sands or sticky, waterlogged clays or slopes too steep for the plough. Just over 5 per cent of the county is wooded – below the national average of 8 per cent but significantly more than most of its neighbours. About three-fifths of Northamptonshire's woods are considered to be of ancient origin, the rest being secondary woods formed naturally or planted on formerly open land since AD 1600. The ancient woods vary from tiny copses

Small-leaved lime coppice and wild garlic on wet ⇨
clay at Collyweston Great Wood, Northamptonshire. The stools were last cut in about 1950. April
(PETER WAKELY)

⇩ *The distribution of ancient woodland in*
Northamptonshire (see text)

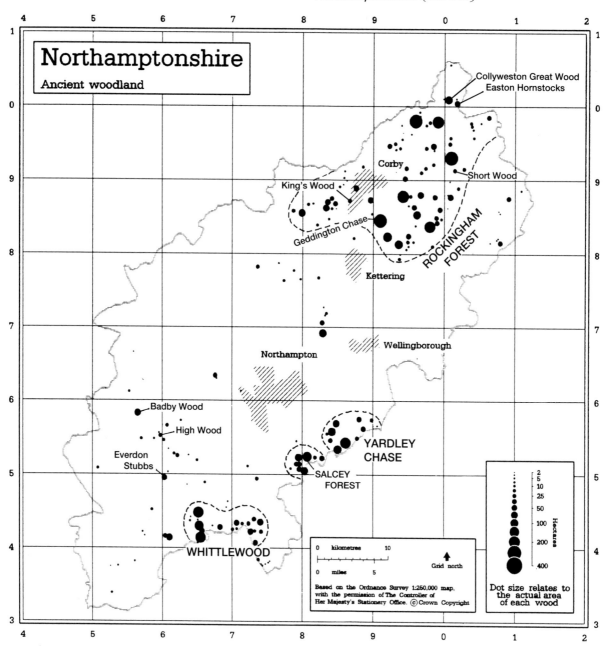

Northamptonshire

Ancient woodland

Collyweston Great Wood
Easton Hornstocks

Corby

King's Wood

Short Wood

Geddington Chase

ROCKINGHAM FOREST

Kettering

Wellingborough

Northampton

Badby Wood

High Wood

YARDLEY CHASE

Everdon Stubbs

SALCEY FOREST

WHITTLEWOOD

0   kilometres   10

0   miles   5

Grid north

Based on the Ordnance Survey 1:250,000 map,
with the permission of The Controller of
Her Majesty's Stationery Office. © Crown Copyright

2
5
10
25
50
100
200
400

Hectares

Dot size relates to
the actual area
of each wood

of only 1ha (2.47acres) or so up to what are by English standards large woods of 200-300ha (494 - 741 acres). Large woods are more prevalent in Northamptonshire than in many other English counties but they are nearly all confined to ancient forests and chases.

Now for the bad news. Fully two-thirds of the ancient and natural woodland existing in Northamptonshire in 1920 has since been cleared away for housing, roads or quarries, or to make room for more farmland, or converted to plantations of mainly non-native coniferous trees. Most woods in this county lie on gentle inclines easily accessible to deep ploughs. After 1945 many of them were purchased by the Forestry Commission, whose mandate was to produce fast-growing timber. The high density of woodland in parts of Northamptonshire added to their potential profitability as plantations.

According to the NCC's inventory, the total area of ancient woodland of 2ha (5 acres) and over in Northamptonshire is as follows:

ANCIENT AND NATURAL WOODLAND	2,277ha (5,626 acres) [32%]
REPLANTED since c 1920	4,230ha (10,452 acres) [58%]
CLEARED since c 1920	713ha (1,761 acres) [10%]

Fortunately nature conservation is now an objective of a good proportion of Northamptonshire's ancient woods. By 1988, some 1,074ha (2,654 acres) of ancient woodland – 15 per cent of the total – were Sites of Special Scientific Interest (SSSI) designated by the Nature Conservancy Council and many of these are nature reserves owned by the Northamptonshire Wildlife Trust or the Forestry Commission.

THE ROYAL FORESTS

The densest areas of woodland in Northampton-shire lie within the perambulations of medieval forests and chases, land on which the king or powerful members of the nobility once held hunting rights. Rockingham Forest in the north was a Royal Forest in which the king owned some of the land and occasionally hunted there from his lodge at King's Cliffe. At the opposite end of the county were three smaller, more compact forests; Yardley Chase, Whittlewood and Salcey Forest. Forests are not always well-wooded – a forest in the medieval sense is a place of deer, not trees, but in Northamptonshire they coincide with the best wooded areas and were indeed originally demarcated for that reason.

Rockingham Forest is well documented[4]. It is a good place to look at how the woods of a medieval forest were used and how they survived into modern times after the legal system that maintained them was abolished. Rockingham Forest was more fertile and better populated than many forests. There were twelve forest villages, each of which held rights in woods. Partly for that reason and also because, unlike the forests of Hampshire or Dean in Gloucestershire, Rockingham Forest was remote from the naval dockyards, it never became dominated by great oaks grown for ship timber. Most of its woods were managed as coppice-with-standards. Coppice crafts were an important mainstay of the local economy down to the early years of the present century, when King's Cliffe was a centre for wood-turning and carving, based on abundant local supplies of cheap or free wood. As late as the 1960s, hazel coppice was still being cut from woods near Pipewell for hedge binders and stakes.

Rockingham Forest contained four or five main blocks of woodland, together with numerous much smaller woods generally of less than 50ha (123.5 acres), which seem to have been ordinary parish woods in which the king's huntsmen and bailiffs took little interest. The larger woods were divided by woodbanks and fences into individually named compartments of about 20ha (49.4 acres). Many of the latter still survive. There were 'thicks' – dense, perhaps thorn-ridden, coppices; 'slades' – valleys or dells, often with alders; 'sales', where woodsales were held after a felling; 'thorns', probably recent thickets on former plains; as well as rustic, descriptive names such as 'stubbs' and 'hornstocks'. 'Hayes', as in Sulehay and Fotheringhay, were areas in which paling fences channelled the deer as, driven by dogs, they ran into an ambush of waiting bowmen. The names first surface in the great survey of Crown woods of 1564, but they are probably much older.

The history of **Geddington Chase,** which has been studied by Mr Burl Bellamy[5], is representative of the Forest as a whole. Originally called Geddington Wood, it used to be the third largest block of woodland in the Forest measuring about 400ha (988 acres). What remains of it can be seen from miles away as a dark line of trees on the crest of a ridge, the usual place for large woods in Rockingham Forest. Within, it has the characteristic bumpy terrain of virgin unploughed soils and is full of dells and banks and winding streams that become sudden torrents after heavy rain. The wood was originally divided into twenty named compartments separated by grass-covered tracks and rides. Most, with names like Little Hames Sale, Rising Bridge Quarter and Blackmore Thick, were cut over on rotation as coppices. Birchtree Lawn and Langley Plain were wood-pasture, that is open, common grazing land, probably with a scatter of pollards to supply winter feed for deer.

The commoners of Geddington, a more significant settlement in the Middle Ages than now (witness its large Norman church, massive stone bridge and the beautiful Eleanor's Cross in the village square), held rights of pasture there for all animals except goats and pigs more than a year old. They could also collect *estover* (firewood) and quotas of 'woodbote', 'cartbote' and 'housebote' for repair work. In exchange for these liberties, each commoner was required to make three ploughings and mowings annually for the king's bailiff and to present him with a hen at Christmas and a dozen eggs at Easter.

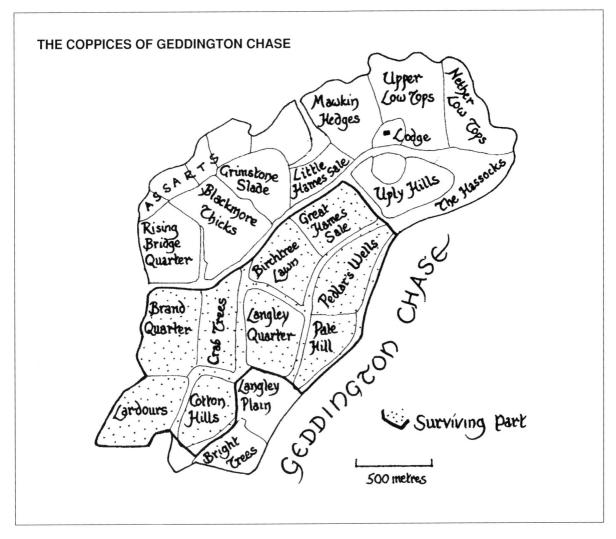

THE COPPICES OF GEDDINGTON CHASE

Surviving park

500 metres

The Crown survey of 1564 itemises 8,781 oak standards at Geddington Wood – about a dozen per acre of underwood. The survey describes the underwood in some detail and it seems to have been then, as now, a mixture of coppiced ash, hazel, maple, thorn and sallow on wet boulder clay. 'Thorn' probably includes both hawthorn and the dense blackthorn thickets that can rapidly establish on open or recently cleared land on these sticky soils. After each felling, the Crown held annual wood sales of timber, underwood, bark and faggots (but not, as in Roman and Norman times, of charcoal). Even as early as 1564 the

forest system seems to have been in decline, and some of the underwood is said to have remained uncut for between eighty and two hundred years, and 'daily wasteth' (though after two hundred years of growth it would hardly have been underwood). King Charles I, realising he could make more money by selling rights than by attempting to manage the wood himself, sold the timber to Lord Montague.

In 1676 the Crown severed all ties with the land, and the Montagues changed its name from Geddington Wood to Geddington Chase. Enclosure followed and the evicted commoners were compensated with land grubbed from the northern half of the wood. The Montagues planted trees as a patriotic duty, as directed by Evelyn's *Sylva*, and set out a radiating pattern of rides from a central forest lodge, thus subverting the old pattern of coppices and plains. Our own time saw the fellings of two world wars and, particularly after 1945, the planting of conifers, intended as a fast-growing cash crop to precede a final crop of oaks. In practice, the native underwood has survived here and there, which is why the old compartments of Great Brand and Crab Tree Hills are today a Site of Special Scientific Interest. In the future, Geddington Chase is likely to be mainly broadleaved high forest, its original identity much eroded but still present in the patches of wet ash-maple coppice, the stools of lime and hornbeam, the crumbling woodbanks and the scatter of wild daffodils along the broader rides.

The small woods of Rockingham Forest have changed less overall than the larger ones and often retain their medieval boundaries. They are also easier to understand, because a walk of only two or three hours can take in their salient features. **Short Wood** (25ha) [52 acres] near Oundle, shows nearly all the historical and biological features of ancient woodland characteristic of this part of England. Equally remarkable is **King's Wood** (31ha) [77 acres] in what is now the suburbs of Corby. This is a Local Nature Reserve and the subject of a mighty and learned treatise by Mr J. A. Best [6]. (When, in *Woodland Heritage*, I wrote that 'a book of this size could be written about every one of Britain's ancient woods', I had in mind Mr Best's *magnum opus*, 321 closely-printed pages in length.) King's Wood used to be a Crown wood with common grazing rights but was enclosed as a privately owned close in the eighteenth century and later preserved for game. Today it has become an overgrown ash-maple-hazel coppice that has been stripped of most of its former standard trees. Unusually for Rockingham Forest, King's Wood has some fine pollard oaks, reminding us of its former use in part as wood-pasture, a landscape in the process of restoration by the pupils of nearby Beanfield School.

Bedford Purlieus: 'the most flower-rich wood in England'

AREA: 185ha (457 acres)

STATUS: Forest Nature Reserve managed by agreement between the Forestry Commission and the NCC. Part of the wood is leased by the Northamptonshire Wildlife Trust as a nature reserve.

ACCESS: Restricted. But the central ride is a public footpath.

TYPE: Overgrown coppice of small-leaved lime, sessile oak-hazel and ash-hazel-maple with valley elm woodland, and planted oak, beech and conifers.

GRID REFERENCE: TL 042995

This fine wood has nothing to do with the town or county of Bedford. It owes its name to the Russell Earls and later, Dukes of Bedford, whose property it became in the late Middle Ages and with whom it remained until 1904. A purlieu is a detached part of a forest, in effect a forest suburb. Our wood stands at the northern edge of Rockingham Forest on the present-day boundary of Northamptonshire and Cambridgeshire. Although it sounds like a medieval survival, Bedford Purlieus is in fact a modern name. It represents the surviving rump of a much larger wood, called Thornhaw Wood ('Thornhaw' is hawthorn transposed), most of which was grubbed up for farmland between 1862 and 1868. The present-day wood's angular outline is the result of a once elaborate system of rides which radiated like wheel spokes from a central point in a French fashion known as *pattes d'oie* – goose-feet – that became popular in Georgian England. Complete sets of such rides survive elsewhere in Rockingham Forest at Geddington Chase and Grafton Park Wood. The hub of a *patte d'oie* was often the place for one or more fine specimen trees. At Bedford Purlieus one of the largest oaks in the wood stands here, though as a result of the

agricultural boom of the 1860s, it is now at the edge and not, as originally intended, in the middle.

As to the native trees and shrubs of the wood, one can do no better than to quote John Clare, the rustic poet who spent most of his life at nearby Helpston, and might have had Bedford Purlieus in mind when he wrote, in *Walks in the Woods*:

> When all around one boughs are twined,
> When naught but green leaves fill the eye,
> When brushing ash and hazel by,
> Cornel and thorn and spindle tree,
> And hazel with the nuts in bud,
> And crab and lime that well agree
> To make a host of underwood.

Clare is unusual among poets in that he describes real woods rather than idealised sylvan settings. Not for him the dryads merry-making

⇧ This large ash stool at Bedford Purlieus conceals a variety of small-scale habitats, often scarce in managed woodland, including moss cushions, dead wood and rainwater-filled holes. March (PETER MARREN)

through the forest fayre. His is recognisably a wood on the Northampton limestone and the reference to spindle, crab, hazel and, above all, lime places the poet among ancient vegetation. Note too that his trees are not tall standards but 'a host of underwood', that is, managed coppice. Elsewhere he writes of coppice stools by their local name of *stovens*. Clare would find many changes at Bedford Purlieus today, but much that would be familiar also. Like virtually all the larger ancient woods in eastern England, Bedford Purlieus is a hotchpotch of the old and the new. Oaks were being planted here in Clare's day, but the present even-aged oaks are nearly all the product of Forestry Commission plantings between 1935 and 1943. Almost the whole wood was clear-felled between these dates, the only areas to escape being a sliver of mixed woodland along the eastern side and the elms of the central valley, which have since succumbed to disease.

The soils of Bedford Purlieus are substantially undisturbed and, as is nature's way, varied and complex. Where limestone reaches the surface, ash-maple-hazel coppice predominates. Sessile oak-hazel coppice marks the more acidic superficial deposits, and somewhere in between lies the lime coppice on moderately calcareous clay. Most remarkably, the ill-drained valley crossing the middle of the wood is or was an elm grove, though it is currently a stark place of dead trees, tufted grass and bramble. Elm once filled the fertile river valleys of the gentle south, but most of it was cleared away in prehistory. Here we have what seems to be a rare survivor of ancient elm woodland[7]. One particularly fine elm coppice stool at the edge of the elm-valley appears to be a Lineage elm, which coppices like wych elm but bears small leaves like East Anglian elms. These curious trees are characteristic of some eastern ancient woods.

But Bedford Purlieus' main claim to fame is its wild flowers. The wood has long been known to botanists as a peculiarly rich place, and Druce's *Flora of Northamptonshire* (1930) claims that it is the single richest wood in Britain. This is still probably true today, although certain woods in Suffolk, Hampshire and Kent contain more species specifically associated with ancient woodland. Most of the interest at Bedford Purlieus is centred on the broader rides and the glades. It is possible to walk along the central ride in late spring, a place of ill-drained lime-rich clay, to see the local specialities lined up along the way like confections in a shop window. I have passed caper spurge, ramsons, deadly nightshade, wild columbine, toothwort and fly orchid in less than a hundred yards. An old

quarry at the southern end adds local plants of wood edges on calcareous soils, such as narrow-leaved everlasting pea and yellow-wort. And a walk along the northern rides in early spring should soon sniff out the dark-green jagged leaf fans and pale drooping bells of stinking hellebore. Bedford Purlieus also marks the southern limit of an attractive northern grass, the nodding melic, and the northern limit of wood spurge.

Here I will touch briefly on one other part of the wood's story: the ironstone industry. Like other woods in the vicinity, Bedford Purlieus stands on top of potentially valuable reserves of ironstone. Ironworks existed here in Roman times and samples of Roman slag have been dug from fields next to the wood, suggesting that the wood was probably being cut over nearly two thousand years ago to supply the smelters with fuelwood or charcoal. In our own times the surrounding land has become pock-marked with stone quarries and gravel pits. In 1964, the British Steel Corporation secured a thirty-five-year lease at Bedford Purlieus under emergency regulations for extracting ironstone. The likely fate of the wood if work had gone ahead is visible in the nearby woods of Easton Hornstocks and Great Morton Sale, where spoil mounds and pits stand in place of former ancient vegetation. Once worked out, the land was to be returned to the Forestry Commission for planting. Thus a corner of Bedford Purlieus known as Cocker Wood was duly 'restored' to the main wood in the 1960s by planting it with Corsican pine. Fortunately, the ore beneath Bedford Purlieus proved of inferior quality, not worth the trouble of removing, and the Steel Corporation have since relinquished mineral options over the site. In retrospect we can now see that their intervention was a blessing in disguise, for the expectation of losing the wood restrained the Forestry Commission's planting programmes. Thus, thanks to ironstone and the vigour of its native underwood, the Purlieus is still composed largely of ancient and natural vegetation. It seems destined to become high forest by singling and planting, but here and there compartments are to be maintained as coppice.

BEDFORD PURLIEUS

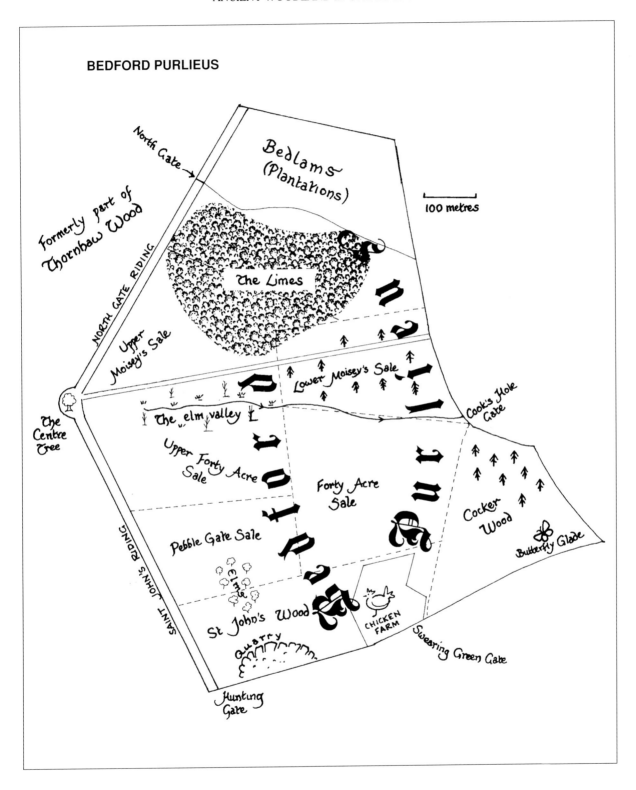

Bedlams
(Plantations)

North Gate

100 metres

Formerly part of
Thornhaw Wood

NORTH GATE RIDING

The Limes

Upper
Moisey's Sale

Lower Moisey's Sale

The elm valley

Cook's Hole
Gate

The
Centre
Tree

Upper Forty Acre
Sale

Forty Acre
Sale

Cocker
Wood

Pebble Gate Sale

Butterfly Glade

elms

St John's Wood

CHICKEN
FARM

SAINT JOHN'S RIDING

Quarry

Swearing Green Gate

Hunting
Gate

Whittlewood

At the opposite end of the county from Rockingham Forest lies the remains of the ancient Forest of **Whittlewood,** a circle of ancient copses, enclosed in the sixteenth century, surrounding what used to be an open lawn but which is now mostly ploughland. At the western end is a large park, enclosed at about the same time. The sturdy solid shapes of the surviving Whittlewood copses, with sinuous borders and rounded corners, is inherited

from the Middle Ages, as are their massive woodbanks. The interior compartments are probably younger, belonging to Tudor times. Until the late nineteenth century these woods were managed as coppice-with-standards, but they have

since grown up to become dense high forest. **Buckingham Thick Copse** (45ha) [111 acres] is the best-preserved Whittlewood copse, an ash-maple wood typical of the lime-rich boulder clays of Northamptonshire, but distinguished by its scattering of large brooding oaks with contorted trunks and branches, together with crooked old crab trees and giant chestnut stools. Some of the big oaks are typical pollards, but others, tall with narrow crowns, may be *shredded trees*, in which side branches were formerly lopped for fodder or firewood, leaving just a tuft at the top. Buckingham Thick Copse also demonstrates *par excellence* the abrupt transition from sand through clay to limestone that we have noted elsewhere in the county. On sandy soils there is oak-birch woodland with a sparse understorey of hazel, holly and elder and a bare, brackeny field layer; while on clay there is dense coppice of oak, ash and maple, with carpets of wild flowers. Running through the wood is an extraordinary 'river' of dog's mercury about two metres wide on top of a gullet of limestone, produced by quarrying operations about a century ago. Both English and small-leaved elm have invaded the wood and consolidated their position by suckering before succumbing to Dutch elm disease in the late seventies. The result is a mosaic of different types of woodland vegetation, but there is nothing random about it. This is a natural patterning, in tune with the underlying soils and water supply.

The Daventry woods

The parishes of Everdon, Badby and Dodford, near the Warwickshire border, form an ancient landscape little changed in essentials since Saxon times. A charter of AD 944 mentions woods, hazel thicks, holloways and springs that still survive, and the villages themselves retain their medieval pattern around the central green. The parish woods are

⟵Wild daffodils at Everdon Stubbs, Northamptonshire
(PETER WAKELY)

worthy of their setting. Unlike the boulder clay woods of the east, these lie on the acidic Northampton Sands and Upper Lias clays, and display abrupt transitions from one to the other. Numerous springs and freshets, banks of fern and golden saxifrage, and groves of well-grown birch and rowan lend these woods a western air, which deepens if you glimpse a redstart or hear a wood warbler. Somewhere between Corby and Daventry we have passed out of eastern England into the Midlands.

The three most interesting woods in this group are High Wood, Badby Wood and Everdon Stubbs. **High Wood** (6.4ha) [16 acres], the smallest and best preserved, is now a nature reserve belonging to the Northamptonshire Wildlife Trust. This is a delightful little wood, at its prettiest in April when its wild cherries and crab trees are in blossom, or in the following month when it becomes awash with bluebells. It is hard to understand why it is called High Wood because it lies in a hollow. Possibly it is a fragment of a larger medieval wood for there are no woodbanks visible. Virtually everything in this wood is wild grown, from the aspen spinneys and ash-hazel coppice on poorly drained clay to the oaks and hazels on loamy sand. And, as a bonus, at its foot lies an ancient meadow, not of the lush riverine type but of tough bents and fescues, furrowed by streamlets and dotted with anthills. Solitary bees and wasps burrow in its sandy soils.

You enter the hilltop wood of Badby through a triumphal arch, and, from its high top, an ancient moot or assembly place called Hazley Knob, you could (until the trees grew too high) look over nearly two thousand years of landscape history, from the Saxon village of Badby with its medieval church tower to the Tudor house and park of Fawsley, in which Roman entrenchments are visible. **Badby Wood** (24ha) [59 acres] retains its sinuous medieval outline and massive woodbank, and a deep holloway forms its western boundary. Inside, however, it has been much modified by the Victorian tree-planter's favourite mix of oaks, sycamores and sweet chestnuts and their descendants, while the east side is a more recent mixed plantation. The native vegetation is mainly pedunculate oak and coppiced hazel with a lot of hawthorn and occasional hollies. Big open-grown oaks crown the rise above Fawsley Park and, together with the absence here of woodbanks or a well-developed understorey, they suggest that this side of the wood was formerly used as wood-pasture. Badby Wood is a famous bluebell wood and a good place to watch badgers. It has large bracken glades on the sandy knolls, but most of the special plants, including wood vetch and wood horsetail, grow at the wood edge or by streams.

Everdon Stubbs is a fine old name, recalling wild boars and coppice stools. Now a Woodland Trust property, it forms the eastern two-thirds of Everdon Wood (12ha) [30 acres], from which it is separated by a steep-banked old lane. Like Badby Wood, Everdon Stubbs is a medieval wood with a mixture of original and planted vegetation, though here, with large non-native hornbeam and chestnut stools present, some of the planting is itself not recent. Inside the wood, though it is now abandoned to bracken and invading oak, was a meadow similar to that at High Wood. It would be a bonus if this could be kept open by mowing and not allowed to turn into woodland, for much of the wild community of the wood probably uses it as a source of nectar, as a basking place and as open sandy soil for burrowing.

This is another wood full of banks and ditches, including a large holloway of uncertain date. It is also a well-known daffodil wood. Wild daffodils have a strangely patchy distribution in eastern England, occurring in nooks and corners of ancient countryside, usually in woods. In Northamptonshire, one never finds the glorious cloth of gold that drapes the meadows and woodland glades at Farndale or Dymock in Gloucestershire. The Everdon daffodils seem to choose their ground daintily, a bunch here, a flowering stem or two there, generally on flushed banks near streamlets. They make a brave display on the eastern side of the wood, solitary yellow stars against dark earth and dead wood – but there are not enough of them to pick.

3
THE ENGLISH HEARTLAND:
Berkshire, Buckinghamshire and Oxfordshire

I apologise to those who believe the heartland of England lies elsewhere. The three counties of the Upper Thames cover an area little larger than Hampshire or Kent, but between them they express in small space much that is characteristic of the landscape of the English lowlands and of its wooded landscapes in particular. For that reason I propose to treat them in some detail before moving on to a brisker excursion through the remaining southern counties.

The best-known woods of 'Berks, Bucks and Oxon' are perhaps those of the Chilterns, especially the tall shady hangers of beech that grace the clay-capped hilltops. There is another concentration of ancient woodland in the Clay Vale running north-east from Oxford, which includes Bernwood Forest, famous for its butterflies and a good example of the problems inherent in trying to reconcile nature conservation with modern forestry practices. On acid, sandy soils near the Thames are two of England's outstanding wood-pastures: Windsor Great Park and Burnham Beeches, the former an enclosed royal 'waste', the latter an open common. Both contain large numbers of ancient oaks and beeches, home to many rare invertebrates, lichens and fungi associated with mature bark and dead wood. Between the greater woods are ancient copses and wooded commons on a variety of soils. These are havens of wildlife in a landscape that has become much more intensively farmed or suburbanised during the past forty years. The changes in the Thames Valley near Bisham, the setting for Kenneth Grahame's children's classic, *The Wind in the Willows*, in which the traditional sweet water meadows have been replaced by ploughland, mirror those of much of the three counties; but fortunately Grahame's Wild Wood is with us yet.

BERKSHIRE

The greatest concentration of ancient woodland in this county lies around the edges of commons, especially on the plateau gravel beds between Newbury and Reading. The commons themselves are now well-wooded, but most of this woodland has formed recently and is dominated by birch. Ancient coppices often lie near the edge of large commons, however. At Snelsmore Common, now a country park and still in part open heath and bog, there are no fewer than six copses on the periphery and, in contrast to the highly infertile common itself, these lie on richer clay soils. **Mapleash Copse** is a well-preserved example with prominent woodbanks that originally supported a fence or hedge to exclude the free-roaming pigs, cattle and sheep of the open common. Ash standards grow on the pebbly soil at the upper part where it borders an ancient track called Pebble Lane. Farther down the slope, we reach clay where the ashes are replaced by pedunculate oaks in the reverse of the usual

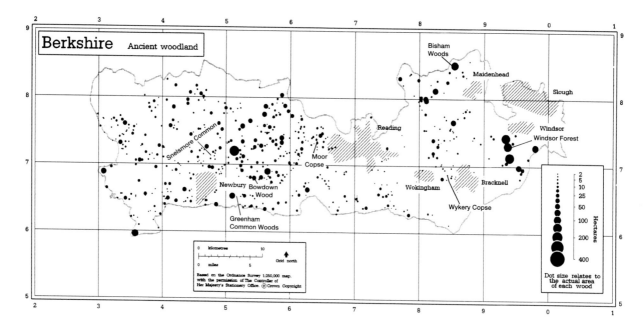

Based on the Ordnance Survey 1:250,000 map, with the permission of The Controller of Her Majesty's Stationery Office. © Crown Copyright

pattern, and at the bottom there are some big wild cherries growing where their roots can reach the underlying chalk. The main problem in this wood today is deer, which have increased to the point where they now threaten the survival of the newly coppiced hazel. One method used to deter them is to pile the tops of cut hazel over the stools to give the regrowth a good start. This wood owes its preservation to the difficulty of extracting timber from steep slopes and to the efforts of its sympathetic private owner over the past four decades.

South of the Kennet we reach **Greenham Common,** 365ha (902 acres) of former heath and rough grazing that was largely destroyed in the 1950s and 1960s when the wartime airfield was lengthened to accommodate jet bombers. Its perimeter is now a 'Via Dolorosa' of chainlink fences, barbed wire and peace camps. But the woods around the common have been largely unaffected by the military takeover. These woods are full of surprises, with much to fascinate anyone with the curiosity to penetrate what appears at first sight to be uniform birchwood. A capping of gravel over the plateau provides a constant supply of water to deep soggy gullies luxuriant with ferns, sedges and both species of golden saxifrage. Both the rich

⇧ *Berkshire is now a well-wooded county: it lost its least-wooded part to Oxfordshire in 1974. Most ancient woods are copses of less than 30ha (74 acres), and there are more of them in the west than the east. The only large woods are Fence Wood near Newbury, Bisham Woods by the Thames near Maidenhead and the woods of Windsor Forest*

flora and the massive stools of ash and alder suggest that man never managed to clear this woodland. Drier ground between the valleys carries venerable open-grown oaks, huge rowans and even hornbeams, groves of aspen and patches of heather and wet heath. The more open areas still support nightjars, tree pipits, grayling butterflies and bog bush crickets. A ramble through the woodland in early summer reveals flushes of wood horsetails and marsh violets; gullies with bog mosses, tussock sedges, lesser skullcap and alder buckthorn; drifts of lily-of-the-valley and Solomon's seal, and rich ancient woodland communities of bluebell, wood anemone, wood-sorrel, moschatel, yellow archangel, yellow pimpernel and thin-spiked wood sedge. The butterflies include white admiral and purple emperor, and at least fifteen species of dragonflies breed in the streams, pools and boggy runnels.

Two of the best Greenham Common woods, both on the north side above the marshes of the Kennet, are now owned by the Berks, Bucks and Oxon Naturalists' Trust, 'BBONT'. **Chamberhouse Great Wood** (16ha) [39 acres] is known as Baynes Reserve after the timber company, Baynes (Reading) Ltd, which first leased the area to the Trust in 1982. It is an enclosed coppice with woodbanks and an external ditch, obscured in one area by clinker from a wartime sewage works, and seems always to have been a private wood with no common rights attached to it. Large coppice stools of alder, maple and ash indicate a long and continu-

⇩*An alder gully at Bowdown and Chamberhouse Wood, Berkshire, in October*
(PETER WAKELY)

ous management as coppice, and Chamberhouse Wood probably supplied wood to the turneries at Thatcham.

Most of the timber was felled for fuel during World War II, after which the wood was left to grow wild for more than thirty years until 1981 when an area of birch and alder was clear-felled. That event drew attention to this hitherto little-known wood, now regarded as one of the finest in the county. In 1982 BBONT started a coppicing programme, weeded out the invasive grey alder and sycamore, and widened the main rides. The wood's ground flora has benefitted from renewed management, and early purple orchids, wild daffodils, herb paris, narrow buckler-fern, wood-spurge and other plants have all made a dramatic return after a long period of scarcity.

The floodplains of most Berkshire rivers are virtually devoid of ancient woodland, and although

the willow and alder groves and poplar plantations of the Kennet Valley look like, and in one place are actually named as, wilderness, they are of relatively recent origin. The exception is the Pang valley near Tidmarsh where, amid an intricate patchwork of meadows and ancient copses, some of them tiny ones of less than 5ha (12 acres), lies one of BBONT's showcase nature reserves, **Moor Copse** (27ha) [67 acres]. This is, in fact, three separate copses linked by old seasonally flooded hayfields: Moor Copse proper, Park Wood and Hogmoor Copse, the latter an interesting name that suggests former common rights of pannage. Although all are on very wet alluvial soils, each has its own special character. Hogmoor, the wettest, is a place of willows and alders. It was badly damaged by the storm of January 1990 and has since been heavily thinned by timber contractors, though part was left as a non-intervention area. Park Wood is a hazel coppice with oak standards and brave springtime shows of primroses and bluebells; and Moor Copse itself is wet ash, alder and birch coppice with oak standards. BBONT have made a great effort to reinstate these woods, fencing, widening rides, laying hedges, cutting bracken and digging ponds. The present aim is to bring Park Wood and Moor Copse back into a permanent coppice rotation.

Widely scattered small copses characterise the low-lying London Clay around Wokingham, Maidenhead and Bracknell. This area has been much built on in postwar years. London Clay is useful stuff for making bricks, and a number of woods, such as Tarman's Copse near Bracknell, were sacrificed for their underlying clay. Tarman's Copse's neighbour, **Wykery Copse** (3.2ha) [8 acres] was spared, but extraction on the periphery left this tiny squarish wood standing high and increasingly dry on a pedestal of clay three or four metres above the surrounding land. To their credit, Bracknell District Council have made elaborate plans to try to maintain the natural water level of the copse by excavating within it a self-sustaining network of ditches blocked at their exit point by a clay bund. It is hoped that this will keep sufficient

water inside the wood and safeguard it from possible pollution from a nearby industrial estate.

Wykery Copse is a remarkably rich little wood and a reminder of what has been lost elsewhere in the Thames valley. Different levels of wetness and dryness have produced at least five recognisable types of woodland vegetation – mixtures of oak, ash and hazel coppice on the slopes, a line of willows and alders strung along the central stream and young aspens and birches regenerating in the gaps. In addition, there has been an incursion of elm from the hedgerow. There are some fine crab apple and wild service trees, the latter regenerating freely as suckers. Where the woodland floor is dry enough, bluebells and dog's mercury abound; but on the prevailing wet clay there are thickets of bramble. Sedges are prominent by rides and ditches, including two that are virtually confined, in this area, to ancient woods: the pale sedge and the thin-stalked wood-sedge. The mosses and liverworts are exceptionally diverse and luxuriant for a small wood, with a rare moss, *Plagiothecium latebricola*, on rotting stumps and tree bases, and a liverwort, *Homalia trichomanoides*, on old ash stools. These delicate, almost translucent plants are sensitive alike to pollution, drying and the removal of dead logs and stumps and, as a result, may be good indicators of relatively undisturbed woodland.

The last main group of Berkshire woods are those of the Chalk. By contrast with most of those we have considered so far, these are relatively dry woods, dominated by ash and maple and usually occupying patches of clay-with-flints or drift soils on the lower downland ridges rather than the bare chalk itself. Herb paris is unusually common in the West Berkshire chalk woods. In the past, these woods were important sources of firewood, both domestic and industrial, as place-names such as Brick-kiln Wood indicate. Many small woods on the open downs were planted during the past 200 years as windbreaks and fox coverts. Downland woods of regular, symmetrical shape and dominated by beech almost invariably prove to be plantations. A few ancient chalk woods, such as

Common Wood at Streatley and the ash-wych elm copses below Coombe Gibbet, cling to steep scarp slopes. But the finest scarp woods in the county are those at the side of the Thames below Cookham Dean, known collectively as Bisham Woods.

Bisham Wood: Kenneth Grahame's Wild Wood

AREA: 154ha (380 acres)

STATUS: A Woodland Trust property

ACCESS: Open to the public along tracks, but presently in dangerous condition from gale damage

TYPE: Beech high forest

GRID REFERENCE: SU 857850

In 1990, the Woodland Trust launched its most ambitious appeal to date, to raise more than half a million pounds for the purchase of Bisham Woods, a series of very steep beechwoods bordering the Thames near Marlow. Those who know that corner of deepest England of boats, regattas, weed-winding banks and islands and well-wooded chalk hills, will recall that between Bisham and Cookham Dean the river passes below a veritable wall of woodland. At first sight, which is all most car drivers will have as they zoom past in their haste to reach the M4, Bisham looks like just another collection of Chilterns beeches, though steeper than most and now much knocked about by gales. But if you enter the wood by foot along one of the ancient sunken lanes that wind through the trees to the hilltop village of Cookham Dean, another more secret wood is revealed, a place of piled leaves, mossed banks and holes, fallen trunks, chalk banks and quarries, hazel coppice, alder slades and a strip of hornbeam coppice about Grubwood Lane. This is the richest ancient wood in Berkshire. Rare helleborine orchids are among some fifty 'ancient woodland indicator' plants found here. They suggest that Bisham is probably primary woodland, saved from the wholesale 'beechification' that has overtaken its neighbours north of the Thames by the vertiginous slope and, probably, by legal restraints imposed by the commonland system.

There is another reason for pausing at this particular wood. Cookham Dean was the home, both in boyhood and in retirement, of Kenneth Grahame, the author of *The Wind in the Willows*, and it is the banks, meadows and woods of this corner of the Thames that form the living backcloth to the adventures of Rat, Mole and Toad of Toad Hall. E. H. Shepard, who illustrated later editions of the book, recalled how the aged Grahame, 'looking like some ancient Viking', spoke of *The Wind in the Willows* as an elegy to the lost idylls of his childhood in rural Berkshire, when he explored the upper Thames by canoe, swam in its clear weedy depths and trod the path to 'the Wild Wood way up on the hill above the river'. Bisham Wood provides the real-life setting for the Wild Wood, the rather sinister place where the stoats and weasels lived and where Mole and Rat sheltered from the snow-storm and sought refuge with Mr Badger.

'Wild Wood' is a phrase with powerful resonances for a woodland ecologist, for wildwood as a single word, lower case, is also the term coined by Oliver Rackham for Britain's original virgin forest, from which all unplanted woods ultimately derive. But Kenneth Grahame's Wild Wood is emphatically not Rackham's wildwood. We have Mr Badger's word for it that the former grew up over the ruins of a city built long ago by 'a powerful people, and rich'. Mr Badger's own home lies in the cellars of a fallen mansion. Clearly this Wild Wood is a secondary wood (though I know of no real-life secondary wood on the site of a Roman city). If Bisham Wood had been that kind of wood, it would not be the richest wood in Berkshire.

Kenneth Grahame never described his Wild Wood in detail, by contrast with his loving rhapsodies on riverbank vegetation. He mentions only one particular kind of tree, the 'deep dark hollow of an old beech'. The real Bisham Wood is present, however, in the deep lanes that tempt the Mole farther and farther into the depths of the wood and

the 'dry leaf carpet' of a beechwood in winter. The 'holes, hollows, pools and pitfalls', which in the book are reflections of the ruined city beneath the ground, happen to be actual features of primary woods, resulting from piles of debris left behind by the retreating ice. The most significant aspect that Bisham Wood lends to the story, however, is its sense of a barrier, a hedge around the enchanted world of the riverbank separating it from the other world of human beings and smoky cities beyond. In summer, the distant Wild Wood appears as a 'background of woodland that darkly framed the water-meadows on one side of the river'; in winter it becomes 'low and threatening like a black reef in some still southern sky'. 'Beyond the Wild Wood comes the Wide World,' says Rat, 'and that's something that doesn't matter, either to you or me. I've never been there, and I'm never going, nor you either, if you've got any sense.'

⇧ *Quarry Wood, Bisham, the 'background of woodland that darkly framed the water-meadows on one side of the river' in September*
(PETER WAKELY)

An ancient pollard oak at Windsor Great Park. ⇨
This tree is hollow and nine-tenths dead, but the living sapwood is still perfectly healthy and it will probably outlive us all
(TED GREEN)

Windsor Forest and Great Park: of lightning, bracket fungi and click-beetles

AREA: 3,150ha (7,783 acres) are owned and managed by the Crown Estate Commissioners, of which approximately 1,200ha (2,965 acres) are woodland. 846ha (2,091 acres) are designated as a Site of Special Scientific Interest

ACCESS: About half of the Great Park is open to the public. The remainder is restricted and visitors require a permit from the Crown Estate, Windsor

TYPE: Oak and beech wood-pasture on acid soils with ancient trees. Young-growth stands include groves of hornbeam

GRID REFERENCE: SU 9373

Windsor Forest and Great Park stand apart from the rest of Berkshire. Here is ancient woodland on a truly royal scale, probably the largest and most important group of trees over 500 years old in the whole of Western Europe. Autumn in Windsor Great Park epitomises the ancient woodland experience. Red deer roar among the yellowing bracken, a medley of bracket fungi and toadstools sprout from fallen trunks, there is an occasional twittering of redpolls or crossbills, a smell of deer musk and decomposition, and all is well with the world. This is the best place in England to see old oaks and beeches in great numbers and variety. At Burnham Beeches, say, or Moccas Park, it is possible to identify a 'typical' old tree, but at Windsor the range of form and size defies description. Both oaks are present and more distinct from one another than usual, the sessile oaks with their great fan vaults of leaves, rather like old rhododendron bushes, the pedunculate oaks with their bunched leaves on heavy, gnarled, spreading limbs.

Many of the oaks are pollards, virtually all of them are hollow, and some are embossed with great burrs, feathered with twigs. A few trees have split open, exposing chimney-like or cavernous interiors. Other oaks lost their tops in the 1987 storm and now bristle like chimney brushes on top of short stubby bollings. Others still are tall trees that show no signs of former pollarding. Their central vertical branch with smaller laterals on either side might be the result of the medieval practice of shredding, where side-branches were regularly lopped for fuel or fodder, leaving a quiver of branches at the top (a practice long extinct in Britain, but still occasionally practised in France). At least one sessile oak is a standard of great girth and soaring trunk of the sort that still grows in the Forests of Fontainebleau and Compiègne, but are otherwise virtually extinct in western Europe (although they are occasionally dug out of Bronze Age peat layers in Britain). Unfortunately, this tree has developed a pronounced lean and may soon blow over. The Windsor trees tell of past thunderstorms, gales and droughts, infestations of caterpillars and fungi and bear the scars of generations of woodcutters and grazing animals. They have seen a score of English kings and have so much to tell us about the past, could we but read all the messages hidden in their mighty boughs.

Windsor is one of the few places where there has been a continuous succession of old trees, probably dating back to the wildwood. In the New Forest there have been only four significant periods of regeneration in as many centuries, but at Windsor there are trees of every age from the past thousand years. The oldest trees are among the oldest in the land, for growth is slow on these infertile Bagshot Sands and veteran trees photographed in 1864 have hardly changed since. Beech is not believed to reach the great age of oak, but the largest beech I have ever seen is at Windsor: a now dead tree about 9m (30ft) in girth and probably more than 500 years old. The oldest oaks in the park, those spectacular living shells with dead tops and billows of foliage coming off the trunk, are reputed to be up to 800 years old. One vast tree by Forest Lodge, its cavernous bolling held together by iron pins and braces, its boughs propped up with crutches, may even have witnessed the establishment of Windsor Forest by William the Conqueror soon after 1066.

I want to concentrate on two aspects of Windsor Forest's natural history: the effects of wood-rotting fungi and of lightning. Wood-rotting fungi are much maligned organisms. We have developed the wrong vocabulary for old trees, words recalling hospitals or battlefields. We say that fungi *attack* them, implying aggression and malevolence. We denounce heart-rotting fungi for ruining the timber without considering possible benefits to the tree. Do we subconsciously liken them to our own bodies and conclude that the infected tree must be sick or even dying? I am as guilty of passing on these misconceptions as anyone. In the first book of this series, *Woodland Heritage*, I declared that 'few bracket fungi attack healthy trees'. *Mea culpa*. In the context of a tree, 'attack' and 'healthy' are heavily loaded words. A tree may be festooned by fungi but only rarely at Windsor Park is the living tissue infected. Most fungi are decomposers, not parasites, and feed only on dead wood, which includes the heartwood at the core of the tree. If a tree with fungus-induced heart-rot can be said to be dying, then the great oaks of Windsor have been dying for most of their lives. Ted Green, who has made a long study of these old trees and their fungi, goes further. He suggests that, far from being malevolent agents, these polypores and 'beefsteaks' are providing an important service for the tree by helping to break down the useless weight of the heartwood and other dead wood and returning it to the soil, thereby enabling the tree to recycle itself by creating an island of fertility within the grasp of its roots. And, in converting the tree to a hollow cylinder, they help to produce a firm and a more windproof shape than a solid trunk, and a much lighter load on the decaying roots.

Windsor is one of the outstanding places in northern Europe for fungi associated with old trees. Many are rare precisely because elsewhere their habitat has been felled, sawn up and removed. In the wildwood, which probably produced six tonnes of dead wood annually for every ten hectares of forest, fungi now rare were probably common. On the large oaks of Windsor Park,

the commonest species are sulphur polypore (now a favourite in London Italian restaurants) and beefsteak fungus, both heartwood decomposers that produce the characteristic red-rotten interior of over-mature oaks. These species are rare on beech where one finds instead spectacular tawny and cream brackets shaped like hooves or Elizabethan frills, and belonging to the genus *Ganoderma*. Most of these fungi are perennials, putting on annual rings like their host tree and growing bigger and bigger. A twenty-year-old *Ganoderma* can be more than a metre (3.25ft) in diameter. Astronomical numbers of snuff-brown spores are produced by such fruit-bodies. In sheltered places they cover not only the fungus itself but also the surrounding bark, leaves and grass blades like spilt cocoa powder.

Bracket fungi are probably present in every tree at Windsor above a century in age. All we normally see of them are the fruit-bodies, which are stimulated when light manages to enter the tree through a chink in the bark. Heart-rotting brackets are most frequent in trees of middling years. On trees in which the heartwood has rotted away completely, they are rare. The completely hollow pollard beeches at Burnham Beeches, for example, are almost bracket-free.

Fungi enter trees through 'wounds', at a broken bough for example, or where a deer's antler, a squirrel's jaws, a farmer's machine or a boy's penknife have scored the bark. At Windsor, a very important wounding agent is lightning. Thunderstorms are frequent in this part of England, and probably two or three trees are struck each year. Ted Green thinks it likely that every old oak at Windsor has been struck at least once, though the scars usually last only twenty years or so. Lightning rarely sets native British trees ablaze, because, with the exception of Scots pine, they are virtually fireproof. Usually it strips away a metre or so of bark to form a triangular or strap-shaped scar. Rough-barked trees such as oak and sweet chestnut probably conduct electricity through the rainwater collected in the bark fissures, which might explain why lightning scars are commonly found

FUNGI OF LARGE STUMPS AND LOGS

⇧Ganoderma adspersum *which forms tiers up to a metre across on large beech stumps and logs*
(TED GREEN)

The 'hedgehog fungus' Creolophus cirrhatus, ⇨ *occasional on beechlogs in the south of England*
(PETER WAKELY)

⇩Phellinus robustus, *a giant hoof-shaped bracket on oak; large specimens can weigh up to 15kg (33lb)*
(TED GREEN)

near the base of the tree. Big redwoods such as Wellingtonia, combining great height with rough bark, are the most lightning-susceptible trees of all. Severe strikes can score into the sapwood and strip away bark from top to bottom along one side of the tree, causing die-back or even death.

Occasionally a direct hit on an old hollow tree causes it to explode, scattering lumps of wood and bits of bark in all directions. This was witnessed by Jack Taylor, Chief Forester at Windsor, while playing bowls one evening under an almost cloudless sky! Suddenly there was an almighty bang and a flash, and the next moment pieces of wood weighing up to half a hundredweight were flying through the air, some landing a hundred metres from what had, a minute before, been a living tree. It is believed that lightning can, under certain circumstances, turn the sap into superheated steam and create enough pressure to blast away the enclos-

46

↑ *The violet click-beetle and its tree in Windsor Forest. On the left is the upper part of a hollow beech trunk, set upright by conservationists after it had snapped in the 1987 gale. To the right are the reassembled fragments of the lower trunk. April* (TED GREEN)

The violet click-beetle, Limoniscus violaceus⇨ (TED GREEN)

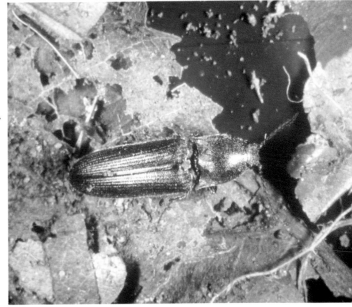

ing bark. In this extreme case the entire tree became a living grenade. I wonder to what extent old oaks owe their bizarre, gnarled appearance to such bolts from the blue.

Postscript: the violet click-beetle story
Consider the inside of a beech tree about 250 years old. Much of the heartwood has already rotted away and has fallen to the base of the cavity. The

lower layers are already compressed into rich black humus. Above that is a lighter compost made not only of wood-pulp and leaf-mould but also of the remains of the nests of woodpeckers and jackdaws, owl pellets and bat droppings, all topped with a crust of fungal threads. There are sodden, partly rotted chips of wood and perhaps the liquefying remains of a dead mouse or bat. Farther up the trunk are pockets and crevices which periodically fill with rainwater, moistening the nameless slimy 'gunge' inside. Add to these the warmth and humidity of slow decomposition and the still, quiet march of time and you have a marvellously nutritious habitat: rather like a thick layer of Dundee cake lying on the floor of a cave.

Many rare beetles, for which Windsor Forest and Great Park is a famous necropolis, live in such environments. One species became better known than the rest when, in 1988, the government decided to place it on their protected list, one of only two native beetles to receive this accolade. This is the violet click-beetle, *Limoniscus violaceus*, rarest of the rare, the ancient woodland denizen *par excellence*. This modest, purple-shot beetle, about two centimetres long, was first discovered in 1937, 'in an old decaying beech trunk, at some depth below the surface of the wood', in the part of Windsor Forest known as High-Standing Hill. Its life-history has been worked out recently by H. Mendel and Professor John Owen[8]. Over the years, it has been found in nearly a dozen hollow beech trunks, usually in trees that have recently fallen or been snapped by the wind. Since it is not possible to see inside the majority of beeches of the right age, the violet click-beetle is perhaps not uncommon at Windsor, though extremely rare outside it. The beetle's larva seems to spend its life wallowing in the aforementioned 'primordial compost' inside half rotten standing trunks. It spends at least two years eating steadily before pupating in a chamber excavated inside hard earth or a wood chipping. The beetle emerges the following year. It can fly and evidently has a taste for hawthorn flowers, so the adults probably move about from tree to tree within the forest. Evidently its habits

chime with those of other rare click-beetles, because one stump may prove to be home for several 'Red Data Book' species.

OXFORDSHIRE

Oxfordshire is a county of limestone heights separated by clay vales, and these contrasting landscapes determine the character of its ancient woods. In the west of the county, the Vale of the White Horse, inherited from Berkshire in 1974, has rather few, widely scattered ancient woods, most of them very small. By contrast, the Chilterns is a densely wooded patchwork of woods, downs and fields, particularly north of the Thames between Goring and Watlington. Between the Chilterns and Oxford we pass through another almost woodless zone until we reach the clay woods north-east and south-west of the city, and the Jurassic limestone woods to the west of it. Two famous woods dominate the neighbourhood of Oxford: Wytham Wood on a hill of limestone and 'Bernwood Forest' in the Clay Vale at the Buckinghamshire border. Moving farther west into Cotswold country, we pass by the great pollard oaks of Blenheim Great Park and the delightful hanging copses of the River Evenlode before reaching another former Royal Forest, Wychwood. We need not bother with the north of the county around Bicester and Banbury, which is a waste of dull improvement countryside despite its prominent place in the literature through Flora Thompson's *Lark Rise to Candleford*. I confess that in the year I spent looking after Oxfordshire for the NCC, I spent no more than a day north of Bicester!

The Oxford Clay stands out on our map as a string of medium-sized woods running south-west to north-east past the city of Oxford. In the Middle Ages the area lay at the heart of three contiguous Royal Forests – Shotover, Stowood and Bernwood. Many of the woods still retain their original

Ancient woodland is concentrated in the Chilterns, *in the Clay Vale and the limestone hills on either side of Oxford, and in and around the Forest of Wychwood. Wychwood is among the largest ancient woods in the Midlands*

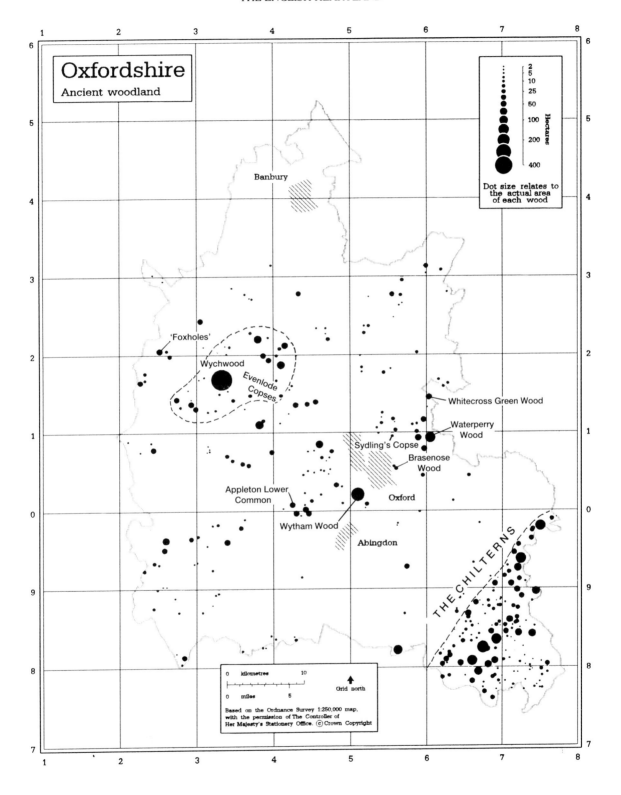

Oxfordshire
Ancient woodland

Banbury

Hectares
2
5
10
25
50
100
200
400

Dot size relates to
the actual area
of each wood

'Foxholes'

Wychwood

Evenlode
Copses

Whitecross Green Wood

Waterperry
Wood

Sydling's Copse

Brasenose
Wood

Appleton Lower
Common

Oxford

Wytham Wood

Abingdon

THE CHILTERNS

0   kilometres   10

0   miles   5

Grid north

Based on the Ordnance Survey 1:250,000 map,
with the permission of The Controller of
Her Majesty's Stationery Office. © Crown Copyright

boundaries and woodbanks. Holly (originally Horley) Wood and Stanton Great Wood are recorded in the Domesday Book. Most of these woods are overgrown coppices which lost their timber during World War II. They are classed as wet ash-maple woods and very wet they are: when not churned by vehicles, the rides can be virtual marshes, full of sedges, tufted hair-grass and wood small-reed. At **Appleton Lower Common,** a Thames-side wood preserved by the late owner of Blackwells Bookshop, depressions in the rides become ponds in wet weather, and are lined with water-pepper. On poorly drained clay too acid for maple, standards of pedunculate oak and ash top an underwood dominated by hazel. Aspen, wild cherry and both kinds of birch are often frequent and the woods are generally fringed by blackthorn thickets.

The limestone woods in the west of the county share some of the characteristics of the clay woods, but on the steeper slopes and where bedrock nears the surface there are rich and well-drained soils supporting ash, hazel and wych elm coppice with standard oaks. The hanging copses along the incised banks of the Evenlode, like Mill Wood and Sturt Copse, have a wonderful vernal flora with rarities such as toothwort and yellow star-of-Bethlehem set among delicious riverine carpets of anemone, ramsons, moschatel and celandine. These woods are particularly rich in mosses, which flourish in these humid riverine conditions. **Wychwood** is by far the largest wood of west Oxfordshire, but because it is very private – the so-called 'secret forest' – and because I have touched on its history already in *Woodland Heritage*, I will be brief. Until it was enclosed by Act of Parliament 1857, Wychwood was one of the last working vestiges of the Forest system left in England. It comprises three square miles of compartmented copses and 'lights' (open grassy areas) with a central plain and an enclosed deer park attached. Unfortunately, enclosure meant that the western half could be grubbed up and, while the surviving east part was saved as a game preserve, the old historical boundaries have become hard to trace in the

uniformly dense high forest. Although it is still among the more significant ancient woods, Wychwood is essentially a Victorian game covert; its medieval antecedents are not obvious. Easier to appreciate, perhaps, and certainly more accessible, is one of the purlieu woods of Wychwood, **'Foxholes'** nature reserve (64ha) [158 acres], otherwise known as Bould Wood. Secretive and tranquil, rather like Wychwood scaled down, this is a wood of contrasting bands of wet clay and well-drained limestone, with wet riverside meads and coppice glades. It is not called Foxholes for nothing; the Heythrop hunt here on two days each year but there has been no noticeable reduction in their quarry.

Wytham Wood: an open-air laboratory

AREA: 426ha (1,058 acres)

STATUS: A private wood owned by the University of Oxford

ACCESS: By permission only

TYPE: Wet ash-maple and ash-hazel coppice with oak standards

Grid reference: SP 462083

Motorists who travel regularly along the A34 will know this famous wood just 3.2km (2 miles) from the centre of Oxford. It's great dome of trees above the hay meadows of the Thames dominates the scenery for miles. Wytham Wood was given to the University by the Ffennell family in the 1920s on condition that its natural beauty was preserved for all time (a condition which one might wish was stipulated more often). This princely benefaction could not have been more opportune, for Oxford at that time was becoming a world leader in ornithology and woodland ecology, under the guidance of such luminaries as H. N. Southern and Charles Elton. In Wytham Wood they were presented with the perfect outdoor laboratory. There

laid bare: a never-ending scramble for food, a relentless matter of checks and balances which prevent one part of the food-web from ever gaining a permanent advantage over the rest. The system depends, above all, on *variety*.

BUCKINGHAMSHIRE

Let us begin in the Clay Vale, which Buckinghamshire shares with Oxfordshire. This is the second most densely wooded part of the county after the Chilterns and consists mostly of former coppices on undulating ground or gentle slopes, many retaining the 'solid' rounded shapes characteristic of medieval parish woods. Because most of them lost their mature growth during World War II, these woods have grown into dense young undergrowth with few large or tall trees [10]. For the past forty years they have been valued more as game coverts than productive woods. The principle ancient vegetation is ash, maple and hazel underwood typical of the Oxford Clay, with ash and pedunculate oak standards. On the more acidic, ill-drained clays, as in Sheephouse Wood or The Straits in Salcey Forest, there are more species-poor stands with oak standards and hazel coppice. Both of these types are susceptible to elm invasion, and many woods contain the glades of stricken elm trees, pushing up suckers from the still-living roots. Aspen and service tree are locally frequent. Here and there are patches of native hornbeam and

⇦ This is a county of extreme contrast: while the Chilterns and Burnham Beeches are among the most densely wooded parts of England, the Vale of Aylesbury has no ancient woods at all. In the north of the county most ancient woods lie on poorly drained clays or infertile sands in the former forests of Bernwood, Whittlewood and Whaddon Chase

alders by springs or in wet depressions. In the woods near Brickhill, between Milton Keynes and Woburn Abbey, Greensand breaks through the surface clay producing light acid soils and stands of sessile oak, otherwise scarce in this county. Small-leaved lime is an occasional tree in such stands in neighbouring Bedfordshire, but not apparently in Buckinghamshire. Conifers grow well on Greensand, so many of these woods have been replanted.

Characteristic flowers of the clay woods, particularly on the rides, are yellow pimpernel, orpine, pale sedge, pendulous sedge and wood small-reed. **Rushbeds Wood** (45ha) [111 acres], one of the Bernwood Forest woods, is, like so many ancient woods on the Oxford Clay, a place of young growth, having lost virtually all of its mature oak, ashes and maples forty years ago. Traditional coppicing continued here well into the twentieth century, and lately has begun again as part of a conservation plan. It is a very wet wood and does indeed contain beds of rushes. It lies at the centre of an oasis of unimproved countryside rich in wildlife, with thick hedges and narrow, ancient meadows. Some of these woods and their surroundings are justly celebrated for their butterflies. **Whitecross Green Wood** (62ha) [153 acres], a medieval wood unfortunately clear-felled and coniferised by the Forestry Commission in the mid-1960s, can boast black and brown hairstreaks, wood white, marbled white, white admiral and purple emperor. These insects depend on sunny ride vegetation. BBONT have widened the main rides and created glades and scalloped woodland margins to encourage such species.

Much of the Buckinghamshire clay country, with its broad vales, intervening rises, irregularly shaped woods, hedged meadows and small villages was under Forest Law in the Middle Ages. Salcey Forest and Whittlewood lie on the border with Northamptonshire; Bernwood Forest with Oxfordshire. The one forest which lay completely within Buckinghamshire was **Whaddon Chase**, which once covered a broad expanse of copses and commons to the west of Milton Keynes. But,

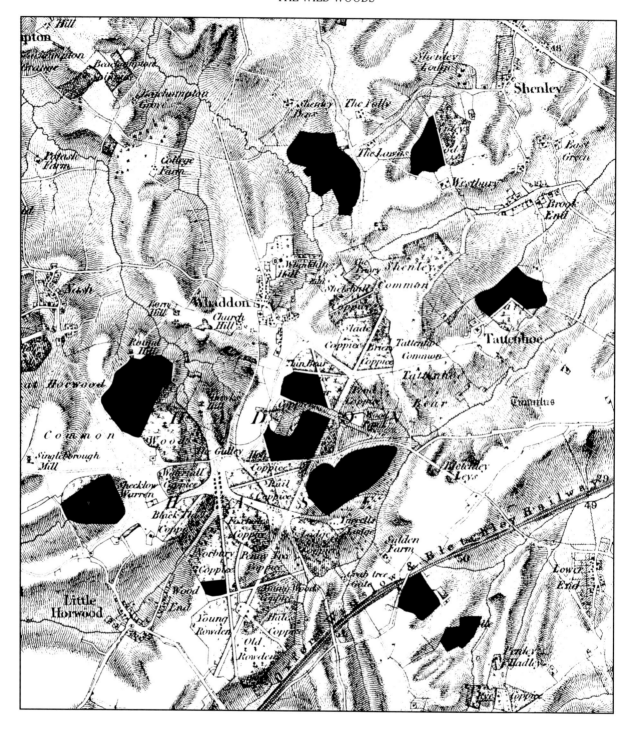

⇦ Whaddon Chase, Bucks, as recorded on this early Ordnance Survey map, used to be an ancient landscape of coppice compartments and commons, through which rides and carriageways had been cut. Nineteenth-century farm improvements transformed it into a chequerboard of large fields with scattered woods. The surviving woods are shown in solid black; most of these were replanted with conifers after 1945

unlike Whittlewood or Bernwood, it has left no important woodland legacy. The Chase was enclosed in 1841 and, as usual, many of its woods were grubbed up soon afterwards. Some survivors, such as College Wood and Broadway and Thrift Wood, were replanted. Others, such as Howe Park, are probably descended from medieval deer parks, of which about sixty are recorded. The country park at Langley is such a place. So is, or was, poor little Hoo Wood, once Le Ho park, now carved in two to form tiny copses shivering at one another from across the M1.

Shabbington and Waterperry Woods: a Forest Nature Reserve

AREA: Shabbington: 309ha (763 acres)
Waterperry: 140ha (364 acres)

STATUS: Forest Nature Reserve by agreement between the Forestry Commission and the NCC. Burrows Reserve, Bernwood Meadow and Oakley Parish Hedge are adjacent nature reserves managed by the Berks, Bucks and Oxon Naturalists' Trust (BBONT)

ACCESS: Open along main rides (but heaven help you if you are seen carrying a butterfly net). Car park at SP 610115

TYPE: Plantations on the remains of oak-hazel and ash-hazel-maple woodland

GRID REFERENCES: SP 615110 (Shabbington);
SP 605090 (Waterperry)

These large woods that straddle the border of Oxfordshire and Buckinghamshire a few miles east of Oxford are often referred to as Bernwood Forest, a modern revival of an ancient name. Bernwood, the Saxon *Byrnewuda*, appears in an entry in the Anglo-Saxon Chronicle for AD 921 as a lawless place, plundered by roving bands of Danes who waylaid unsuspecting folk and 'took away great spoil both in captives and cattle between Byrnewuda and Aeglesbyrig (Aylesbury)'. Bernwood became a Royal Forest under the Normans, centred on the then well-wooded but now bare country north of the town of Brill. Whitecross Green Wood and Rushbeds Wood are among the surviving medieval woods of Bernwood Forest. Shabbington and Waterperry Woods, on the other hand, seem to have been excluded from the Forest proper, though the king evidently retained some vaguely defined hunting rights there, an example of a royal wish to have his cake and eat it. Both woods had parted company with the last vestige of Forest Law by the time the *Mayflower* set sail for America. Perhaps it would be less confusing, therefore, if we left the name Bernwood to the historians.

Shabbington and Waterperry Woods lie not on a hilltop, like the majority of ancient woods on the Oxford Clay, but in a flat-bottomed hollow, notorious for mire and frost. A few miles away, in a larger, slightly deeper hollow too wet for trees, lies Otmoor, that famous wilderness in the heart of England. At the demise of the original Bernwood in the early seventeenth century, many woods, including Panshill Wood, a great provider of timber in the Middle Ages, were grubbed up as allotments for displaced commoners or as pasture for sheep. But the clearance of Shabbington and Waterperry Woods seems to have been beyond the resources of the day, and they were kept on as coppices. Waterperry retains its medieval boundary exactly, a dumpy cottage loaf of a wood snug inside its bank and ditch. Shabbington Wood, on the other hand, is a shapeless mass, a conflation of four earlier woods – namely, Shabbington Wood proper, York's Wood, Oakley Wood and the memorably named

Hell Coppice. The boundary of this composite wood has shifted over the years as bits were taken out for cultivation, while unsuccessful former fields tumbled back again into woodland. Only Hell Coppice stands within its original banks – its hellish sticky clay defeated everybody.

For at least a century, these woods have been a famous locality for butterflies. At one time, every woodland species in southern England bar one occurred here, and the woods still have the reputation of being 'the best butterfly wood in Britain'. However, those who come here hoping to see large numbers of hairstreaks, fritillaries and purple emperors are likely to be disappointed. Butterflies can indeed be very numerous, but nearly all of those that abound along the grassy sides of the broad woodland rides are typical of hedgerows and wood-edges rather than woodland interiors. Moreover, at first sight Shabbington and half of Waterperry look like everyday conifer plantations, dense squares of young trees segregated by hard-surfaced rides. Here and there are islands of native trees and shrubs along the ride edges, but none is very large. The ancient woodland seems to have been all but obliterated.

Yet this is supposed to be a showcase wood, a Forest Nature Reserve, where one expects to see something out of the ordinary. It is, in fact, a more fascinating place than it looks. Intended to display a supposed compatibility between nature conservation and commercial timber growing, its recent history reveals more clearly than that of most woods the difficulty of long-term planning for either. Foresters and conservationists both lay great store by management plans. From a city office it is all too easy to confuse what is laid down in a plan with what happens on the ground. If trees are planted, foresters assume that they will grow. If a butterfly reserve is designated, conservationists assume that butterflies will use it. In the 1950s, both were reasonably confident that they knew what Shabbington and Waterperry Woods would look like forty years hence, and indicated as much in their plans. As it turned out, they were both wrong.

Fellings during World War II removed virtually all the mature timber from Shabbington and Waterperry Woods, and turned their tracks to quagmires. The Forestry Commission, which purchased both woods very cheaply in 1950, described them as 'a classical example of devastated woodlands at their worst'[11]. There was never much doubt about what should be done to restore them. Forestry methods then had little use for unplanted trees. The native 'scrub' must be stripped away and replaced by profitable trees: that is, a first crop of conifers with a final crop of oaks in AD 2010. At that time the Commission had had relatively little experience of getting rid of natural vegetation on the scale required at Shabbington and Waterperry Woods. Most prewar conifers had been planted on open ground, especially upland moors. The situation called for experimentation. The Commission built broad made-up rides lined by ditches across the soggy clay. The old coppices of Waterperry Wood – Drunkard's Corner, Riding's Sale, Polecat End – were sliced up into a chessboard of square blocks for practising silvicultural experiments. Early problems for the new plantings were frost and weed growth, especially the tufted hair-grass, *Deschampsia cespitosa*, which thrives on waterlogged ground. The Commission soon found that better results were achieved by leaving a scatter of scrub birches to provide a dappled shade, than by indiscriminately cutting everything down. But the resurgent coppice needed more drastic treatment. It culminated in a blitz of poison sprays in the early 1960s. Foresters' memories of that time are of mud and diesel oil. One worker recalls that, after having sprayed the undergrowth with a mixture of hormone weedkiller and petrol for a few minutes, he noticed that the fluid had started to melt his rubber boots. At one giddy moment of technological messianism, a helicopter was hired to spray the stuff onto the tree-tops, an experiment that was presumably judged a failure because it was abandoned after only seventeen acres.

Then, in the mid-sixties, the government moved the goalposts. The Forestry Commission was told that its woods had to be made more profitable and bring a greater return to the government's investment in forestry. That meant that oak had suddenly become an unaffordable luxury. The confident long-term plans for Shabbington and Waterperry were set aside. The future now lay in softwoods and nothing but softwoods, so the oaks, those 1950s oaks that had been established at so much trouble and expense, were to be poisoned in their turn. Or at least they should have been, and were on paper. Fortunately it is not unknown for people on the ground, who know their woods and like them, to mitigate the zeal of distant senior managers.

In the meantime, how were the butterflies getting on? In 1955, Waterperry Wood was declared a Forest Nature Reserve, by agreement between the Forestry Commission and the Nature Conservancy. In those days, conservationists were obliged to regard a few crumbs of loaf as better than no bread. They had little money to buy land or compensate owners for reduced production and so were reduced to making a plea on behalf of the wild inhabitants of the wood. The pleading in this case was persuasive, because the petitioners included the great Oxford ecologist, Charles Elton, and an entomologist of repute, Marcus Goddard. At first, however, the transformation from overgrown coppice to plantation seemed to encourage the butterflies, some of which, like the fritillaries, appeared in greater numbers than for years past, enjoying the sudden floods of sunlight and flushes of spring flowers. The species in greatest danger were thought to be the purple emperor, which needs big sallows in woodland glades, and the black hairstreak, which lives among blackthorn thickets.

What did the conservationists get out of the 1955 nature reserve agreement? Apart from a certain amount of window dressing (signs, wardens, access rights), it boiled down to four hectares worth of glades in Waterperry for the emperor and a promise to retain patches of blackthorn in Shabbington for the hairstreak. The butterflies had to make do with these morsels because, as the naturalists were forever being told, 'this is a working wood'. The measures were reasonably successful. The black hairstreak, whose breeding haunts had been covered with hessian bags to protect them from the helicopter's lethal rain, has not declined noticeably – black hairstreaks ask very little from life so long as their breeding thickets are not disturbed. And the purple emperor flies there still, albeit in reduced numbers. The fritillaries, on the other hand, began to decline once the growing trees started to shade the clearings of the 1950s. The high brown fritillary has not been seen in either wood for many years.

Since 1985, the Forestry Commission has switched to planting broadleaves in ancient and natural woodland. Once again there is to be a final crop of oaks at Shabbington and Waterperry after the conifers are taken out. It may well be that the conifers of Shabbington and Waterperry will turn out to be but a short-lived phase in their history, marking the high tide of the industrial era when ancient woods were treated as shop floors for timber factories. If the story of these woods suggests anything it is that the future is unpredictable, but it seems likely that these woods will be transformed eventually into broadleaved high forest with big grassy ride junctions and a scatter of glades, some of them sheltering ponds. Perhaps there will one day even be a woodman or two, harvesting firewood and rustic poles from restored coppice in Drunkard's Corner.

THE CHILTERNS

In his short story *Other Kingdom*, E. M. Forster declared that 'Other Kingdom Copse is just like any other beech copse, and I am therefore spared the fatigue of describing it'. Walking in the Chilterns almost anywhere between Henley and Tring one can see what he meant. The chalk slopes and clay-capped plateaux of the Chilterns are to a large degree a natural and historical unity. It is the second largest wooded area in England, measuring some 64 by 40km (40 by 25 miles), and has been so since the Norman Conquest. For most of its history it was thinly populated and, despite a wealth of woodland, was never subjected to Forest Law nor harnessed to the industrial effort. Today's landscape policies emphasise the area's special character with the Chilterns Standing Conference and the 1971 Plan for the Chilterns. In the mind's eye, then, the Chiltern woods are places of soaring, even-aged beeches and bare, leafy floors. If I had to name one place that typified that view of the Chilterns it would be along the steep hill road west of Marlow between the woodbanks of Pullingshill and Hollowhill Woods which, until the gales of the late 1980s, formed an arcade of huge beeches like the nave of a Gothic cathedral. The cathedral effect, so widely admired, actually depends on the trees being the same size and, in all probability, planted at the same time. Unmanaged English beeches are rarely so tall or so symmetrical. In this section we will look at the nature of the ancient woods that still survive within the uniform mantle

of beech, like heather under snow, and how the Chilterns came to be as they are today.

The nurture of beech

How much beech was there in the woods of the Chilterns before the age of enclosure and plantations? Beech is not much good at looking after itself in English woodland. Its regeneration de-

Coppiced beech stools at Hodgemoor Wood, ⇨
Buckinghamshire. September
(PETER WAKELY)

⇩ *Broad rides and an open 'box junction' at Shabbington Wood in 'Bernwood Forest'. The contraption in the middle of the ride is a mercury vapour moth trap (for this is an outstanding place for moths as well as butterflies). August*
(PAUL WARING)

pends on long warm summers needed to ripen the nuts: good mast years and good wine vintages tend to go together. But how often do you find ripe beechnuts? And even after an exceptional mast year such as 1976 or 1990, most beechlings succumb to frost and damp if their fleshy initial leaves have not already been devoured by caterpillars or pigeons. Grey squirrels and their great liking for beechmast and bark are a further major problem that our forebears did not have to contend with. Sometimes their gnawing precipitates that strange phenomenon known as beech-snap, when the tree suddenly breaks in half in the wind, leaving a rotten stump some 4 or 5m (13 or 16ft) high.

In these circumstances Chiltern beechwoods have to be nurtured with care. Most beech is of planted origin and is encouraged to grow up as tall forest trees. Some of the woods are secondary, having been planted on former farmland from the late seventeenth century onwards. But more than half are believed to be ancient and are dominated by beech only because past silviculture involved the suppression of competing trees. However, beech was not unimportant before the expansion of the furniture trade. Woodmen seem to favour beech in this area since the Middle Ages, probably because beech makes good firewood. In 1677, the Oxford natural historian Robert Plot wrote that 'the most frequent tree in this county is the beech which yields the most healthy firing in the world, it curing all the maladies of low situations'. Descriptions of the Chilterns landscape in the eighteenth century, before the great expansion of the furniture trade, confirm Plot's account, speaking of 'perpetual woods of beech'. Abbey Wood near Woodcote in south Oxfordshire, for example, seems to have been managed intensively as a beech coppice to supply firewood for the abbot's kitchens[12].

There are, nevertheless, major differences between the Chilterns then and now. We are used to seeing large high forest woods covering hill and dale alike in a blanket of beech. Early maps indicate that the original landscape was much more finely detailed, a patchwork of copses, commons managed as wood-pastures, and sometimes tiny meadows and fields *inside* the woods. Big tall beeches were probably rare. The medieval idea of a beech was a gnarled old pollard or a bristly coppice stump, not a soaring, smooth-skinned maiden. An effort of the imagination is needed to visualise the Chiltern woods as they were when the commonland system prevailed: scenes of leafy bushes of foliage on large stumps, winding tracks and wood lanes, woodbanks with hornbeam hedges and, on the plateau in autumn, the almost surreal sight of beech leaves turning gold over a mantle of flowering heather. It is even harder to persuade the non-specialist that these woods were closer to nature and richer in wildlife than the present forests.

Coppicing, bodging and pegging

Practically the only value for beech coppice is for fuel: beech small round-wood has none of the special uses of ash, oak, hazel or chestnut but, like hornbeam, it burns well, producing the intense high temperatures needed for bread ovens and furnaces. Before 1800, there were dozens of wood-burning kilns in the southern Chilterns, using local clay for brick-making or chalk for quicklime. Beech wood also supplied the Henley-on-Thames glass-works. Many Buckinghamshire parishes operated 'intercommoning' arrangements, whereby the wooded Chiltern parishes supplied firewood to their partners in the valley in exchange for grazing rights on the rich meads of the Thames. In our own time beech smallwood continued to be cut to supply brush factories at Chesham and Henley, and is still cut for firewood on a very limited scale.

The most celebrated traditional woodland-based industries in the Chilterns are chair leg and tent peg-making. Chairs, like forks or sandwiches, are surprisingly recent inventions. In England they were not much used in private houses before the seventeenth century: instead people sat on stools or benches. As living standards improved, however, there was a growing demand for wooden chairs, particularly the classic 'Windsor chair', whose legs and backstands were individually slotted into the seat. The chair legs were generally made of beech, with seats of elmwood and, for high class chairs, backs of yew, cherry-wood or walnut. The early chairmakers worked in or near the woods, but the manufacture of seats and backs and the assembly work soon became a cottage industry and was eventually centred in factories at High Wycombe. Nevertheless, the basic sawing and turning of green wood on simple foot-treadled pole lathes continued to be done in the open, usually in autumn and winter when the sap was low. This became the work of travelling pedlars with the now comic name of bodgers – perhaps from the German *botcher*, meaning a cooper, not because they necessarily bodged or botched their work. Bodgers preferred sawn wood from young straight-trunked standard trees, not roundwood from coppice. Their heyday was from around 1870, when High Wycombe was producing some 4,500 chairs every day, until 1914. Until that date, all chairs supplied to the government had to have their legs cleft from the log by a bodger, a lucrative contract indeed. But once the bodgers were called to the front to fight for king and country, inferior machine-made chair legs became a necessity. During the next forty years the craft gradually died out.

At Woodcote in south Oxfordshire, the first bodger appeared in 1871, and ten years later seven of them were employed in the surrounding woods. The career of the last full-time bodger in the area, who retired in 1961, aged eighty-four, spanned almost the entire history of the craft. Like charcoal burners in the west, bodgers (for they preferred to work in pairs) were part of the local woodland scene, with their shacks of calico-covered brush-wood, the piles of chair legs stacked to dry, 'the ashpole of their lathe jutting out at front, and a hanging kettle singing over a wood fire nearby'[13]. A skilled bodger could make a chair leg out of a log in ten minutes, and might produce well over six hundred turned parts per week, enough for ninety chairs, and bargain for them at the factory gate. But even so he rarely made a fortune: five shillings a week was a chair-bodger's average takings in 1900.

The decline of chair-bodging led to a lessening demand for small trees, and this has resulted in overstocked woods, cluttered up with third-rate trees. The bodgers continued to make a somewhat uncertain living by making tent pegs from small billets of beech, which used similar methods of sawing, splitting and turning. The Boer War and the two world wars saw an enormous demand for tent pegs for the army, and south Oxfordshire, the centre for this industry, produced about thirty million pegs during world war II alone. A good pegger could manage about 120 tent pegs per hour. Like bodging, this craft survived into the 1950s on a reduced scale, and a few people still turn out pegs for boy scouts, or put themselves on display at country shows. As with coppice crafts such as hurdle and thatching-spar making, chair bodging might be ripe for economic revival. Mike Abbot, a latterday enthusiast who taught himself the craft from books, set up a training course in the mid-eighties, and three of his ex-students are now established full-time bodgers working woods in the Bath and Bristol area [14]. Abbot even foresees a future when DIY enthusiasts can buy their wood direct from the forester and perhaps cleave and turn it on the spot, just as people now troop happily into the fields and orchards to pick their own strawberries and apples. Such a future is entirely compatible with conservation objectives.

Ancient vegetation

Much of the flora of Chiltern woods depends on small patches of variety amid uniformity, and only occasionally on whole woods. Most of these patches differ from their surroundings in being less shaded, or, as in the case of some of the rare orchids, are centred on woodbanks, well-rotted beech litter or other localised features. On the gravels and clays of the plateau there can be a great deal of oak as well as other trees tolerant of acid conditions, such as hazel, aspen, birch, rowan, cherry, yew and holly. On the more shallow lime-rich soil of the slopes one can expect to find much ash, maple and whitebeam as well as shrubs such as dogwood, spindle and guelder rose in the more open situations. Significant pointers to ancient woodland in this area are sessile oak, wych elm, aspen, and, much more rarely, 'lineage' elm and wild service tree. Sessile oak occurs also as large trees on former commons, such as Naphill Common in Bucks, or as coppiced trees at Offal Wood and Pishill Bank.

Chiltern oak coppices have a fairytale atmosphere to them, a strange architecture of swollen bases and spreading, twisting stems rather like antlers. They generally lie on very poor, acidic soils and are almost bare of other vegetation. Wych elm, by contrast, prefers rich moist soils. There are large oak coppice stools at Mongewell Woods and one still occasionally finds healthy maiden trees. Near Goring there are some coppiced 'lineage' elms on large high-cut stools, known otherwise mainly from East Anglia. Hornbeam is a surprisingly scarce native of the Chilterns and was probably selectively removed in the past to make room for beech. It has, however, been much planted on woodbanks to form hedges or, in pure stands, probably for firewood to service brickworks. The strip of hornbeam coppice acting as a thick hedge at Quarry Wood, Cookham Dean, may, however, be a remnant of the original vegetation. Aspen is sometimes found as small standard trees in mixed coppice, but a more characteristic place for this tree is on damp, formerly wooded commons where its unpleasant taste provided it with some protection from grazing. Big old aspens are rare in the Chilterns; evidently fungal disease cuts down most aspens while they are still adolescent. Sycamore is widespread, often successfully competing with ash for colonising vacant ground and contesting a space in the woodland canopy with beech.

The majority of woodland in the Chilterns however is composed of the familiar 'cathedral-like' high forest, composed almost entirely of beech, with just a few oaks or hollies or the occasional giant cherry tree. There is little light, no flowers, and hardly any undergrowth except for non-flowering brambles (which leap into life after thinning) and ivy scrambling up the trunks. At its most sepulchral, the forest floor is, in Chris Smith's words 'shin-deep in fallen leaves whatever the time of year, or so bare of litter as to give the impression of having been swept by a broom'[15]. Two of the most characteristic flowers of Chiltern beechwoods are the leafless, honey-coloured spikes of bird's-nest orchid, whose weird lifestyle is as an outsize parasite feeding off the fungi in its roots, and the wall lettuce, a plant of little spurts of yellow and flat paper-thin leaves, as if they had been pressed in a book, and often covered in mildew. One could make a long list of other Chiltern woodland specialities: coralwort, green and stinking hellebores, wood barley, fly orchid, red, narrow-lipped, violet and green-flowered helleborines, early dog-violet, wood melic, southern wood-rush, mezereon, lesser wintergreen. But most of these need at least a dappling of light at flowering time and are more likely to be found near the edge of the wood or in islands of less modified vegetation, especially on steep slopes. Wood barley and wood melic are found most often on woodbanks. In general, Buckinghamshire woods are richer botanically than their congeners in Oxfordshire, perhaps because a much greater proportion of the latter are bramble-dominated plateau woods with fewer steep hangers.

Conservation

There are about 7,790ha (18,949 acres) of ancient woodland within the Chilterns Area of Outstanding Natural Beauty, compared with 6,830ha (16,877 acres) of recent secondary woodland. Some 3,077ha (7,603 acres) – nearly half of it – has been converted to plantations in recent years. A relatively small proportion – 602ha (1,488 acres) – has been designated as Sites of Special Scientific Interest, 306ha (756 acres) in Oxfordshire and 242ha (732 acres) in Bucks.

Since 1945, lime-tolerant conifers such as Norway spruce and Corsican and Austrian pine have become part of the Chiltern forest scene. The prospect of creeping coniferisation in the Chilterns was unwelcome to many, and guidelines, published in 1971 as the Plan for the Chilterns, limit the size of felling coupes and provide for a final crop of 'native broadleaves' – that is, beech – with conifers relegated to the role of nurse crops. But while the Plan was welcomed by conservation bodies as an improvement, it was mainly concerned with landscape matters and failed to distinguish between the relatively dull plantations and the much richer ancient and natural woods. Since 1985, the Forestry Commission's Broadleaved Woodland Policy has acknowledged the need for more sympathetic management in ancient and natural woodland. Since there was by then a pressing need to identify such woodland in the Chilterns, a survey of every wood over 2ha (4.9 acres) was undertaken for the NCC by Jean Buchanan and Janet Welsh, using a range of ancient woodland indicators. They looked for stands with an unusual diversity of trees and shrubs, especially where sessile oak, living wych elm or lineage elm, wild service, aspen or hornbeam were present, stands with twenty-eight or more species of flowers or ferns associated with ancient woodland, and places where rare flowers grew. They also kept an eye open for ancient earthworks, pollarded trees and other historic features. In all, about 2,000ha (4,942 acres) of woodland fitted one or more of these criteria. In most instances these areas lay on sloping ground where planting was difficult. The NCC has called them 'heritage woods' and urges their owners to consider natural regeneration, rather than planting, as a means to perpetuate them and to favour native trees such as oak, ash, birch and wild cherry as well as the ubiquitous beech [16].

One of the many remarkable beech pollards at ⇨ Burnham Beeches, a living sculpture of wood and leafage, cut in 1989 by selectively thinning the heavy branches. September
(PETER WAKELY)

Burnham Beeches:
from common to open space

AREA: 219ha (540 acres)

STATUS: Owned by the Corporation of London. Part of Dorney Wood is owned by the National Trust. SSSI

ACCESS: Open to the public. A booklet is available

TYPE: Strongly acid beech, oak and birch with ancient trees; oak-hazel on clay, valley alderwood

GRID REFERENCE: SU 950857

Virtually at the doorstep of upmarket Marlow and downmarket Slough lies a remarkably wild stretch of ancient countryside. Around the edge are large houses, huge trees, gravel pits and deep circular pools secluded in woodland; and here and there, traces of furtive wrong-doing – burnt-out cars and piles of rubbish. Then there is an inner belt of old fields, coppice woods enclosed by earth banks, areas of towering high forest, bogs and swallow holes and dells. And at its heart lies Burnham Beeches proper, part overgrown common, part wood-pasture with ancient oaks and beeches, mysterious banks and moats and areas of dense woodland with almost bare floors. This is marvellous walking country for the cramped city dweller. Those who have read George Orwell's *Keep the Aspidistra Flying* may remember a description of it and, because the City Corporation's wardens have police powers of arrest, it is also perhaps one of the safest places near London to wander at will.

Eighteenth- and nineteenth-century maps reveal that Burnham Beeches was then an open landscape, a common of heather and grass on a plateau of infertile sand, gravel and clay. It is classed as ancient woodland today because of its famous pollard trees, 'the largest collection of old beech trees in the world', which are thought to have originated around 400 to 450 years ago, probably during a period of slack grazing. Older yet are the moats and banks marking former areas of cultivation amid the common waste. 'Hardicanute's Moat', for example, used to surround a medieval homestead. The moat and its mighty inner bank, once topped by a hedge, were designed not so much to resist human enemies as to keep out the commoners' free-ranging cattle, pigs and goats. Larger enclosures were later made to protect woodland, beginning with New Coppice in the fifteenth century, to which Fleet Wood was added 300 years later. But the coppices around the edge are ancient woodland with well-preserved woodbanks. Dorneywood and Egypt Wood display a great variety of woodland soils and vegetation, from tall, bendy oaks competing with spindly 'snags' of birch, giant rowans and jungly groves of holly, to coppice stools of oak, beech and hazel, with occasional 'indicator species' such as service trees and alder buckthorn.

Burnham Beeches itself is a modern name, first surfacing around 1837. When the City of London Corporation purchased the area in 1880 as a public open space, it was still in part an open heath, noted for nightjars, woodlarks and a magnificent view of London. But by 1914, common grazing had declined to a few cows, ponies and donkeys, and soon ceased altogether. Thus much of Burnham Beeches is recent, secondary woodland, a place of dense birches, bracken, and rhododendron, although the original cover of heather still survives in places.

On these acid soils one would not expect to find lush carpets of woodland flowers. The heart of Burnham Beeches is almost flowerless, the bare ground being broken only by scattered tufts of hair-grass, bramble sprigs and the distinctive pale-green cushions of the moss, *Leucobryum glaucum*. The richest places tend to be gullies and swallow holes (locally, 'swilly holes' from the Saxon 'swylie', a hole in the ground, full of water), natural dells where the underlying chalk has dissolved away causing the land to subside. One such gully, whose underground stream emerges in a Victorian brick culvert, has a particularly splendid slade of tall straight coppice-derived alders in which the feathery whisks of wood horsetail are prominent. The great rarity of Dorneywood is a real oddity, an umbellifer with the resounding name of Cornish bladderseed *(Physospermum cornubiense)*. This is most at home in milder Mediterranean climes and has only a few outlying colonies in Britain, mainly in Cornwall. Its status at Dorneywood is uncertain. It is confined to a single large patch the size of an average garden beneath a close canopy of birch and rowan, and it has not shifted its ground significantly since its discovery in 1904. Druce, the author of the *Flora of Buckinghamshire* (1926), suggests that these bladderseeds originated from the grounds of Bulstrode, three miles distant, where they are believed to have been planted near an ornamental pond among other rare flowers introduced by the Duchess of Portland. At Dorneywood only one plant in twenty produces flowers and it would probably benefit from some thinning of the overlying canopy. In Cornwall it has a decided preference for managed coppice.

The glory of Burnham Beeches are its magnificent pollarded trees. As the name implies, most of them are beeches cut about 2.4m (8ft) from the ground, but there are also pollard oaks such as the battered old Druid's Oak, nine metres in girth. Some of the old pollard beeches also have whimsical names. A great beech at the bottom of Pumpkins Hill was called 'His Majesty'. About the same size as the Druid's Oak, it was said to be the largest beech in England. Mendelssohn is said to have composed *A Midsummer Night's Dream* beneath another great pollard called Mendelssohn's Tree in his honour. This was among the pollards badly damaged in the gale of January 1990, though the hollow bolling remains alive. Gone altogether, alas, is the venerable beech that stood by the stream below Stag Hill, which is believed to be the original of the tree in Gray's 'Elegy', that

. . . yonder nodding beech
That wreathes its old fantastic roots so high,
His listless length at noon-tide would he stretch,
And pore upon the brook that babbles by.

Burnham has about 700 old beech pollards, each of which is an individual with its own little metal plate. Some are scored by oak-like fissures quite unlike the usual smooth, limb-like bark. Others have blackened crowns, rotting where rainwater has collected at the top, and sprouting hedge garlic, polypodies and other plants in the humus collected in the clefts. They were 'lopped and topped' regularly between about 1500 and 1820. The wood so obtained belonged to the Lord of the Manor, and was used as firewood and, in the earlier years, as winter fodder. There is a legend that Cromwell's soldiers lopped the trees to make musket stocks, though branch loppings were hardly suited to that purpose. Another story is that the Duchess of Monmouth beheaded the trees in memory of her husband the Duke, lately pollarded by his uncle, King James II.

No one knows how long these great trees will last without treatment. Careful and selective cutting of the largest branches relieves the trunk of its heavy burden, makes the tree less susceptible to windblow and prolongs its life. Neglected trees are apt to shed their boughs, a worrisome hazard in a public place such as Burnham Beeches. Some trees, notably hornbeam in woodland and riverside willows and limes in town and village streets, have a high success rate when repollarded after a long interval. With others, such as oak, the result is unpredictable with weak trees often dying. Beech is among the more difficult trees. Repollarding any large neglected pollard is a risky operation, both to the cutter and the tree. As Peter Mitchell puts it, it effectively means 'felling small to medium-size trees while standing on a small platform with awkward footholds two to three metres up in the air' [17]. In these circumstances chain-saws can be deadly weapons, as ready to pollard the woodcutter as the tree. Many prefer therefore to use slower but safer axes or bow-saws. Even then the work is dangerous enough, given the unpredictable twisting and kicking of a cut limb as it falls.

4

WESSEX

This chapter is about the woods of Wiltshire, Dorset, Hampshire and the Isle of Wight. Here are found some of the more extensive and famous of England's ancient woods: the 'ancient and ornamental' woods and wood-pastures of the New Forest; Cranborne Chase, the great provider of hazel sheep hurdles; Parkhurst Forest in the Isle of Wight, once a New Forest in miniature; and the wonderful beech hangers near Selborne in Hampshire, which figure so prominently in the letters and journals of Gilbert White. For the most part, however, their ancient woods lie within farmland. Most were managed previously as coppice, but less worked coppice survives here now than in the south-east or East Anglia. As elsewhere, the smaller woods are often intact but neglected, while the larger ones have been much replanted with the more profitable conifers. Some large woods, such as Langley Wood in Hampshire, are managed high forest with broad rides.

Thomas Hardy's Wessex has some of the most wildlife-rich woods in England, the result of a warm climate and a variety of soils and ancient habitats working in combination. More than a quarter of England's managed hazel coppice was in Hampshire and Wiltshire. Hazelwoods still dominate much of Cranborne Chase and many other copses in the region, and are of two main types: mixtures of hazel, ash, maple and pedunculate oak on poorly drained but base-rich soil, and oak-hazel woods on more acid soils. Sessile oak also occurs, generally in the less disturbed woods on acid soils where it is sometimes accompanied by dense groves of holly. Beech woodland dominates the hangers of east Hampshire, but it thins out as one travels west (although there are some mighty individual trees in the New Forest and Savernake Forest), reaching the limits of its natural range in Dorset and Somerset. There is very little native hornbeam or lime except in north Dorset.

The history of woods in Wessex has not been worked out in the same detail as those of East Anglia, but they are likely to have a lot in common. Much of Hampshire and Wiltshire was Royal Forest in the Middle Ages, not so much because they were better wooded than other counties but because the king owned more manors there. The New Forest, safeguarded by its unique legislation, is the supreme survivor of the old unenclosed, unimproved landscape of heaths, woods and bogs. Woods used as pasture were widespread in the region, although working examples, such as Binswood in Hampshire, are now very rare. The main woodland industry was hazel coppicing for hurdles, thatching spars, hedge binders and other purposes where flexible 'withies' were required. Such woods are often very rich in wild flowers and with an intricate pattern of banks and rides. Let us explore each county in turn.

WILTSHIRE

In Wiltshire, the pattern of ancient woodland has not changed substantially since the advent of the Domesday Book. In the Middle Ages, much of the county was under Forest Law, though in reality only a small proportion of it was woodland. The physical forest was concentrated on great parks such as Clarendon which, in its heyday, measured 11km (7 miles) in perimeter with twenty coppices, 'every one a mile round'. But most of the forests of Wiltshire were disafforested under the early Stuarts, and much grubbing of woodland followed. Aubrey attributed the loss of the pine marten in north Wiltshire to these seventeenth-century clearances. It is unlikely that the forests were much more densely wooded than the rest of the county. It is interesting that Cranborne Chase, the most densely wooded area of all, was never Royal Forest, although it was owned by the Plantagenet kings. The largest area of wooded forest to survive is **Savernake**. Before it was privatised in 1549, contemporaries speak of it as an expanse of heath, bracken and open wood-pasture with ancient pollards and 'severely neglected coppices' [18]. Planting has since changed its nature drastically and, grand though it is, most of the Savernake Forest is of comparatively recent origin. Traces of its pre-plantation past survive in the great pollard oaks, with their communities of rare lichens, mosses and beetles, and in the ground flora of the original coppice compartments.

The lush woods of the limestone north-west form a distinct group of ash-wych elm woodland. These are all woods of 50ha (123.5 acres) or less that cling to moist valley sides and coombes and were formerly managed as coppices. **Monk's Wood** near Slaughterford and the adjoining **Colerne Park** (48ha) [118 acres], both owned by the Woodland Trust, have a particularly rich flora that was documented in great detail by Donald Grose in the 1950s [19]. They owe their excellent preservation to New College, Oxford, to whom they were given as a benefaction by the College's founder, William of Wykeham, in the fourteenth century and with whom they remained until 1945. A magnificent avenue of

trees, now swallowed up in woodland, leads to Euridge Manor where Sir Walter Raleigh stayed shortly before his last fateful voyage to the West Indies.

On the clay in the north-west of the county lie **Picket and Clanger Woods** near Westbury (52ha) [128 acres], which are among the best-preserved woods of the Forest of Selwood, which straddles the border with Somerset. 'Clanger' is a corruption of Clay Hanger, which describes the wood perfectly, a steeply sloping wood on wet Oxford Clay. It also suggests a sonorous wood, which indeed it is in May and June when the wood echoes to a massed choir of songbirds, including up to twenty pairs of nightingales. Much of the wood was unfortunately clear-felled and replanted with Norway spruce and larch in 1967, but today the natural vegetation is increasing again under the sympathetic management of the Woodland Trust, with the help of local volunteers and school parties.

Wiltshire's chalk woods lie mostly on the steeper scarp slopes or in coombes, or on the plateau where the chalk is overlain by acidic clay-with-flints. By contrast with the Chilterns, native beech is rare in Wiltshire, and, where found, is a tree of the acidic gravels south-east of Salisbury, not of the chalk. The scarp woods are similar to those of the limestone north-west, that is ash-maple or ash-wych elm coppices with oak and ash standards. **Great Ridge Wood** (a baldly descriptive name, characteristic of this county) is the largest wood on the chalk, and contains a wide range of stand-types, including areas of acidic oak-hazel woodland as well as base-rich ash-dominated woodland. Like most big woods, it has been extensively replanted. **Great Yews** is an isolated ancient wood on the windy chalk plains south of Salisbury, hard against the Saxon Grimes Ditch. Recorded in a ninth-century charter, this is, as the name implies, a place of large yews, some of which are at least two hundred years old. This is the only pure yew-wood in the county and, unlike the steep Sussex yew-woods, it stands on a gentle slope.

Clouts Wood (12ha) [32 acres] clings to the side of a valley near Swindon and, like many woods on

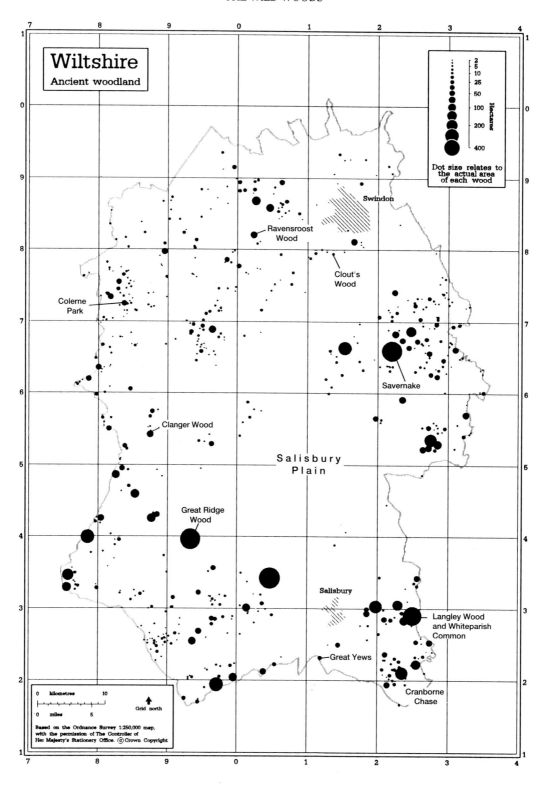

Wiltshire
Ancient woodland

Hectares
2
5
10
25
50
100
200
400

Dot size relates to
the actual area
of each wood

Swindon

Ravensroost
Wood

Clout's
Wood

Colerne
Park

Savernake

Clanger Wood

Salisbury
Plain

Great Ridge
Wood

Salisbury

Langley Wood
and Whiteparish
Common

Great Yews

Cranborne
Chase

0   kilometres   10

0   miles   5

Grid north

Based on the Ordnance Survey 1:250,000 map,
with the permission of The Controller of
Her Majesty's Stationery Office. © Crown Copyright

68

the Wiltshire chalk, was used mainly to provide hazel rods for making sheep hurdles. Though it has since grown shady through neglect, and was battered by gales in 1990, it is still a delightful little wood. It is full of interesting wild flowers and ferns around springs and runnels where chalk meets clay, including groves of giant horsetails with their graceful whorls of leaves that blur from a distance into a dense green mist. The spiked star-of-Bethlehem, a rare lily of subdued green-and-white colouring, is quite common here. What the herbalist Gerard called its 'greene starre flowres' are easily passed over, but its tight knives of buds are very similar to asparagus and used to be gathered for the kitchen as 'Bath asparagus'. This must be one of the very few rare plants that were sought after for food – offhand I can otherwise only think of sea kale, once eaten as rather salty 'greens', and wild orchids, whose testicular tubers were renowned in their day as aphrodisiacs.

The nineteenth-century shepherds of the Wiltshire downs, whose lives were so evocatively described by W. H. Hudson in *A Shepherd's Life* (1910), used vast quantities of hazel hurdles, and large woods at the edge of Salisbury Plain, such as Bentley Woods and Cranborne Chase, were organised into copses for hazel production on a scale unparalleled anywhere in Britain. At Cranborne Chase this was possible only after the deer were rounded up and evicted in 1829 (they have since returned). Exceptionally, the native stocks of hazel were here boosted by planting on former pastureland, as at Bridmoor Green and Farnham Common. Cranborne hazels reputedly made the best hurdles in England. Aubrey, the seventeenth-century author of a natural history of Wiltshire, distinguishes between these, whose withies were 'white and tough' and whose nuts were particularly delicious ('they sell them at Woodbery Hill Faire etc, and the price of them is the price of a buschell of wheate'), and the poorer quality hazels from the north of the county which were 'red and not so tough, more brittle'. Wattle hurdlers still practise their craft at Cranborne Chase today, though on a much-reduced scale and mostly as rustic furniture for suburban gardens.

The acidic clays, sands and gravels in the southeastern corner of the county form another contrast. Here we are close to Hampshire and the New Forest and much of the present-day woodland is secondary, having sprung up on former heaths once kept open by common grazing. **Whiteparish Common**, famous for its woodland butterflies, was still being used as common wood-pasture as late as the 1950s. This is a good place to compare the vegetation of former open wood-pasture, with big pollard beeches, and enclosed copses which have little beech but many coppice stools, including some native lime. The nearby **Blackmoor Copse** is a well-preserved ancient wood having oak and ash standards over a hazel-dominated understorey with ponds, rides and coppiced glades.

Ravensroost Wood: a Wiltshire coppice

AREA: 40ha (98.8 acres)

STATUS: Nature reserve owned by the Wiltshire Trust for Nature Conservation. Part of the Braydon Forest countryside management project, managed by the Trust

ACCESS: Open along main paths and bridleway

TYPE: Wet ash-wych elm and ash-hazel woodland

GRID REFERENCE: SU 022882

The raven was once a familiar sight in the woods of

The great chalkland heart of Wiltshire – Salisbury Plain and the Marlborough Downs – is almost woodless. Elsewhere some 13,250ha (32,741 acres) of ancient woodland are scattered on infertile soils, on hillsides and hilltops and in former forests and chases near the borders of the county, notably at Savernake, Selwood and Cranborne Chase. More than half of the ancient woodland, especially the larger woods, has been replanted

southern England. The Rev A. C. Smith, who wrote a book about the birds of Wiltshire in c 1830, knew of twenty-three breeding places in his county, mostly in woods or ruined buildings. These grand, glossy-black birds used to choose tall, prominent trees, often called raven-trees in their honour, to build their nests, using the same site year after year. The same woods would often play host to noisy gatherings of non-breeding birds that croaked and tumbled lazily above the treetops. Gilbert White's beech hanger at Selborne was such a place. What finally banished the raven to the wilder moors were the rewards offered under a late-sixteenth-century statute, by churchwardens for raven heads, in the belief that they caused serious losses of new-born lambs and poultry. Their regular nesting habits made them easy prey. Superstition might have preserved a few pairs. W. H. Hudson recalled a farmer whose sheep each year fell dead of a pestilence, bringing him to the brink of ruin. His shepherd shook his head: 'Tis not strange, master, he shot a raven.' But by the time A. C. Smith's book was published in 1887, only three pairs of ravens still nested in Wiltshire, and today there are none at all.

In Britain, some twenty-seven ancient woods are named after ravens (though some of them may commemorate unknown persons called *Mr* Raven). Ravensroost Wood, in the Clay Vale west of Swindon, seems to have been a place of ravens until the early 1800s when persecution finally drove them out. An alternative name, mentioned in a lease dated 1632, was Ravenshurst Wood, the wooded hill of ravens, a reference to the wood's position on the crest of a low hill. The birds may well have used an outsize tree, the Charlton Oak, which used to stand in a prominent place near the hilltop.

Ravensroost Wood lies in ancient countryside, characterised by small irregular-shaped fields and ancient hedges with oaks in them. This used also to be a place of old meadowland with cowslips and orchids. The woods in this area supplied firewood and building material to villages such Minety and Cricklade, and so were cut over regularly. Today the Braydon Forest project aims to develop mod-

ern markets for such traditional woodland produce. Ravensroost Wood is one of only a handful of woods in Britain which are known to have been coppiced almost uninterruptedly for centuries. In the 1950s and 1960s, when the majority of ancient woods were game coverts or plantations, this one still possessed a full-time woodman-gamekeeper who maintained the rides and supplied nearby villages with pea sticks, hazel thatching spars and hethers for hedge laying, as well as faggots for fuel. The sledge used to remove the cut wood is still there, propped up next to a delightfully carved rustic lodge in the middle of the wood, the past scene of roistering Boxing Day shooting parties. Coppicing continues under the stewardship of the Wiltshire Trust for Nature Conservation, who bought the wood in 1987. The unbroken tradition of management at Ravensroost has preserved spectacular vernal carpets of wood anemones, primroses and lesser celandines, and a vigorously regenerating underwood dominated by hazel, together with some ash and wych elm and a wide range of shrubs.

The Clay Vale of Wiltshire is notorious for its sticky blue-grey 'Minety clay', so poorly drained that the hillsides are almost as wet as the valleys. At Ravensroost, pendulous sedge, normally a plant of ditches, smothers the surface of the rides. A previous owner, who liked to drive his carriage through the wood, employed one Jake Hobson to dig up clay from the wood and bake it to spread over the main rides. This crude form of metalling was remarkably effective, and, fifty years later, the surface is still covered with what looks like crumbled red brick. Jake's steep-sided clay pits have since become ponds. One of them, recently dredged and freed from overshadowing tangle by the Trust, is full of remarkably clear water through which you can peer down into a miniature underwater forest of stoneworts.

Jake Hobson's carriage ride through Ravensroost ⇨
Wood, Wiltshire. The pines were part of the
wood's 'beautification' earlier in the century. April
(PETER MARREN)

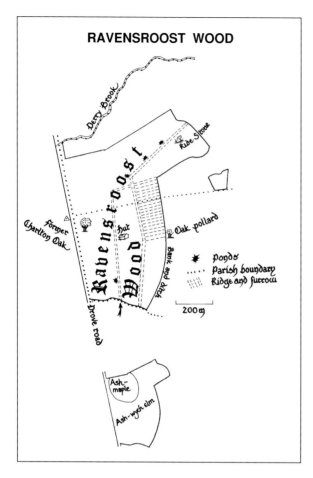

RAVENSROOST WOOD

Derry Brook

Ride Stone

Ravensroost Wood

Former Charlton Oak

Hut

Oak pollard

Bank and ditch

Drove road

✱ ponds
···· Parish boundary
||| Ridge and furrow

200 m

Ash-maple

Ash-wych elm

may have tried to augment the natural supply by pushing hazelnuts into the soil. The secondary nature of this part of the wood is immediately made clear by its impoverished flora, and especially the near absence of wood anemones and primroses.

Like most woods, Ravensroost records the foibles and eccentricities of its owners and users, past and present. Ninety years ago it was thought a good idea to plant oaks there. Some of the trees survived but, with their feet stuck in cold sodden clay, they are poor, crabbed specimens, useless for timber. Fortunately they did not succeed in entirely suppressing the underwood and the Wiltshire Trust is now wisely thinning the more oak-dominated parts. But even the Trust cannot resist unnecessary planting experiments. In the midst of some young ash and hazel coppice, a dozen whips of wild service tree have been planted, which, even if successful, will suppress the coppice without contributing anything of value. Much of the interest of wild service lies in its rarity and natural pattern of distribution.

Before leaving Ravensroost, a word should be said about its ride system whose close chequerboard pattern suggests intensive use. Ride-making is usually undocumented and, as a result, impossible to date, although we are safe in assuming that it is post-medieval. But here, in the north-eastern corner of the wood, is a fine inscribed stone dated 1770, recording the creation of the rides by the then owner Captain J. N. P. Nott of the Royal Navy (contemporary maps refer to Ravensroost as 'Nott's Wood'). The reverse side commemorates Harry Hughes, 'woodward, forty years servant in the family', who doubtless supervised the work.

DORSET

Dorset is a county of small woods and copses, many of them associated with physical features such as scarps, springs, steep-sided valleys and hilltops. Virtually all lie on poor soils. The densest concentration of woodland is in the north-east of the county at Cranborne Chase. Elsewhere many of the larger woods are former wood-pastures or

Its wet, intractable clay probably saved most of Ravensroost Wood from the plough once the medieval Forest of Braydon was privatised by Charles I (a typically arbitrary act which caused commoners' riots). But the eastern side of the wood was grubbed up and ploughed. The ridge-and-furrow is very well preserved, well enough indeed to make a tired walker feel seasick, but the experiment was evidently a failure for the field is once again part of the wood. It is said to have been planted with hazels, and hazel certainly dominates the ground today. Hazel-planting in woodland is probably rare because there was more than enough hazel around already, but in these Wiltshire woods at the edge of the downland sheep-walks, enormous quantities of hazel withies were used to make hurdles for sheepfolds, and some owners

overgrown commons, as at Holt Forest and Powerstock Common, or lie within medieval parkland, such as Melbury Park. One of Dorset's best-known natural features is the great loop of chalk downland that passes from Cranborne Chase, across Blandford Forest and Chetterwood, to the famous chalk cliffs around Lulworth Cove. On its north-facing scarp, lie sinuous 'hanging' woods and woods nestling inside steep-sided dry valleys whose ground is too steep to cultivate.

The chalk scarp of the Isle of Purbeck is also well-wooded for much of its length. Great Wood and Kings Wood at opposite ends are steeply inclined oak-ash-maple woods with small stands of small-leaved lime. There are also ancient secondary woods near Langton Maltravers on disused quarries of Purbeck marble. At the top of the ridge the chalk is displaced by more acidic clay-with-flints supporting dwarf oak trees, their canopies sheared by south-westerly winds. Like those at Cranborne Chase, these woods were extensively coppiced in the past but have since matured into closed-canopy high forest. Among their special flowers are wild daffodil and the pretty narrow-leaved lungwort, a rarity elsewhere confined to ancient woods around the old Solent River.

West Dorset is more like Devon with its commons, parks, deep-banked lanes and small steep woods, including the narrow streamside gullies known as gwyles. One of its pearls is **Powerstock Common** (115ha) [284 acres], a large island of wild countryside that owes its preservation both to the restrictions imposed by commonland and former Royal Forest status and to its extremely infertile soil. Its name is well earned: Powerstock is pronounced 'poor stock'. In this part of Dorset acidic Greensand and Gault Clay overlie heavy Fullers Earth clay to produce a jumble of landslips well watered by flushes and springs. The common was not enclosed until the mid-nineteenth century, and most of the present woodland dates from that time. Nevertheless Powerstock Common has an undeniable air of antiquity, with many stumpy moss-covered oaks which present a tangle of spreading limbs, stunted and contorted butts and

exposed intertwining roots.

Elsewhere in this part of Dorset there are some unusual little woods clustered around the springs emerging at the junction between the free-draining chalk and Greensand and the impervious underlying clay. The permanently waterlogged ground has produced alder and sallow woods on a layer of deep black peat, traditionally maintained as copses or withy beds. Now full of marsh marigolds, golden saxifrage and impressive mounds of tussock sedge, these woods have an extremely rich (though largely hidden) invertebrate fauna.

Melbury Park (255ha) [630 acres] is one of the finest medieval parks in the country and has changed little since its origins in the fifteenth century. The open launds are set with magnificent ancient oaks (one of which is called Billy Wilkins), bottomland groves of alder, birch and willow, lines of springs and enclosed hazel woods. On the bark of well-grown oaks, elms and ashes is one of the richest lichen floras in western Europe.

Duncliffe Wood (88ha) [217 acres], a great dark wood that rides the twin-topped saddle of Duncliffe Hill in the Vale of Blackmore, is said to have inspired Thomas Hardy's novel, *The Woodlanders*. The wood sits astride an island of infertile Greensand and Kimmeridge clay set amid the lush pastures of the Vale of Blackmore. It was certainly used by woodlanders, and as late as 1938 men in leather gloves and aprons were still cutting hazel to make thatching spars and for weaving into hurdles, stripping oak bark to sell to the tanyards and bundling brushwood into faggots. Signs of deep antiquity abound: through the wood passes an ancient track, Hort's Way; parish boundaries are marked by earth banks and lines of pollard or high-cut coppiced limes; an ancient spring still flows with clear water near the summit, and there are at least two dozen species of flowers, trees and ferns indicative of ancient woodland. In one place there are huge stools of small-leaved lime that may be a thousand years old, possibly the oldest living things in Dorset.

The western side of Duncliffe Wood has been grubbed and straightened since 1747, but the side facing Shaftesbury remains as a sinuous line of bays and headlands, bordered in places by big lime and ash stools, as irregular as a piece of jigsaw. None of these considerations prevented the Forestry Commission from clear-felling much of the wood in the 1950s and restocking it with plantations of larch and Douglas fir. Even so, the wood could not be made profitable and in 1984 the Commission decided to sell it. Fortunately the Woodland Trust was able to acquire Duncliffe Wood with financial aid from local authorities and the Countryside Commission. In places the natural vegetation has survived, including the irreplaceable ancient coppice stools and pollards, and the Trust is gradually restoring the original cover by thinning the conifers and creating open glades to encourage natural regeneration. There is, however, far too much planting taking place.

A mile or two west of Duncliffe Wood is another

⟵Spiked Star-of-Bethlehem (Ornithogalum pyrenaicum), one of Wiltshire's special woodland flowers and surprisingly difficult to spot in partly shaded wood borders and glades. It was once gathered for consumption as wild asparagus (PETER WAKELY)

Woodland Trust property, **Fifehead Wood** (20ha) [49 acres] near the village of Fifehead Magdalen. But whereas Duncliffe stands on a hill, Fifehead lies in a wet hollow, criss-crossed by drains. Ferns and mosses flourish in the humid atmosphere. On the other hand, ash standards, plonked unkindly into cold, waterlogged ground by some previous owner, have developed trunk canker and other ailments. Fifehead is really two small square ancient woods turned into one by the planting, with an old osier bed tacked on at one end. The ancient parts have large hazel stools and dense carpets of bluebells. To turn away deer and rabbits from newly coppiced hazels, the Trust's volunteers use a trick that might have been familiar to Thomas Hardy, of building a wigwam of twigs and branches over each stool to protect the buds and leaves until the shoots are well established.

It is fitting that Hardy's county should be the home of the Parnham Trust, a charitable foundation based at Hooke Park College near Beaminster, the brainchild of the furniture designer, John Makepeace. Coppicing has declined steadily in Dorset since 1900, but nearly half its ancient woods were still being coppiced in the late 1940s. During the 1950s, however, the practice all but died out and many woods ceased to be managed regularly. The result, as elsewhere, has been dense, shady woods, much poorer in wildlife than their predecessors. The aim of the Parnham Trust is to bring neglected woodlands back to sustainable use by developing new applications and markets for traditional roundwood timber and other coppice products.

A distant view of Duncliffe Wood, Dorset, on its ⟹ high saddle in the midst of the Blackmoor Vale.
August
(PETER WAKELY)

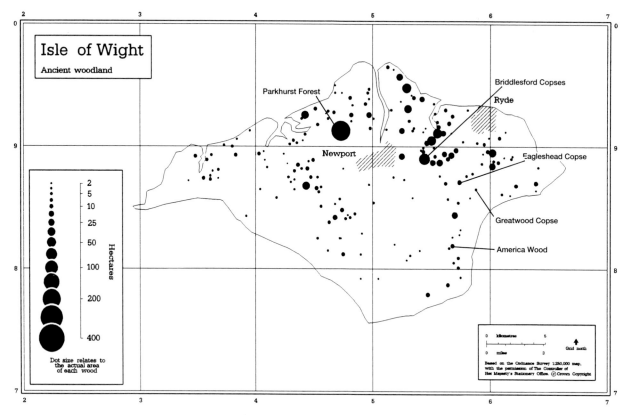

Isle of Wight

Ancient woodland

Parkhurst Forest

Briddlesford Copses

Ryde

Newport

Eagleshead Copse

Greatwood Copse

America Wood

Hectares

2
5
10
25
50
100
200
400

Dot size relates to
the actual area
of each wood

Based on the Ordnance Survey 1:250,000 map,
with the permission of The Controller of
Her Majesty's Stationery Office. © Crown Copyright

ISLE OF WIGHT

At only 38,000ha (93,898 acres), the Isle of Wight is now the smallest county in England (it was severed administratively from Hampshire in 1974). Its diminutive size belies its varied scenery, which is rather like central southern England in miniature. The northern half is an area of gently undulating countryside of mixed farming, small copses and hedgerows on poorly drained clay and acidic plateau gravels. It is here, along the coastal landslips where the clay has slid into the sea, as well as around the narrow creeks and estuaries penetrating far inland, that many of the island's most interesting ancient woods are to be found. Originally most of them were managed quite intensively as coppices. The Isle of Wight needed to be self-sufficient in wood products, and a major use was for firewood for heating the island's greenhouses. On the central spine of chalk and the southern chalk plateau, smaller copses nestle along the coombes and valleys below the escarpment. The

⇧ The northern half of the Isle of Wight has a good sprinkling of small copses and a few larger woods, notably Parkhurst Forest near Newport, and Briddlesford and Firestone Copses near Ryde. Most woodland in the southern half is recent

Upper Greensand formation which outcrops at the foot of the chalk also has several fine woods clinging to its steepest scarp slopes. The central vale and the southern part of the island, by contrast, have few ancient woods. The undercliff between St Catherine's Point and Luccombe is mostly a jumble of recent regeneration and planted trees, although the presence of plants such as Italian lords-and-ladies, Irish ivy and an abundance of wych elm hint that some of it is older. Originally this was probably rough, brambly country, of boulders and landslips, with islands of ash and wych elm woodland.

Perhaps it is the absence of those two marauders of woods, grey squirrels and feral deer, allied to a humid, maritime climate, that explains the lushness and vigour of Isle of Wight woods. At the same time, these woods have fewer flowers than their counterparts on the mainland because many flowers familiar in Hampshire woods, such as Solomon's seal and herb paris, are absent from the island. Perhaps they failed to cross the land bridge in time before the island was severed by the rising sea level at the end of the Ice Age. Certain woodland birds, too, are rare or missing, notably the tawny owl, nuthatch, willow tit and wood warbler. For three of these birds, this may be due to a lack of suitable nesting places rather than an inability to cross the Solent. The place of the tawny owl, however, seems to have been taken up by the barn owl, which here commonly nests in holes in trees and is widespread throughout the island. On the other hand, the island is a very good place for bats, with at least ten out of the sixteen British species resident, including the rare Bechstein's bat, which is particularly associated with ancient woodland.

The island's woods still have fairly good numbers of our two native arboreal mammals, the dormouse and the red squirrel. This is one of the few places in England, outside the Lake District, where the latter still inhabits native broadleaved woodland. The squirrels number between three and four thousand, and were the subject of a detailed study during the 1980s by the wildlife broadcaster Jessica Holm. A project to give the squirrels a helping hand based on her recommendations is presently underway.

The woods bordering the Solent east of the River Medina are the most complex and varied on the island. **Briddlesford Copses** form an intricate snaggle of woods on the valley sides and tributary arms of Wootton Creek. A steam railway runs through the middle, a nostalgic scene straight out of the children's classic, *The Railway Children*, with cottages, tiny stations and a trail of smoke through the trees. This is a complicated wood that takes days, if not weeks, to survey, with tall forests of sessile oak on the most acidic soils and ash-wych elm woods on the most lime-rich. At the sides of

the creek, woodland blends naturally into salt-marsh and seawater in one of those rare natural transitions that ecologists seek out in order to study the mysteries of plant succession.

Wild service trees are abundant both in these copses and others on the coastal landslips, and its medlar-like fruits, known as 'chequers', are said to have been gathered for sale. Another rarity, quite common along the rides in these woods, is the narrow-leaved lungwort, called locally Jerusalem cowslip or Good Friday flower, because its pretty flower clusters, pink in bud, gentian-blue when open, often appear at Easter. The Jerusalem cowslip can claim to be one of the island's special flowers. It occurs also in parts of south-west Hampshire and Dorset but thrives best here. The curious feature about its distribution is that it is virtually confined to the vicinity of ancient woods in the catchment of the old Solent River, which once drained this part of England before the 'peninsula of Wight' became an island. There are several insects that have a similar distribution, of which the best known is the wood cricket, whose gentle churring can often be heard in glades and along the side of sunny rides in Briddlesford Copse between late June and November. On the mainland it occurs in a handful of sites, usually sun-traps, in the New Forest, Dorset, Devon and Cornwall but, like the Jerusalem cowslip, its stronghold is in the ancient woods of the old Solent River and its tributaries.

The Isle of Wight is the only abode of one of our rarest woodland flowers, the wood calamint. This attractive, sage-like plant flowers in late summer along the edge of a copse at the foot of a down, where it has been known since 1900. Over the years it seems to have been forced out to the very edge of the wood by increased shading, and its purple-spotted flowers now spill through a wire fence and onto a tarmac layby. The conservation body, Plantlife, has lent it a helping hand by cutting back some of the young scrub that threatened to engulf it altogether.

The largest and best-known area of woodland on the island is **Parkhurst Forest.** Until the early

1800s, Parkhurst must have resembled the unenclosed parts of the New Forest on the opposite side of the Solent, a desolate expanse of open heathland, bog and wood-pasture with large oaks and beeches and woods of holly. As in the Hampshire forests of Bere, Delamere, Woolmer and Alice Holt, however, the Crown decided to enclose and plant Parkhurst with oaks, in the hope that it would eventually be able to supply the Royal Navy with high-grade ship timber. The Commissioners' reports to the House of Lords, unearthed and studied by Clive Chatters, indicate that this was a difficult place to get acorns or saplings to grow, and that early attempts generally failed. As a result, some of the original vegetation, including stands of old trees, survived. Old Parkhurst did not pass away without some feelings of regret. In 1898 a travel writer commented that

> Parkhurst Forest . . . is a very good example of what a national forest ought not to be and what the New Forest would have become had the old Act empowering its enclosure as a state timber farm not been modified. (Parkhurst) is an ancient royal Forest. But instead of remaining in its natural condition of a wild furze heath and woodland it is now a solid mass of timber, mainly Oak and Chestnut, viewless, and also impenetrable except by the roads cut through it. If anyone desires to know how dull a thousand acres of scientific plantation can be they only need spend an hour in Parkhurst Forest. On the other hand it is an economic success. [20]

A few small woods on poor sandy soils elsewhere on the island retain the characteristics of former wood-pasture – large over-mature trees with their special communities of old forest lichens and insects. One of these is called **America Wood** near Shanklin (11ha) [27 acres], the story being that oaks felled from here were used to build fighting ships that took part in the American War of Independence. Unlike most woodland legends, this one is probably true. Before the 1770s, the wood was called Little Castle Wood. America Wood

stands in a steep valley west of Shanklin, which cuts through the Lower Greensand and provides the unusual experience of walking on soft wet sand past great trees. Rain scores ripples on the path resembling tidal sand-flats and streams have carved great tawny chasms through the surface. This is a place of large mature oaks set in bracken and bramble, with a few huge old chestnut and sycamore coppice stools and a patch of hazel near a natural landslip called Tinker's Hole. Some of the oaks are heavily burred or wreathed in honeysuckle. Lichens, especially the big yellowish *Parmelia caperata*, plaster the bark.

The oldest trees probably pre-date the America fellings, which would have selected the best timber trees of that generation. I suspect, however, that most of the present oaks were planted later, along with sycamore and chestnut. Oak, sycamore and chestnut is a typical early nineteenth-century planter's mix. The wood owes its present mature and natural appearance to the difficulty of extracting timber from it. Today, if left to itself, America Wood would eventually turn into a sycamore wood. The Woodland Trust is wisely resisting that change by removing seedlings and saplings. America Wood has a delightful surprise for the visitor in summer: in a secluded dell, reached only by a steep flight of steps, lies a seventeenth-century keeper's cottage from which the Trust's resident wardens sell teas and ice-cream, a thoroughly civilised notion and all too rare an experience in English woods.

The Greensand offers another spectacular wood at **Cliff Copse** (8ha) [20 acres] and **Greatwood Copse** near Shanklin which, as you approach from the north, rear up as a veritable wall of trees. These precipitous woods are virtually unique in Britain and almost defy classification, though they appear to be aberrant stands of ash-maple-wych elm woodland. Their nearest counterparts lie in Hampshire on the Upper Greensand escarpment between Selborne and Petersfield. Cliff Copse shows few signs of use and is probably the most natural wood on the island, a cliff-hanging wood of mature ashes, wych elms and beeches, flushed by lime-rich springwater bearing thickets of wild gooseberry and carpets of golden saxifrage. Huge contorted whitebeams project from crevices, and beneath the beeches are dense masses of greater wood-rush, a rare and probably ancient combination. The oldest trees are smothered in moss and large lichens, including lungwort, a reliable indicator of ancient, undisturbed woodland in the south of England.

The chalk copses lack the drama of the Greensand, but are also excellent botanical hunting grounds, particularly because some are associated with unspoilt pockets of downland. One of the best is **Eaglehead and Bloodstone Copse** (7ha) [17 acres], a dramatic name for a peaceful wood on one side of a winding valley between rounded chalk hills. This wood of mature ash standards over ash, maple and hazel coppice was hard hit in the gale of October 1987, which scooped out gaps in the canopy and created glades of sunlight and riotous vegetation. Prominent flowers in this rich, lush wood include stinking iris, toothwort and a green sea of mercury and ivy scrambling over thin, flinty soil. At the join of the two copses is a sheltered natural chalk bank, full of moon daisies, hay-rattle and trefoil. On the short cattle-grazed chalk turf opposite are the embanked terraces of a medieval rabbit warren. Exactly how these warrens worked is one of the minor mysteries of the ancient landscape. As Della Hooke points out in her study of pre-conquest woodland 'there is little descriptive detail in the literature about matters with which almost every peasant in England would have been familiar'.[21]

I cannot leave the woods of the Isle of Wight without a brief mention of the remarkable wood of holm oak on St Boniface Down above Ventnor. The holm or evergreen oak is a popular tree of park and gardens, but only rarely does it grow wild in this country. But here, on one of the mildest and sunniest banks in the British Isles, it forms a dense wood of thousands of trees, which somehow spread *upwards* over former grassland, no doubt with the aid of acorn-burying jackdaws and jays. It is not an ancient wood; the first trees are said to have been sown as acorns about a century ago by a local man who always carried a pocket full of them on his walks across the down. The wood is almost impenetrable and you risk your neck scrambling down over the slippery carpet of leaves. The evergreen shade and deep leaf litter produce a hostile environment for woodland plants, but already a few tough pioneers, such as clematis and wild madder, are appearing, along with other exotic escapes from the Mediterranean such as Turkey oak, walnut and Laurustinus *(Viburnum tinus)*. It will be interesting to see how this, our own 'Mediterranean wood', will develop in the future, assuming, of course, that people can be persuaded to leave it alone.

HAMPSHIRE

Hampshire is famous for its woods. Apart from the New Forest, a unique expanse of wood-pasture, heath and bog inherited from Norman England, there are the wooded hangers of the Wealden Edge, alderwoods along the Hamble River kept wet by the tide, large acidic oakwoods at Pamber and Harewood Forests, extensive hazel coppices on the chalk at Little Somborne and Cranborne Chase, and a beautifully preserved medieval common at Binswood. It is not possible to do justice to such a county in the few pages at my disposal. Fortunately the task has already been well done by others, notably by Colebourne, Brough and Gibbons, and Tubbs [22], and I refer the reader to these authors for a more detailed treatment. Here I can highlight only a few aspects of the character of Hampshire's ancient woodland.

The broad pattern of woodland distribution in Hampshire is ancient. At the height of the Royal Forest system under King John, the greater part of the county was forest. Here, as elsewhere, legal forest does not always equate with physical woodland. Some of the Hampshire forests, like Chute, probably had very little woodland. The wild game of the forests lived in a landscape of grassland or heath with scattered large trees, which was also used in common by the villagers for rough grazing. Where conflict between tree regeneration and grazing arose, the trees were cut as pollards. In the

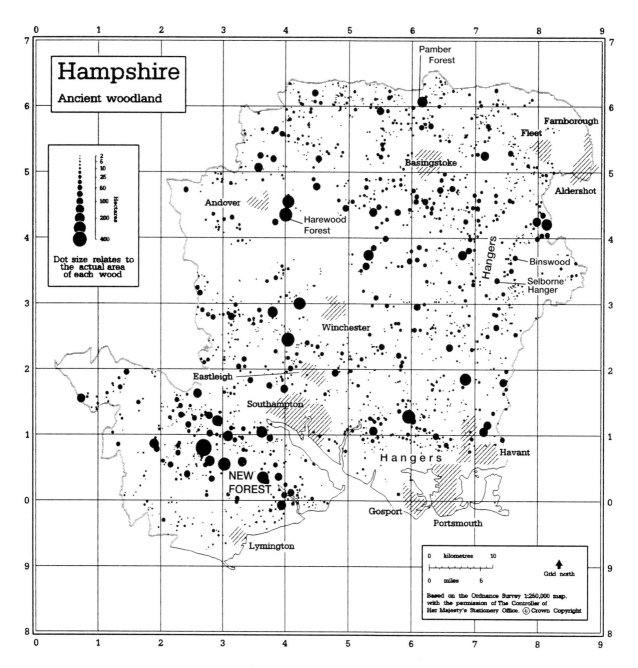

Hampshire

Ancient woodland

Hectares
2
5
10
25
50
100
200
400

Dot size relates to
the actual area
of each wood

Pamber
Forest

Farnborough

Fleet

Basingstoke

Andover

Aldershot

Harewood
Forest

Hangers

Binswood

Selborne
Hanger

Winchester

Eastleigh

Southampton

Hangers

Havant

NEW
FOREST

Gosport

Portsmouth

Lymington

0   kilometres   10

0   miles   5

Grid north

Based on the Ordnance Survey 1:250,000 map,
with the permission of The Controller of
Her Majesty's Stationery Office. © Crown Copyright

⇧ *Hampshire is a well-wooded county, containing some 25,000ha (61,775 acres) of ancient woodland. About a third has been replanted since 1945. The map shows a concentration of large woods in the New Forest and lines of small 'hanger' woods in the east and along the chalk escarpment between Southampton and Havant.*

The chalk plain around Andover is poorly wooded, although Harewood Forest, just east of Andover, is one of the largest ancient woods in the county

New Forest, where this practice had already ceased by the seventeenth century, the oldest trees are oak and beech pollards, which had once stood in open pasture rather than, as now, in woodland.

One of the last working examples of a wood-pasture common is **Binswood** near Alton (62 ha)[153 acres], which represents the lower half of a medieval deer park carved out of Wolmer Forest. Here the ancient boundary survives as a series of curves funnelling into corners where lanes enter the common. Its survival owes everything to the determination of its commoners to exercise their rights and, today, twelve to fourteen commoners still graze a quota of cows allotted to them by the 'common warden'. Much of the pasture has never been improved and is full of wild flowers of acid grassland and heath such as tormentil, lousewort and bitter vetch. In the wetter parts there are woods of alder and sallow. Much of Binswood's atmosphere depends on its old oaks and beeches, some of them pollards, among more recent thickets of holly.

Among Hampshire's most exciting woods are those which border the estuaries of the North Solent, particularly along the Beaulieu River and **Upper Hamble**. These are remarkably rich in trees and flowers. Twelve distinct types of ancient woodlands can be found along the Upper Hamble, where the heavy London Clay intergrades with light sands and gravels. Wild service tree is unusually common. There are also stands of small-leaved lime and a rare estuarine alderwood on river silt kept wet at low tide by freshwater springs. In places, gnarled old coppice oaks dip their feet in saltwater. Between them, the copses of the Hamble contain 186 species of woodland plants, including at least 62 that indicate 'a long continuity of woodland cover', making this area one of the richest in southern England. Together with those along the north shore of the Isle of Wight, the Solent woods are also the best examples in the British Isles of a natural transition from ancient woodland into saltmarsh.

The best examples of ancient and naturally wooded forests lie in the north of the county at **Pamber Forest** (115ha) [284 acres] and **Harewood Forest** near Andover. These lie on some of the poorest soils in the county, almost wholly acidic and alternately thirsty or waterlogged. Both forests are probably in large part primary woodland. Pamber is a wonderful place where one can walk from dry open heathland through dense hazel coppice to lush stream valleys lined by alders and willows. It is made up of twelve former copses separated by woodbanks and bearing names such as Beggars Bridge Copse, King's Hogsty Copse and Gold Oak Copse. Its hazels have been coppiced every seven to eleven years for a couple of centuries, producing bavins (bundles of firewood) for fuel, hoopsticks for barrel-making, hurdles for sheep pens and modern gardens and crate rods for Staffordshire chinaware. The lack of large coppice stools and the scatter of big eighteenth-century oaks at Pamber suggests a switch from wood-pasture to systematically managed coppice perhaps two hundred years ago.

Harewood Forest is a former oak coppice that once supplied bark to the Andover tanneries. Its soils are strongly acidic and, in places, the floor is almost as bare as a Chiltern wood, with scattered pale green cushions of the moss *Leucobryum glaucum*. Harewood was one of the haunts of W. H. Hudson, and some of the acute observations of nature in his *Hampshire Days* (1903) were made here. It seems that Hudson could not make up his mind about Harewood Forest. In one breath he complains that he had 'found little wild life to interest me except the jays', and in the next he describes lyrically the flight of a purple emperor high up among the oaks and the antics of great green grasshoppers fighting and stridulating in a heathy glade. Woods are like that; one visit can be disappointing, another inspiring and memorable. At the end of his life Hudson also wrote a novella about Harewood Forest: *Dead Man's Plack*, 'a tale from a hotter, fiercer world'. The book was inspired by a great granite cross in the heart of the forest that is said to mark the place where 'over nine centuries ago King Edgar, with his own hand, slew his friend and favourite, Earl Athelwold'.

The Hampshire Hangers

Between Binsted and Petersfield lies one of Hampshire's most distinctive landscapes, a billow of woodland clinging to a steep winding scarp of chalk and greensand with pockets of downland and scrub in the corners. These are the Hampshire hangers, so-named from the Old English word *hangr* meaning wooded slope. These are tall beech-woods with ash and wych elm coppice near the foot of the slope, where the soil is kept moist by downwash and calcareous springs. Their flora is among the richest in the land, and the best woods contain between thirty-five and fifty ancient woodland indicator plants among the ubiquitous carpets of dog's mercury, Solomon's seal and sweet woodruff. There are 185 hangers in all spread over about 800ha (1,977 acres) and linked by broad ancient hedgerows and sunken lanes.

Before about 1800, these slopes held grass and woodland in roughly equal measure. The woods were divided by banks, especially along the parish boundaries, and were managed in different ways as coppice simple, coppice-with-standards and high forest. Beech, though always important, was not the dominant tree it has since become. Today's beeches are fairly even-aged, and indicate a change to high forest some 150 to 200 years ago, possibly assisted by mass plantings. On these steep, rather unstable slopes, natural change is also a permanent feature of the scene. Greensand slumps over clay, producing springs and landslips on which the rare Italian lords-and-ladies finds its main English base. Gales overturn tall trees, especially the shallow-rooted, top-heavy beech, ripping up the bank in the process. Yew is presently spreading into the chalk-stained gaps along the ridge.

Much of this beautiful landscape is publicly owned. For the past five years, a special project funded by East Hampshire District Council has been encouraging an approach to woodland management of *little and often*: conservation in a nutshell. This involves light thinning, scrub clearance on recently invaded downland and re-coppicing hazel. The area is well served by public footpaths, but there are no plans to build coach parks and new roads. This is walker's country, and so far remains refreshingly uncommercialised.

The landscape of the Hampshire Hangers as they appeared in the second half of the eighteenth century lives on for ever in the letters and diaries of one of Hampshire's most famous sons, Gilbert White. Selborne is the subject of the next short woodland portrait.

Selborne Hanger and Common:
the cradle of English natural history

AREA: 101ha (250 acres)

STATUS: A National Trust property, including registered common land

ACCESS: Open to the public. The Hangers Way footpath passes through Selborne Hanger

TYPE: Beechwood on chalk scarp

GRID REFERENCE: SU 734332

Many people on visiting Selborne for the first time find they are in an already familiar, oft-imagined landscape with its church tower, its steep-banked lanes and above all the scarp with its 'long hanging wood, called the Hanger' that extends long shadows towards the village in winter. Selborne is so infused with Gilbert White's sense of place that we can continue to use his *Natural History* as a practical guide as well as a work of inspiration. That there have been many changes since the book was published, however, becomes clear on comparing the contemporary engravings of the parish with what we see there today. Mature woodland has swallowed up most of the open scrubby down of Gilbert's day. The fields are bigger, the meadows mostly reseeded. With the demise of their habitat, Gilbert's field and mole crickets have gone, along with the ravens that used to congregate above the Hanger and the summer-long crex-crex of the corncrake down among the hayfields. On the other

hand, recent surveys have revealed rare and wonderful things that Gilbert hardly mentions: a rich
assortment of soldier flies and crane flies in the
springs at the base of the Hanger, and ancient
woodland beetles in the rot-holes and cavities of
beech pollards on the Common, not to mention a
newly discovered 'worm-like slug', *Boettgerilla
pallens*. The thousand-year-old yew of the churchyard was blown over in the great gale of January
1990, but local forestry students have managed to
lever its trunk back into place, minus the spreading limbs. Let us hope it lives on, a link with the
remote age that called this place *Seleborne*, the
stream winding past the sallows.

There are many scarce and exciting flowers on
Selborne Hanger. Of those that Gilbert himself
recorded, stinking hellebore, spurge laurel, bird's-
nest orchid and toothwort are still there, possibly
in much the same places (his green hellebore still
grows 'in the deep stony lane on the left hand just
before the turning to Norton farm'). The colony of
winter-flowering mezereon, on the other hand, has
disappeared; very likely some gardener dug them
up. Gilbert excavated truffles from the Hanger and
the common 'High-wood', a feat repeated by June
Chatfield during a foray there in autumn 1989. The
richest parts of the Hanger are the permanently
moist hollows, springs and seepages along the
base of the slope. Here grow rarities unknown in
White's day, the elusive green-flowered helleborine
and Italian lords-and-ladies. If he had been as good
a botanist as he was a zoologist, he would surely
have added these to his impressive list of 'firsts'.

In contrast with the Hanger, the woodland of
Selborne Common lies on wet, acid soils. It is
interesting to compare the open common of White's
day with W. H. Hudson's view of it in the early
1900s as the 'most forest-like, the wildest in England'. In fact, most of this wilderness has sprung up
since Gilbert White's day, since the commoners
ceased to use it for grazing. As we have noted
before, the primeval appearance of some
unmanaged commons is wholly illusory. The earlier wood-pasture phase of Gilbert White's time
survives in an ancient pond and a scatter of great
pollard beeches, though these have been battered
severely by recent storms. The National Trust is
currently pollarding selected maiden beeches to
replace those that have fallen.

5

LONDON AND THE SOUTH-EAST

South-eastern England is one of the most densely populated parts of Britain, both for people and for native trees. Ancient woods of more than four hundred hectares are found mostly in Kent and Sussex, the Forest of Dean and the Scottish Highlands. Kent and Sussex are also the last bastion of traditional coppicing, largely of sweet chestnut and mainly for pulpwood and fencing. Worked coppice has maintained suitable conditions for many declining animals and plants. The 1987 storm hit this area particularly hard and changed the structure of many woods. Three years on, its impact is much muted, and many of the gaps created by windblow are being filled by replanting or natural regeneration.

One of the distinctive types of woodland found in this region is the sessile oak-hornbeam woods that characterise areas of poor soil in Hertfordshire and the Blean in Kent (in the latter, the natural woodland has been replaced extensively by sweet chestnut). Another is the ash-maple woods that are particularly widespread in the Weald and the Downs. In the past, such woods were usually managed as coppice or coppice-with-standards, but in many instances they now have a high forest structure. Coppicing for conservation purposes increased during the 1980s, but the collapse of the major market for coppice products – pulpwood – makes its future uncertain.

Special types of woodland include many areas of old parkland and commons that were managed as wood-pasture and are noted for their giant pollarded trees with their rare invertebrates and lichens. These are particularly widespread in Sussex. That county shares with Kent and a small area of Surrey the deep humid valleys known as ghylls, which form an outpost for 'Atlantic' ferns, mosses and liverworts associated with western Britain. A recent discovery is the rare large-leaved lime, present in a few old coppice woods in Surrey and Sussex, the basal stools of which may be up to a thousand years old. Box Hill in Surrey is the main area for another rare tree, the box, which is certainly native here and forms steep hanging groves known to have been present since the seventeenth century.

These are among the types of woodland that lend a special character to the ancient woods of Kent, Sussex, Surrey, Greater London and Hertfordshire, which we will now consider in turn.

KENT

'Kent, sir – everybody knows Kent – apples, cherries, hops, and women,' at least according to Mr Jingle of *Pickwick Papers* (though Dingley Dell sounds more like Herefordshire than Kent). I suppose many people also know Kentish woods – crab apples, chestnuts, hop poles and lady orchids – although their history is less known than their wildlife. Kent is (or was) the last stronghold of commercial coppicing in England, the most densely wooded county, the stronghold of many rare woodland flowers and insects, with some of the most inspiring nature reserves and some of the most beleaguered scenery in the land.

The Weald, which Kent shares with Sussex and Surrey, was *the* great woodland fastness of Old England. An estimated 70 per cent of it was still wooded in Norman times, which means about 3,883 sq km (1,500 square miles) of woodland; it was thus five times more heavily wooded than the rest of Kent. Generations of historians have imagined it as a vast trackless forest full of boars and wolves, barely penetrated by man (though King Harold and Duke William managed somehow to find each other and fight the Battle of Hastings in it). However, recent research has overturned this view: woodland is not necessarily wilderness. In fact, in Oliver Rackham's cogent words, it was 'nowhere possible in Norman England to penetrate

into woodland further than four miles from some habitation. . . . The landscape of Norman England was not like that of Borneo but like that of modern France'[23].

Although the Weald was only very sparsely settled until the later Middle Ages, it was traversed by numerous drove roads, and every inch of it was in some form of use. In Roman times the Weald was

⬇*Kent has more ancient woodland than any other county in Britain – some 30,000ha (74,130 acres). It also has a larger proportion of large woods than any other: look at the enormous 'blobs' at the Blean near Canterbury. This is a landscape more akin to northern France than England. However, even here there are woodless places: the marshy districts along the Thames estuary, Thanet and Romney Marsh. Urban development and farm improvements have devoured 4,000ha (9,668 acres) of ancient Kentish woodland since 1930*

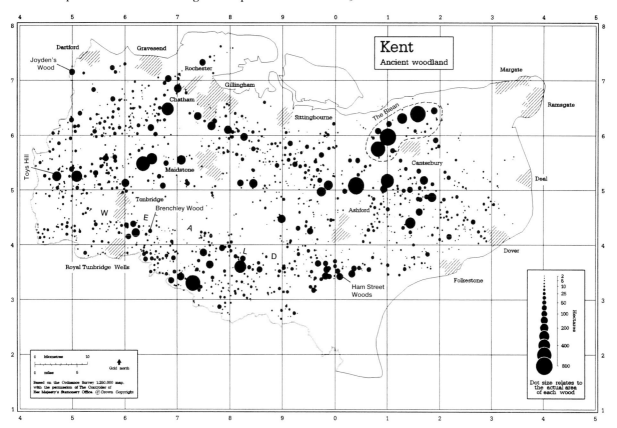

Recently coppiced sweet chestnut at Church Wood ⇨ in the Blean. [Inset] The Heath fritillary owes its survival to Kentish coppicing
(PETER WAKELY)

the base of an intensive iron-smelting industry exploiting its timber for firewood and charcoal, an industry revived again in the fifteenth century. For the Saxons, the Weald was above all a vast common where cattle and pigs would be taken in summer from the parent village to out-pasture in the woods and glades. The Kentish Weald was divided into twelve commons, each belonging to a distant settlement. The common at Tenterden, for example, belonged to the men of Thanet some thirty miles away. Another, called *Weowerawealde*, meant, and was, the 'wood of the men of Wye'. One of the lost sights of old England is that of swine-herds driving their snorting herds of wild-looking pigs mile after mile along the steep-banked drove roads to the woods where they would range freely, gorging on acorns and beechmast before being slaughtered and salted down in barrels. Pig grazing was a common right known as pannage, for which the Lord of the Manor received a rent in cash or kind, that is, salt pork. Large woods were needed because good acorn crops are erratic in England, and beechmast yields still more so. Pannage was already in decline by the time of the advent of the Domesday Book, though it continued later here than in most other counties. Today it survives as a common right only in the New Forest.

More significant in the later Middle Ages was the grazing of cattle and sheep in large open glades or 'dens'. The effect of continuous grazing would have been to widen the dens and eventually to convert much of the High Weald to a rather open park-like landscape, with large areas of grass and bracken and knots of dense woodland along sandstone gullies and other places where the animals could not reach the shoots. The near absence of the highly palatable native lime suggests that common grazing was widespread over the entire area. In turn, the dens eventually became the sites of permanent hamlets and, later, of towns with woodland names ending in -hurst or -ley. Battle was a medieval new town, founded around the abbey on the site of Harold's last stand. The clearance of the Weald began in earnest during the land-hungry years before the Black Death. P. Brandon estimates that an average of five acres of woodland

86

were grubbed up for farming every day for more than 200 years, 'an achievement without parallel in medieval England' [24]. The second great clearance began in Victorian times when new technology and an 'improvement' ethic enabled landowners to drain the soggiest field and enclose and fertilise the sourest common. Many woods have since grown up on the sites of these abortive cultivation experiments.

Today the main survivors of the old Wealden wooded commons and parks lie in Sussex. In Kent, we are left with the woods which have long since been sundered from pasture and have, for a couple of centuries at least, been managed as coppice, supplying poles for hop yards and charcoal for oast houses and gunpowder works. These woods come in all sizes, but most of them are raggle-taggle in shape with rectangular bites taken out of them on all sides by fields. Strips of woodland called *shaws* border and occasionally surround open fields. These often look like original woodland, but may equally be an encroachment of trees and scrub on banks.

In Kent, ancient woodland species such as wild service often grow in hedges and should not, by themselves, be taken as evidence of ancient woodland. Here, the most frequent type of ancient woodland is a dense coppice of hazel, hornbeam and sometimes sweet chestnut with standard pedunculate oaks and some of the most dazzling displays of wood anemones and bluebells in the country. On richer soils, such as the bottoms of valleys and along the courses of streams, ash and maple coppice is found, generally with a dense carpet of dog's mercury beneath.

The woods of the High Weald often contain narrow, steep-sided valleys known as ghylls, similar to those in Surrey and Sussex. **Brenchley Wood** (7ha) [17 acres] is one example. Here, the Tudely Brook has cut through Tunbridge Wells sandstone to produce a steep, moist slope covered in spotted orchids, bugles and primroses and a wonderful variety of mosses and liverworts on bare clay banks and exposed roots. Rusty brown seepages, with sphagnum moss and feathery wood horsetails, remind us of the iron-rich rocks beneath. Many of these ghyll woods were 'damaged' in the October 1987 gale. Of **Hunstead Wood**, a nature reserve guide relates that 'the steep sloping beech woodland falls to a stream and pond'. That is exactly what did happen in the small hours of 16 October 1987. In general this gale did more good than harm to ancient woods, but an exception must be made of these narrow ghylls whose interesting flora depends to some extent on overshading by mature trees.

The Weald and the Blean, near Canterbury, formed the 'wild interior' of Kent. Elsewhere the county presents an ancient landscape that has been well settled since the Romans. Few parts of Kent were forest, and those few not royal. Nor was much of the county affected by the enclosure movement of the eighteenth century. Kent has always been a county of commoners and prosperous yeomen, of independent outlook and, at one time, traditionally rebellious. Except in wholly woodless areas, most manors owned a wood or two as a source of wood and timber. 'Housebote' was an important common right in a county where virtually all houses were built of timber frames and wattles. The woods in the Chatham area presumably yielded their share of ship timber to the naval dockyards. Those near London were a source of firewood for the growing city of London. In 1724, Daniel Defoe remarked on the vast quantities of faggots laid up at Woolwich, Erith and Dartford, but even by that date London taverns had started to use coal and the trade in faggots was dwindling. As a result, more and more Kentish woods were 'yearly stubbed up and made fit for the plough'.

One of the large woods that escaped this fate is **Joyden's Wood** (130ha) [321 acres] near Dartford, purchased by the Woodland Trust in 1987 after a major appeal. On a clear day one can look down from its vantage point on the downs to the endless suburbs and their green spaces, with the great towers of the City only twelve miles away. Inside the wood is evidence of the past two thousand years. An impressive earthwork, the Faesten Dic (Dyke), winds through the wood and probably marked the western boundary of the Saxon Kingdom of Kent. It lies within a few hundred yards of the present county boundary. At one end a Roman pottery kiln has been excavated. Elsewhere the ground is punctuated by funnel-shaped depressions known as deneholes, the collapsed remains of underground chalk mines. Thus the wood was, at different times, the site of a pottery and a fertiliser industry as well as a source of firewood faggots for Defoe's London.

Although Joyden's Wood lies on the chalk, surface deposits mean that much of the soil is unexpectedly acidic, bearing coppices of hornbeam, chestnut and sessile oak and even glades of heather or bracken. The small-scale differences between ridge, slope and valley bottom are often more significant in Kent than the underlying geology. Yew comes into its own on dry chalky banks, and while Kent has nothing to compare with Kingley Vale in Sussex or the Druid's Grove in Surrey, it does have **Westfield Wood** (5ha) [12 acres], a steep hanging yew-wood above the Pilgrim's Way near Kit's Coty. The most exciting places for wild flowers are often very steep banks where chalk shows through the thin skin of soil. Woods on Kentish downs are celebrated for their orchids, notably violet helleborine, greater butterfly orchid, bird's-nest orchid and fly orchid, that often flower in shade, and the stately lady orchid, which prefers open banks within woods. The lady orchid is among our most beautiful wild flowers and quite a few have been dug up in consequence. The Kent Trust for Nature Conservation reveal only one site, at Yocklett's Bank in East Kent.

Unique among English woods is the old holly wood at Holmstone Beach on Dungeness. This tiny wood – a few hectares of windswept bushes, 2-4m (6.5-13ft) high but up to 17m (56ft) in diameter, rooted in bare shingle – has excited the interest of travellers and naturalists for more than four hundred years. It has been present for even longer. A charter of King Aethilberht of Kent, dated AD 741, alludes to 'the wood called Ripp' (ie *ripae*, meaning shingle banks) between 'the marsh which is called Bishop's Wick' and 'the boundary of Sussex, as Romanus formerly had it', which clearly indicates the Holmstone Beach wood in roughly its present position. It was therefore already old when Leland's *Itinerary* (1539) mentioned that 'ther is a place beyond Lydd wher as a great numbre of holme trees groueth upon a bank of baches (ie, shingle beaches) throwen up by the se and there they bat fowle and kil many birdes'. Despite their alleged hazards for birds, the hollies used to play host to a heronry. The ecology of this fascinating place has been investigated by Peterken and Hubbard (1972) [25].

Before leaving Kent, it is worth taking a brief look at the ridge of Greensand which follows the outer edge of the great horseshoe of clay that is the Low Weald. Here the woods have seen much re-planting with beech and conifers and, partly for that reason, they suffered a severe battering from the 1987 gale. **Toy's Hill** (152ha) [375 acres], one of the highest hills in Kent, lost many of its mature trees, including the fine pollard beeches left over after the enclosure of Brasted Common in 1853. The storm opened up long-lost vistas and view-points, rescued some of the heaths from pine and birch and put new life into the bluebells. In 1989, for the first time in many years, the thrilling reel of nightjars was heard. The Trust courageously resisted the temptation to tidy everything up. A third of the trees remain where they fell, and a 'non-intervention zone' was declared so that we could watch nature repair the wood in her own way. Only three years after the great storm the only obvious signs of damage were those exposed ridges on the Greensand and the North Downs and along some of the ghylls; elsewhere one had to look hard for evidence that it ever happened.

The Blean: of butterflies and sweet chestnut

AREA: Church Wood, 530ha (1,310 acres); Ellenden Wood, 91ha (225 acres); East Blean Wood, 157ha (388 acres)

STATUS: Church Wood is a nature reserve owned by a consortium of conservation bodies, including English Nature ('Blean Woods NNR'), RSPB, the Woodland Trust and three local authorities. Most of Ellenden Wood and parts of East Blean Wood are nature reserves of the Kent Trust for Nature Conservation

ACCESS: The Blean is well served with public footpaths. A convenient starting place is the RSPB car park at Rough Common

TYPE: Lowland sessile oak-hornbeam. Some areas are virtually pure chestnut coppice, others oak and beech high forest

GRID REFERENCE: TR 109603

The Saxons called this large tract of rough ground visible from St Augustine's church *blacha*, comparing its shaggy contours with a coarse mat or rug. The Blean, as it had become known by the time Chaucer's pilgrims were riding past it on their way to Canterbury, is the collective name for the series of large woods of oak, chestnut, beech and hornbeam on the infertile gravels and clay beds between Canterbury and the Thames estuary. Confusingly, within the Blean are three separate woods, each called Blean Wood, not to mention 'Blean Woods National Nature Reserve', which is the northern part of Church Wood. Here I use the name in its ancient sense to describe the whole district. The Blean is among the most densely wooded parts of Kent, although not all of it is ancient: much formerly open ground has been planted with conifers or sweet chestnuts. It is also one of the best protected tracts of ancient woodland in the country. Virtually all the most interesting parts are now nature reserves of one kind or another, the most recent addition being a major 250ha (618 acres) purchase made by a consortium of local authorities and conservation bodies in 1990.

Church Wood was among the elite woods earmarked by Lord Rothschild's Society for the Promotion of Nature Reserves in 1915. However, in their judgement, its value lay not so much in the woodland itself (coppice woodland was much commoner then) as in the rare insects and other small beasts that lived there. The NCC's Nature Conservation Review (1977) describes the Blean as 'a stepping stone by which many continental species enter the British Isles and become established', in the same way as did the Saxon invaders and St Augustine's holy men back in the *blacha* days. Among the odder insects present is a small black and orange beetle *Acritus homeopathicus* which lives only on bonfire sites in recently coppiced glades – incidentally, an ancient habitat, once frequent in woods managed for charcoal production. Another beetle, *Triplax lacordairii*, seems to be restricted to oyster mushrooms on decaying elm or beech trunks. The Blean's innumerable army of wood ants sublet to a whole ecosystem of nest-living scavengers. And I understand that it was in one of the Blean's woods that the most bizarre investigation in entomological history took place: a survey of the insects found on the body of a dead tramp.

To most naturalists, however, the Blean is synonymous with a single species: the heath fritillary. This is a daft name, one might think, for a woodland insect, but this attractive chequer-winged butterfly does indeed occur in heathland in some of the sheltered coombes of Exmoor, and the Blean itself was considerably more open and heath-like in the past. The principal food plant of the heath fritillary caterpillar is cow-wheat, a parasitic plant so abundant at the Blean that it often dominates the ground a year or two after coppicing. Conserving this rare butterfly is simple in theory, but involves a great deal of trouble in practice. Like many of the rare species of ancient woods, the heath fritillary is a traditionalist; it prefers regularly managed coppices with their warm open glades and connecting networks of broad rides[26]. When coppicing was revived in Church Wood in the late 1960s, the fritillary, until then in decline, suddenly reappeared in large numbers. The earlier idea of keeping 'disturbance' to a minimum on nature reserves had nearly proved fatal to it. Fortunately parts of the Blean were still coppiced regularly for chestnut palings and, as a result, the Blean's most celebrated species was for a time more common in commercial woods than in its own nature reserve!

Today, the National Nature Reserve at Church Wood is managed very largely to suit the heath fritillary. This has been criticised as scientifically misguided. Ecologists, particularly the botanical variety whose views have dominated nature conservation in Britain, are brought up to believe in the sanctity of natural *habitats*. If you get the make-up of the habitat right, the species will all look after themselves. But like most of us, rare butterflies need sunshine and flowers, and they will not find either in Kentish woodland unless the trees are thinned and the underwood cut regularly and often. The real significance of the heath fritillary conservation programme at the Blean is that it has guided woodland managers along a beneficial path which they might not otherwise have taken: the tail has wagged the dog. A vast range of Blean wildlife from nightingales to bonfire beetles have the heath fritillary to thank for returning neglected woodland to productive coppice. In turn the Blean has helped to set the new fashion for woodland nature reserves: a revival of coppicing on a scale not dreamed of back in 1970 (though the recent collapse in the market for wood pulp for paper means that alternative markets must be found to sustain it). The hundreds of heath fritillaries you see in Church Wood in some years are a bonus.

The proximity of the Blean Woods to the European mainland is reflected in the two dominant types of vegetation here: coppiced hornbeam and sweet chestnut, with or without sessile oak standards. On some of the clay valley sides there is a more mixed high forest of pedunculate oak, beech, elm and ash, and Ellenden Wood is crowned with a rare ancient beech coppice. But the overall impression is of remarkably uniform coppice-derived woodland. Hornbeam we will consider in the context of the Hertfordshire and Essex woods, but this is a suitable place to consider the special nature of sweet chestnut. Chestnut is frequently dismissed as a planted import: Tansley, for example, hardly mentions it. But, although chestnut was almost certainly introduced by the Romans, it behaves like a native tree in the warm dry climate of southeast Essex and Kent, forming a characteristic community on acidic soils, often with sessile oak, beech or hornbeam. Large chestnut stools are not infrequently among the oldest trees in a wood.

Chestnut is rarely grown for timber today because, as one can deduce from its characteristically twisted bark, its wood has a spiral grain and is prone to internal stress fractures known as *shakes,* which ruin its value. Most chestnuts are therefore coppiced, although some woods also retain a scatter of standard trees. Until about 1850, chestnut does not seem to have been valued more highly than other underwood trees. What set it

apart was the remarkable durability and speed of growth of its coppice wood. A single season after cutting, the stools are a bristling mass of poles bearing huge saw-toothed leaves; three years later they may be 3m (10ft) high.

With chestnut, decay-resistant heartwood forms very early in the growing poles, which restricts the sapwood to a narrow band beneath the bark. This makes them ideal for outdoor use, and in late nineteenth-century Kent there was a ready local demand for such wood for hop poles. (The traditional method of growing hops was to train the vines up slender poles about fourteen feet [4.2m] high.) The yards used around 2,000 hop poles per acre and, because the replacement rate was rapid, the continual demand and high prices paid led to chestnut planting on a significant scale – though probably always on open ground. In ancient woodland, a more effective means of propagation is by layering. The fall in demand, once hop poles began to be replaced by wire, was soon more than compensated for by the growing market for cleft chestnut palings, known as *spiles* in Kent. For palings the poles are cut when ten to twelve years old and 10 or 12cm (4 or 5in) thick at the base. A skilled cleaver can make a mile of fencing, using some 25,000 pales, from an acre of chestnut coppice [27]. Since chestnut is also used as pulpwood, it is, in Kent at least, in the financial 'big league' of broadleaved forest trees. In the mid-1960s there were about 12,900ha (31,876 acres) of simple chestnut coppice, mostly in Kent and East Sussex, compared with only 1,700ha (4,201 acres) of managed hazel coppice. Indeed, on Forestry Commission figures, there was more chestnut coppice than all kinds of managed coppice-with-standards woodland put together.

In 1990, however, a hitherto buoyant market for chestnut spiles and pulpwood suddenly collapsed. In the previous year chestnut coppice had been worth an average of $400 an acre at auction, rising to $1,000 or more for prime sites. Major buyers included local authorities, who bought vast quantities for snow fences to prevent drifting on main roads, and builders who used chestnut for temporary fencing on building sites. Suddenly, with poll tax and allied difficulties, councils were spending less, and in those green times pulpmills switched from using hardwoods to recycled paper. The chestnut coppices of Kent, seemingly so secure in the 1980s, faced an uncertain future.

SUSSEX

With no less than 18 per cent of its surface under trees, Sussex is among the most densely wooded counties in England and is nearly as wooded as France. Furthermore, about three-fifths of its woods are long-established ones and many of them are large by English standards. A century ago, the county was divided into eastern and western halves which, since 1974, have become separate counties. The division cuts across natural features of the landscape. Sussex scenery is divided between the open spaces of the 'champion' country of the coastal plain and the South Downs and the 'bocage' (hedges and woods) landscape of the Weald. The latter is further divided at around the 150 metre contour into the Low Weald, described by Camden in 1586 as 'garnished with meadows, pastures, cornfields and groves' and the High Weald to the north, which was then, and is still, 'shaded most

⇩East Sussex has two contrasting landscapes: the well-wooded Weald and the open 'champion' of the coast. There are an exceptional number of large woods

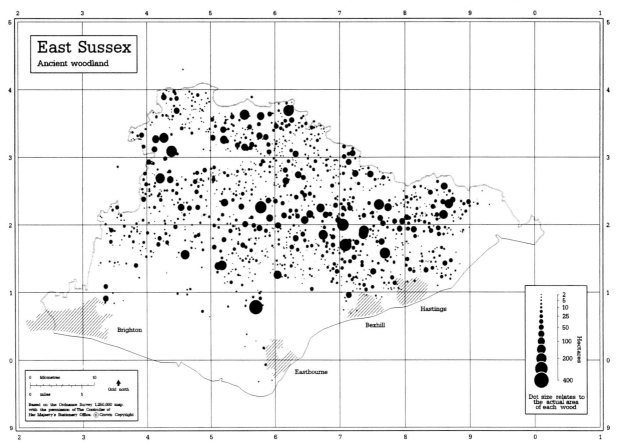

pleasantly with woods'. The Low Weald *looks* better wooded than it really is because of its multitude of copses, hedgerows and wooded strips or shaws; in fact the High Weald of East Sussex is the more densely wooded landscape. There are also concentrations of ancient woodland in places on the Greensand and the Gault Clay that lie between the Downs and the Weald. Only the coastal plain, the Downs of East Sussex and the built-up areas are poorly wooded.

Problems of ancient woodland identification in Sussex

The natural woods of Sussex are a mixture of ancient woods and more recent secondary woods that have grown up on old commons and other places no longer maintained for grazing. Over much of eastern England it is usually possible to distinguish the two by the judicious use of 'ancient woodland indicator species'. This is not the case in Sussex. The reasons are partly climatic, partly historical. The Sussex Weald is influenced by westerly airflows which in places bring a rainfall of 75-87cm (30-40in) and results in well-watered woods with enough internal humidity for sensitive oceanic plants to survive far to the east of their range. Secondly, secondary woods have often developed next door to, or even within, older woods. The old Wealden wood-pasture commons of The Mens and Ebernoe Common, for example, consist largely of recent woodland, but with a core of ancient, probably primary, woodland and a scatter of old trees in former pasture land. Even when woods are more isolated, they are often linked by ancient hedgebanks, sunken lanes, shaws, wooded ghylls or roadside commons. Finally, in Sussex, woods of different ages have been managed in a similar way, producing a similar structure of coppiced underwood and standard trees. Even planted woods were, between the seventeenth and nineteenth centuries, often managed as coppice.

Ghyll woods

The High Weald of Sussex and Kent is rainier than the rest of south-east England and more compara-ble with lowland Devon or the Pennine Dales. As a result, there is plenty of surface water which drains in a radial pattern from the watershed on the High Weald to produce a series of narrow ghylls. 'Ghyll' is a Victorian prettification; the original word was *gill*, a narrow, steep-sided gully formed by streamwater cutting through the underlying sandstone and clay. What makes them interesting botanically is their high humidity and absence of grazing and other disturbance that provides a refuge for plants that need moist, shady conditions. One highly drought-sensitive fern, the Tunbridge filmy-fern, was first discovered in a ghyll near the town of that name, although its centre of distribution is along the Atlantic seaboard. Ecologists believe that the communities of ferns, mosses, liverworts and lichens found among the rock underhangs, tree roots and wet unstable slopes of the ghylls are relics of the Atlantic period, some 6,000 years ago, when the climate was generally milder and damper than today. They mark some of the oldest, least disturbed woodland in the south-east.

The greater part of the old woods in the High Weald are described scientifically as oak-bracken-bramble woods, often with a formerly coppiced underwood of hazel and hawthorn, and sometimes also sweet chestnut and hornbeam. Many contain spectacular drifts of bluebells and spangled wood anemones, and are scored through by wet runnels deepening into ghylls, bearing narrow, more base-rich lines of ash, alder, maple and dog's mercury.

Sussex commons and parks

The ancient woods can often be distinguished by names such as 'thrift', 'frith', 'holt', 'hurst' and 'grove', all of which mean 'wood'. The distinctions between them have been lost in the mists of time, but they were probably legal rather than physical (friths, for example, were freemen's woods with rights attached to them). It is important to remember that in Saxon times and for much of the Middle Ages, the Weald was wood-pasture, not 'solid' woodland. For much of the High Weald we must imagine a landscape not dissimilar to that of Ashdown Forest today, an expanse of high windy ground covered with heath, bracken, bramble and gorse, kept largely free of trees by burning. Dense woodland was probably confined to heavy soils (and possibly kept confined by fire). Even in woodland, commoners had rights of cattle grazing and pannage. Woodland was not managed primarily for wood production until the Weald began to be industrialised in the late Middle Ages.

About half the original extent of Ashdown Forest remains a common to this day. But the best examples of ancient wood-pastures are elsewhere. **The Mens** (155ha) [383 acres] a few miles southwest of Billingshurst, is a famous wooded common, whose past has been pieced together in detail by Ruth Tittensor[28]. Here, an uncultivated Saxon landscape is preserved in most of its details, except that where there was once pasture there is now young woodland. The straggling outline, typical of old commons, funnels into the lanes at their point of entry. Earthworks surround areas of private woodland that supplied wood and charcoal to the blast furnaces and glassworks in Tudor times, and also mark the parish boundaries and divide the common into compartments. Around the edge there are scattered houses but, with a few exceptions inside private enclosures; there are none on the common itself. A long and relatively stable history, coupled with the continued survival of some primary woodland, has made this place one of the richest in wildlife in southern England. Today, however, almost the only vestiges of the wood-pasture system are the giant pollarded trees now swallowed up among their pigmy neighbours.

Eridge Park was carved out of the High Weald in the fourteenth century, and is one of the best preserved of several hundred medieval parks known in Sussex. Parks originally looked very like commons – the Arcadian scene of deer and scattered trees at Petworth Park is captured on famous canvases painted by J. M. W. Turner. But, unlike commons, parks were private property and, instead of a highly irregular boundary that has evolved from natural features such as soil infertility and high ground, they were usually oval or circular to keep fencing costs as low as possible. Eridge Park forms a great circle of uninhabited countryside enclosing about 400ha (988 acres). Some of it has been 'improved' but the Old Park still retains its old oaks, maples, ashes and beeches rooted among bracken and heather. The lichen flora on their bark is exceptional by any standards, with at least 167 species recorded. This is among the few places in south-east England where lungwort grows on the older trunks and boughs.

Some parks, such as Sutton Park near Birmingham (qv) are compartmented with enclosed copses and 'hays' around the edge of the open launds. At Eridge Park however the woods lie adjacent to, but mostly *outside*, the park perimeter. One of these, **Nap Wood** (43ha) [106 acres] lies beyond the south-eastern boundary on a spur of Tunbridge Wells sandstone. This is a well-preserved wood typical of the High Weald, with acidic oak-birch woodland on the high, dry ridge contrasting with alder-lined ghylls full of ferns and golden saxifrage. Parts are overgrown coppice, but scattered old pollard beeches on the highest ground attest to past divisions within the wood between coppice and wood-pasture. Most large woods in the Weald are similarly complex, and their present appearance reflects not only the natural variability of the underlying soils and drainage but also the way in which previous generations of stock holders, woodcutters and quarrymen (and many commoners were all three) used them.

The South Downs

The South Downs were traditionally grassy sheep-walks which, with the decline of sheep, are reverting back to scrub and woodland with disconcerting speed. Long-established woods lie mainly on the superficial soils above the downland escarpments rather than the chalk itself, and are more numerous in the west than the east. The beechwoods of the South Downs are nearly all plantations on former open land, although some of the older ones have since acquired flowers and molluscs associated with ancient woodland. Near the Hampshire border, however, are some unquestionably ancient woods formerly managed as coppices. **Rook Clift** near Treyford is an astonishing place where huge coppice stools of large-leaved lime up to one thousand years old grow inside a deep ravine cut through the chalk. Despite their size and prominence, these great trees went unnoticed until their discovery, in 1989, by Dr Francis Rose. It is not unlikely that large-leaved lime was among the commonest trees on steep chalk escarpments in prehistoric times. Several more such sites have since been discovered, all of them in ancient woods formerly managed as coppice-with-standards. At The Miscombe, an ancient lime marks the Saxon county boundary.

West Dean Woods near Chilgrove is one of the finest downland woods, a well-structured wood with oak standards and a dense hazel underwood. From its deep soils of red acidic clay and exceptionally rich flora, this is thought to be a primary wood, hence a useful point of reference to compare with the much more man-modified land outside. However, Celtic field banks within the wood indicate a previous agricultural phase over at least part of it, while the dominance of oak and hazel suggests a selective removal of non-commercial trees and, in the case of oak, possibly even planting. The rich flora and fauna of West Dean Woods is being maintained today by coppicing by the Sussex Wildlife Trust. Much of the work is financed by sales of firewood – you can collect a car bootful for about £4.

The best-known woods of the steep downland scarps and coombes in Sussex are yew-woods, of which the largest is the Great Yew Wood at **Kingley Vale**. There is a popular belief that yews are so long-lived as to be almost immortal. At Kingley Vale magnificent trees of great girth spread their evergreen boughs over what W. H. Hudson calls the 'sacred dim interior, with its silent, cavernous air of antiquity'. But, for all their atmosphere and fascination, pure yew-woods are not ancient. As long ago as the 1920s, A. S. Watt demonstrated from a study of ten separate Sussex yew-woods that they are rather woods in motion, spreading amoeba-like over the downland slopes and gradually turning into more mixed woods with beech, whitebeam, ash and other trees [29]. Ecologists now believe that yews are younger than they look, and that yew-woods stand on slopes that were bare downland only two hundred years ago. Most of Kingley Vale's yews date from as recently as 1870-80, when changes in sheep husbandry allowed yew seedlings to invade former sheep-walks, though its core of large trees is undoubtedly older. Possibly, as Ruth Tittensor suggests, the seed source of downland yew-woods were the old trees that line the parish boundaries, one of which passes through the Vale [30].

SURREY

Surrey is a well-wooded county; indeed, with Sussex and Kent it contains the highest proportion of woodland (18 per cent) of any English county. Much of this consists of former downs, heaths and commons that have turned into woods through the abandonment of grazing, or forestry plantations on previously unwooded sites. Nevertheless, a total of 9,700ha (23,969 acres) (5.7 per cent of the whole county), of Surrey woodland is believed to be of ancient origin. Surrey's ancient woods reflect the diversity of its landscapes, from Wealden ghyll woods and downland hangers to Greensand bluebell woods and clay copses full of sedges. In this county, extensive commonland and the protection of large areas by the National Trust and local authorities, together with the limited amount of high grade land, has restricted intensive farming: agricultural land covers only 43 per cent of the county. Rural Surrey remains a place of hedges and woods, of prosperous smallholders and well-protected landscapes (except for trunk roads and motorways, from which there seems at present to be no protection), despite its dense population of over one million inhabitants.

As in Sussex, distinguishing old plantations from ancient and natural woods is particularly difficult in this county, since planting for amenity and timber was widespread throughout the eighteenth and nineteenth centuries, stimulated by the silvicultural writings and experiments of John Evelyn, himself a Surrey landowner. Indeed, certain plantations in Surrey are earlier than AD 1600 and therefore fall into our definition of ancient woodland! The oldest recorded tree plantings in England were carried out by the monks of Chertsey Abbey in 1307 and, by Elizabethan times, exotics such as Turkey oak and Scots pine were being planted in wooded parks.

From about the thirteenth century, Surrey's woods were divided to accommodate the conflicting needs of pasture and wood production. Some areas remained in use as wood-pastures, commons and parks, others were enclosed by banks and cut over regularly as coppices. Wood-pasture has been in decline since the Middle Ages and the ancient habitat of aged trees set in grassland and bracken is now rare in the county and confined mostly to the Wealden clay. **Staffhurst Wood** (38ha) [94 acres] is in part an ancient wooded common with old pollard oaks, but much of it was enclosed at some stage and is now hornbeam coppice with wet hollows, some magnificent service trees and numberless bluebells. Ashstead Common is the most important site in the county for ancient pollard oaks. On the majority of Surrey commons, however, the woodland is mostly young and secondary, sometimes with a scatter of mature oaks, as at Bookham Commons, left over from the days when these woods were open grassland and heather.

Otherwise the majority of Surrey woods are coppices, usually with standard trees, and modified to a greater or lesser extent by modern silviculture. More than half are on the clays and sandstones of the Weald, densest in the west in the neighbourhood of Haslemere, Chiddingfold and Hambleton, but also scattered across a broad band across the south of the county as far as East Grinstead on the Kentish border. Elsewhere, there are concentrations of ancient woodland on the North Downs, especially in the Box Hill area. The north-west of the county, by contrast, is heath country on the infertile Bagshot Sands where ancient woods are few and far between.

In the Weald of Surrey, the most common type of ancient woodland on both clay and sandstone is of pedunculate oak standards over a dense underwood of hazel. There are also sessile oakwoods on the Greensand ridge, as at Leith Hill, which have carpets of bilberry and small sphagnum bogs with groves of alder. Hornbeam coppice and, less frequently, small-leaved lime, are widespread and, when the stools are sufficiently widely spaced, spectacular carpets of wood anemone and drifts of bluebell may be found. The clay woods of the Lower Weald are noted for their wild service trees and, in places, the rare herb paris. On the sandy Hastings Beds around East Grinstead, less floristically rich sessile oak-birch woodland predominates.

Edolph's Copse (24ha) [59 acres] and **Glover's Wood** (25ha) [62 acres], both owned in part by the Woodland Trust and within a runway's length of Gatwick airport, are fine examples of Wealden woods. Both are subdivided by numerous banks, some straight, others sinuous, indicating a complex history. Old maps reveal that 150 years ago some areas now wooded were open 'furzes' and fields. At Edolph's Copse the fields were surrounded by narrow belts of ancient woodland known as shaws. Today the ancient and secondary woodland are easily distinguished. The former includes areas of hummocky ground, has old coppice stools of ash, maple, hornbeam and small-leaved lime and ancient woodland plants such as yellow archangel, Midland hawthorn and wild service tree. Glover's Wood contains a shallow ghyll, narrowing at an outcrop of sandstone to form a humid gully with ferny banks and a profusion of mosses and liverworts. There is a dense scattering of wild daffodils. Nearby place-names hint at great age: the village of Charlwood, next door to Glover's Wood, means the wood of *ceorls*, Saxon freemen 'who never bent to a lord'. Mountnoddy Wood, now attached to Glover's, may be a Celtic name, commemorating the Sun-god, Nod.

By contrast the flora of the secondary woodland and plantations is still dominated, after the passage of more than a century, by colonising species such as willow-herb, bramble and pasture grasses. But since management (until the Woodland Trust took over) had been concentrated on these areas, they have better-maintained rides and a more open structure. The old coppice, by contrast, has hardly been touched in decades, is up to 12m (40ft) tall and, in places, casts a deep dank shadow.

Edolph's Copse and Glover's Wood were, like many others in Surrey, formerly cut over regularly by charcoal burners to supply fuel to the ironworks and glassworks of the Weald and charcoal for the gunpowder industry. The drift of smoke from the turf-covered mounds in clearings in the wood were part of the eighteenth-century rural scene (later the burners also took to slow-burning wood in big cast-iron pans). The iron industry has left its mark on Glover's Wood in the form of circular bell-pits, so-named because the opening shaft is much narrower than the cavity in the ore-bearing seam beneath. Once abandoned, the pits collapse into a funnel shape, fill with water and become bell-ponds. They are normally deeper than field ponds (Glover's has one of these, too) and surrounded by mounds of spoil. Elsewhere in Surrey there are hammer-ponds, made by damming the headwaters of a stream to drive forge-hammers and bellows. These too often lie in, or near, ancient woodland; Vann Lake is a particularly fine example.

Box Hill: box-groves and giant limes

AREA: 253ha (625 acres)

STATUS: A country park owned by the National Trust

ACCESS: Open (though part of the ancient box-groves is fenced off)

TYPE: Chalk box-woods and mixed beech, ash and yew woodland with occasional large-leaved lime

GRID REFERENCE: TQ 175516

Most visitors to Box Hill will see more grassland and scrub than mature woodland as they toil up the well-worn route to the summit. The scrubby flanks of the hill, with their dark tints of juniper, box and yew, flecked by the silver of whitebeam and the pale green of beech in the spring, have turned into woodland in recent times, like so much of Surrey. But on the steep, slippery banks above the River Mole, in places projecting over the water, is one of the rarest kinds of ancient woodland in Britain: mature box-groves. We know they are ancient not only from the large size of some of the stools but because they are mentioned in a document dated 1602, cautioning the grazing tenant to safeguard these valuable trees from livestock and requiring half-yearly accounts for any wood cut and sold. Box Hill, too, is an old name, clearly commemorating the strange, serpentine groves at its foot.

Box does not look much like a native plant. Its smooth-barked, corkscrew stems and ragged crowns of pungent, evergreen leaves seem reminiscent of Mediterranean vegetation rather than associated with our own wet, seasonal climate. The woods of box and yew at Box Hill seem to be a northern outlier of woodland more common in limestone gorges in central France, and surviving here in a particularly warm, dry and sun-drenched locality. Box does not get on very well with our other native trees. On the less steep slopes its main companion is yew, but the undercut banks of the Mole are almost solid box, snaking up in a sinuous bend above a grey-white bank of chalk as steep as a roof. Some are old coppice stools, others apparently natural pollards, living stumps covered with epicormic twigs. There is a school of thought, still occasionally expressed, that because boxwood is valuable, someone must have planted it. The Romans, perhaps. A more plausible reason for doubting the nativeness of box is its absence from northern France, except in places where it has clearly been planted as cover for game. Arthur Tansley, the pioneer of plant ecology in Britain, certainly had his doubts and Tansley's opinion had a way of becoming accepted fact.

⇧*A tangle of timber in the damp defile of the*
Welland Gill, winding through young beech at
Glover's Wood, Surrey. November
(PETER WAKELY)

More recently, box charcoal has been found in association with Neolithic camps on the South Downs, suggesting (since Stone Age farmers are not known to have been planters or importers) that it then grew wild. The Saxons, who were not given to planting exotic trees, knew box and named villages after it. Most box place-names are now boxless, but the village of Boxwell in the Cotswolds has a fine nearby box-grove mentioned in documents dating back to the early Plantagenets. This wood and another in the Chilterns, as well as Box Hill itself, are believed to be native. Box, like beech and hornbeam, probably colonised southern England some 6,500 years ago when the climate was at its warmest and driest. The rarity of its pollen and other remains suggest that it was never an important constituent of the wild wood, and was perhaps then, as now, confined to steep unstable slopes facing the sun where no other native tree, not even beech or yew, is comfortable. Box is valuable wood and most old trees have been cut over many times, but at Box Hill the steepness and inaccessibility of the main groves may have preserved them from over-exploitation.

There is another rare tree of chalky slopes at Box Hill: the large-leaved lime, *Tilia platyphyllos*. The leaves can indeed be large: recently coppiced trees often bear great leaves the size of dinner plates. *T.platyphyllos* leaves have an under covering of dense hairs best appreciated by placing one in your mouth, when it feels like felt. While the leaves of its commoner relative, the small-leaved lime, are pleasant to eat when fresh, few would care to chew *T. platyphyllos*. They can be distinguished from planted hybrid limes, which also occur at Box Hill, by their beautiful heart-shaped (cordate) leaves and downy twigs. The large-leaved limes are the oldest trees on the hill. Each is a coppice stool cut about 30cm (1ft) or so above the ground. The largest, perched at the rim of a large swallowhole, is a giant of some 7.8m (26ft) in girth. Perhaps it was once a riverside tree, standing at the point where the old course of the Mole vanished underground. Inside the now dry hole, among abandoned prams and other rubbish, lurk rare wood-lice and springtails, old forest relics of the wild wood (maybe trapped there, unable to get out). This tree may be the oldest living thing in Surrey because at a conservative estimate it is at least eight hundred years old. It is surprisingly little known, perhaps because at first sight it appears to be a grove of separate trunks, each of which have but a century's growth in them. Old limes are remarkably good at hiding in woods; perhaps that is one reason why they have survived.

The Box Hill limes grow in well-developed ancient woodland at the base of the chalky hillside, among a mixture of beech, ash, maple, yew and whitebeam. There are other rarities hereabouts: green hound's-tongue, stinking iris and stinking hellebore. Dr Donald Pigott, the leading authority on native lime in Britain, has seen similar ancient vegetation on cliffs and screes in the Dordogne and the Cevennes in southern France [31]. By contrast, recent woodland in the Box Hill area consists of little more than beech and yew.

Native box-woods elsewhere

This seems a convenient point to pause and look briefly at the remaining two English box-groves that are undoubtedly ancient and natural: **Boxwell** in the Cotswolds and the groves on the steep-sided chalk coombes of **Chequers** estate in the Chilterns. Boxwell is well-documented[32]. People were cutting boxwood from this steep valley seven hundred years ago, and botanists have visited it for nearly half of that time. Aubrey, the author of *Brief Lives*, mentions that the trees were then cropped regularly by a Mr Huntley to sell to 'the combe-makers in London'. The grove was evidently cut on a long coppice rotation of about thirty years, because craftsmen using box generally needed small pieces for fashioning chessmen or combs, not unworkable logs. The Boxwell grove must have changed size and shape over the years, because box seedlings establish only on open ground. Today, it occupies about 5ha (12 acres) along 800m (0.5 miles) of the valley. One end has been trimmed ignominiously to form a hedge. Until the 1940s,

another fine box-grove grew nearby at Kingscote. The usual explanation for its demise is that it was cut down during World War II to supply wood for tool handles and instruments, the usual source from Turkey having been blocked by U-boats. But that would not necessarily have hurt the trees, which were well used to cutting. Unfortunately, beech was planted on top of them. A few straggly box bushes still gasp for light beneath their dull-green shroud.

The chalk coombes at Chequers are the most extensive box-groves in Britain, but here most of the trees are elderly and unfit. The groves are becoming gappy, and remind one of the similarly tattered state of juniper on southern downs. However, on a particularly steep slope called Happy Valley, young box bushes are appearing through raw chalk scree, together with other chalk shrubs and, a great surprise, young walnut trees sprung up from nuts shed by their planted parents. Here is another scene from southern Europe, literally baking hot at the height of summer, in which this least celebrated of native trees is at home among some of its companion trees of far-off lands.

GREATER LONDON

Greater London was created in 1974 from the former counties of Middlesex and the City of London, plus urbanised bits of Essex, Hertfordshire and Surrey and a still partly rural portion of west Kent. In terms of its geology and woodland, this administrative chimera has an accidental unity. Beneath the houses and pavements lies a single vast deposit of London Clay, with superficial deposits of sand and gravel along the northern periphery, and with gravel beds and chalk at the south-eastern limits. Before the great expansion of London in the nineteenth century, this was fairly well-wooded countryside. On the evidence of the Domesday Book, Middlesex was once among the most thickly wooded English counties with woodland enough to support 20,000 swine. Early maps and paintings reveal a patchwork of enclosed meadows and pasture, orchards and crop fields, heathy commons and woods on hillsides or ill-drained ground. Virtually every settlement once had a wood. And a surprising number still survive, usually much fragmented, as open spaces in the present-day townscape. The result is that despite its overwhelmingly urban character, Greater London is by no means the least-wooded English county. With about 2,500ha (5,977 acres) of ancient woodland, it has more woodland than Leicestershire or Warwickshire, not to mention the other 'metropolitan' counties. Moreover, London's woods are largely natural and have the smallest proportion of replanted woodland of any county in Britain.

London's woods are described in some detail in a number of published works, notably David Goode's *Wild in London* (1986) and the excellent series of illustrated natural history booklets produced for each borough by the London Ecology Centre [33]. For those who have never visited them, the great surprise of the London woods is their wild character. While a few have been stripped down to bare essentials – trees and ground, plus or minus daffodils – in most of them you soon find yourself among hazel coppice, boggy streams lined with sedges and tall grass, carpets of bluebell and anemone, groves of flowering cherries and austere hornbeam springs. Some, such as Perivale Wood in Ealing, sit in their own island of ancient countryside with ancient hedges, brackeny hillsides and flowery old meadows and pastures. Their excellent state of preservation owes much to the far-sightedness of the London Corporation which, recognising that 'man does not live by bread alone', began in the 1870s to purchase open land for public enjoyment. Spurred on by the newly formed Commons, Open Spaces and Footpaths Preservation Society, their first great acquisition was Epping Forest, followed by Burnham Beeches in Buckinghamshire and Highgate and Queen's Woods in Middlesex.

Perivale Wood (8ha) [19.7 acres] in the lower Brent valley is one of the world's oldest nature sanctuaries, purchased by one of the pioneer conservation bodies, the Selborne Society, in the 1880s. This is a well-preserved wood of the London Clay, with standards of pedunculate oak and ash over a dense hazel underwood. There are some big maples, crabtrees and service trees and a good variety of flowering shrubs and wild flowers. But alas, despite its status as a sanctuary, street hawkers seventy years ago dug up nearly all of Perivale Wood's famous primroses. They would have become much reduced anyway, once regular coppicing was abandoned and the wood shaded over. The Society's recent policy of planting primroses *and* reinstating some of the coppice should successfully restore this most loved of all London's wild plants to at least an echo of its former glory at Perivale.

Many London woods were hard hit by the gale of October 1987. At **Pett Wood**, (54ha) [133 acres], named after a family of Elizabethan seafarers, about a third of the trees were blown over. But, although the wood looked a terrible mess the next morning, the wind had made up for several decades of neglect, toppling the surplus oaks and birches, but leaving the ancient elements intact. It is perhaps easier to appreciate now what Pett Wood really is: not a monotonous collection of oaks and birches but an ancient coppice, divided from a former common by a woodbank lined with big pollard oaks. In its heyday this was an open place of coppice glades, open wood-pasture with open-grown trees, rich in wildlife. The big open-grown trees, now buried in woodland, still support stag beetles and spotted woodpeckers.

London Clay produces fairly acidic soils, characterised by oak-hazel woods, often underwashed by bluebells. Many woods also have stands of hornbeam, formerly cut over for firewood but which are now in places dense thickets suppressing much of the ground flora. **Park Wood, Copse Wood** and **Mad Bess Wood** in Ruislip are well-preserved examples of hornbeam coppice with oak standards. Some ancient woods have patches of damper, heavier soil richer in lime, and these areas are closer to the boulder clay woods of the East Midlands – ash-maple-hazel woods with a rich flora containing flowers such as moschatel, dog's mercury, yellow archangel and early purple or-

↑*Native box, snaking up from a bare, chalky bank above the River Mole near Box Hill, Surrey. November*
(PETER WAKELY)

chid. **Lesnes Abbey Wood** (128ha) [316 acres] in Bexley and Greenwich, contains a unique and delightful carpet of wild daffodils beneath singled stools of sessile oak.

I shall do no more than sketch an outline of London's largest and most famous woodland, **Epping Forest** (1,730ha) [4,274 acres] which lies mostly across the county boundary in Essex. Epping is well documented both historically and biologically [34]. The formal description of the area as a Site of Special Scientific Interest runs into five pages. Epping and its neighbour Hainault were the physical woodland of the larger legal Forest of Waltham, of which little else survives except the name. The pollen profile indicates that this area has been wooded for at least 4,000 years. For the past 800 years, commoners have held undisputed rights of grazing and woodcutting here, and for that reason Epping and Hainault Forests were never enclosed or compartmented. Grazing would have harmed any regrowth near the ground, so the trees were lopped out of reach of animals from pollards: of beech on the gravelly plateau and of hornbeam, with scattered oak and ash, on the clay slopes beneath. We owe the rescue of Epping Forest from Victorian improvers to its commoners, one of whom insisted on his right to lop hornbeams under a grant made to local parishioners by Queen Elizabeth I. The ensuing dispute against those who wished to enclose the forest brought about the intervention of the London

Corporation and the Epping Forest Act of 1878, a landmark in the modern conservation movement. The forest today is not that of a century ago: too many pollards were misguidedly felled to make room for ordinary standard trees that were foreign to Epping Forest. Those that remained were allowed to become overgrown, thus shading out Epping's erstwhile carpets of primroses and heather. But it might have been much worse – it could have become a municipal park, or a beech plantation. Today, the Conservators are fully aware of the forest's special nature and bizarre beauty, and a programme of repollarding the ancient trees has begun.

Hainault Forest was less fortunate. Formerly a twin of Epping Forest but of more compact shape, most of it was pointlessly destroyed in 1851 to produce third-rate farmland, now largely occupied by a country park and golf course. The tenth (129ha) [319 acres] that did survive gives a good impression of what these great pollard woods were like in their heyday: great, gnarled tree-men

Giant oak pollards with wonderfully fissured bark⇩ line an ancient trackway at Richmond Park in Greater London. July
(PETER WAKELY)

of hornbeam, oak and thorn with swollen heads and crabbed limbs, prickly jungles of holly beneath, interspersed with open 'plains' of grass, bracken and heath. Even less survives of London's third great wood-pasture common, **Enfield Chase**, which was privatised and enclosed in 1777. But on Monken Hadley Common, where Warwick the Kingmaker received his come-uppance at the Battle of Barnet, the same pattern of plateau beech and clay valley hornbeams, oak and ash survives, though here most of the trees are mature standards with few pollards and little underwood.

HERTFORDSHIRE

In Norman times, Hertfordshire was among the most densely wooded English counties: around 30 per cent was then woodland, concentrated on the infertile sands, gravels and clays in the south and west. Despite this, none of Hertfordshire was ever designated as forest, though later in the Middle Ages many woods were enclosed and preserved as deer parks. In the eighteenth and early nineteenth centuries, the woods of southern Hertfordshire became major suppliers of firewood for the expanding London market. There may have been some selection in favour of hornbeam at that time because one of this tree's virtues is to burn without spitting at a steady intense temperature. Hornbeam faggots were especially in demand as a roasting fuel in the maltings. As a result, nearly all woodland hornbeams are coppice stools or pollards. The woodmen of Hertfordshire who harvested these woods were said to be 'difficult to equal in the use of an axe or bill, and rarely surpassed in the masterly way they did their work'. Their sense of *esprit de corps* went as far as a woodman's 'uniform': a leather jacket, leather breeches and leather gaiters. Some Home Counties Hardy should have written a novel about them.

Hertfordshire's ancient woods fall into three main types: ash-maple woods, on the calcareous boulder clay in the west; beech woodland on the chalk scarps and clay-with-flints plateau in the Chilterns; and the cool, shady sessile oak-hornbeam woods on the London Clay. Of the first two we need say little, for they have much in common with neighbouring Buckinghamshire. There are fine Chiltern woods on the National Trust's Ashridge estate, although Trust ownership used to be no safeguard against replanting. In their care Frithsden Great Copse and Aldbury Common have become dreary and meaningless plantations. **Frithsden Beeches** is a former wood-pasture common now swallowed up in secondary woodland with some magnificent old pollard beeches to remind us of its past. Tring has a string of beechwoods on the west-facing chalk escarpment that are good places to hunt for rare flowers.

Hertfordshire's sessile oak-hornbeam woods are its greatest prize, for such woods are best developed in this county, and in Essex. They were the subject of one of the pioneer scientific studies of British vegetation by E. J. Salisbury, made during World War I [35]. Salisbury was interested in the changeable nature of woodland vegetation, the ebb and flow of 'the shade flora' and 'the marginal flora' under a coppice system, then still widely used. In the course of his investigations, he noticed that there were two distinctive types of oak-hornbeam woods: those with predominantly sessile oaks and those with pedunculate oaks. Comparing their respective floras, he discovered that the former woods were invariably much the richer in associated plants. No fewer than fifty-six kinds of wild flowers and ferns were confined to sessile oak-hornbeam woods, including many that are now regarded as ancient woodland indicators in the south and east, such as pale sedge, saw-wort and alder buckthorn. Salisbury also looked at the fungi, plants shamefully neglected by his successors, with similar results. Horns of plenty, earth fans and uncommon boletes were among the 450

Hertfordshire's ancient woods are concentrated ⇨
in the south-east of the county,
where its famous sessile oak-hornbeam
woods are. Note that the suburban parts have
more woods than the more rural parts

kinds of fungi found associated with sessile oaks only; the pedunculate oaks had not half so many. To some extent the disparity can be attributed to the greater range of soil and slope in the sessile oak woods compared with the more uniform clay typical of pedunculate oakwoods. But the fundamental difference is historical: the former are almost always ancient and natural woods; but pedunculate oaks were the trees favoured by the tree planter. We know, for example, that there was a great planting of oaks in Northaw Great Wood between 1780 and 1850.

At the heart of the Hertfordshire hornbeam country, between Hertford and Potter's Bar, is an area known as 'the Broxbourne Woods', part of the Cecil Hatfield Estate. The wealth of the Cecils may have saved the woods from undue commercial pressure until the late 1970s when a programme of clear-felling and replanting was begun. Fortunately the Woodland Trust was able to step in and pur-

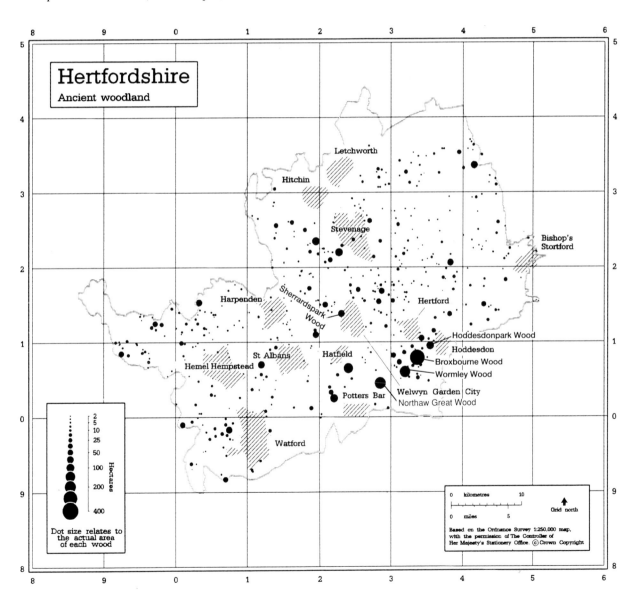

⇧*Sessile oak standards and hornbeam coppice at Northaw Great Wood, Hertfordshire. October*
(PETER WAKELY)

chase the two finest woods of all, Wormley Wood and Hoddesdonpark Wood, before their character could be changed irreversibly. **Wormley Wood** is perhaps the archetypal oak-hornbeam wood, a cool shady dome of sessile oak, laced by meandering streams with carpets of moss and ferny dinglenooks. Away from the streams are bare leaf carpets with an occasional cluster of brambles and honeysuckle, or a glade of bracken and bluebells. Stout hornbeam pollards mark the old boundary banks. These are bird-rich woods, and among the best places in England to watch for hawfinches.

Hoddesdonpark Wood, by contrast, was converted to oak forest in the nineteenth century. Beneath the oaks this is another wood of streams and banks, with a fine row of pollard hornbeams on one side where the Roman road of Ermine Street marks the western boundary of the wood (straight ancient tracks are a characteristic of Hertfordshire woods; Wormley Wood, for instance, is crossed by an old road that took coal wagons to London). Its nonconforming grid of rides was present by 1692, and it may have been made for the sport-loving second Cecil Earl of Salisbury, 'a man of no words, except in hunting and hawking'. Unusually for lowland oakwoods, Hoddesdonpark seems to be regenerating well with a broad age structure, including oak saplings and seedlings. Other oak-hornbeam woods in the area have their own distinct character. **Sherrardspark Wood**, for example, now in the suburbs of Welwyn Garden City, lies on thin clay with chalk just below the surface. Some chalk has dissolved to form swillyholes that flood in winter. In another place, a railway line has thrown up chalky soil that is sprouting a thicket of spindle, dogwood and guelder rose, typical of the Chiltern scarp but strangely out of place against the sombre backcloth of hornbeam coppice. The management of these suburban woods has its problems. At **Fir and Pond Woods**, a remnant of Enfield Chase now in the care of the Hertfordshire Wildlife Trust, 1990 was a busy and successful year. Then, reports its warden, John Scivyer, 'the blow fell. Vandals attacked the (new) footbridge. Despite being disturbed at their task, they came a second time, and when they finally left, only the concrete and steel girders remained. . . . We do not know if there was a motive, or if it was just mindless vandalism. Which bodes worse for the future?'[36]

Perhaps the most complex wood in Hertfordshire is the large **Great Wood** of Northaw (100ha) [247 acres], which was transferred to the county as a public amenity in 1937, and is now a country park. This wood is described in detail in a book by Bryan Sage[37]. Like many of the large Hertfordshire hornbeam woods, Northaw Great Wood lies astride a plateau of infertile gravel beds, once a large expanse of commonland. Despite some encroachment along the edge by houses and gardens (the modern equivalent of the medieval *purpresture*) and some planting of oak and chestnut, the Great Wood retains its ancient shape and much of its traditional character. Its history has been traced back to the early Middle Ages when its tenant, Peter de

Valoinges, paid twenty-five shillings and two hawks per year to St Albans Abbey for the timber and hunting. Today the oldest trees in the wood are the pollard hornbeams near a school camp, survivors of the old commonland system that came to an end in 1781. Some of these trees have been carefully repollarded by the park wardens, a wise precaution in view of the gales of the 1980s. Much of the hornbeam coppice has been 'stored' by singling the long-neglected stools and converting them to high forest. This creates an environment of deep shade in which the wells of sunlight above the still-coppiced sweet chestnut 'groves' become a welcome relief to walkers. Coppicing the overstood hornbeam might improve the wood for wildlife. In the Middle Ages, the Great Wood's resident hermit complained to the Almighty about the nightingales, whose night-long chorus interrupted his sleep. The three or four pairs that nest in the wood's blackthorn thickets today would scarcely bother him.

6

THE SOUTH-WEST

The ancient woods of Cornwall, Devon and the western half of Somerset are dominated by a single tree: sessile oak. Natural oakwoods are characteristic of the upland fringes of Britain: in the South-West, in Wales and its border counties, in the North Pennines and along the west coast of Scotland. In the humid and comparatively unpolluted air of the western seaboard, sensitive mosses, liverworts and lichens abound on tree bark, rocks and stream sides. In certain woods in Cornwall and Devon, lichens seem to be everywhere, plastering the bark, hanging from the treetops like tangles of wool and stubbling the rocks in various hues of orange, yellow-green and grey. The best site of all is not a wood but a medieval deer park full of well-lit old trees at Boconnoc in Cornwall, which has been described as the richest place for lichens in the whole of Europe.

When it grows well and is free of 'shake', oak can be a valuable timber tree, but in most woods in south-west England it was valued more for two products: charcoal and bark. No trees, apart from alder and juniper, provide as high a quality of charcoal as oak, and in Cornwall and Devon this material was needed in large quantities for smelting tin and lead, and, in Somerset, for smelting imported pig iron. Oak bark is rich in tannic acid, the main natural agent for curing hides into leather, and high prices were paid for it by tanners between about 1700 and 1850. Both of these products

were obtained not from big timber oaks but from oak coppice, and it was therefore as coppices that most of these woods were managed. With the availability of coke and manufactured substitutes for charcoal and bark from the nineteenth century onwards, however, many south-western woods fell into disuse or were converted into tall timber forests. Coppicing had all but ceased in Cornwall and Devon by about 1914. Today many old coppices have been replanted or have grown up as dense, jungly woodland of low commercial value. Their conservation as ancient and natural woodland presents a considerable challenge to our generation.

Oak is not the only tree with which we shall deal. Eastern Somerset and the new county of Avon have more mellow landscapes in which limestone is prominent. Among the best-wooded districts are the Mendips, with its beautiful hanging ashwoods, the steep gorge of the River Avon at Bristol and Bath and the little-known ancient Forest of Selwood on the rolling hills along the Wiltshire border. Somerset is a county of great contrasts, from the flat, treeless levels to the grand coombes of Exmoor where woods fill the valleys and blend into open moor. Here east meets west, and in the space of a few miles one can pass from ash-maple hilltop woods that would not be out of place in Suffolk to more elemental scenes of waterfalls and crags in deep wooded valleys.

CORNWALL

Cornwall's salt-laden winds and thin moorland soils are a harsh environment for trees; indeed the county as a whole is a rare example of a woodless ancient landscape. Trees grow tall only in sheltered ravines. On coastal bays and river valleys the treetops are pruned by the wind as efficiently as if a giant hedge trimmer had run over them. The Dizzard, one of the few woods on the north coast, is an 'elfin wood' in which all the trees are dwarfs, some contorted into weird shapes. They have even been mistaken for bracken at a distance. Even tall Cornish oaks can be as twisty as corkscrews. The clean damp air is ideal for epiphytes, so that many Cornish trees wear a rich natural decoration of moss and lichens, and sometimes sprout wood-rushes and ferns from humus collected in their clefts. The treetops above the Golitha Falls on the River Fowey are permanently drenched by the spray and are smothered with luxuriant feather lichens, including the long, trailing strands of the spectacular *Usnea articulata*. I have heard it claimed that this is Britain's closest approximation to Andean cloud forest!

Cornwall is one of the areas, generally those in rather extreme conditions, in which oak outnumbers all other native trees. In terms of tree composition, therefore, Cornish woods are rather

The Helford River, winding between ancient ⇨
oakwoods near Merthen Quay, Cornwall.
September
(PETER WAKELY)

⇩*Bastard balm* (Melittis melissophyllum), *a speciality of woodland banks in Cornwall and Devon. May*
(PETER WAKELY)

predictable. Oak lines the slopes, with cherry and other trees in pockets of deeper soil and, in inland woods, with alders at the bottom of the valley. Some woods are almost pure sessile oak with a patchy understorey of holly and hazel (see the Helford River Woods below). The great majority of ancient woods were coppiced. They usually lacked standard trees, but supplied firewood, charcoal and pit props for Cornwall's tin mines and bark for the tanneries. A few deep gorges, such as **Draynes Wood** (40ha) [99 acres] at the edge of Bodmin Moor, carried stands of oak high forest used for boat building. This separation of standard trees from coppice is peculiarly Cornish; more often, of course, the two are combined on the same patch of ground as coppice-with-standards. Most Cornish coppices were last cut before 1914, but some coppicing was carried out locally for firewood until the early 1960s. In some woods the oak coppice has been converted to high forest by singling, but more often the stools have been left to their own devices and have grown up to produce dense young stands of oak.

In general, Cornish woods are better protected from their enemy the sheep than comparable woods in Wales or the north. Around the edge of Bodmin Moor and in the ravines of some of the southern valleys are ungrazed, wonderfully jungly

woods, perpetually humid with cascades of greater wood-rush, bilberry and ferns, rock overhangs and boulders and below the river tumbling through deep pools, falls and rapids. Here are niches galore for the many oceanic mosses, liverworts and ferns confined to the Atlantic coast. There are also Cornish specialities among the flowering plants. **Nance Wood** (10ha) [25 acres] has the largest British population of our most attractive spurge, the Irish spurge, which grows on wet, shaded streambanks. At the Cornwall Wildlife Trust's **Luckett Reserve** (29ha) [72 acres] the star is Cornish bladderseed, a Mediterranean umbellifer with a toehold in south-west England.

Wood-names in the ancient Cornish language are good evidence of the wood's antiquity, though in general they are borrowed from the nearest settlement. Names beginning or ending with *lan-* or *cos-* are likely to be Cornish. Old maps show a whole crop of strange-sounding wood-names by the Helford River, among them Calamansack, Coose-Carmynowe and Cosabnack. The Woodland Trust's **Lantyan Wood** by the Fowey, which appears in the Exeter Domesday Book as 'Lanthien', may well be the 'Lancien' of Arthurian romance, the physical setting of the Tristram and Iseult stories. If so, the backcloth to Wagner's opera should be a broad tidal river, snaking between great mounds of woodland, a meeting of wood and seawater where seaweed catches in the overhanging boughs and is blown onto the cow-wheat by southerly gales. These wooded creeks, parts of them almost inaccessible, are almost unique to Cornwall. Along the Fal estuary there are even tidal woods of alder and sallow, rather like mangroves, forming a narrow band between the saltings and the oaks.

Many of the more accessible Cornish woods have been modified by planting. In the nineteenth century the main trees planted were beeches and sycamores both of which have become widespread as self-sown trees, along with rhododendron and laurel bushes. Modern forestry has radically changed the character of most of the larger inland woods, especially those at the edge of Bodmin Moor and along the Looe Rivers. The gales of January 1990 damaged some plantations (though much less than in north Devon). In broadleaved woods, mature beeches were uprooted, blocking paths and making access difficult. At Kennall Vale sewer pipes were splintered by falling trees with hideous, though probably temporary, consequences. Cornwall shares with Devon the enterprising 'Project Silvanus' which aims to help woodland owners, especially small owner-occupied farms, to restore neglected and damaged woods to productive high forest or coppice of native trees.

The Helford River Woods and Cornish tin-mining

AREA: 45ha (111 acres) [Merthen Wood only]

STATUS: Tremayne Great Wood is a National Trust property. The other woods are private

ACCESS: Tremayne Great Wood is open to the public. A public road passes through Gweek Wood, but the best way to appreciate these woods is to hire a boat

TYPE: Acid sessile oak woodland

GRID REFERENCE: SX 730263

Helford River was 'drowned' ten thousand years ago, when Cornwall started to sink like an overladen raft allowing the English Channel to enter its southern valleys and penetrate far inland as winding brackish creeks. The result is a unique landscape, justly celebrated in Daphne du Maurier's *Frenchman's Creek*: good smuggling country with narrow, steep-sided creeks or 'pills' winding past places with names such as Reskymmer, Calamansack, Trelowarren, Gweek. This is one of the few places in northern Europe where ancient woodland meets the sea, where thrift is introduced to primroses. At the highest tides the overhanging branches of oak skim the floodwater and seaweed catches in the clefts. On the Fal, storms can blow debris onto coppice stools, though a steep bank prevents similar spectacles at the Helford River Woods. From an oyster boat in the narrows – the best possible view of these woods – one looks out to sea past a grand sweep of wind-pruned woods, the checkered and flecked hues of Cornish oak above the patches of cord-grass, the mudflats and the river. These are wild sessile oaks in an astonishing range of shapes and sizes, from salt-pruned dwarfs to corkscrew giants 27m (90ft) high, each bursting its buds or shedding its leaves at slightly different times from its neighbours to produce a medley of hues and colours in the spring and autumn. Farther down the coast at Cadgwith a natural funnel in the cliffs is clothed by a dwarf elmwood with tops so smoothed by the wind one could almost walk on them. The smooth contours of the treetops disguise the irregularity of the ground: the tallest trees stand not at the bottom of the slope but in the middle.

The Helford River woods have been investigated in detail by Oliver Rackham [38], to whom I am indebted for much of the following account. With those of the Fal, these creek woods are the most extensive areas of ancient woodland left in Cornwall. Except for the National Trust woods they are very private woods, and in parts almost impenetrable. As a group they are remarkably uniform, sharing a common pattern of old sessile oak coppice, crabbed and windswept at the top of the slope. In the middle, they are tall and twisty above sheets of bluebells and glades of bracken; below, where we might expect the most fertile ground to be, we find open woodland and heather. Evidently the soil nutrients disappear into the river.

The oak stools vary in size; commonly they are about 1.5m (5ft) across, which means that they are several hundred years old, because these Cornish oaks, blasted by wind and rooted in poor soil, grow slowly. There are some 3m (10ft) giants in Calamansack Wood, which may date back to Celtic Cornwall. Here we see no loss in vigour from the repeated cutting of sessile oak experienced in some other parts of Britain. In places there are prickly jungles of holly and, more locally, patches of hazel coppice. These woods are the westernmost hazel coppices in England. More or less pure hazelwood was probably widespread in the Cornish wildwood, and these hazel hollows in Merthen Wood and elsewhere may be survivors of prehistoric vegetation. But for much of the area the ground is too acidic, and too ferny and wood-rush dominated for a more mellow vegetation to develop. Here and there, however, are Cornish specialities – wild madder, tutsan, and one of our most exotic woodland plants, the faintly clownish-looking bastard-balm (*Melittis melissophyllum*).

Many of the Helford River woods are enclosed by enormous revetted earthworks. The time and labour that must have been invested in them suggests that woodland was considered a valuable property in a county that had been chronically short of trees since the Bronze Age. Documents show a close association between these woods and the Cornish tin industry. Most fuel-using industries, such as potteries, glassworks and iron-smelters, were based in well-wooded areas. Cornwall had perforce to make what it could of its more meagre supply. Between the Middle Ages and 1700, when coal began to take over, wood charcoal was used to roast the ore. Small-bore wood was cut from coppiced oaks and reduced to charcoal *in situ*, in the great smoking mounds that were then a familiar sight in western woods. The tin-smelters nearby added their own arsenic fumes produced by a first roasting of tin ore. The more sensitive liverworts and lichens were permanently reduced thereby, and no doubt human beings suffered too. Rackham estimates that at peak production in the mid- to late seventeenth century, the area centred on the Helford River produced about 150 tonnes of tin per year. At that time, tin-smelting probably used up the entire wood production from Helford River. In these circumstances, it is unlikely that any of these woods, however remote today, escaped intensive production. Each and every one has been cut over again and again. Despite that, the vegetation is still almost entirely natural.

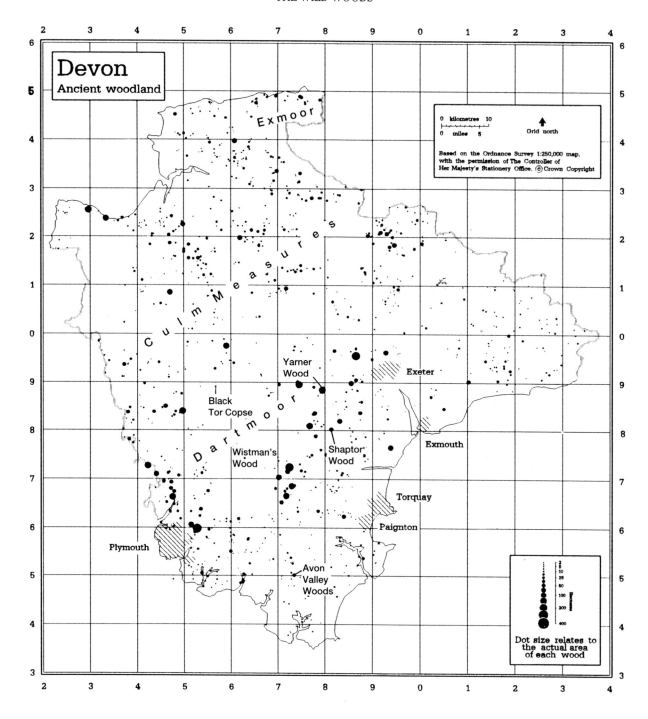

Devon
Ancient woodland

Exmoor

Culm Measures

Dartmoor

Yarner
Wood

Black
Tor Copse

Wistman's
Wood

Shaptor
Wood

Exeter

Exmouth

Torquay

Paignton

Plymouth

Avon
Valley
Woods

0 kilometres 10
0 miles 5
Grid north

Based on the Ordnance Survey 1:250,000 map,
with the permission of The Controller of
Her Majesty's Stationery Office. © Crown Copyright

Dot size relates to
the actual area
of each wood

⇦Devon is moderately well timbered, though only about one-quarter of its woods are of ancient origin. The larger ancient woods are concentrated in the valleys on the fringe of Dartmoor, and on limestone hillsides near Plymouth. Tiny hillside woods are frequent on the Culm Measures in the north

DEVON

The traditional way of the woods in Devon is oak coppice. Devon oak was cut for use in mines as pit props and for shoring up the shafts. Because the county had no coal, oakwood and charcoal were used by the potters and iron-smelters as fuel, while Devon tanners used oak bark to cure leather. Coppice oak was cut to make fish barrels and fence posts. Oak timber from standard trees in woods and hedgerows supplied beams, rafters and ship timber. As in other areas, however, improved roads and new railways eventually brought in coal to replace wood as fuel, while the rural mining and tanning industries also found cheaper substitutes. By the mid-nineteenth century, therefore, the principal need was not wood but timber, and many of Devon's oak coppices were converted to high forest. Today, oak coppicing is no longer practised. As a result, Devon is full of coppices gone wild or coppices that their owners have tried to convert into something else. Yet in the 1960s, Devon was still second only to Somerset as an oakwood county, with about 1,000ha (2,471 acres) of ancient woodland classified as 'scrub oak'.

A detailed survey of South Devon by the NCC in 1983 found two main types of natural woodland. By far the most widespread is acid oakwood. Most woods have both species of oaks plus hybrids between the two, and Devon seems to be one of the counties where both oaks are unquestionably native. Sessile oak tends to be the dominant tree in the valleys that fringe Dartmoor, while pedunculate oak appears in strength at the extremes of altitude: at Wistman's Wood high up in the middle of the moor and around the coast in sheltered estuaries. Most of these woods lie on steep slopes with relative dry acid soil uppermost, and deeper, more fertile soils in the valley bottoms. In the former, oak grows with birch; in the latter with rather leggy hazel, alder and sometimes ash. Occasionally small-leaved lime is present, notably at Holne Chase in the Dart valley. Many of these woods are important habitats for mosses and lichens.

Much more local in distribution are woods on base-rich soils. The main such group is associated with outcrops of Devonian limestone near Plymouth and around Torbay and Newton Abbot, but another is associated with Cretaceous limestone and chalk on the East Devon coast. These are mixed woods, often so modified by felling and planting that they defy classification, but commonly they contain as much ash as oak, an abundance of field maple and occasional small-leaved limes. They used to contain a great many fine tall wych elms before Dutch elm disease struck them down. Beech and sycamore were planted in many estate woods after 1918, and young growth of ash and sycamore is filling many of the places vacated by felling. Carpets of woodland flowers are much more frequent in these limestone woods than in the acid oakwoods, and characteristic species include spurge laurel, stinking iris and butcher's broom.

Planting has long been practised in Devon woods. Some woods contain large coppice stools of sweet chestnut, which was a fashionable tree in the eighteenth century and possibly even earlier. Pedunculate oak was also much planted between about 1780 and 1830, in the hope that when well grown it could fetch a fine profit from the shipyards. Most of the big oaks and chestnuts on the Powderham estate, for example, were planted during that time, either as new plantations or into existing coppices. Sycamore and beech were also popular in estate woods as a source of fast-growing, turnable wood, and both have since seeded in as wild trees; sycamore is now a widespread nuisance.

We must be cautious about using flowering plants as indicators of long-established woodland in Devon. In the maritime climate of the south-west, few plants are confined to woods, and the most reliable indicators of antiquity are large coppice stools and particularly rich *communities* of epiphytic lichens. A good clue to ancient woodland in Devon is that old wood-names are often named after their parish. Most occupy steep slopes and few have the familiar rounded outline of old lowland woods (Yarner Wood is an exception), but rather the linear shape and ragged boundaries of upland woods. Nor do they have the massive boundary banks of ancient woods in Cornwall or East Anglia.

Before looking at Devon's best-known woods in more detail, let us remember the poor field workers who braved the mud, rain and biting insects to survey the woods of this county. Woodland survey is not always a pleasant stroll through primroses. Here is Andrew Pinches on some of the problems they faced in Devon:

The woods were stocked with particularly nasty sweat flies and dense brambles. This made work exhausting, difficult and very unpleasant . . . It was difficult to park near some woods because the lanes were just too narrow and this meant a long walk to reach the wood. The general access to the woods was also poor, often involving long treks across open land only to find there were no paths or rides inside the woods. The maps were totally unreliable, often showing tracks that had long since disappeared. The brambles were so dense that a slasher would have been necessary to cut a path. Instead, the surveyors usually had to bash through them as best they could. This was time consuming and made bathing in acid seem quite a pleasant prospect . . .

The Dartmoor Woods

Only half of the Dartmoor National Park is bare moorland. The quaking bogs and mysterious pools of the high moor feed streams which, in this rainy climate, swell rapidly into rivers that tumble through rocks and gullies, and finally gouge steep-sided valleys through the soft slates and shales surrounding the moor. These are the setting for many of Devon's wildest woods, particularly those along the River Tavy and its tributaries in the west, along the Avon and the Dart in the south-east, and by the Teign and its tributaries farther to the east. The appearance of these woods is perfectly expressed in the Devon word *cleave*, a deep wooded cleavage between rounded bosomy hills. Virtually all of them are oakwoods that were formerly cut over as coppice.

In the past, few of the trees were allowed to grow tall, and so long as the demand for oak smallwood continued, there was little growth in the wood over twenty years old except in inaccessible places. These were woods of dense, bushy, stumpy oaks, ideal for making charcoal and 'black poles'. Some woods, such as **Shaptor Wood**, were also pockmarked with mineshafts, which suggest scenes of bustle and smoke from charcoal mounds and iron-smelters. The tall, tangled woods of today are the product of neglect and mismanagement of the past century. **Avon Woods** (40ha) [98 acres], for example, one of the first woods to be purchased by the Woodland Trust, was oak high forest between about 1850 and 1914 but lost most of its timber quality trees during World War I. The oak stumps sprouted again and were later singled to produce a wood of dense straight-grown oaks, quite different from the scrubby appearance of oak coppice. These changes have tended to blur the original small-scale differences on the ground and turn what were originally separate coppices with individual characteristics into larger, more uniform woods. Thus, 'Avon Woods' is historically not one wood but three, whose names were Woodleigh, Titcombe and Bedlime Woods. The large Shaptor Wood includes Sunny Copse, Pixey Copse and Furzeleigh Wood, as well as the stunted, writhing oaks on the rocky hillside of Shaptor itself. Shaptor Wood is an ancient secondary wood overlying former fields whose walls can be traced inside. Possibly they are a reminder of the distant time when cultivation reached the heart of Dartmoor before the climate changed and fields were once again swallowed up by the advancing moor and woodland.

One of the few woods which is not confined wholly to the valleys is **Yarner Wood** (149ha) [368 acres], one of the largest ancient woods in the county and among the first in England to become a National Nature Reserve. It fills two steep-sided stream valleys and occupies the intervening plateau, a place which, in other circumstances, would now be a conifer plantation. Yarner Wood retains some big oaks of the sort that were otherwise removed wholesale from Devon woods during the wartime emergencies. Like its neighbouring cleaves in the Bovey Valley, this is an acid wood with a scatter of holly, birch and rowan above a knee-deep jungle of bilberry, ferns and moss-covered rocks. In autumn, fungi are prominent and include many rarities. In the spring, the wood is alive with breeding birds, including pied flycatcher, redstart, wood warbler and raven. The first named makes good use of the reserve's nest boxes. The year 1990 was a record-breaking season with 360 young fledged from 70 pairs of flycatchers, all of them using nest boxes. In his annual warden's report for the wood, Mr Phil Page notes that this attractive bird has become remarkably aggressive. On 29 April one attacked a nuthatch and took over its nest and eggs. On another occasion a pair of them mugged a grey squirrel and then went on to mob a woodpecker!

Wistman's Wood: woodland at the limits

AREA: 3.45ha (8.5 acres)

STATUS: Forest Nature Reserve by agreement between the Duchy of Cornwall and the Nature Conservancy Council

ACCESS: You need permission to enter the wood, but a public footpath runs past it

TYPE: High altitude acid pedunculate oakwood

GRID REFERENCE: SX 613770

This is a famous wood, the ultimate in arboreal deformity, a phantasmagoria of greenleaf and granite where limbs of stunted trees twist like serpents over a rubble of mossed boulders. The old oaks – and, until fairly recently, all the trees of Wistman's Wood were old oaks – have been named Methuselahs after the oldest man in the Bible. Their air of great age is not due to their girth, which is modest, but from their crooked branches festooned with moss and lichen, with ferns and even young trees sprouting from their clefts. The atmosphere is that of a prehistoric forest, with wild, mad trees shaped like wooden king crabs and octopuses. 'Wistman' may mean 'Wisht-man' – an unworldly spirit. Antiquarians were sure that this was a sacred grove of the Druids: it *must* have been.

The wood's appearance from across the valley of the West Dart is surprisingly bland and fails to prepare the visitor for the scene within. Entry is a matter of clambering and ducking, taking care not to slip on the moss (a broken ankle for you, but death for the moss) or fall over a creeping branch (or is it a root?). For safety, Wistman's Wood should be admired from a stationary position. There is much about this wood that remains mysterious, but the deformity of the trees is really no more than one should expect from a wind-blasted situation four hundred metres above the sea in the heart of Dartmoor. What is surprising is that the wood should be here at all. However, woods do not grow in places that are best for trees; they occur where the trees cannot be eaten. All three high-level woods of Dartmoor – the other two, at opposite ends of the moor, are called Black Tor Copse and Piles Copse – are made up of twisted oaks sunk in rocky 'clitter'.

Tree establishment and growth in a harsh climate and a moor full of hungry sheep, cattle and ponies is only possible in the shelter of rocky crevices and holes where the seedling is given some respite from winter gales and frost, and above all protection from grazing. Granite blocks also retain solar heat, like storage radiators, cocooning the seedling in relatively warm, moist air. The oakling may have two or three years of incubation in this natural nursery before peeping above

↑*A view of Wistman's Wood on the boulder-strewn bank of the West Dart. The trees are little more than man-height. May*
(DAVID ROGERS)

the rocks to face the everyday horrors of moorland life. Very few oaklings ever survive to become Methuselahs, but, since these apparently decrepit trees produce plenty of healthy acorns, a less than one-in-a-million chance is probably sufficient to

But there are real mysteries at Wistman's Wood. Why, for example, when the woods of the valleys at the edge of Dartmoor are of sessile oak, are Wistman's trees all of pedunculate oak, a peculiarity also shared with Black Tor Copse and Piles Copse? The answer doubtless lies in the distant past. It cannot be that these high woods are 'relic' woods, pushed out by the invading sessile oaks, because sessile oak is the hardier tree and scientists believe that it colonised England before pedunculate oak. A plausible explanation eludes us.

Another mystery, well attested by the observations of travellers over the past three hundred years, is that Wistman's Wood is not as it seems, a static array of distorted timbers frozen in time, but what ecologists would call a dynamic ecosystem. Today's wood is not that of Miller Christy and Hansford Worth [39], who visited it in 1923, still less is it the extraordinary intermingling of rock and branch illustrated in Carrington's *Dartmoor* (1826). The earliest record we have, that of one Tristram Risdon writing in 1620, notes that the trees were 'no taller than a man may touch to top with his head'. Today their average height is 6m (20ft), four times as high as Tristram Risdon's trees and twice the height of those of Christy and Worth. It seems there is plenty of life left in these strange old trees. The wood has also doubled in acreage in the past fifty years, advancing outwards into its apron of bracken so that young oaks now grow on what used to be bare 'clitter', and deformed trees which grew up outside the wood have been overtaken by new growth.

Apart from the contorted trees, the most remarkable feature of Wistman's Wood is its luxurious blanket of moss. Here again there has been change. Victorian botanists were thrilled to find large masses of a rare and handsome moss *Antitrichia curtipendula* which carpeted the level branches and hung jungle-like from the twigs. Today you could search all day without finding so much as a single tuft of it. The growth of the past half-century seems to have opened up the wood with a consequent loss of humidity and the down-

regenerate the wood. As the trees mature, they provide shelter in turn for seedlings on their leeward side. And because the leeward side of Wistman's Wood is upslope, the wood tends to creep uphill, as if propelled by the wind.

fall of sensitive plants such as the filmy ferns and the oceanic liverwort *Douinia ovata*. Air pollution too, may have taken its toll of these plants. In the early sixties, much of the remaining *Antitrichia* moss was struck by a mysterious calamity, leaving it withered and dead in places where it had abounded only a few years before [40].

The most probable reason for the changes at Wistman's Wood is an improvement in the climate. The seventeenth and eighteenth centuries, when Wistman's Wood was no more than a tiny island of dwarf trees, were a 'mini-Ice Age'. With oak at the limit of its endurance on Dartmoor, the difference of a couple of degrees centigrade is probably enough to determine whether or not the trees can regenerate. Today we find a rapid advancement of oak which shows no signs of abating. The new oaks, however, are straight grown and scarcely different from their lowland congeners except in size. We seem to be witnessing a gradual transformation from a wood of spectacularly twisted trees to a relatively 'ordinary' wood of corkscrew oaks with their feet sunk in grassy clitter. The gain in area will be at the expense of Wistman's Wood's peculiar character and aura of primeval decay.

SOMERSET

Few English counties can rival Somerset's dramatic range of scenery from the Levels to rugged hills, from limestone and marl to acid ancient rocks, from dairy fields and cider orchards to deep coombes and wooded sea-cliffs. As our map indicates, the county's densest concentrations of ancient woodland lie in the west, in the coombes and river valleys of Exmoor, the Brendon Hills and the Quantocks, and in the east on the slopes of the Mendips and along the Wiltshire border in the former Forest of Selwood. The Blackdown Hills and the hilly fringe of the Somerset Levels are sparsely wooded but the Levels themselves have no ancient woods at all; indeed they are almost treeless. Thus although Somerset's average of 5.6 per cent of land under trees places it among the less-wooded English counties, certain parts are among our most well-wooded landscapes.

The limestone hills, valleys and rocky gorges of the Mendips include some of the most distinctive and beautiful woods in the country. It was probably from these woods that small roundwood of oak, ash, lime and hazel was cut to build wattle hurdles for use as duckboarding on the wet and treeless Levels, nearly 6,000 years ago. The hills have been mined and quarried for coal, stone, lead and other minerals for at least the past 2,000 years. Pits and spoil heaps of Roman age abound, some of them with rare plants that thrive on lead-rich sites. The woods have been cut over again and again for wood and bark during the past millennium, used as cattle shelters, enclosed, pared away to create new fields, planted with foreign trees and gouged into by roadstone quarries. That this remains a well-wooded area is a testament to woodland conservation. Each manor owned at least one wood and sometimes went to the trouble of building dry stone walls around them. Many hilly areas have either lost their woods through overgrazing or seen them succumb to modern forestry. Fortunately, in the Mendips native wood products remained of value until at least the 1940s, and amenity and conservation interests have taken care since then to ensure that the best woods are managed in sympathy with their character.

It is time to try to define what that character is. The dominant tree in the Mendips is ash, but we must beware of assuming that this is the natural state of things, for ash regenerates well from seed in woodland, whereas oak, hazel and lime do not. Examination of the coppice stools shows that, although there are some ancient ash stools, the majority are between forty and one hundred years old and have seen no more than two cycles of coppice. If one subtracts the ubiquitous young ash, a more complex ancient pattern emerges. Ash with wych elm predominates on the steeper slopes, with yew where rock breaks through, but elsewhere ash is outnumbered by hazel and small-leaved lime. Here and there are unusual types of woodland such as ash, hazel and maple on *dry* soils, maple-lime woods and oakwoods with an understorey of ash and lime.

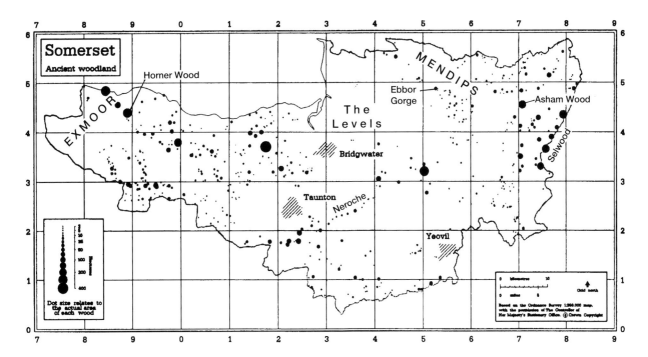

Somerset — Ancient woodland

Horner Wood

EXMOOR

MENDIPS

Ebbor Gorge

The Levels

Asham Wood

Selwood

Bridgwater

Taunton

Neroche

Yeovil

Dot size relates to the actual area of each wood

⇧*Somerset's ancient woods often mark the course of rivers (in the west) or the crests of hills (in the east). Large woods are found mainly in the deep valleys and coombes east of Exmoor or, at the other end of the county, on the Mendips and at Selwood on the Wiltshire border. Exmoor, the Somerset Levels and the 'improvement country-side' between Taunton and Yeovil are, by contrast, virtually woodless*

Different woods have their individual features, from the coppiced lime of Cheddar Wood to the big pollard ashes in Vigo Wood and the varied collection of boundary stubs and low-cut pollards in Asham Wood. What unites many of them is a south-facing aspect on a steepish slope, producing warm, dry, sunny woods. Their flora is often very rich and distinguished by rare flowers and trees. Characteristic species include herb paris, lily-of-the-valley, angular Solomon's seal, toothwort and, more locally, wild daffodils. The most celebrated plant of all is the blue gromwell, whose vivid 'midnight blue' flowers occasionally appear in quantity in early summer a season or two after coppicing. The blue gromwell is otherwise found commonly only in parts of South Wales and amid scrub on the landslips of the South Devon coast. An even rarer plant, the starved wood-sedge, has one of its two British stations on a dry bank beside a Mendips wood.

Asham Wood (140ha) [346 acres] is the largest of the Mendips woods and contains the greatest variety of scenery, with a steep limestone gorge, woodland on the plateau as well as the slope, and alders at the bottom of a deep valley. It was managed as coppice-with-standards until about 1950. Some of the oaks were coppiced, providing bark for the Cheddar tannery. However, like most woods in the Mendips, Asham's mature standards were felled during World War II, leaving it a wood of mostly young stands of ash, hazel and lime, except for some boundary pollards. The flora and fauna are extremely rich; there are rare snails such as the bulin, *Ena montana*, left over from prehistoric woodland and a wonderful array of scarce flowers, including narrow-leaved bitter-cress, columbine, wood vetch, small teasel and meadow saffron. The whole wood ought to be a nature reserve; but

⇧*The great oak-filled coombe of Horner Wood and
Holnicote Water, Somerset, as seen from the
moors to the west*
(PETER WAKELY)

instead, part of it has fallen victim to a competing interest in the Mendips, a giant roadstone quarry that has by stages bitten into the centre of the wood, almost cutting it in half. Sixteen hectares (40 acres) of Asham Wood were thus destroyed in 1984. Today the demand for stone is the major threat to Mendips woodland; and, although quarrying is nothing new historically, mechanisation has changed the scale from modest bites into natural cliffs and banks to monstrous cavities that dominate the landscape for miles.

Edford Wood (15.6ha) [38 acres] belongs to a second, contrasting, group of Mendips woods. This is a moist riverine wood with wild daffodils that are regularly raided by gypsies, and an abundance of that rare western flower, the monkshood, along well-watered banks. There are yews along the edge of the wood – a good dodge in cattle country, for the poisonous yew compels the farmer to maintain his fences. The wood was clear-felled in 1938, and now consists almost entirely of dense fifty-year growth from stools. In the past it contained a colliery, reminders of which can still be seen in depressions with black coal-water where the ground has subsided over collapsed pits. Part of the wood is secondary, having grown over old workings and slag mounds. Badgers have dug into the slag and thrown up lumps of coal in their excavations. There is also the remains of a leat which had the dual purpose of channelling river water from the wood to the pit, and also watering the meadows farther downstream to provide an early bite for cattle. Such traces of an industrial past are found in several other ancient woods in the Mendips. Long Wood, for example, possessed a spectacular mile-long elmwood water conduit built in about 1850 'for buddling the lead slimes'. Thus places such as Edford Wood are not only interesting for their wildlife but also for their evidence of a half-forgotten industrial past, when the uses to which these woods were put ensured their survival.

In the Middle Ages, Somerset had several rather ill-defined forests, not because it was a well-wooded county but because kings owned manors and pal-

123

aces there. One of the great palaces of the Saxon kings of Wessex was near Cheddar Gorge, where King Alfred's grandson, King Edmund, once nearly came to grief while hunting. The Forest of **Selwood** is one of the oldest known, and is mentioned several times in Saxon chronicles and charters. It seems to have formed a densely wooded border-land along the chain of ridges between Frome and Penselwood (which means the hill or *penne* of Selwood), then as now dividing Somerset from the heartland of Wessex. It was at Egbert's Stone in Selwood that King Alfred famously rallied 'all the men of Somerset, Hampshire and Wiltshire' before going on to defeat the Danes at *Ethandun*. Alfred's biographer, Bishop Asser, who relates these events, also offers a rare nugget of information by divulging Selwood's previous *British* name – although as *Coit Maur* means nothing more exciting than 'big wood' it may be that Ancient British names are no great loss. Selwood's woods survived almost intact into the twentieth century, but nearly all have been turned into conifer plantations during the past forty years. From Ashen Copse near Frome we can deduce that the woods of Selwood were more like the boulder clay coppices of East Anglia than those of the Mendips or the Quantocks, that is, big hilltop woods with impressive woodbanks, ill-drained clay soil, pedunculate oak standards and dense underwood dominated by ash and maple. They even share the east's fallow deer problem.

The primroses that adorn this corner of Somerset in their thousands are unusual in that all the flowers' styles are the same length, which means that they can set seed without first being cross-pollinated from another flower. The condition, known as homostyly, is peculiar to this primrose population; those elsewhere are a mixture of 'pin-eyed' flowers with long styles and 'thrum-eyed' flowers with short styles. Because these different arrangements are controlled by particular genes, they shed light on heredity and evolution. For that reason, the primroses of Postlebury Wood in Selwood have been studied since the 1940s.

The **Forest of Neroche** used to lie on the northern edge of the Blackdown Hills in that part of deepest Somerset full of narrowing lanes that lead eventually to villages with names like Curry Mallet, Beercrocombe and Staple Fitzpaine. Neroche was an infertile area of hilly pasture, managed as an open common by the surrounding villages, with woods around the edge. Although it was disafforested and 'improved' in 1830, some of its woods and commons survive thanks to the resistance of the commoners and the difficulty of enclosing steeply sloping ground. Where the woods were grubbed up, their outline sometimes remains in 'ghost hedges' full of hazel and wych elm. One of the best-preserved Neroche woods is **Thurlbear Wood**, where Ernest Neal conducted his classic studies of the badger in the 1940s and 1950s. Thurlbear is partly ancient woodland, partly secondary woodland on former open fields. The oldest trees are sessile oak coppice stools and a single stool of small-leaved lime. Much of the wood is overgrown hazel coppice on lime-rich clay with some maple and hawthorn stools under a canopy of younger pedunculate oak and ash. A lime kiln was built here in about 1850, no doubt to produce fertiliser for liming the newly cultivated land (some of which is now woodland again!). Part of the wood, in the care of the Somerset Trust for Nature Conservation, is an experiment in 'Wildwood management' whereby a more natural woodland of mixed age and composition is being promoted by thinning and coppicing. The project is paid for partly by sales of firewood.

The coombes, valleys and sheltered coastal bays of Somerset's western hills are the most densely wooded parts of the county. Here, in the steep-sided combes of the Porlock and Minehead district, ancient woodland dominates the scene, pressed against the hillsides, pruned by the salty winds, with the sound of running water never far away. Signs that we have reached the Atlantic fringe are indicated by mosses and liverworts covering wet rocks and banks and feathery bark lichens luxuriating in the moist, clean air, while in early summer you will probably not go far before disturbing a redstart or a pied flycatcher. These are sessile oakwoods, prime examples of the moist, rocky woods that girdle our Atlantic coast from South Devon to Ardnamurchan. Most of them were once managed as oak coppice to supply wood, bark and charcoal. Much of the Quantocks was never enclosed and was farmed in common by the valley dwellers, and hence woodbanks and other indications of private property are rare. Until modern times, this was a patchwork landscape of small meadows and farmed plots and mill-based industries set among managed woodland (see Horner Wood below). Today the ancient and natural woods are distinguished from the more recent ones by the presence of large coppice stools of sessile oak, alder, hazel, of stands of ash, wych elm and maple on pockets of deeper soil, and by a relatively rich ground flora including a great variety of lichens, mosses and ferns.

The steep cliff woods of the Exmoor coast, stretching from Porlock westwards into Devon, are among the most dramatic in England: 9km (5 miles) of continuous oakwood rising on the windy bluffs and falling to narrow coombes where silvery streams ripple through the trees and tumble down the sandstone and shale cliffs onto the rocky beach below. In one place the steeple of Culbone parish church projects from the trees. The sessile oaks are former coppice trees, left uncut for so long that some have crowns up to 27.5m (90ft) high. In rocky and windy places there are, by contrast, stunted spread-limbed oaks no higher than a man. Much of the floor is carpeted by greater wood-rush, and here and there among the oaks are two rare whitebeams, *Sorbus vexans* and *Sorbus subcuneata*, found nowhere else in the world.

Horner Wood: rural enterprise and big game

AREA: 405ha (1,000 acres)

STATUS: A National Trust property

ACCESS: Open to the public along paths and tracks.

TYPE: Upland hazel-sessile oak

GRID REFERENCE: SS 897440

Horner Wood is the finest of all the magnificent wooded coombes that fringe the treeless moors of Exmoor. By great good fortune, it passed into the ownership of the National Trust in 1918 and hence has not been subjected to modern commercial pressures. The Trust's management plan aims to preserve 'mature, self-perpetuating oak high forest' by singling old coppice stools or, in areas zoned for 'non-intervention', by doing nothing. The visitor, looking down at the marvellous billowing of oaks which fill this winding valley, wind-stunted near the top, tall and graceful at the bottom, may be surprised to learn that this 'high forest' has developed during the course of a single human life-span. Once again, we are gazing not at virgin forest but at the overgrown remains of a once populous vale that has only lately gone wild.

Horner Wood stands in a great funnel of Old Red Sandstone. From the relatively fertile bottomland, with its mixed woodland of oak, hazel, ash, wych elm and other trees, the funnel rises through hundreds of acres of almost solid sessile oak, fizzling out near the top where the wood merges with open moor in a ragged stubble of birch, rowan and whin. Lungwort and other large lichens on the bigger oaks and the unusual abundance of plants such as hay-scented buckler-fern and soft shield-fern, proclaim Horner Wood to be ancient, possibly primary, woodland. The majority of the oaks are coppice stools, last cut (until present-day conservation management began) about seventy years ago. There are few young oaks at Horner, because the last burst of regeneration took place about one hundred and fifty years ago when the grazing pressure suddenly relaxed after poachers shot most of the deer. The National Trust's policy of singling the stools 'stores' the coppice, leaving options open for the future, but it also shortens the life of the tree without producing any valuable timber. Horner Wood, like so many West Country oakwoods, is frozen in time against the day when woods can be managed profitably without ruining their value for amenity and wildlife.

Documentary records, studied by Olive Hallam and Rosemary Teverson [41], add a social dimension

to the physical evidence of the past provided by Horner's redundant coppice trees and strange islands of younger growth. The wood in its heyday was an integral part of rural life in the Porlock area. A valuation survey of 1809 reveals a complex system of ownership, probably inherited from the Middle Ages, in which tenants of the manor held scattered tenements of woodland, meadow and ploughland within the valley. The Lord of the Manor retained as his own desmesne the land between his lodge at Cloutsham and the Horner Water and decorated it with the then fashionable planted avenues of sweet chestnut and beech. Some of these park trees still survive, though the advance of woodland has long since swept over them.

The majority of the wood used to be simple oak coppice, cut regularly on rotation and secured against cattle and deer until the regrowth was

⇧Ancient pollard oaks in former wood-pasture at Horner Wood. September
(PETER WAKELY)

Young ash dominates the woodland on⇨ steep limestone hillsides at Cheddar Gorge, Somerset. May
(PETER WAKELY)

browse-proof. The fine oak pollards near Cloutsham, some of which were repollarded recently by the Trust, indicate an area of wood-pasture. Some of the coppices also contained a scatter of standard trees, but their timber value may have been less than the owner hoped, because there are few big timber sales in the record. Horner Wood saw the usual push and pull between

126

graziers and woodmen. A lease granted in 1580 complains that lessees sometimes failed to fence the coppice 'sale' after the 'fall' of wood, with the result that the commoners' cattle waded in to gorge on the young shoots leaving the growth 'very thinne and badd'.

At the time of the 1809 survey, the most important coppice products from Horner were charcoal and tanbark, typical of West Country oakwoods. The wood provided enough bark for three local tanneries and there remained a still sizeable surplus to ship across the seas to South Wales and to Ireland (whose own big oakwoods were already a thing of the past). A tannery at Porlock continued to use local bark until 1939. Some of the charcoal was also used locally for smelting iron ore imported from Wales. The Horner Water was dammed in a number of places to power a series of mills, among them a fulling mill which leased 3.2ha (8 acres) of coppice. In Elizabethan times, there was also a trip-hammer mill for beating iron, similar to the great ironworks of Dean and the Weald. The picture that emerges then is of a valley well populated with people as well as trees. This was not a great uniform oakwood but a patchwork of woods, variously managed, with intervening open commons and meadowland, and a hive of wood-processing works underscored by a time-honoured rural economy.

On top of all this, Horner Wood was, and is, a place of deer. It is often said that Exmoor's herd of red deer is descended from prehistoric herds, though their genetic make-up suggests otherwise. Today, about 300 deer use the wood regularly. In view of its importance for game management, it seems strange to us that Horner Wood and its neighbouring wooded coombes were carefully excluded from the perambulation of the Royal Forest of Exmoor. Exmoor is the classic example of a largely treeless forest. But it may be that the king exercised an indirect control over the woods, because their manorial lords took care to preserve the deer by forbidding entry into the coverts during calving time on pain of forfeiture of livestock and suspension of common rights.

The modern form of West Country stag hunting with hounds began in the eighteenth century. Horner Wood's richest owner, Sir Thomas Acland, bought the estate for its hunting, and it helped him to become Master of the North Devon Staghounds. But the disafforestation of Exmoor in 1819 removed legal penalties for killing deer and left them at the mercy of the poacher's rifle. Deer numbers decide when and by how much a wood will regenerate. The decline of the deer after 1819 gave the trees a respite, and many of the present-day mature trees originated in the burst of regeneration at that time. Deer numbers increased again after the re-establishment of the Devon and Somerset Staghounds in 1855, and today there are fallow and roe deer present as well.

The well-publicised controversy over the morality of hunting deer with hounds, and whether or not the National Trust should allow it on their property, distracts us from the fundamental ecological problem of woodland regeneration. Too many deer (and now also too many sheep) means too few young trees and reduces management options to one, high forest, which has little or nothing to do with the historic Horner Wood. In the long term, Horner Wood will degenerate unless a way is found to reduce the grazing pressure on it. In the shorter term, coppicing inside deer fences would benefit the wood's wildlife and prolong the life of the trees, as well as restoring a broken historical tradition. In that sense, perhaps the Trust's policy of perpetuating oak high forest should be regarded as a holding action.

AVON

Avon is a small sparsely wooded county created in 1974 from the cities of Bristol and Bath and parts of north Somerset and south Gloucestershire. It has inherited some of the woods of the Mendips and the southern Cotswolds, which are described under Somerset and Gloucestershire. If there is a common pattern to ancient woodland in this artificial county, it is that they generally lie on the highest ground of a parish, particularly on infertile patches of limestone or clay. Over the past century, ash and sycamore, and to a lesser extent birch, have increased through their readiness to regenerate from seed. Hazel, formerly the commonest coppice tree, is declining. Oak, having been widely planted in the last century, lost ground to wartime lumbermen, while elm, still common in woods near Bath, has been decimated by disease. The mild, wet climate is favourable to tree growth, except where it is inhibited by salt-bearing winds or thin soils.

Game management on country estates has maintained a large proportion of broadleaved woods in Avon. Victorian planting for amenity and timber production also took place on a substantial scale. Here there are no great forests of ship oak or furniture beech, nor is there much old wood-pasture or medieval parkland. Instead there are many mellow woods such as those at **Clevedon Court** (118ha) [291 acres], a characteristic mix of original and planted woodland on a large estate. Forming a dense green backcloth to the mansion, the part called Norton's Wood is an ancient mixed coppice of hazel, ash, small-leaved lime and maple, with scattered oak and beech standards pruned by coastal winds and ash and sycamore maidens. But tacked onto this ancient core is an extraordinary collection of holm oaks, Scots pines, leylandia cypress, redwoods, monkey puzzles and anything else that took the owners' fancy, a kind of fashion parade of imported trees from the 1890s to the 1960s. The most recent plantations are near the crest of the hill on top of a former flower-rich warren and Neolithic hillfort.

Norton Wood stands at the coastal end of one of the county's most beautiful natural landscapes, the Gordano Valley, a peaceful scene of rhines, thick hedges and wet cattle-grazed meadows, small reedbeds and pollard willows. Along the slopes of the valley are woods used mainly for pheasant rearing, interspersed by grassy commons. **Weston Big Wood** (38ha) [94 acres] is leased by the Avon Wildlife Trust, who have restored its overgrown great ride and brought increased order to the tangle. Coppicing here has a continuous 900-year history, from the *Sylva minuta* of the Domesday

Book to the Trust's activities today. The underlying limestone and acid sandstones produce sudden contrasts in the ground vegetation, from massed bluebells under oak and lime to lush ashwoods flecked by whitebeam. **Prior's Wood** near Portbury is another fine Gordano wood of oak, lime, ash and maple on acid soil, which has nurtured some giant beeches and sweet chestnuts.

The Wetmoor Woods:
the archaeology of ancient woodland

AREA: Lower Wetmoor Wood (20ha) [49.4 acres] is part of a much larger woodland complex of 285ha (700acres)

STATUS: Lower Wetmoor is a nature reserve owned and managed by the Gloucestershire Trust for Nature Conservation. The remainder is private woodland

ACCESS: By permission from the Gloucestershire Trust. A booklet and leaflet are available

TYPE: Wet ash-maple-hazel coppice

GRID REFERENCE: ST 743877

From Tudor times, and probably much earlier, woods were often divided between rounded coppices of about 20ha (50 acres) and open pasture, variously called plains, greens or lights. Both areas allowed the commoner his grazing rights but also managed to produce wood: in the coppices by excluding animals until the regrowth was well away, and in the plains by cutting the trees high as pollards, out of the reach of deer, cattle or ponies. Large woods were thus an intricate mixture of coppices and grazing greens, together with patches of thorn scrub, connected by broad green lanes leading in from the open common outside. In Northamptonshire we met with such a wood called Geddington Chase, but there, as in most woods, the open ground has long since turned into woodland.

↑ *A view across the Avon Gorge from Nightingale Valley. July*
(PETER WAKELY)

An unusually well-preserved example of a woodland common is found on low-lying wet ground at the foot of the Cotswolds near Wickwar. These are the 'Wetmoor Woods', a series of coppices within rounded woodbanks between the open commons of Inglestone and Hawkesbury. Common pasture rights still exist, though they are not exercised, and the cost of draining the sticky clay soils has deterred modern forestry experiments. The Saxon name for this area was *Horwudu* – the muddy wood. The most remarkable features of these woods are the broad grassy lanes that wind between the coppices. They are known here as 'trenches', an old word derived from the French *trenchée,* meaning a cutting through a wood. Where two or more trenches meet there are plains, some still grassy, others scrubbing over from disuse. Some of the trenches are plains in themselves: Horton Great Trench is of motorway width. In all there is more than 1.6km (1 mile) of them, though one trench has been metalled over for use as a carriageway.

Coppice sales of hazel and oak from Wetmoor supplied a variety of markets, notably oak bark for tanning leather (a huge industry between 1780 and 1850), oak underwood for pit props, cooper's staves and posts and rails, hazel for sheep hurdles and all kinds of wood for firewood. There are surprisingly few sales records for charcoal, despite the proximity of the gunpowder factories and glassworks of

Bristol. As coppicing became increasingly uneconomic in the nineteenth century, great efforts were made to grow oak on ground previously cleared and prepared by ditching. Most of these were eventually felled by lumberjacks from New Zealand during World War II. The native underwood survived the oak phase, and its constituent hazels, ashes, maples and service trees later served time as a fox covert for the Duke of Beaufort's hunt. For the past twenty years, Lower Wetmoor Wood has been a nature reserve [42].

Lower Wetmoor is one of the few ancient woods (as opposed to antiquities inside woods) to have been investigated by archaeologists [43]. Apart from its spectacular trenches, the wood can boast no fewer than eleven well-preserved saw-pits, a woodbank topped by a beech and thorn hedge, internal compartment banks, a charcoal hearth and an elaborate network of old drains. Its internal tracks, which may be medieval or even earlier, follow natural contours and peter out in the middle of the wood. Probably they were used to gain temporary access to a particular place. Added together, the various earthworks measure 6.5km (4 miles) long, representing a remarkable amount of work in a smallish wood of only 20ha (50 acres).

The saw-pits of Lower Wetmoor are coffin-shaped and sometimes shored and lined with stone. When in use, the sawyer would secure a log across the pit with ropes and trestles. His mate, the pitman, would stand beneath it at one end of the long saw, while the sawyer would straddle the log from the other. It must have been difficult, back-breaking work, pushing and pulling at the unco-operative wood. The men took their creature comforts with them. One of the Wetmoor saw-pits contained an empty wine bottle and a twin-handled 'posset cup'. Such earthworks have much to tell us about the past use of this particular wood and, by analogy, many similar woods elsewhere. The archaeologists of Wetmoor concluded that it would be as well to forget the popular image of the solitary woodman with axe on shoulder. The evidence suggests, rather, that the wood was worked over by a resident group of skilled men bearing not axes but picks and shovels, with barrows for stones and with big six-foot-long saws. Now and again they were joined by itinerant coppice workers, hurdle makers and the odd charcoal burner. Their story otherwise survives only in the dry evidence of bills and accounts but, read with scientific knowledge and historical imagination, the earthworks of a wood can be as meaningful as the walls of a church or castle.

7
THE MIDLANDS AND EAST ANGLIA

If current trends in agriculture continue, much of the former dairy pastures of the Midlands and their well-maintained hedges are likely to change to arable, to the swaying corn and big open skies of present-day Norfolk or Lincolnshire. What at present unites this large slice of middling and eastern England is that nearly all of it is lowland and is for the most part fertile and cultivable. The soils are predominately clays: calcareous boulder clay and London Clay in East Anglia, soft grey Lias clay and red Keuper marl in the Midlands. Ancient woods are sparsely scattered over the whole area, but they are more frequent in areas of poor soil and in 'ancient landscapes' formed over many centuries than in the less detailed 'improvement landscapes' produced by the enclosure movement in the last two hundred years. Leicestershire, largely an 'improvement' county, has few ancient woods; Essex, largely an 'ancient' one has many. In both kinds of landscapes, however, ancient woods tend to be of medium size – between 20 and 50 hectares (50-125 acres), have permanent boundaries and are surrounded by farmland. In the past they served the farming community as a source of firewood, timber and building material. Today they are mainly private property, growing poor quality timber or acting as cover for pheasants. An increasing number, especially in East Anglia, are managed as nature reserves.

The ancient woods of Cambridgeshire and East Anglia are among the best known in the country, largely because of the writings of the Cambridge-based historian and ecologist, Oliver Rackham. Because they figure so prominently in published books about woodland, I have touched on this area only lightly. The woods of the Midlands are much less well documented; indeed less has been written about them than of almost any other part of England. Among the more distinctive ancient woods there are the limewoods of Lincolnshire, the oak-holly woods of Staffordshire and the oak-birch woods on the acidic sandstones of Sherwood Forest in Nottinghamshire. But throughout the Midlands, as in East Anglia, the most widespread type of ancient woodland is a mixture of ash, maple, hazel and pedunculate oak ('ash-maple woods'), formerly managed as coppice-with-standards but in most cases now left to mature as even-aged high forest. Wood-pasture is a valuable part of the region's wildlife and landscape heritage. Normally situated on poor, often sandy, soil, places such as Bradgate Park in Leicestershire, Woburn Abbey in Bedfordshire and Grimsthorpe Park in Lincolnshire form the last stands of wildlife dependent on old, partly decayed trees.

This chapter falls into three sections. First, we amble through the ancient woods of the Midland counties, Warwickshire, Leicestershire and Rutland, Nottinghamshire (lingering among the mighty oaks of Birkland in Sherwood Forest), Staffordshire and the West Midlands. Next we pay brief respects to the woods of Lincolnshire and Humberside. Finally we take a whistle-stop tour of Cambridgeshire, Bedfordshire and the three counties of East Anglia. It is a big area to cover in a single chapter, but I hope to demonstrate that the ancient woods of each county have a particular flavour, and that no two woods are alike.

WARWICKSHIRE

In Warwickshire, nearly nine woods out of ten are of ancient origin, although four of them will be replanted with conifers. Most woods used to be managed as coppice-with-standards. Perhaps because almost all the land is cultivable, there is very little surviving wood-pasture, medieval parkland or wooded commons in this county: most woods have long been private land.

Warwickshire can be divided roughly into three parts: the northern 'Arden' (meaning steep or high) has hard rocks and acid soils; the centre is red clay country which, as in Shakespeare's time, is 'baren of woode but plentifull of corne'; and the 'Felden' (ie, field) country along the marches with Northamptonshire is a district of rolling hills on soft, fertile clays. One thinks of Warwickshire as the quintessential Midlands landscape, a patchwork quilt of small square fields bordered by hedges set with elms, the product of parliamentary enclosures on former open fields. But, in the north and west of the county lies a less fertile and more ancient landscape in which the majority of the larger ancient woods now lie. A more widely scattered concentration of ancient woodland lies on the scarp slopes and ill-drained hilltops of the Felden.

Many a pilgrim to the birthplace of the Bard at Stratford-on-Avon must wonder whatever had happened to Shakespeare's Forest of Arden, that fabled 'desert inaccessible under the shade of melancholy boughs'. Stratford itself lies in largely woodless countryside. But Shakespeare himself probably never saw it: the Arden of *As You Like It* is almost as legendary as Camelot. A few place-names remind us of a district bearing that name,

but the historical record is a virtual blank. Evidently Arden was a short-lived Royal Forest lying north of the Avon which, if it was ever well-wooded, succumbed to farming improvements during the Middle Ages. Some of the present-day ancient woods and parks on acidic soils in the north of the county may have been forest 'wastes' in Norman times. Today, the best of them are on large private estates, such as the Bentley Park and Monks Park Woods (103ha) [257 acres] near Atherstone. **Clowes Wood** (21ha) [52.5 acres] in the west of the county is an 'Arden wood' characterised by carpets of bilberry, cow-wheat, hairy wood-rush and an unusual abundance of lily-of-the-valley. Like other well-preserved ancient woods in this area, its canopy is dominated by sessile oak, but there are also boggy slades of alder, groves of birch, rowan and holly, and occasional wild service trees. Some woods also contain coppiced small-leaved lime. **Hartshill Hayes** (55ha) [137 acres] near Nuneaton, an otherwise largely replanted ancient wood, contains giant lime stools up to fifteen feet across that were already old in Shakespeare's day. Similar stools are to be found in Ryton Wood, Oversley Wood and Piles Coppice [44].

A particularly fine group of Arden-type ancient woods lies around Princethorpe, between Coventry and Rugby. **Ryton Wood** (68ha) [176 acres], the brightest jewel in the crown of the Warwickshire Nature Conservation Trust, is a well-preserved oak-hazel and oak-lime wood with large bracken glades and wet, flowery rides. This is one of those woods that seem to be 'good' for nearly everything, from nightingales nesting in thorn thickets to white admiral butterflies fluttering at the edge of their native range, to rare hoverflies associated with large old trees. Ryton and its neighbours are noted for their fine carpets of bluebell, wood anemone, red campion, violet and wood-sorrel, to be succeeded later in the season by brambles, honeysuckle and bracken.

The rolling clay country of southern Warwickshire has more in common with the neighbouring counties of Oxfordshire and Northamptonshire than the rest of the county. Here ancient woods are larger on average and generally occupy the highest and poorest land in the parish. They are often north-facing and usually surrounded by arable land. Here ash is at least as common as oak, and shrubs such as spindle, dogwood and privet are frequent. The lime-rich nature of the soil is revealed by the rich flora, characterised by dog's mercury, sweet woodruff, lesser celandine, yellow archangel, ramsons (wild garlic) and primrose.

In Ufton parish, a few miles east of Royal Leamington Spa, is **Long Itchington and Ufton Woods** (80ha) [200 acres], a privately owned wood which is one of the most important woods in the Midlands. Until the Warwickshire Nature Conservation Trust began to coppice the overgrown underwood on their nature reserves, this was the only wood in the county that presented a woodland scene plucked straight out of the Middle Ages, with open-grown pedunculate standards and a vigorous hazel underwood cut on rotation. The long and stable history of management of this wood has helped to preserve a rich flora, which includes a number of plants otherwise scarce in this county such as water avens, herb paris, lesser butterfly orchid and bird's-nest orchid. **Wolford Wood** (64ha) [160 acres], on the heavy calcareous clays in the south of the county, is a more typical 'Felden' wood. It is of horticultural interest as the origin of garden Polyanthus flowers, bred from primroses gathered in 1661 from 'great Woolver Wood in Warwickshire' by the Welsh botanist Edward Morgan.

THE WEST MIDLANDS

The 'metropolitan county' of West Midlands was set up in 1974 to detach the cities of Birmingham, Wolverhampton and Coventry from their shires. This is a largely urban county – 'the endless village' of housing estates – but a surprising amount of rural land remains in the 'Meriden gap' between Birmingham and Coventry, where there are several small woods, such as Frogmore and Millinson's Woods, that may be survivors of the mysterious Forest of Arden (see Warwickshire). The county's modest extent of ancient woodland – only about 730ha (1,825 acres) – is overshadowed by the magnificent Sutton Park, one of the largest and best-preserved medieval parks in all England. Even among the interminable suburbs there are islands of greenery and ancient woods of surprising quality.

The majority of ancient woods are very small: nearly three-quarters of them are only 5ha (12.5 acres) or less. Of the area's biggest woods, Meriden Shafts (40ha) [100 acres] was turned into a conifer plantation and Chelmesley Wood (38ha) [95 acres] cut down to make room for the housing estate that now bears its name. One of the best woods in the county, Hampton Coppice (27ha) [67 acres], was partly cleared to make room for more farmland. The largest wood intact is now Holly Hurst (37ha) [92 acres] in Sutton Park. Though a total of 110ha (275 acres) of ancient woodland has been lost to urban development, urban woods were on the whole treated more sympathetically than the rural ones.

Sutton Park

Few modern cities have anything to rival this, an oasis of heath, bog, marsh and ancient woodland covering some 1,000ha (2,470 acres) of medieval parkland. Sutton Park was presented to the town of Sutton Coldfield by Henry VIII in 1528 and has been maintained for public use ever since. Sutton is one of the best examples of a *compartmented park*, carved out of an earlier Royal Forest and divided into separate woods and open deer launds of open grassland and heath. There are six ancient pools, made in the Middle Ages by damming the streams to power a series of mills (modern planning notions of 'multi-purpose use' are nothing new). The woods retain their ancient names and identities. There are hursts, usually a name for a wooded hill but here used for woods on the flat, together with alder slades and small rounded copses that make up the 'Seven Hays' or hunting enclosures of the park. The woods lie on acid soils and are dominated by oak, holly and rowan, joined more recently by birch. The oldest trees, in Streetly Wood and Gum Slade, are all sessile oaks. The pedunculate oaks, which stand on the higher ground, are probably planted, as are the enclosures of beech, pine, larch and sweet chestnut. A striking feature of some of the woods is a luxuriant jungle of holly, which rivals the famous holly groves of the New Forest and Staverton Park in Suffolk. These jungles probably formed after grazing animals were removed. Most of these woods were used as wood-pasture, as indicated by the impoverished heath-like nature of the woodland floor, with its acres of bracken, bramble, bilberry and wavy hair-grass.

Today, Sutton Park is showing signs of wear and tear. The Boy Scout Jubilee Jamboree, held here for a fortnight during the summer of 1957, is said to have put paid to the last breeding nightjars. Former deer launds have been drained and turned into a golf course and nibbled away by car parks and paths. Ancient earthworks have been damaged, and on summer weekends, Sutton Park is starting to look like Hyde Park. It is a place to visit at quiet times, perhaps at dawn or when the snow is piled thick over the hard standings and the only bright colours are the scarlet beacons of holly.

STAFFORDSHIRE

About half of Staffordshire's 15,230ha (37,618 acres) of woodland is considered to be of ancient origin. In Norman times, this county was, with Cheshire and Worcestershire, one of the most densely wooded parts of England, with nearly one-third of it classed by the Domesday Book as woodland. But, like those counties, it has since lost four-fifths of its woods, some to farmland, some, through overgrazing, to heaths such as Cannock Chase. The surviving ancient woods tend to be concentrated on valley sides, eg, the Churnet complex, or on areas of poor or heavy soils, as in the former Forests of Needwood and Lyme and on the area of thirsty sands south-west of Stoke-on-Trent. Many of Staffordshire's ancient woods are quite large and on land suitable for growing conifers, and nearly half of them have been replanted.

This is one of the transition counties of the West Midlands, partly upland moors, craggy bluffs and dales, partly a flat Midlands landscape of villages and country houses, power stations, cows and hedges. Falling roughly halfway between the two is a plateau of acidic sands and clay east of Stafford, which was at the core of the former **Forest of Needwood**, a common for the poor and needy, and once a refuge for outlaws. There were no fewer than seven medieval forests and chases in the county, but this is the only one to have retained a substantial number of its original woods, thanks mainly to the Duchy of Lancaster which prevented a wholesale loss of woodland after Needwood was disafforested and carved up into farm plots in 1801. The best surviving ancient and natural woods are **Bracken Hurst** (26ha) [65 acres] on the plateau and **Forest Banks** (45ha) [112 acres] on the northern scarp slopes. An unusual aspect of these woods is that they contain an apparently natural mixture of both pedunculate and sessile oaks, some of them very old. They are accompanied by both kinds of birch. As at Sutton Park, the woodland floor is covered by grass and bracken.

On the richer soils, there is some oak-hazel woodland and, at Forest Banks, a small area of ash-wych elm woodland with both native limes that closely resembles the Magnesian limestone woods farther north. The most evocative scene, however, is an ancient *hollin*, a group of old pollarded hollies once lopped for winter browsing which perhaps presents a vista little changed since the seventeenth century – the last vestige of the common wood-pasture system at Needwood. These woods, and others like them at Cannock Chase and Burnt Wood near Market Drayton, are rich in rare insects, especially those that live in dead wood or require open woodland. Here I shall do no more than list three of the scarcer moths of Needwood for the sheer delight of their names: the *argent and sable*, a heraldic name that perfectly describes the moth's black-and-white chequered wings; the *ruddy highflier*, that flies high up out of reach and thus annoys collectors; and the *Blomer's rivulet* that was discovered by Captain Blomer, but has nothing to do with rivers.

Cannock Chase, another infertile waste in the heart of the county, is mostly heath or recent birchwoods, and need not detain us long. The last of the woods that formerly bordered the Chase is **Brocton Coppice**, which retains its circular medieval boundary, though it is well on the way to becoming a heath itself. Here ancient standard oaks, set in an ocean of bilberry and heather with upstart birches, have outlived the coppiced underwood, except for a fine alder slade that lines the Sherbrook valley.

Woods on neutral or calcareous soils are scarce in Staffordshire. Two of the best are at Wrinehill Wood on the Cheshire border and The Wilderness, near Kidderminster, where there is an intricate mosaic of natural woodland types with hollows, flushes and mysterious little streams. Acid woods of oak and birch are more typical of the county and are particularly common in the Churnet valley, between Stoke-on-Trent and Alton Towers with the village of Oakamoor amidmost. This was one of the birthplaces of the Industrial Revolution and, like Coalbrookdale in Shropshire, woods were therefore preserved and managed intensively to produce charcoal for the forges. Farther north we pass into the moorland of the Dark Peak, a place of peat hags and hardy sheep, in which woods become ever smaller as we climb the hill, and are soon restricted to deep 'cloughs' and steep rocky hillsides. The limestone White Peak is better wooded, especially in the upper reaches of the Rivers Dove, Hamps and Manifold. Dovedale and the Manifold Valley are soft mellow landscapes, with woods of ash and yew, interspersed by flower-rich grassland and white outcrops and crags.

In the Hamps and Manifold Valleys there are also some of Staffordshire's characteristic oak-holly woods, again containing very old pedunculate and sessile oaks. Typical ancient woodland plants in these valleys include alpine currant, a pretty shrub with delicate three-pointed leaves and a mass of erect flowers in the spring, side by side with lowland flowers such as toothwort, herb paris and spurge laurel. Here and there, usually on craggy ground well out of reach of hungry sheep, are massive stools of both small- and large-leaved limes.

Leicestershire's 2,575ha (6,362 acres) of ancient woodland is concentrated in three areas: at Charnwood Forest between Leicester and Loughborough, in the 'Owston Group' north of the Eye Brook, and around Exton Park and Cottesmore on the Lincolnshire border. The fertile clay lands and the Vale of Belvoir have very little ancient woodland

LEICESTERSHIRE AND RUTLAND

Leicestershire and Rutland are hunting country and their pattern of woods has been shaped to no small degree by the Quorn, Cottesmore, Belvoir and Fernine Hunts. Many of their woods are fox coverts, planted around the end of the eighteenth century. Their names – 'covert', 'spinney', 'gorse', 'plantation' and the like – indicate their recent origin. Ancient woods are centred on the craggy dome of Charnwood Forest in the west and on the scarps, hills and vales of 'High Leicestershire' in the east. The larger woods are often associated with medieval deer parks, such as Shepshed or Oakley Parks, or large estates such as Exton Park and Burley, both in Rutland. Many of the larger woods have been replanted. Barnsdale used to be a particularly fine example of a medieval park until most of it was drowned by Rutland Water.

Charnwood Forest is a place of bracken and granite, of hillsides crowned or spired with stone with a scatter of mature trees, and woods on the valley sides. It seems to have been not so much a royal game reserve as a gigantic common on which grazing rights were held by the commoners of Groby, Barrow, Shepshed and Whitwick. Many of its present woods are planted or of recent origin, and the original forest was probably mainly open. The surviving ancient woodland lies near the edge, and may have been excluded from the forest proper. Some ancient woods, such as Outwoods near Loughborough and Martinshaw Wood by

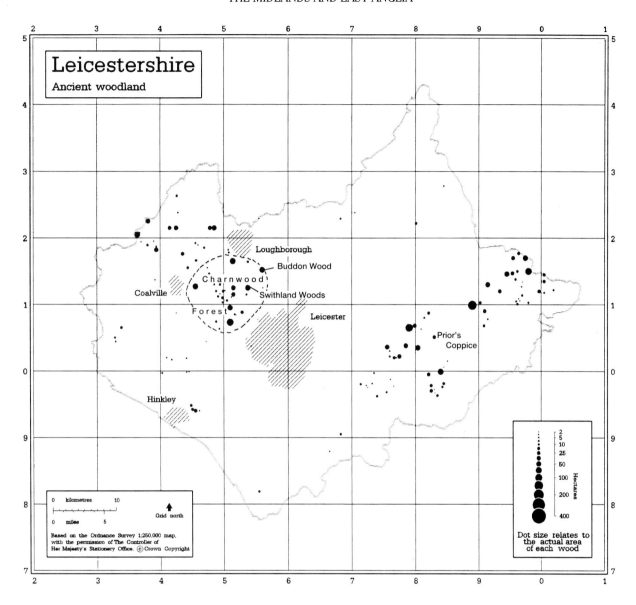

Leicestershire
Ancient woodland

Loughborough
Buddon Wood
Charnwood
Coalville
Swithland Woods
Forest
Leicester
Prior's Coppice
Hinkley

0   kilometres   10
0   miles   5
Grid north
Based on the Ordnance Survey 1:250.000 map,
with the permission of The Controller of
Her Majesty's Stationery Office. (c) Crown Copyright

2
5
10
25
50
100
200
400
Hectares
Dot size relates to
the actual area
of each wood

Groby, have been largely replanted in recent years; others such as Bardon Hill have been eaten away by quarries. **Swithland Wood** (58ha) [145 acres] is the best preserved. This is an ancient secondary wood formed over old slate quarries. Gnarled and stunted oaks mark places where the slate lies close to the surface. Swithland is a remarkable mixture of natural types of woodland, dominated by sessile oak with birches on the light, acid soils and coppiced hazels on the richer clays. Alders occupy the poorly drained, low-lying ground and there are also substantial areas of small-leaved lime coppice. The wood was originally managed as coppice, but parts have remained uncut since about 1850 and have developed into mature high forest. No fewer than ten kinds of ancient woodlands have been identified in this wood [45].

I mourn the partial loss of **Buddon Wood** near Quorn, a great camel's hump of trees among whose glades, crags and disused quarries I used to trespass in my schooldays. It was here that I first found a bee orchid and watched the extraordinary courtship ritual of crested grebes on Swithland Reservoir below the hill. Naturalists have been visiting Buddon Wood for more than 200 years. Its greatest rarity, the spreading bellflower (*Campanula patula*) was presumed extinct for almost the whole of that time, until refound recently by a hawk-eyed Loughborough naturalist. Buddon, unlike Swithland, is probably primary woodland. At least half of every kind of ancient woodland ever found in the county was in it somewhere. In addition, there were seepage lines and small sphagnum bogs along the hillside, stunted heather pressed against granite crags, alder carrs and birch groves and, at the base of the hill, some vast and unfathomably ancient lime stools. It was a famous place for rare mosses, beetles and spiders, many of which survived a clear-felling and a great fire during World War II, only to disappear in the 1960s when the Mountsorrel Granite Company extended its activities into the wood. Today, after fifteen years of working the hard red roadstone, the great hump has become a rim of trees surrounding a deep quarry. Fortunately, the lower slopes of Buddon Wood are still intact and little changed.

Fate has dealt more kindly with the ancient woods of East Leicestershire and West Rutland. These are ash-maple woods of solid medieval shapes with enclaves of elm overlying wet, lime-rich boulder clay. **Prior's Coppice** (29ha) [72 acres] near Braunston is typical of the group. This is a pre-Reformation name; the priors in question lived a mile away at Brooke Priory and probably owned the timber. The parish boundary runs along the northern side of the wood where big ash pollards stand on the field side. The western half was clear-felled about sixty years ago and is now a dense stand of young growth. But the eastern half remains coppice-with-standards in structure, though now overgrown with shaded muddy rides currently being restored by the Leicestershire and Rutland Nature Conservation Trust. (This is one of the places where I'm proud to say I have wielded a billhook myself.)

NOTTINGHAMSHIRE

What distinguishes the ancient woods of Nottinghamshire? At first sight the best of them are similar in many respects to East Anglian woods. There are woods on ridges, generally on wet clay soils and near parish boundaries, a coppice-with-standards structure, a wide range of trees and shrubs, big coppice stools and recent invasions of elm and sycamore. But then, particularly in the north of the county, one begins to notice subtle differences. Where are the big earthbanks that surround so many woods farther south? Treswell Wood, for example, has only a modest external ditch to mark its thousand-year-old borders. Equally one sees little or nothing of the internal banks, compartments and moats that tell us so much of the past of old woods in Cambridgeshire and Northamptonshire. Oak standards are surprisingly scarce, and more often found in hedgerows than woods. Ash is the dominant tree of Nottingham woods, possibly because of its past usefulness as hop poles. The minor trees – crab apple, service, aspen, holly, gean, Midland hawthorn – though often present in ancient woods are generally scarce, while native lime is very rare [46].

Nevertheless, many Nottinghamshire woods do have a distinctive flavour. Particularly characteristic of this county are the narrow steep-sided channels known as *dumbles*, which score through the surface 'Mercian Mudstone' around the town of Southwell. These are formed by small streams cutting through the soft marl and coming to rest on a bed of hard sandstone, known in Nottinghamshire as *skerries*. Many dumbles are wooded and provide valuable nesting space for finches and other birds that feed mostly on the surrounding open farmland. The appearance of dog's mercury, archangel, ramsons and herb paris on the sides of many dumbles suggest that they are ancient woodland. Possibly the maple and oak, hawthorn and bryony that grow in the dumbles were the models for the exquisitely carved foliated capitals of Southwell Minster, one of the most exuberant celebrations of nature from the darkness of the Gothic age. Even the lovely rusticity of the word

⇧ *The strange stag-headed oaks of Birklands in Sherwood Forest lend this area its special character and are host to one of the most important beetle faunas in Britain. October*
(PETER WAKELY)

dumble is somehow characteristic of Nottinghamshire. While many ancient woods are named simply after their parish or manor – with down-to-earth Saxon names such as Eaton, Gamston and Kirton – other names seem to tell us something more about the wood. What images are summoned up by Pudding Poke Wood, Conjure Alders, Collier Spring, Gosling Carr and Spitfire Bottoms (which, I'm assured, predates the Battle of Britain)!

Treswell Wood (48ha) [120 acres], a gem among Nottingham woods, is recognisably the same place as the wood at the manor of 'Tireswelle' in AD 1086, landlords Godric and Roger, with 'wood for pannage 4 furlongs in length and 1½ furlongs in breadth'. It was then worth 50 shillings, about the same as in the good old days of King Edward. The boundary has changed little, except for an eighteenth-century field that took a big bite out of the eastern side. One possible reason for this astonishing stability is that between the union of the parishes in the sixteenth century and 1946 the wood was owned by just one family. It seems to have been a useful source of income to the estate. A sales account dated 1824 lists fencing stakes, hedge binders, round poles, hop poles and bark from Treswell Wood, amounting to about £90, less the seven-shillings-and-sixpence-worth of beer consumed by the bark-peeling gang. The list fails to mention timber, implying that the wood was managed as simple coppice, nor does it mention firewood, which might have been given free to the poorer tenants.

More turbulent times began in 1938, with perhaps the first almost clear-felling Treswell Wood had ever received. In 1946, the wood was sold to a firm of timber merchants, which stripped the wood of its remaining timber, turning it into a quagmire in the process. By the early 1970s, the wood was an economic ruin, ripe for restocking with conifers. Fortunately the Nottinghamshire Trust for Nature Conservation was able to purchase the site in the nick of time. That is not, of course, the end of the story. Looking after Treswell Wood is hard work. As in scores of ancient woods from Cornwall to Caithness, volunteers from the Trust have been busy laying hedges, coppicing underwood, widening and strengthening rides, stacking cordwood, putting in drains, censusing nesting birds, selling hazel spar-gads for hedging and thatching, and dozens of other tasks. In the space of a dozen years, Treswell Wood has been brought back successfully from the brink of disaster to what it has been for a thousand years: a managed ash-maple wood, rich in wildlife and untroubled so far by deer or gales.

Treswell belongs to a close-knit group of ancient woods around Retford, on the ridges of the small, often steep-sided, hills that separate the broad Vale of Trent from the valley of the River Idle. This is ancient countryside, an area of heavy red 'Mercia Mudstone' known as 'the Clays', and characterised by hedged fields, green lanes, and red-brick and pantiled villages with big woods named after their respective parishes. From their high vantage point you can see far beyond the cooling towers of the Trent to the spires of Lincoln Cathedral and the distant Derbyshire Pennines. These are all ash-maple woods, with dense hazel coppice, huge stools of wych elm and, where light permits, a lush and colourful vernal flora. Yellow pimpernel, field briar, early purple orchid, sweet woodruff, wood millet and yellow archangel are common along the rides and, in places, the borders are fringed by the dainty wood melic grass. **Eaton** (24ha) [60 acres] and **Gamston Woods** (41ha) [102 acres] lie opposite one another on the ridge, separated by a minor road with flower-rich verges.

For twenty-five years they were owned by the Forestry Commission who put in a lot of conifers and neglected the woods thereafter. The native underwood struck back, smothering most of the conifers and producing a chaotic mixture of native and planted trees. Put on the market as part of the Commission's sell-off campaign in the 1980s, the woods were acquired by the Trust, which had campaigned hard to meet the purchase price. The task of restoration here was at least as great as at Treswell Wood, but Eaton and Gamston Woods, too, have been restored from the 'pine plantation' of the Commission stock maps to ancient ash-maple woods. At Gamston Wood, the Trust has left a block of the more vigorous Corsican pines to grow up until they are of saleable size. Parts of this wood are more acidic than Treswell or Eaton Woods, and both pine and oak did better than usual: a turn of the century oak planting is now worthy of a registered seed source for oak.

The woods considered so far are all on heavy, often waterlogged clay. The second widespread type of woodland in Nottinghamshire, ash-wych elm woodland, lies on better drained, more calcareous soil. Good examples are **Kirton Wood** (18ha) [45 acres], not far from the famous open-field system of Laxton, and **Bunny Old Wood** (32ha) [80 acres] on a north-facing ridge of marl and Rhaetic beds in the south of the county. The history of both woods has been traced back to the early Middle Ages, when their respective names were Kyrketune and 'Boneyris'. In 1487, King Henry VII and his army 'lay al nyght in the felde, under a wode called Bonley Rice' on their way to Stoke to fight the Yorkists. 'Ris' or 'rice' evidently refers to the new brushwood in felled coppices. Boneyris had become plain Bunny Wood by 1558, and was later dubbed an Old Wood to distinguish it from the new wood, planted nearby when the parish was enclosed in the eighteenth century.

In their traditional management as coppices with dense underwood and a rich flora, these woods have much in common with Treswell and Eaton Woods. The main difference lies in their much greater abundance of wych elm, which in

Bunny Old Wood is actually the dominant tree. The difference has been accentuated by Dutch elm disease, which has so far killed many elms and injured more, yet mysteriously spared others. There are still many big healthy coppice stools. Other elms are dead from about halfway up the trunk but are bushing out vigorously farther down. In Kirton Wood the elms are widely spaced and evidently more resistant to the disease, but Bunny Wood has areas where almost all the old growth is dead, producing a haunted wood that groans and creaks even when the air is still. The release of minerals from dying elms has provided a bonanza of phosphates and nitrates for weeds such as cleavers and stinging nettles, and in open spaces a meadow-like flora of buttercups and grasses seems to be displacing the primroses and bluebells. Cut elm logs, used to strengthen the main ride, sprout great dryad's saddles and oyster mushrooms. Bunny Old Wood may take a long time to settle down again after this crisis, and might even change in the process from an elmwood into an ashwood.

Birkland and the legend of Robin Hood

AREA: 185ha (460 acres)

STATUS: A Country Park administered by Nottingham County Council

ACCESS: Along waymarked paths

TYPE: Acid oak and birch wood-pasture with ancient trees

GRID REFERENCE: SK 625675

In somer, when the shawes be sheyne,
And leves be large and long,
Hit is full mery in feyre foreste
To here the foulys song

Here is the most popular, or at any rate the most populated, wood in England, thanks to the enduring myth of Robin Hood. The inevitable visitor centre lies at one end, next to enormous sylvan car parks, and a waymarked path from the centre takes the visitor past numerous aged trees to a clearing where stands the biggest tree of all, a vast hulk called the Major Oak. It is so-named not to distinguish this tree from relatively minor oaks but (rather disappointingly) to commemorate one Major Hayman Rooke, who wrote about these trees in the 1790s. Curiously enough, although Robin Hood is firmly rammed down our throats by every sticker and placard, there is no Robin's oak, only the remains of 'Robin Hood's Larder', once a hollow oak which gradually 'weakened until it looked like a huge old barrel held together with iron bands . . . (until) a summer gale in 1966 brought it crashing down, and only a decaying stump remains'.

Most really old trees in Britain, by which I mean those of four hundred years and more, are pollards standing on land used formerly as wood-pasture. Elsewhere in this book we have met, or will meet, the lightning-scarred trunks at Windsor, the squat oak-men of Moccas Park, the embossed pedestals of Burnham Beeches. The great oaks of Birkland are among the oddest of all. They have been called 'blasted oaks' or 'giraffe pollards', trees cut short about 12m (40ft) above ground. It is hard to imagine why woodmen would clamber so far up the tree before lopping boughs (even giraffes cannot reach this high). Surely these are, rather, natural pollards topped by the wind long ago. A characteristic shape is a spire of dead barkless wood, like a dunce's cap, projecting above the living canopy. Shakespeare may have known such trees in his native Warwickshire for his 'high top bald with drie antiquity' describes them perfectly. These ancient wood-pastures probably preserve much of the natural genetic composition of primeval forest, so that each of the six hundred or so old trees at Birkland is an individual, leafing at different times, some with fluted bark, others grotesquely distorted with cankers and bosses and great swirls of blackened bark. Most are hollow with red-rotten interiors stained by bracket fungi. Their age has been estimated at between three hundred and six hundred years, old but not old enough to be contemporaries of Robin Hood. The Major Oak and its companions belong to the age of the halberd and the arquebus, not the longbow.

The County Council's nature trail echoes the popular belief that such trees are diseased and dying. Legend attributes their dramatic spires and antlers to bolts of lightning. They are more probably the result of die-back, an often misunderstood phenomenon in which a tree comes to terms with a slower growth rate by reducing its leafage to a smaller, inner crown and abandoning its original spreading branches. Such an adjustment might have been caused by sudden stress, such as defoliation by caterpillars to which oaks are prone, but it should not be confused with ill-health. Whatever its nature, the event that produced these strange shapes happened long ago. Visitors from Major Hayman Rooke onwards have admired them and speculated about their origin. Some of the supposedly decrepit trees are in fact, bursting with flowers and acorns, and the county's foresters are not averse to collecting the latter for planting. There are dead trees among the living but in all probability their demise was caused by human agency. They seem to have weathered a period of air pollution in the 1920s and 1930s so severe that wire rabbit-fences would corrode and fall to bits within a few years. But the porous Bunter sandstone soils of Sherwood Forest are vulnerable to water abstraction. Industries have used vast quantities of ground water in recent times and the water table has fallen. The trees died of thirst.

Great efforts have been made to prolong the life of the Major Oak. This famous tree has become an ancient monument and is treated like a cross between an elderly patient and a ruined abbey. Inside its hollow trunk is a pedestal of concrete. The great spreading boughs, each the size of a normal trunk, are suspended by wires and propped up with crutches. Dead limbs have been removed by tree surgeons and the cut ends treated with salves and sprays. Visitors must keep their distance, lest a child, swinging on a bent limb, should bring the whole tottering wreck crashing down on

top of it. There is not much more one can do. The Major Oak would have benefitted most from pollarding a couple of centuries ago.

It is impossible to overemphasise the importance of such trees for nature conservation. Without its ancient oaks Birkland would still be of interest for the invertebrates that live among tussocky grass and birch trees, both of which have been present continuously for hundreds of years. But it would be no more exciting than a score of other such places in northern England. As it is, Birklands has the most exciting community of rare spiders in the whole of Great Britain, and is among the best half-dozen places for insects of dead wood. Some 1,500 species of beetles have been found here, of which a large proportion, including most of the rare ones, live under loose bark or inside the hollow trunks of over-mature *living* trees. Most invertebrates need the humidity lent by the living sapwood as well as the warmth generated by rotting heartwood; completely dead barkless trees in open wood-pasture provide a much drier, harsher environment, inimical to invertebrates except for those few, such as some of the larger beetles, that have evolved drought-resistant life-styles. A second reason for its importance is that Birkland spans the divide between north and south; many species with a southerly distribution reach their northern limit here, and vice versa. It is, for example, probably the only place where the marbled brown, a moth belonging to big oakwoods in the south and west, meets the angle-striped sallow, a fellow moth of upland birchwoods.

Sherwood's ancient trees and their wildlife bring to mind the mythical Greenwood inhabited by Robin Hood and his men; Robin's spirit is ever-present (it would be cynical to suggest his entrepreneurial sense also). As a leaflet coyly informs the visitor: 'You're not alone. You're being watched by the unseen men of the Greenwood – Robin's men.' It is perhaps fitting that Robin should be the embodiment of the English Greenwood for his is a refreshingly down-to-earth presence, the product of medieval low-life, of penny ballads, alehouse songs and May games. In the original Robin Hood stories, the forest lanes are busy with travelling folk, tinkers, beggars, wandering friars and minstrels, wood-cutters and tanners. There is a great deal of eating and drinking and singing on the way, accompanied by gratuitous violence and a complete disregard of the law and its enforcers. There is no nonsense about robbing the rich to pay the poor in the original rhymes – the outlaws robbed for themselves! Despite the fictional cast of the stories, the background is authentic enough. One reads of similar lawless feuds and pranks in the record of real forests, such as Needwood and Pickering (qv) and, centuries later, in Cranborne Chase. The Visitor Centre rightly concentrates on medieval forest life, using Robin and his men as convenient symbols of real outlaws, friars and woodmen. Robin's fame perhaps owes much to the chord of blood memory he strikes in us, of a life close to nature in which we can discard the suffocating apparel of civilisation and be daring outlaws again.

Birkland is so much the epitome of how a medieval wood is popularly imagined – a place of big oaks, deer and bracken – that it seems unsporting to suggest that in Robin's time (which I take to be the late twelfth century) Sherwood Forest was more like Egdon Heath. Birkland is a Viking name, *Birkilundr*, meaning birch wood. It seems to have been a deer exclosure in ancient times, a wooded locality on a largely woodless common. Whether there were always oak trees present is unknown. Oak regenerates well on commons only when the normal level of grazing is reduced for some reason. Judging from the present age-range of oak at Birkland, there have been only about four such periods in the past five hundred years (we are living through one of them). As for Robin, Professor Holt makes a strong case for Barndale in Yorkshire as the birthplace of the tales, arguing that it was only from the seventeenth century onwards that his exploits became associated with Sherwood [47].

Professor Holt's book is not on sale at the Sherwood Forest Visitor Centre.

LINCOLNSHIRE

Lincolnshire is a big spacious agricultural county with no industrial towns and fewer people per square mile than Cornwall or Clwyd. Three-quarters of it is low-lying and flat, all wind and sky. The Lincolnshire Wolds, though graced with upland names such as 'cliff', 'gap', 'plateau' and 'vale', nowhere exceeds 167m (550ft) in height. This is self-evidently not a well-wooded county: there are places where the landscape recedes for miles with hardly a hedgerow tree. However, Lincolnshire is better wooded than is often imagined. About 27,000ha (6,670 acres) of its surface is under trees, and although less than a quarter of this is considered to be woodland of ancient origin, the county does contain woods of great interest and national importance.

Until 1940, afforestation in Lincolnshire was limited and largely confined to former heathland. Postwar advances in agriculture have tended to push plantation forestry into existing, often ancient, woods, with the result that more than half of the total area of ancient woodland has been replanted. The relatively large, flat woods of Lincolnshire are physically well suited to forestry ploughs, though the dry climate and heavy soils are less amenable. Few woods of any size are entirely free from twentieth-century planting. Rather surprisingly, only a relatively small area of ancient woodland, involving thirty-eight woods, has been cleared altogether since 1930. This is because there were so few woods left to clear, and those mostly on the poorest soils. Nineteenth-century woodland clearance was on a much greater scale. Digging for victory in World War II and afterwards destroyed Lincolnshire's natural heaths, downs and meadows, but left the less tractable woods almost intact.

In Lincolnshire, many woodland flowers are confined to ancient woods and wood relict hedges, among them wood anemones, lily-of-the-valley, yellow archangel, sweet woodruff, great woodrush, bird's-nest orchid, greater butterfly orchid, herb paris and primrose. Woods planted between 1700 and 1850 and thereafter managed as coppice

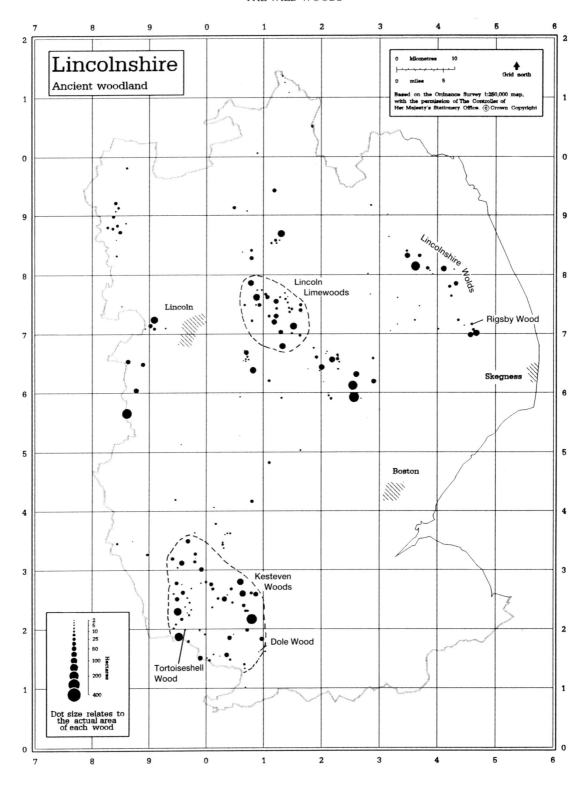

Lincolnshire
Ancient woodland

0 kilometres 10
0 miles 5
Grid north

Based on the Ordnance Survey 1:250,000 map,
with the permission of The Controller of
Her Majesty's Stationery Office. © Crown Copyright

Lincolnshire Wolds

Lincoln
Limewoods

Rigsby Wood

Lincoln

Skegness

Boston

Kesteven
Woods

Dole Wood

Tortoiseshell
Wood

2
5
10
25
50
100
200
400

Hectares

Dot size relates to
the actual area
of each wood

In Lincolnshire, ancient woodland is concentrated in three areas. In the south are the Kesteven Woods on a plateau of lime-rich clay between Bourne and Stamford. In the middle are the Lincolnshire limewoods on a ridge of infertile clay and sand at the edge of the Fens. The third group lies in the east on the dip slope of the Lincolnshire Wolds

look superficially like ancient woodland but completely lack these species. Indeed, they often retain plants from open heathland or grassland, more than a century on [48]. The most famous Lincolnshire woods are its limewoods, a knot of medium-sized or large woods in the Wragby area in which small-leaved lime is the commonest tree. This may be the last stand, as it were, of Lincoln lime because the tree was evidently commoner in the past to judge by the numerous *lin-* or *bass-*place-names. The latter refers to the fibrous bark or *bast*, once used for matting and to make carrier bags known as *basses*. Lime was a better known tree in the Middle Ages than today; a coat of arms from the parish church at Linwood depicts accurately the elegant heart-shaped leaves of small-leaved lime. Unlike the limewoods of the Northamptonshire limestone, these lie on neutral to acidic soils, sour, heavy clays with surface deposits of even more infertile sand and gravel. The prevailing type of woodland is a mixture of overgrown lime, ash and hazel coppice, with oak standards and a great deal of birch. Some stands lie on richer soil and include more base-demanding trees such as maple and Midland hawthorn; others, on soil too poor for ash, are classed as oak-lime woods. The combination of so many different types of lime-dominated woodland is exceptional.

These are old coppice woods, most of which were converted to high forest in the late nineteenth century and have since become dense, heavily shaded places of about a hundred years' growth. Some have older standards of oak and ash, others, like much of **Newball Wood**, are simple coppice with only a scatter of oaks. **Stainton Wood** is a rare example of a limewood managed as high

forest – rare because lime is of little value as a timber tree and was nearly always coppiced or pollarded. The Lincolnshire limewoods were sold to the Forestry Commission after World War II, and were partly converted to plantations of conifers and oak between 1945 and 1970. However, the lime coppice proved impossible to eradicate. Though sensitive to grazing, lime is otherwise virtually immortal, and ready to regenerate from half-rotten stumps or even bits of buried root. By the late 1960s, ecologists had begun to notice limewoods and alert woodland managers of their conservation value. Today, the Lincolnshire limewoods are the subject of a nature reserve agreement that aims not only to 'perpetuate their broadleaved character', but also their natural diversity of structure and composition. **Hatton Wood** (29ha) [72 acres] and **Great West Wood** (27ha) [66.7 acres] are designated as 'minimum management areas', part of a series of ancient woods throughout Britain that have been set aside to study natural processes in woodland (see also Lady Park Wood, Gloucestershire).

Kesteven District was densely wooded in Norman times: the name *Kesteven* is believed to be derived from the Welsh for a wood, *coed* and, if so, it is a rare and interesting example of a pre-Saxon place-name. Although they contain some lime, the Kesteven woods in the south-western corner of the county have closer affinities with the boulder clay woods of Northamptonshire. These are calcareous woods of pedunculate oak, ash and hazel with local enclaves of elm, formerly managed as coppice-with-standards. Maple, service, Midland hawthorn, wild cherry and aspen are often frequent. **Dole Wood** near Bourne is a small but well-preserved fragment that is once again being managed as a coppice by the Lincolnshire Trust for Nature Conservation, with the help of local school-children. In the spring, when the ground becomes a beautiful patchwork quilt of bluebell, archangel, mercury, woodruff and anemone, the flowers distract one's eyes from the canopy, which seems at first sight to be mostly of oak, much of it dead. Closer inspection reveals a much more compli-

cated pattern. The centre, on a slope of sandy clay, is fairly uniform oak-hazel woodland, but the more ill-drained periphery is a mosaic of wet ash-maple and ash-wych elm woodland, a patch of acidic oak-lime woodland very like the Lincoln limewoods, with the occasional wild service tree along the banks. The oldest tree is not oak but a large coppice stool of ash at the south-eastern corner. Dole Wood, it turns out, is not a natural oakwood but an ashwood that a previous owner tried unsuccessfully to turn into an oakwood; and long ago it was probably a limewood. This subtle patterning and interplay of several centuries and half a dozen distinct types of ancient woodland covers precisely 4ha (10 acres) – not much more than the corner of a field: you could walk round it in ten minutes.

Another interesting wood in Kesteven, also managed by the Lincolnshire Trust, is **Tortoiseshell Wood** (9.4ha) [23 acres] near Castle Bytham. This, too, is a surviving fragment of a large wood with a sinuous edge and a medieval woodbank corresponding to the parish boundary on one side, and the contrasting straight borders made by nineteenth-century clearances on the other. It has developed a three-layered structure typical of long neglected coppice, and for its size is another remarkably rich little wood, packed with flowers indicative of ancient woodland. There are some magnificent standard service trees spared by previous owners, perhaps for their beauty, and strange gnarled and bent oaks snaking up from ill-cut stools. The Trust's attempts to reinstate coppicing are bedevilled by deer, a growing problem in this county. Yet the alternative to management is a cold dark wood with old decaying stools, no regeneration and bramble scrambling everywhere.

Rigsby Wood (15ha) [37 acres] near Claxby, another Lincolnshire Trust reserve, belongs to the third concentration of ancient woodland at the

⇦ *Small-leaved lime coppice, now singled and developing as high forest, at Chambers Wood in Bardney Forest, Lincolnshire. May*
(PETER WAKELY)

foot of the Wolds. This is a composite wood with bits and pieces having been tacked on at different times to the original core, producing a geometric shape of squares and right angles which at first sight looks like a plantation. The ancient 'Old Coppice' stands next to an 'Old Plantation' to which the more recent 'Furze Piece' has been connected by a strip of woodland called 'The Pingle'. A parish boundary bank marked by big maples passes along one side, dividing Rigsby Wood from the tiny Ailby Wood. The ancient part of Rigsby Wood can be picked out at a distance in May as a wash of bluebells under ash-hazel coppice with oak and ash standards. This wood is probably a small parish coppice that later became a shooting covert. In the spacious country of the Wolds and its coastal apron, The Marsh, the survival of ancient woodland owes much to fox hunting and game preservation, the main historic counterbalance to arable farming in a flat and predominantly fertile area.

HUMBERSIDE
The intensively farmed landscape of Humberside is the most poorly wooded in all of lowland England except for the completely treeless fens, levels and coastal marshes. Its entire area of ancient woodland – 600ha (1,483 acres) – would scarcely fill an average parish, and amounts to only one five-hundredth of the county's area. The majority of the ancient woods are small and the only dense concentration is in the Manby district south of the Humber. As in Lincolnshire, postwar agricultural improvement has tended to push plantation forestry into the ancient woods, so that nearly half of the latter have been replanted, including both the richest wood and the two largest woods in the county.

Some of the earliest evidence of woodland clearance comes from the fenny carrs and *garths* on the wet, peaty levels of the Humber. This area has very little ancient woodland today, but Low Wood at the head of Hornsea Mere may be an ancient carr wood occupying a site that has never been completely cleared. There is evidence that the drier, thinner soils of the Wolds were probably in extensive cultivation from as long ago as the Bronze Age, thus restricting the surviving woods to the steep western scarps and pockets of heavy clay which they occupy today. At Castlethorpe, the limy silt of fen ditches preserves fossils and charcoal that indicate a sudden change from woodland to an open landscape around 3,400 years ago – the work of early farmers.

The chalk woods of the Wolds are free-drained and dominated by ash. Some, possibly most, are secondary woods that have sprung up naturally over former open sheep pasture after grazing declined. **Millington Wood**, the finest of them, has a magnificent suite of woodland plants, which suggests that the core of it is a primary wood. It lies in one of the characteristic winding valleys of the Wolds called Lily Dale, perhaps in honour of the lily-of-the-valley that still lingers here. Once an ashwood, Millington Wood fell victim to Forestry Commission operations in the 1960s, when most of it was replanted with larch, Norway spruce and beech. A token corner of ancient ashwood was spared, and there, fortunately, some of the wood's botanical treasures survive, among them baneberry, greater and nettle-leaved bellflowers and toothwort. It is now owned by Humberside County Council, which is trying to return it to a mixed-aged broadleaved wood.

Burton Bushes (12ha) [30 acres] near Beverley is one of the few woods in the county to have been investigated in detail [49]. This is a common, until recently grazed by cattle, and much of it is open and grassy with a park-like perimeter and a cross of broad rides – on the map the wood resembles a hot-cross bun. Most of it is of pedunculate oak standards and an understorey of holly. Hazel is scarce, because cows eat it, but the presence of crabtrees, wych elm and maple suggests a long continuity of woodland, and the name itself has an ancient ring to it. The wood was fenced in 1980 to keep out the cattle and, rather to everyone's surprise, the regeneration of oak has been spectacular.

The woods near Broughton in former Lincoln-

In Cambridgeshire, ancient woodland is found ⇨ *mainly on the chalky boulder clay around the edge of the woodless Fens. Among the 2,800ha (6,919 acres) of ancient woodland are well-known woods such as Bedford Purlieus, Castor Hanglands, Monk's Wood and Hayley Wood*

shire are the most extensive in the county, and the evidence of ancient banks and of poorly colonising plants such as small-leaved lime and lily-of-the-valley suggests that **Manby Wood** and **Far Wood**, at least, are of ancient origin. They lie on an area of poor soil that in the Middle Ages supported heath and enclosed copses. The former was planted with trees by the Earl of Yarborough in the early nineteenth century, and later on the coppice woods were converted to high forest by planting and singling. Today, Far Wood's appearance may represent the future of ancient coppice woods if the Forestry Commission's present guidelines for broadleaved woodland continue: a wood of youngish trees, including non-indigenous sycamore and beech, with woodbanks and a Roman road swallowed up inside, and a few large coppice stools of sessile oak and small-leaved lime near the edge to remind us of its former identity. Such a regime will preserve a great deal, though not all, of Far Wood's wildlife. It is certainly preferable in every way to the outright coniferisation that at one time seemed the probable fate of most large ancient woods.

CAMBRIDGESHIRE

Since 1974, an enlarged Cambridgeshire has swallowed up the county of Huntingdonshire and the Soke of Peterborough. It is still a predominantly agricultural county with a very low proportion of woodland (less than 1 per cent) and scarcely any uncultivable land. For that reason, there has been no postwar afforestation of open land.

Although Cambridgeshire is a low-lying county rising to no more than 146m (579ft) above sea level near the Essex border, many of its ancient woods

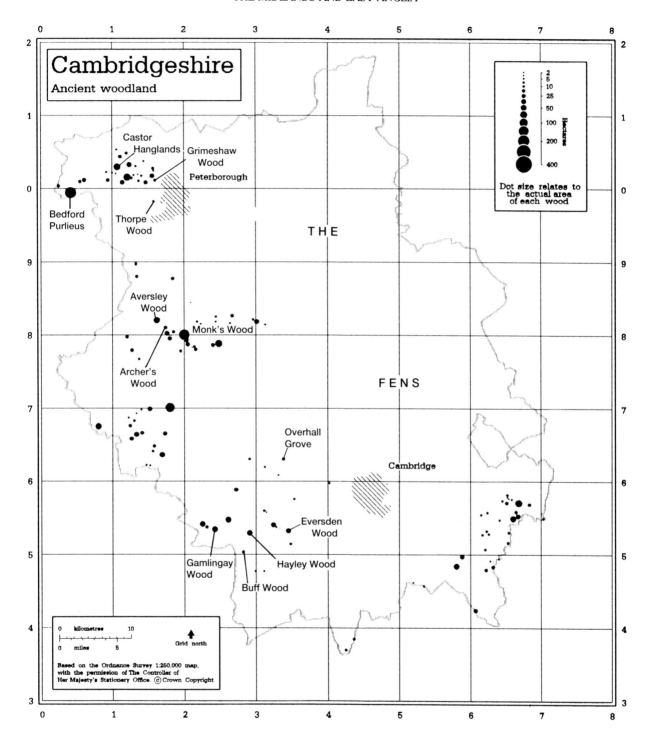

Cambridgeshire

Ancient woodland

Castor
Hanglands

Grimeshaw
Wood

Peterborough

Bedford
Purlieus

Thorpe
Wood

T H E

Aversley
Wood

Monk's Wood

Archer's
Wood

F E N S

Overhall
Grove

Cambridge

Eversden
Wood

Gamlingay
Wood

Hayley Wood

Buff Wood

Hectares

2
5
10
25
50
100
200
400

Dot size relates to
the actual area
of each wood

0   kilometres   10

0   miles   5

Grid north

Based on the Ordnance Survey 1:250,000 map,
with the permission of The Controller of
Her Majesty's Stationery Office. © Crown Copyright

⇐ The Red Well at Overhall Grove, Cambridgeshire, an ancient site perhaps named from the reddish rust stain produced by its iron-rich water. It lies close to Knapwell church and probably supplied water to the medieval village. April
(PETER MARREN)

Dead and fallen elm at Overhall Grove, ⇒ Cambridgeshire – a common sight in ancient woods in eastern England. In some instances elm will live on as underwood; in others it may be destined for replacement ash and other colonising trees. March
(PETER MARREN)

Deer fencing at Monk's Wood, Cambridgeshire, ⇩ now necessary to safeguard the young growth against rapidly increasing deer numbers. March
(PETER WAKELY)

are on hilltops. Typically, they occupy patches of ill-drained clay near the parish boundary that are often waterlogged in winter but can turn as hard as a board in hot weather. The predominant type of woodland has dense ash-hazel coppice with oak and ash standards. Associated trees and shrubs are many, among the most regular being maple, Midland hawthorn and aspen, with blackthorn and common hawthorn at the edge. Most Cambridgeshire woods have one or two stands of elm, and in the case of Overhall Grove, Papworth Wood and Buff Wood, elm has taken over a large part of the original wood. Woodland elms are not easy to name. Two species, the 'English' elm *Ulmus procera* and the small-leaved 'East Anglian' elm *Ulmus carpinifolia* are involved, but a close study of **Buff Wood** revealed no fewer than twenty-nine distinct varieties of elm which have invaded the wood at different times, either from root suckers, from

seed or possibly by planting [50]. The elm stands are now stark and dangerous places, strewn about with fallen trunks, creaking ominously in the wind and often waist-high in nettles in the summer.

The woods west of Cambridge are well known for their beautiful displays of oxlips in April. Oxlips are confined to woods on the East Anglian boulder clay and have long been considered a good indicator of ancient woodland. Unfortunately for the oxlips, wild fallow deer have increased greatly in this area during the last twenty years. Oxlips smell, and presumably taste, delicious and greedy deer have reduced former oxlip carpets to bare ground and brambles. They are also severely damaging the coppice regrowth in managed woods. In **Hayley Wood** (49ha) [121 acres], which has been coppiced at an acre per year since 1964, much of the formerly dense underwood has been devoured and a prominent browse line has developed. On my last

visit to the wood, at oxlip time in 1990, more than one deer carcass was decomposing malodorously and immense swarms of bluebottle flies were about, blackening the trunks as they basked in the spring sunshine. Deer are perhaps the greatest crisis the wood has faced in its otherwise remarkably stable history.

Some Cambridgeshire woods, like Hayley and its neighbour Gamlingay Wood, have permanent borders at least 750 years old. Others, such as Aversley Wood near Sawtry, were partly grubbed up and ploughed during the Middle Ages, only to revert to woodland again as the land was abandoned. Such vicissitudes probably reflect the changes in population before and after the Black Death. Some woods have swallowed up ancient settlements. Archer's Wood lies partly on top of a Cistercian grange, Overhall Grove on a moated manor house. Buff Wood buries part of a lost

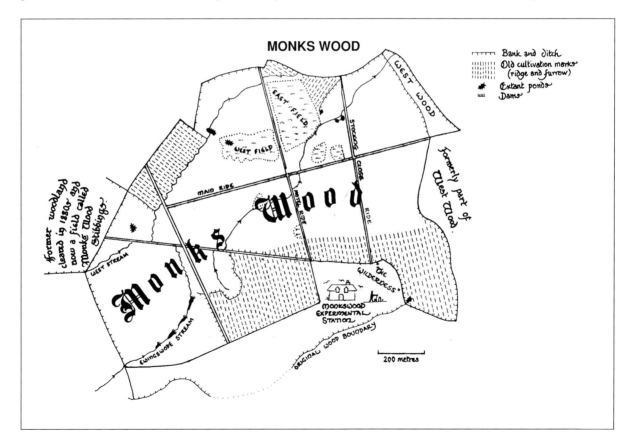

village. These changes generally pre-date our arbitrary time-post of 1600, and so we class these woods as ancient, though most of them contain areas of secondary woodland as well as land that has probably always been wooded.

Non-Fenland Cambridgeshire has been a densely populated county for at least a millennium. Most parishes had at least one wood that provided underwood for firewood, hurdle-making, fence posts and other uses. There are no known wooded commons in the county; all the woods seem to have been private property and were often, as with Hayley Wood and Monk's Wood, owned by abbeys.

Apart from its well-preserved boundary bank and ditch, Hayley Wood has few earthworks. Other woods such as Overhall Grove, Buff Wood and Eversden Wood are full of woodbanks, moats and patches of ridge-and-furrow, indicating a more complex history. **Overhall Grove** (17ha) [42 acres] is overshadowed by the magnificently gnarled pollard elms that once marked the streets of the shrunken medieval village of Knapwell. At the farthest end from the village at the top of a hill stood the manor house. All traces of it above ground have gone, but judging from its location and massive defences – a large moat and deep ditch (in which badgers burrow) – the Lord of the Manor must have been on poor terms with his commoners. He seems to have used the ground below as his dustbin: tall nettles, elder, goosegrass and hogweed all attest to phosphate-rich soil. From the manor house, the wood slopes downhill to an embanked, waterlogged section which may be the original core of the wood; the existence of an original wood is inferred from the presence there of oxlips [51].

Eversden Wood (50ha) [123.5 acres] is another complex wood of partly secondary origin. Its history was worked out by Oliver Rackham from an examination of the abundant earthworks within the wood. The original Saxon wood (*Eversden* is Old English for 'boar hill') lay on high ground at the conjunction of three parishes, each with banked lanes running along the boundaries. Each parish took care to look after its own bit of the wood,

further subdividing them into compartments marked by banks and pollards and named after their respective owners. Later in the Middle Ages, some of these compartments were grubbed up and ploughed, but later were allowed to revert naturally to woodland. In one compartment, a scatter of big pollarded trees indicates its former use as wood-pasture. Another became a building site, a large house inside its fashionable moat. To baffle posterity further, a mid-nineteenth-century owner superimposed a grid of rides on the wood that fails to conform to any of the earlier tracks and banks [52].

Aversley Wood (61ha) [151 acres] near Sawtry and Hayley Wood contain a characteristic feature of Cambridgeshire: armed ponds. In both cases the pond lies over former ridge-and-furrow, and hence is man-made and unlikely to be earlier than the fifteenth century. Armed ponds have three or four narrow arms extending starfish-like from the centre and seem designed to present a long edge, perhaps in order to accommodate as many drinking cattle as possible. The Aversley Wood pond stands close to an ancient track called Bullock Road, down which as many as 200,000 cattle were driven each year to be fattened in the sweet pastures of Huntingdonshire before being taken to the London markets. The one at Hayley is about 1.5m (5ft) deep with steep sides and a lining of cobblestones. Its purpose is a mystery, since there is no recorded use of the wood as cattle pasture.

Peterborough, now the largest town in the county, owns **Grimeshaw Wood**, a 'community wood' looked after by local residents and conservation volunteers. This is another ash-hazel wood, typical of ancient woodland on the East Anglian boulder clay, with some large ash stools, a lot of wild garlic and early purple orchid, and beautiful displays of primroses (they spill over onto the road bank where a dual carriageway cut through the nearby Thorpe Wood in the early 1980s). Grimeshaw Wood is surrounded by roads and houses, and adoption by the city was considered to be its best defence against fly-tipping and vandalism.

*The Great Pond at Hayley Wood, an armed pond⇧
designed to accommodate drinking cattle. April*
(PETER MARREN)

CAMBRIDGESHIRE WOODLAND PONDS

⇦ *The broad moat which formerly guarded a
medieval manor house above Overhall Grove*
(PETER MARREN)

BEDFORDSHIRE

Bedfordshire is a small, sparsely wooded county. Ancient woodland accounts for roughly half of the total woodland of 5,800ha (14,321 acres) and, as in other densely settled agricultural counties, virtually all ancient woodland occupies land too poor or too steep to be worth farming. While the pattern of ancient woodland in Bedfordshire has not changed much in nine hundred years, no more than a quarter of the woods survive. Like other mainly fertile counties, Bedfordshire saw large-scale medieval woodland clearances in favour of agriculture. The county can be divided physically into four main geological strata and these are the main influences on the natural vegetation. To the north and west is boulder clay, with scattered ash-maple woods, some of them quite large – Odell Great Wood, West Wood and Potton Wood on the Cambridge border are all around 100ha (247 acres).

These are similar in character to the West Cambridgeshire woods, although the Bedfordshire woods have received less attention from historians and naturalists and rather more from foresters. The heart of the county lies on Gault Clay and is intensively farmed with just a scatter of small woods, again mostly ash-maple copses. By contrast with that of Buckingham and Oxford, the Bedfordshire Chalk is very poorly wooded. The scarp slopes are relatively gentle and pitted with quarries. Leete Wood on the slope of the predominantly grassland Barton Hills NNR, may be a native beechwood, for it has an underwood of hazel, spindle and yew, and there is ash as well as beech in the canopy. George Wood and Slaughters Wood are tiny dip slope woods in the suburbs of Luton and have a wider range of stand types, including hornbeam and planted sweet chestnut.

Nearly half of the county's woodland is concentrated on the infertile ridge of greensand around Woburn Abbey and the villages of Flitwick, Maulden and Clophill. If there is a distinctive character to Bedfordshire woods, it is in these woods of contrasting light sand and heavy boulder clay. The sandy parts are well known for the lily-of-the-valley, and still in places 'offer a wonderful sight of this plant despite the raids that have been made on it in recent years', as the botanist Claridge Druce pointed out in 1926 [53]. This area was particularly well-wooded in the Middle Ages and many woods were owned by abbeys and priories, raising revenue from rents and the sales of firewood and other products. Large areas were incorporated into deer parks such as Woburn and Luton Hoo. The woods reached their peak of production in the early nineteenth century when parliamentary enclosure led to a large demand for fencing stakes and for wooded pipes to underdrain fields, and also coincided with the peak of the London firewood market. At this period, prices paid for coppice products were such that timber production was neglected.

Later in the century, however, as coal replaced firewood as fuel, the situation was reversed. Many woods were converted to high forest and some were later replanted with conifers, including the well-recorded Maulden Woods. In the latter, the wildlife interest is centred on the still open marshland and the edges of the rides. Today the only coppicing in the county is for conservation purposes, mainly at Bramingham Wood near Luton, Clapham Park Woods near Bedford and at Marston Thrift nature reserve.

King's and Baker's Wood, a few miles north of Leighton Buzzard, is one of the larger ancient woods of the East Midlands. The Roman road of Watling Street skirts its northern side separated from the wood by a medieval anti-highwayman trench. Sessile oak, birch and planted Scots pine on the light, acidic soils of the greensand contrasts with the dense underwood and pedunculate oak and ash standards on heavier, poorly drained boulder clay. Hornbeam coppice is prominent on the clay and there are also small stands of small-leaved lime. As befits its size and largely natural vegetation, this wood has the longest list of ancient woodland plants in the county, including lily-of-the-valley, wood vetch, wood spurge, yellow archangel and great wood-rush.

Bramingham Wood, in the northern suburbs of Luton, is one of the Woodland Trust's community woodlands, managed by local volunteers. This is a well-documented wood, whose records date back to 1227 when the tenant, one Simon de Bramblehanger, planted a hedge around the wood, an action that landed him in the dock of the manorial court. Old maps show that this was once two woods, Great and Little Bramingham, separated by a strip of open ground. As late as the 1920s, it was still being cut over regularly to supply fencing stakes, poles and firewood, but fell into disuse thereafter. The Trust volunteers have a major task in restoring the wood after sixty years of near neglect, during which the underwood grew dense and shady and top-heavy ash trees fell to pieces. Since 1985, the Trust has begun to reinstate the historic management of the wood as coppice-with-standards, cutting an acre of underwood a year on a projected fifteen-year cycle and financing the work from sales of rustic poles and firewood.

EAST ANGLIA

The ancient woods of East Anglia epitomise many of the historic and natural features that have come to be associated with ancient woodland: sinuous fixed boundaries, prominent woodbanks and ditches, wet clay soils, ponds and dells, carpets of woodland wild flowers and a dense and well-defined underwood. Nearly all of the ancient woods lie on near level ground, on modest inclines, or, most typically, on hilltops and ridges. They occupy land that would have been difficult to clear and cultivate, notably ill-drained, heavy clays, alternately waterlogged and rock hard. Most East Anglian woods were managed on rotation as coppice or coppice-with-standards. East Anglian underwood was used for making tool handles, hurdles, hedge binders, thatching spars and the like, or for firewood. More often than not, the fate of these woods in the past fifty years was to have been exploited for their remaining timber and then abandoned to the pheasant or cleared and re-

⇩*Essex is unusual in that most of the land is on London Clay, and hence ancient woodland is distributed more evenly than in most counties. Large woods are confined to Epping Forest in the south-west. The low-lying land near the coast is woodless*

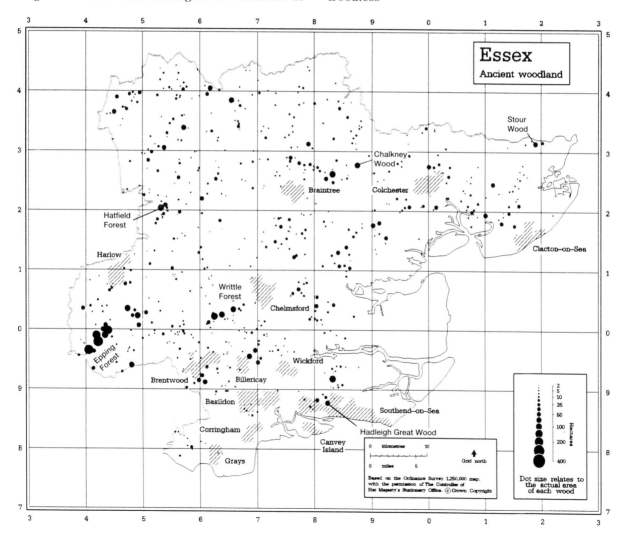

⇧ *Woodbank and pollarded tree at*
Bradfield Woods, Suffolk. April
(PETER WAKELY)

placed by arable fields or conifer plantations. In a few woods, however, rustic products are still made from coppiced underwood, thus continuing a tradition of management and woodmanship that reaches back to antiquity.

Bradfield Woods near Felsham in Suffolk is unique in that it has been managed continuously in this way for at least seven hundred years, and its underwood is still used to make rake handles, hedging stakes and other rustic products. **Combs Wood** near Stowmarket Colne, a hilltop wood mentioned in the Domesday Book has supplied firewood and thatching material since at least the eighteenth century. Such examples have helped to inspire a remarkable revival of coppicing in East Anglia during the past ten years. The prevalence of large trees such as ash, hornbeam and lime has meant that there is a potential market for coppice as pulpwood and firewood. There is also a modest demand for good quality hazel coppice by the thatching trade. At the Swanton Novers woods in Norfolk, coppice wood is sold to the local river authority to make fascines for shoring up eroding banks.

Between Saxon times and the Industrial Revolution, the counties of Norfolk, Suffolk and Essex were among the most densely populated in England. Most East Anglian woods are surrounded by land that has long been farmed intensively. Virtually all the land is cultivable, and the least fertile area, the Breckland, was also among the least wooded until afforestation began there in the 1920s. Woods sometimes occupy much the same boundaries as they did in the Middle Ages. Those of **Chalkney Wood** near Earls Colne in Essex have changed not at all since a remarkably accurate map was made of the area in 1598; even its inner tracks are probably medieval. **Priestley Wood** in Suffolk is the same place as the 'grove which is called Prestele' mentioned in the Ely Coucher Book of 1251, except for the loss of its southern end to farming improvements in the nineteenth century. Both woods are bounded by broad medieval banks, characteristic of East Anglia.

Norfolk is much less densely wooded than Suffolk and Essex, although some woods that survive are of the highest quality. At the time of the Domesday Book Norfolk was better wooded than Suffolk, but it lost three-quarters of its medieval woodland in the zeal for farming improvements that characterised the seventeenth and eighteenth centuries. Norfolk was as much the cradle of the Agrarian Revolution as Coalbrookdale was of the Industrial Revolution [54]. Unlike Coalbrookdale, Norfolk had no heavy industry to safeguard its woods as sources of bark, charcoal and pitwood. Ancient woods become gradually more frequent as one travels south through the region, culminating in Epping Forest, the largest single area of ancient woodland in East Anglia. The whole of Essex, even the towns, was a Royal Forest under King John, and although four-fifths of it was cultivated land even then, there were also substantial areas of densely wooded *physical* forest at Epping and its neighbour Hainault, at the smaller forests of Hatfield and Writtle, and at Kingswood near Colchester. Most of Kingswood and Hainault have since been cleared, but **Hatfield Forest** has been handed down to us miraculously intact. This, claims Oliver Rackham, 'is the only place (in England) where one can step back into the Middle Ages to see, with only a small effort of the imagination, what a forest looked like in use' [55].

The commonest kind of ancient woodland in East Anglia is ash-maple woodland, often with enclaves of elm, on wet boulder clay very similar to those of Cambridgeshire. More localised, but important where they occur, are woods composed of lime, hornbeam and sweet chestnut. Woodland dominated by small-leaved lime is found mainly in two well-defined areas: in north Norfolk and, more extensively, between Ipswich and Chelmsford. Lime can grow either as pure stands or mixed with other trees. In East Anglia it usually forms part of the coppiced underwood, and large standard native limes are rare. The **Swanton Novers woods** have some wonderfully gnarled, high-cut lime stools that look like bristly shaving brushes a season or two after cutting. Here coppiced lime and sessile oak standards grow together. Swanton Novers is also one of Norfolk's special bird cherry

woods. This northern plant, one of our most beautiful native shrubs with its delicate sprays of white flowers against fresh green leaves and almost black bark, finds a southern outpost in Norfolk but is otherwise virtually absent south of a line drawn between the Humber and the Severn. It is seen at its very best at **Wayland Wood**, where, despite its proclivity for cold climates, bird cherry is one of the first trees to burst into leaf.

Hornbeam and sweet chestnut belong as native trees to the most 'continental' parts of England, with hot summers and cold winters. They grow together in eastern Suffolk and Essex, a combination otherwise confined to a few woods in Surrey, Sussex and Kent. Hornbeam is commonest in south Essex, where the grotesque pollards of Epping Forest and the shady coppices of **Hadleigh Great Wood** near Southend are among the best-known ancient woods. Hornbeam is also found, less commonly, in Suffolk and Norfolk, reaching its northern limit at Sexton Wood in the latter county. The widespread planting of sweet chestnut in East Anglian woods has obscured its ancient status, but in at least a few places, such as Stour Wood near Harwich, it was certainly present in the seventeenth century, and the larger coppice stools, 2.7m (9ft) or more in diameter, may be older still. In some of the woods and parks along the coast of Essex the sweet chestnuts may be descended from Roman plantations.

Chestnut coppice-with-standards dominates **Stour Wood** and its neighbour Copperas Wood, on their hilltop between the River Stour and the Ramsey creek. Chestnut palings used to be made in quantity at a sawmill situated at the edge of the wood and were transported from here by rail all over the country. The standard trees, which are also chestnut, plus oak, provided timber for the Harwich shipyards. Despite the prevalence of chestnut, this wood is undoubtedly ancient, and its historical features include a medieval sinuous woodbank with an oak hedge studded with large hollies. On the seaward side, this unusual wood blends naturally with saltmarsh and mudflats.

As a native tree, beech is almost confined in

East Anglia to the remains of ancient wood-pasture, such as the Felbrigg Hall woods in Norfolk and Epping Forest in Essex, where old pollard beeches are now embedded in younger woodland. **Felbrigg Great Wood** is reminiscent of the New Forest with its mighty 400-year-old beeches growing with almost equally large oaks and dense groves of holly. The parks of East Anglia are mostly the creations of landscape gardeners, although ancient features such as fish-ponds and enclosed coppices associated with their medieval forerunners were sometimes retained. At Felbrigg Park and Sotterley Park in Suffolk there are vast oak trees with deep fissured bark and cankered boughs, a haven for lichens and invertebrates otherwise rare in the region. The most stunning park of all is **Staverton Park** in the Sandlings of Suffolk, where the squat pollard oaks, with small crowns nursing natural seed-beds for ferns and saplings, resemble the limbs of giant elephants. Together with the oaks are outsize rowans, birches, hawthorns and hollies, bent and twisted into a fantastic range of shapes. Even here, however, most of the shapes are not wholly natural but the product of regular pollarding at roughly fifty-year intervals between 1600 and 1850. Staverton Park seems always to have been a place of awe and wonder. For that reason, perhaps, no landscape architect was ever hired to 'improve' it.

Ancient woodland conservation has been very successful in East Anglia, and many more woods have survived than seemed likely twenty years ago. One reason is that efforts to turn these clay woods into conifer plantations not only involved a huge cost in labour and materials but were also, as often as not, rewarded by failure. The operation made commercial sense only on an official's balance sheet. Foresters (and, for that matter, conservationists) underestimated the resistant qualities of a strongly established and vigorous underwood combined with heavy, badly drained clay and a dry climate. By the mid-1970s, woodland owners, if not their advisers, had more or less given up the struggle. This might have resulted in the clearance of woods for agriculture, had it not been for a renewed interest in native woods by conservation bodies and by the farmers themselves. The County Councils have lent support both in their planning policies and by promoting special campaigns to subsidise the active, sympathetic management of small woods. It is only too easy to appreciate, when looking towards the almost treeless horizon of the Norfolk prairies, the contribution that traditional woodland makes to the beauty of the landscape.

The Suffolk Wildlife Trust has been particularly active in woodland conservation, launching in 1985 a project, now called Woodland Care, which supplies advice and practical support to a growing number of woodland owners in the county. In most cases, the aim is to maintain the vigour of the underwood by renewing coppice management, and this, in turn, rests on the development of local outlets and markets. Today, despite the decreased demand for pulpwood because of increased paper recycling, we can begin to be cautiously optimistic about the future of ancient woodland in East Anglia.

8

THE WELSH MARCHES

Along the Welsh border lie four of the better-wooded counties of England: Gloucestershire, Herefordshire, Worcestershire and Shropshire (I have ignored the unnatural fusing of the very distinctive counties of Hereford and Worcester). This area is roughly divided by the River Severn into the hard rocks of the west, where oak and birch are the commonest woodland trees, and the softer limestones and clays to the east, where beech rules in the Cotswolds and ash-hazel coppices predominate on the richer clays.

I will admit to a bias and say that this is my favourite part of England. It is predominantly rural in character; the impact of intensive farming on the scenery has been softer here than farther east, and more of the old pattern of pasture, meadow, orchard and wood endures. Since Victorian times, woodland management has tended towards high forest rather than coppice, for the mild, humid climate is particularly favourable for oak or, in the Cotswolds and Wye Valley, for beech. On the whole there has been less of a thoroughgoing emphasis on oak coppice than in Devon or the Lake District, although the Wyre Forest and the woods of the Upper Severn used to be important sources of bark and charcoal. A relatively high proportion of the ancient woodland has been re-planted – from as early as the 1660s in the Forest of Dean – though most plantations date from after 1945.

In this area, the woodland explorer will do a fair amount of climbing and descending, of slipping and sliding down clay banks and hillsides of bracken. There are rocky promontories in the Wye Valley and narrow dingles farther north where the explorer might even need a rope. The climb is worthwhile, because this is a wonderful area for views, whether from the hilltop woods of Hereford, some of them crowned by a prehistoric camp, from the sinuous edge of the Cotswolds or from the narrow edge of those spines of hard limestone at Wenlock Edge and the Malverns. Among the woodland delights are the oldest hollies, the oddest oaks, the most abundant limes and the most attractive beeches in England. Let us enter the woods of each county in turn, beginning with the most well-wooded of them all: Gloucestershire.

GLOUCESTERSHIRE

Gloucestershire includes some of the most impressive ancient woods in the country in some of the sweetest settings: the lower Wye Valley, the scarp and plateau of the Cotswolds and the hills and deep valleys of the Forest of Dean. They fall into five distinctive landscapes: the Severn Vale,

The Cotswolds escarpment in October, looking⇨ towards the village of Sheepscombe from Workman's Wood
(PETER WAKELY)

162

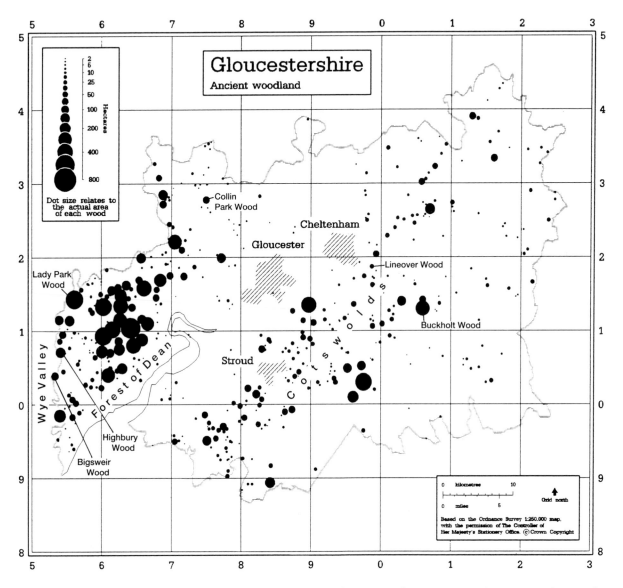

the Cotswold Scarp, the Cotswold Plateau, the Over Severn in the rising hills west of the river, and, tucked away on its outcrop of acid Coal Measures, the Forest of Dean. The majority of ancient and natural woods are former coppices on steep slopes or patches of impenetrable wet clay.

The identification of ancient woodland in Gloucestershire relies heavily on documentary and field evidence. The use of flowering plants as indicator species has to be used with the greatest caution in this mild, humid climate, where flowers

such as wood anemone, primrose, early purple orchid and pignut, confined mostly to old woods in parts of eastern England, are here to be found in hedgerows and even unimproved grassland as well as woods. Lily-of-the-valley, wild service tree and both wild limes are perhaps the plants most associated with Gloucestershire ancient woodland, but the most reliable 'indicator species' are probably two obscure snails left over from the Bronze Age, *Ena montana* and *Zenobiella subrufescens*. A more expedient approach is to

⟵ Some 17,600ha (42,572 acres) or 70 per cent of all woodland in Gloucestershire is believed to be of ancient origin. About one-half lies in the Forest of Dean which, although largely replanted, contains some of the largest woods in western England. The Cotswold Scarp below Cheltenham is also well-wooded. By contrast, the Severn Vale and the dip slope of the Cotswolds in the east have no more than a broad scatter of small farm woods

look at the appearance of the standard trees. Wild populations of trees are full of variety and irregularities, and native Cotswold beech in particular is often a crooked and knotty tree, and so rarely planted. The big furniture beeches of the Cotswolds and Chilterns are European imports.

Gloucestershire has a wealth of Anglo-Saxon and medieval charters and other documents that reveal the antiquity of many wood-names in the county. Old names are commonly based on words such as -ley (leah), -holt, frith, grove (graf) and shaugh (scaga), though their original meanings are obscure. In the small-scale hilly scenery around Stroud and Dursley, wood-names are often descriptive, with -ridge woods on the top of the rise and -combe names in the bottom. The Cotswold area also includes names that allude to former uses, such as Collier or Coaley Woods that were used by charcoal burners. Sometimes, however, names can be misleading. Cowcombe Wood, for example, has nothing to do with cows; the name is a corruption of 'Cowkeham' meaning 'the valley where charcoal ("coke") was burnt'. Other names have changed over the years. Lambricks Farm Wood was originally Rookwood, earlier (with that medieval sense of literary economy) 'Rocwde'. Old woods are frequently linked by name to their village or hamlet, such as Stanley Woods, which is connected to Leonard Stanley by Woodside Lane.

The Cotswold Commons

The Cotswolds form a great arc of soft limestone hills from Chipping Sodbury in the south to the high ridge above Cheltenham. This area contains one of the most extensive areas of wooded com-

mon land in lowland England. Most of the commons lie on the steep scarp slopes and incised valleys that border the Severn Vale. Some, such as Painswick Beacon, are open limestone grassland, formerly 'sweet grazing' for sheep and still wonderful ground for the naturalist. About 400ha (988 acres) of common land is woodland, mostly of beech high forest and preserved by its steepness. Other commons, now open, were once woodland. **Minchinhampton Common**, for example, once had 940ha (2,222 acres) of beechwood, all subject to rights of pasture and wood gathering, although the timber was privately owned. Before the Middle Ages was over, most of it had gone. The commoners blamed the loss on coppice sales and charcoal burners, but it is more likely that they themselves were responsible through overgrazing. Commoners' animals graze Minchinhampton Common still, though problems with road traffic have lately led to a reduction in the numbers of livestock [56].

On the other hand, the common-land system helped to prevent the wholesale clearance and replanting of some former coppices and the removal of 'weed' trees such as whitebeam and holly. The wooded commons in the neighbourhood of Painswick and Birdlip contain magnificent woods on the scarp and valley sides, mostly of beech high forest but also with pedunculate oak, ash, hazel and maple on the deeper plateau soils and valley bottoms. Beech is certainly a native tree in the Cotswolds, and was probably among the dominant trees in the original prehistoric woods. **Buckholt Wood**, part of the Cotswold Commons and Beechwoods National Nature Reserve, was a provider of coppiced beech firewood in the Middle Ages, first to St Sepulchre's Hospital in Gloucester and later to Llanthony Priory. It was enclosed in the seventeenth century when it supplied charcoal and wood for gunstocks until about 1850 when the coppice was 'promoted' to beech high forest. Buckholt itself means 'beech wood' in Old English (it has the same origin as the word 'book').

Workman's Wood and some of its neighbours are managed partly on a shelterwood selection system in which small glades are cleared to encourage natural regeneration. The result is not the familiar monoculture but a more interesting wood containing trees of all ages from saplings to 200-year-old standards. As the NCC's leaflet proclaims, such woods are useful working examples 'of how management for forestry and conservation can be successfully combined'. Comparative stability – no mass plantings or holocausts of native species – has preserved a very rich flora, including many of the rarer woodland flowers of the Cotswolds such as wood barley, stinking hellebore and narrow-lipped helleborine. One of these woods has the largest British colony of the fingered sedge, a choosy plant with a taste for the 'bare soil around the exposed roots of mature beeches and crumbling, over-hanging banks above forest tracks' [57]. Like many woodland plants, it needs light to flower, and hence only flourishes under selection regimes that do not steep the floor in darkness for decades at a time.

Lineover Wood: the bank of lime trees

AREA: 50ha (123 acres)

STATUS: A Woodland Trust property

ACCESS: Open to the public

TYPE: Calcareous ash-lime woodland

GRID REFERENCE: SO 987187

⇩ *Workman's Wood is managed by a shelterwood system which produces mixed-age stands of trees, arguably more attractive and certainly better for wildlife than the usual beech monoculture. September*
(PETER WAKELY)

The view from the Cotswold scarplands near Cheltenham is majestic in its panoramic sweep. There the ground falls away from your feet, plunging several hundred feet into the shadows to reveal the hedges and fields of the Severn Vale, the switchback of the Malverns beyond, the dark stubble of the Forest of Dean and, in the blue, hazy distance, the tops of the Black Mountains and the Brecon Beacons of Wales. It is a landscape writ in stone, the end of the soft rounded rocks of the south and an abrupt switch to the craggier, more elemental scenery of the Welsh Marches. This view inspired the Father of British Geology, William Smith, to investigate the ages of different rocks and produce the first geological map of Britain in the year when the guns were thundering at Waterloo.

The limestone ramparts that soar above the southern outskirts of Cheltenham are the highest and steepest in the Cotswolds, so steep that in places the bare rock juts through the skin of soil and, broken by the weather, crumbles into aprons of scree below. This is the unlikely setting for a remarkable ancient wood owned by the Woodland Trust: Lineover, the place the Saxons called *lind-ofer*, the bank of lime trees. The name is recorded in an early charter of AD 823 granting the wood to the secular canons. There are still limes here today, mostly the rare large-leaved lime and, like most wild limes, they are not maiden trees but coppice stools, circles of stems on a mighty pedestal of living wood 6m (20ft) or more across. Judging from their size and known rate of growth, these giant Lineover limes may be the same trees that grew in *lind-ofer* in the lost Kingdom of the Hwicce. They are older than Methuselah, older than Gloucester Cathedral, possibly older than the county of Gloucestershire itself. From among their roots sprout scarce lilies of ancient woodland – lily-of-the-valley, meadow saffron and angular Solomon's seal – set in a bottle-green sea of dog's mercury. Here place-names, aged trees and rare flowers converge. We are in a place of deep antiquity that has never been other than woodland since mammoths browsed scrub willows in the

Severn Vale, twelve thousand years ago.

Lineover Wood survives because of its steepness. Coppiced hazel, sessile oak, maple and hawthorn, some contorted into grotesque shapes, show that the wood used to be cut over regularly, although how woodmen managed to wield their cutting tools on a stance like the roof of a house is hard to imagine; perhaps they were suspended on ropes from the stout beech trees at the edge of the drop. In Victorian times, Lineover Wood was purchased by Cheltenham Borough Council to safeguard the catchment area of Dowdeswell Reservoir at the foot of the beetling slope. The imperative of the town's water supply precluded the use of agricultural fertilisers and herbicides near the reservoir but that did not, unfortunately, prevent ill-advised forestry experiments from taking place. Not realising what a treasure they held in trust, the Severn-Trent Water Authority set about replacing the native trees with Western red cedar and other Pacific Coast delights 'in accordance with modern forestry practice'. Fortunately the steeper parts of the wood, including the precious limes, escaped the authority's misplaced enthusiasm, and now the Woodland Trust has, very properly, started to restore the wood to its former glory although I hope they will spare a few cedars as a monument to the passing fads of our own time. It is probably too late to save the less steep northern part of the wood, where stumps of oak can be glimpsed through the evergreen shroud (the quality of oak timber provided by Lineover Wood between 1700 and 1812 was surprisingly high and judged suitable 'for military and naval purposes').

I visited Lineover Wood on a bitterly cold day in April in the teeth of a biting north wind blowing squalls of sleet. Squinting down over the edge, the trees seemed no more than grey shapes in a cauldron of vapour. Beyond the wood, the reservoir and the northward marches of the Cotswolds were dimly visible. Slipping down the Woodland Trust's path, needing every yard of the rustic fencing thoughtfully provided, I passed twisted trees, limestone rubble and islands of grass, down to the

Cotswold Way, which passes by an old meadow, kept verdant by springs rising through a carpet of golden saxifrage. This is a wonderful wood, one of the precious islands of primeval vegetation in our crowded country, situated not in some remote mountain ravine or lake island but where the residents of Cheltenham housing estates can look out on it every day.

Over Severn and the Forest of Dean

West of the Severn lies an area of acid rocks in and around the Forest of Dean, whose woods form a strong contrast with those of the limestone and clay farther east. The best-preserved woods lie not within the forest itself but among the woods around Newent, and the star is without doubt **Collin Park Wood** (67ha) [165 acres], part of which is a nature reserve belonging to the Gloucestershire Trust for Nature Conservation. Collin Park Wood is a former coppice, once managed intensively as a provider of charcoal for the iron industry. Many of its rides are former tramways, and what appears to be a disused lane on one side is a former railway line, part of an unsuccessful plan to link the coalfields of Dean with factories in the West Midlands. The principal trees are sessile oak and small-leaved lime, some of which are being thinned and singled by the Trust to produce potentially profitable high forest. There are also unusually large numbers of wild service trees. The wood lies on ill-draining Keuper Marl. Its flora is almost entirely one of acid soils, with bluebells on the drier ground, greater wood-rush carpeting the wetter parts and great wreaths of honeysuckle smothering the stumps. For some reason, the wood lacks the constellations of wild daffodils that are the distinguishing feature of the nearby **Betty Daw's Wood**.

Although almost the full extent of the medieval Forest of Dean survives as woodland, most of its woods are plantations. This is one of the few places where England provides a 'forest experience' on a continental scale. Dean's original coppices and pastures had already fallen into ruin and riot by Stuart times. After 1660, a major enclosure and replanting programme was begun, which over the next forty years, turned 4,450ha (11,000 acres) of the forest into oak plantations, intended to produce ship timber for the Royal Navy. The oldest age-class of standard oaks today date from that time. There was another major planting of oaks during the Napoleonic War, and oaks continued to be set there until the 1950s. The last vestiges of the former common-land system of wood-pasture, huge pollards of oak, beech and holly, stand near Speech House, once the verderer's court and now a hotel. One great tree, the Newland Oak, alas blown over in a gale in 1956, measured 13.5m (44ft) around the trunk and was probably a contemporary of Dean's famous wild boars and wolves. But to see Dean as it was when the Newland Oak was in its prime, a visit to the unenclosed parts of the New Forest will be necessary; the last open greens at Dean disappeared in the nineteenth century, although a few small patches of natural grassland and bog still remain.

Since 1924, the Forest of Dean has been managed by the Forestry Commission on behalf of the Crown. In recent years the priority has switched from timber production to amenity considerations. In 1990, the Commission published new management proposals designed to perpetuate the 45 per cent of the forest that presently grows broadleaved trees and to create a more uneven age-structure, including that rarity in managed woods, the mature tree. Of some 5,000ha (12,350 acres) of broadleaved woodland, about a fifth is regarded by the Commission as ancient. This fifth, which contains most of the oldest oaks, is to be classed as 'conservation woodland' in which a third of the trees will be 'left to age and die naturally' and the rest managed on a long rotation with felling restricted to small coups. Woods near the forest villages are to become 'community woods', which means felling 'dangerous trees' and planting saplings. The remainder of the broadleaved woods will continue to be managed commercially, but with an increased emphasis on non-oak trees such as ash, beech and chestnut. To succeed fully, the plan depends on the willingness of generations yet unborn to adopt it.

The RSPB nature reserve at **Nagshead** lies on acidic sandstone soils in the middle of the forest. Like most of Dean, it is an oak plantation – the oldest trees were planted about 1814. Grazing animals have been excluded from part of the wood since the 1940s, and it has since developed a dense understorey of holly, rowan and other trees contrasting with the bare forest floor outside. Nagshead has one of the best-documented bird populations in the world. Long-term studies began in 1942, when interest was aroused by the large numbers of pied flycatchers that had started to use the nest boxes. Scientific study was soon broadened to redstarts, blue tits and great tits, which also nest almost entirely in boxes at Nagshead so that their breeding numbers and breeding success can readily be monitored. Only Wytham Wood near Oxford has a longer run of scientific data. From such long-term studies, general biological principles can emerge which shed important light on how animal numbers are regulated.

The Wye Valley

The gorge of the River Wye, that separates England from Wales, is one of our most glorious woodland spectacles, a magnificent billowing of colours and textures from nearly all of our native trees set amid a grand scene of limestone crags and sweet grassland with ruined abbeys overlooking the winding loops of the river. No words of mine can do it justice: the Wye must be witnessed. I list some of its scientific superlatives in the account of Herefordshire's woods below. Here we will linger at the Gloucester woods which crowd the western fringe of the Forest of Dean and share some of its history. The Wye Valley is best known for its limestone woods, but on the Gloucestershire side there are also substantial tracts of woodland on acidic sandstone, some of which is common land. The history of these woods has yet to be worked out, but many have internal compartments divided by stone walls or earth banks, sometimes marked with rows of pollards. What seems to be a single big wood today is generally an aggregation of small woods or *groves*. **Bigswier Wood** (48ha) [118 acres],

for example, is made up of Wyeseal Wood, Slip Wood, New Wier Grove, Moon Grove and Quicken Tree Wood.

As in nearby Dean, much of the coppice used to be cut to make charcoal or lime, and at Bigswier some of the charcoal burners' hearths are still detectable by great circles of blackened earth. Their position is sometimes marked by a pollarded lime tree, suggesting that the same site was used over and over again: a permanent glade. The wood is also full of banks, the biggest of which is none other than Offa's Dyke itself, the greatest earthwork in Britain. Offa's Dyke runs through several woods just above the valley and, because it must have been built over open ground (the purpose of a boundary is to be seen), it indicates that the woods now in its path have developed since the reign of King Offa in the eighth century AD.

The Wye Valley today is a mixture of overgrown simple coppice, coppice-with-standards, high forest and plantations. Behind these differences are past divisions between common land and enclosures. **The Hudnalls** (75ha) [185 acres], for example, included both commons managed entirely as coppice and private land in which trees were cropped for timber as well as underwood. To confuse matters, present-day coppicing at The Hudnalls takes place in secondary woodland on the flatter, more accessible sites and no longer in the ancient coppices of the gorge.

The steep sides of the Wye are distinguished by unusual types of woodland: beech and lime coppice under oak standards, or mixtures of beech-sessile oak coppice and ash-lime coppice. This is one of the places in Britain, generally in warm, dry areas, where there are natural beechwoods. The Wye Valley as a whole is strongly reminiscent of wooded gorges in central France. An attractive grass, the wood fescue, normally a rare crag plant in England, grows here in large patches on the woodland floor as it does in beechwoods on the European mainland. The flora of woods on limestone, such as **Highbury Wood** National Nature Reserve (46ha) [114 acres], is exceptionally rich.

There are rare trees such as large-leaved lime and Cheddar whitebeam, a spurge found nowhere else in Britain, and a host of characteristic plants of undisturbed woods, such as wood barley, oak fern, Forster's wood-rush and giant bellflower.

Lady Park Wood:
an experiment in non-intervention

AREA: 45ha (111 acres)

STATUS: National Nature Reserve

ACCESS: Because of the experimental nature of this site, visitors are not encouraged

TYPE: Sessile oak-beech-ash and oak-lime woodland on limestone

GRID REFERENCE: SO 547145

This steep hanging place, anciently called Hodenoc or Hadnock Wood, is one of the least accessible woods of the Wye Valley, a semicircle of woodland hugging the inside bend of a tight loop in the river. It is unlikely that this wood was ever managed very intensively. It was detached from that hive of medieval industry, the Forest of Dean, in the fourteenth century to become part of a deer park owned by England's richest landowner, John of Gaunt. Later it passed into the broad acres of the squirely Hall family, who gave the wood its present name. In 1817 it was transferred to the Crown. There is no record of any extensive replanting. No doubt people have helped themselves to its wood over the years, but Lady Park Wood lacks the intricate banks and other hints of strong organisation in many other ancient woods in the valley. It seems to have been passed down to us almost intact from the prehistoric wildwood. This is as good a place as anywhere in England to observe the workings of a natural environment.

There was, however, at least one moment of violent discord. It came halfway through World War II when the demand for timber was such that even this remote wood was considered worth felling. The lumberjacks descended on the old oaks, beeches and limes and clear-felled two-thirds of the wood. Of the mature timber, only a stand of oaks up to 200 years old and some large beeches at the top of the wood were spared for 'amenity'. Thus, when the Forestry Commission, the British Ecological Society and Oxford University's Forestry Department agreed a year later that Lady

⇐ *The upright or Tintern spurge*
Euphorbia serrulata *is confined in Britain to woodland rides and glades on limestone in the Wye Valley. July*
(PETER WAKELY)

> *Lady Park Wood as seen from across the Wye at* ⇨
> *Biblins Centre. The variety of woodland textures and shapes on precipitous slopes is characteristic of the Wye Valley. October*
> (PETER WAKELY)

Park Wood was to become Britain's first official non-intervention woodland, much of it was lying flat on the ground. Fortunately there had been no attempt to poison or remove the stumps, so a young even-aged growth stand developed that resembled coppice and preserved the natural composition of lime, sessile oak, ash, beech and associated trees and shrubs (most of the wood is, as we conservation bureaucrats like to say, 'a fine example of an 8Eb').

The importance of long-term recording, to see what actually happens to wild woods rather than merely theorising about them, has already been borne out by events at Lady Park Wood. In their attempts to see order, pattern and, above all, predictability in the workings of nature, scientists have tended to underrate the power of human psychology. Under the influence of the master plant ecologists of the 1930s and 1940s – Sir Arthur Tansley (a student of Freudian psychology himself, as it happened), A. S. Watt and their contemporaries – our understanding of natural vegetation is heavily influenced by *succession*, whereby bare ground is expected to turn inexorably into woodland dominated by one or two species of trees. We imagined the logical end product, the 'climax forest', to be a peaceful sort of place, an eternity of tall forest trees, each living for hundreds of years. Some virgin forests in places as far apart as Poland and the Appalachians tend to confirm this picture (though George Peterken assures me that most do not). What ought to happen at Lady Park Wood, according to this predestined pattern, is a stately progression to permanent dominance by long-lived, shade-bearing trees, especially beech. Trees would grow up and eventually die in an almost mathematical way: six dead trees in every hundred per decade. Only the death of a giant tree would produce a gap in the canopy and a sudden flurry of regeneration on the forest floor.

What happened instead was a tale of disaster, violence and disease. On four occasions since 1945, tree growth across the full profile of the wood in both the old growth and young growth stands has been recorded and the results published recently by E. W. Jones and George Peterken[58]. The first twenty years went more or less according to prediction. In the young growth areas there was regrowth from the stumps and an opportunistic burst of seedling birch. A closed canopy had formed by about 1955. In the old growth stands, nothing much happened. A few trees died or fell over, a few dead stumps crumbled into moss and sawdust. Then, in the mid-1970s, the tempo suddenly accelerated. The droughts of 1975 and 1976 killed many old beech trees. Dutch elm disease destroyed the mature elms (but not the young growth). Gales in the 1980s threw down more big beeches, some of which had been permanently weakened in the droughts, though curiously enough the strongest gale of all, in 1990, had scarcely any effect. Because of its tolerance to shade, beech was supposed to gain a mastery over its competitors. Events have proved otherwise: beech high forest is not, after all, the likely destiny of Lady Park Wood.

The young growth stands proved equally unpredictable. There the drought hit the maiden birch trees the hardest. More birches were crushed by heavy snow in 1981. The regenerating beech survived, only to be torn to shreds by grey squirrels in 1983. Fallow deer have increased and their browsing began seriously to impede the new growth. Oak is hardly regenerating in either stand. The main beneficiaries seem to be ash, which regenerates well both from coppice stools and from seed, and possibly lime, which has an almost immortal ability to spring up from stumps or buried bits of root. Thus what we have seen so far leads not to a stable high forest but to a mixed wood of uneven age with gaps and, deer permitting, patches of new growth.

Because of its steep slope and exposure to westerly winds, Lady Park may be an inherently unstable wood, for ever being knocked about by storms and landslips. This may be an important clue to the richness of the woods of the Wye Valley: that trees often perish before reaching maturity, and the gaps created produce spaces for the smaller trees and shrubs and an opportunity for herbs to flower and set seed. It explains why coppice regimes, which are almost windproof, are more stable on steep slopes than top-heavy, high forest trees. Beech, which was mollycoddled by the Victorians, is what Oliver Rackham has called a 'catastrophic tree' which comes and goes according to the vagaries of the weather. If our weather is becoming more violent, as the gales of 1987 and 1990 seem to indicate, beech will be at a considerable disadvantage in Britain, even in its native stands. Like elm, its future may be as coppice.

Woods on more level ground seem to be less prone to disturbance. Madingley Wood near Cambridge has been monitored photographically every year for almost as long as Lady Park Wood, but has lost only a few big maples and ashes and its general character is little changed. Nevertheless the experience of Lady Park Wood is changing some ecologists' views of natural processes in undisturbed forest. In the concluding part of his paper, George Peterken suggests that 'climax' woods are not stable at all and that their history is unpredictable, since one can never know when the next hurricane, drought or swarm of insects will strike – only that it will.

WORCESTERSHIRE

At the fringes of the Clent Hills near Bromsgrove, within audible distance of the M5 motorway, lies a knot of ancient woodland descended from the medieval Forest of Feckenham. **Chaddesley and Randan Woods** (170ha) [420 acres] are mostly oak high forest on an island of infertile ground: wet, heavy clay capped with sand. The woods are intersected by brooks, green lanes and small herb-rich meadows. Chaddesley Wood became a National Nature Reserve in 1973, originally intended to demonstrate ways of integrating wildlife conservation and modern forestry. Because the wood is half ancient and natural – half conifer plantation on former oak coppice and open ground – it was considered an ideal site.

An alternative strategy, perceivable perhaps as 'bottom-up' rather than 'top-down', has been put into practice at Pepper Wood, a Woodland Trust property no more than a mile from Chaddesley Wood. Pepper Wood, named after a Mercian king called Pyppa, is one of the Trust's community woods, in which local people are encouraged to participate in management activities ranging from footpath repair to green wood turning on pole lathes, all with the purpose of forging links between the local community and the wood. In essence it is an attempt to instil care for ancient woodland by restoring the lost *cultural* community of woodland. In the case of both Chaddesley Wood and Pepper Wood, the local managers realised that care for ancient woodland is about much more than 'scientific management' alone. They recognised a wider human dimension, whether as an 'exhibition wood' designed to demonstrate common ground among woodland managers, or as a new kind of working common, a medieval revival in tune with our own times of leisure and concern for the countryside.

Many woodland nature reserves in Worcestershire represent unsuccessful attempts at plantation forestry. **Shrawley Wood** (103ha) [254 acres], on the banks of the Severn near Stourport, is, on paper, a conifer plantation, but in practice the planted trees were unable to compete with what is perhaps the most magnificent limewood in the land. Today it is hard to find a single living conifer. The wood has reverted to type: a rare example of lime and ash underwood beneath standard limes, an authentic whiff of prehistory. A more prolonged 'deconiferisation' struggle is necessary at **Tiddesley Wood** (81ha) [200 acres], an ancient wood on heavy clay near Pershore. Tiddesley Wood had been clear-felled and restocked with Scots pine and other conifers in the 1950s and 1960s, but only about a quarter of the planted area was a success. The rest is a mixture of resurgent underwood and planted timber, some of which can be reinstated as coppice, while other areas are likely to be managed as high forest. The Trust aims to produce a 'diverse broadleaved woodland of native species with a well-developed understorey of small trees and shrubs wherever possible'.

This does not preclude timber sales by any means – Tiddesley Wood has too much timber anyway – but the over-riding objective of the Trust is nature conservation. Here, as elsewhere, it is still necessary to explain to the public why woodland nature conservation often benefits more from cutting trees down than by planting more of them.

Several ancient woods in Worcestershire, among them Uffmoor Wood near Halesowen and Monkwood, were owned by the Harris Brush Company, which used large quantities of turned wood, taken from local woods, for brush handles. The company's management practices were a great deal more sympathetic to nature conservation than most commercial woodland owners because, although they replanted parts of their woods, no herbicides were employed and the wild coppice was allowed to grow up with the planted saplings of grey alder, sycamore and beech. The perpetuation of coppicing kept these woods reasonably open, and attractive for warblers, butterflies and wild flowers.

Nunnery and Perry Woods: the Worcester Woods

AREA: Nunnery Wood: 17.6ha (43 acres); Perry Wood: 12.4ha (22 acres)

STATUS: A country park administered as 'The Worcester Woods' by the County Council

ACCESS: Open to the public

TYPE: Lowland oak-hazel woodland

GRID REFERENCE: SO 877545

There cannot be many ancient woods within a mile of the centre of a cathedral city, but Perry Wood at Worcester is one: it stands on a steep north-west-facing bank looking directly onto the cathedral tower. Perry Wood and its neighbour, Nunnery Wood, are together known as the Worcester Woods Country Park, formed in 1987, and their story has been pieced together by J. G. Kingsbury [59]. In es-

Perry Wood in November, with the tower of ⇨
Worcester Cathedral just visible in the distance
(PETER WAKELY)

sentials, theirs is the story of many a small wood in England, but what may be surprising is the degree of past management. Both woods have been cut over repeatedly and often since at least 1635, and until Victorian times their value was for coppiced underwood, not timber. Only in the past fifty years has it been possible to dismiss such a valuable commodity as 'worthless scrub'.

The names of these woods are interesting. Nunnery Wood, like Monk's or Abbot's Woods, is a medieval name, or at least a medieval memory, pre-dating the dissolution of the monasteries in 1538. In this particular case, however, there is a problem. The wood was not owned by nuns but by the male-run St Wulfstan's Hospital in Worcester. The name might however enshrine a story that the nuns or White Ladies of Whistan claimed the wood as their own. Since the late sixteenth century, the wood has been owned by Christchurch College, Oxford. 'Perry' is certainly medieval. The wood might be named after a pear tree *(pirian)* mentioned hereabouts in a charter of AD 966. It had become 'Pirywode' by 1370, when the wood was about double its present size. Unfortunately, the original pear tree has left no successors, and it might not be a bad idea to plant a new one.

Both woods were cut over more and more frequently from the Middle Ages onwards; they seem to have been providers of tanbark and oak 'black poles' for hop yards. It would be surprising if they did not also provide commoners of the town with firewood. The earliest document, dated 1635, mentions the excellent quality of the bark, adding that the coppice was 'anciently felled at twenty years growth and now at twelve years'. At that time the woods seem to have been coppice-with-standards, for we learn of a 'great destruction of timber' there a few years later. For the succeeding century or more Perry Wood at least was managed as pure coppice. In 1757 there was 'not any Timber in this Wood except Oliver's Tree wch *(sic)* is a very bad

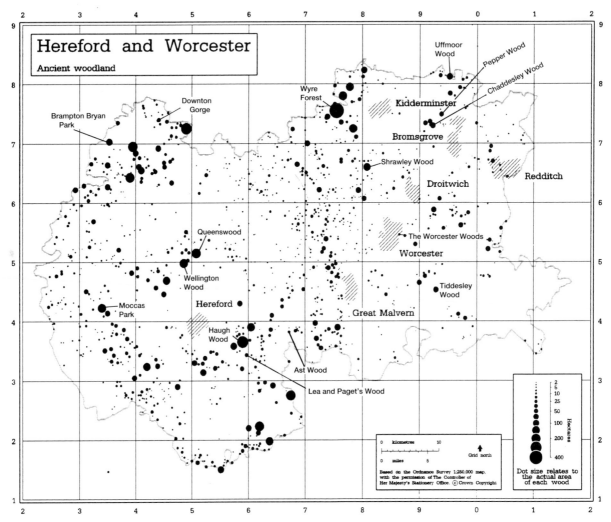

Hereford and Worcester
Ancient woodland

Uffmoor Wood
Pepper Wood
Chaddesley Wood
Wyre Forest
Kidderminster
Downton Gorge
Brampton Bryan Park
Bromsgrove
Shrawley Wood
Droitwich
Redditch
Queenswood
The Worcester Woods
Worcester
Wellington Wood
Moccas Park
Tiddesley Wood
Hereford
Great Malvern
Haugh Wood
Ast Wood
Lea and Paget's Wood

kilometres
miles
Grid north
Based on the Ordnance Survey 1:250,000 map, with the permission of The Controller of Her Majesty's Stationery Office. © Crown Copyright

Hectares
2
5
10
25
50
100
200
400
Dot size relates to the actual area of each wood

one'. This is probably 'Oliver Cromwell's Oak' which appears on an estate map of 1790, by which time both woods had been knocked into roughly their present-day shapes. Oliver Cromwell had fought and won the Battle of Worcester on the nearby banks of the Severn, although it was his fleeing adversary, King Charles II, who was the more noted for his association with big oaks. At Nunnery Wood, as in Perry, the emphasis was on pole growth from the underwood. By 1772, a brisk coppice rotation of eight years produced six-and-a-half-acres-worth of poles annually. Most were used in 'the harvesting', but some wood was also sold for agricultural and building purposes, as well

as bark for the then thriving Worcestershire tanning industry.

The advent of Napoleon and rising prices to meet the needs of war led to a still more rigorous approach to the management of both woods. Perry Wood was judged 'inferior to the other wood, of a stunted growth and very bare in the middle'. Whatever the precise cause of this, it is remarkable that Perry Wood is still bare in the middle nearly two hundred years on: a large glade of scrubby birch, whin and bracken. But the climax of two hundred years of intensive wood and bark production lasted less than a decade, because after the defeat of Napoleon at Waterloo came a slump in prices. The

This is at first sight a complicated map – the result of the administrative blending of two quite different counties. Worcestershire is a hybrid county: fertile and intensively farmed in the east (scattered largish woods) but hilly in the west (many more, but generally smaller, woods). The most densely wooded area is the Wyre Forest in the north-west. Herefordshire, though about the same size as Worcestershire, has twice as much ancient woodland, and more woods of over 100ha (247 acres). Its best wooded landscapes are in hill areas: the Malverns and Wye Valley in the south, the central hills around Dinmore and in the valley of the River Lugg in the north

new fashion was for oak timber, a product notably lacking in Nunnery and Perry Woods. The latter had no large trees at all except a few boundary pollards 'which are much injured for want of cutting many years ago' – in other words, top-heavy and falling to bits. At least one old pollard remains in Nunnery Wood, the barrel-like remains of an oak more than 1.8m (6ft) across, with an elder tree within. In the 1820s, the estate surveyor urged the clearance of the underwood and the mass planting of oaks. The lessees, on the other hand, saw more profit in parcelling up the woods into plotland for houses and paddocks. Grubbing the coppice was considered necessary one way or the other because, apart from anything else, 'owing to the nearness of the wood to the town there are many depredations committed on it, so that it is necessary to keep a man to look after the wood'.

Fortunately there was an alternative. As early as 1809, the college's surveyor had advised that 'Pury Wood' was a great ornament to the City of Worcester, a remarkably early appreciation of the amenity role of traditional woods near town centres. Today, Nunnery Wood is a well-managed, rather even-aged wood dominated by oak and ash standards with some hazel, wild cherry, wych elm, aspen, service. In the spring, there are carpets of wood anemone and bluebell, and there is a pond in which all three kinds of newts breed. No longer a rural wood, it backs onto the County Hall and a big

comprehensive school at one end and the city hospital at the other. It is tidy, but not too tidy. The well-laid paths wind enticingly through the trees and for the weary there are rustic seats donated by Tesco. Perry Wood, by contrast, has a neglected air. Ropes dangle from trees; ivy and litter strew the otherwise bare clay slope; on a wet day in November it looked rather glum. But the documented history of the woods can be corroborated on the ground, because in both there are large oak stools, now singled as forest trees, which might well have helped make some of the wooden and leather products on the shelves of the city museum.

The Wyre Forest
AREA: The Wyre Forest Site of Special Scientific Interest, which includes most of the ancient and natural woodland, measures 897ha (2,218 acres)

STATUS: Mostly owned by the Forestry Commission. Part (357ha) [881 acres] is a National Nature Reserve. Betts (2ha), Fred Dale (23ha) and Knowles Coppice (7.7ha) are nature reserves of the Worcestershire Nature Conservation Trust

ACCESS: Open along main public paths

TYPE: Lowland birch-sessile oak with ash-hazel-lime woodland in the valleys

GRID REFERENCE: SO 730760

In 1969 I spent, like Benjamin Disraeli, A Year in Hartlebury. One of the then highlights of the weekly paper, the *Kidderminster Times*, was a column about the wildlife of the nearby Wyre Forest by the late Norman Hickin. With the aid of a lively pen and fine scraperboard drawings, Hickin sketched life portraits of the wild plants and animals of the Forest, familiar and obscure, one by one, week by week. Thus, I learned about the mysterious whitty pear tree, of the enormous Seckley Beech, 11m (36ft) in girth with twenty-six separate trunks, of the Mawley Oak whose boughs spread over quarter of an acre,

Stripping the bark from a pole using a barking ⇨
iron. The Wyre Forest, Worcestershire
(JOHN ROBINSON)

of a rare and wonderful caddis fly that lives not in ponds but in woods and whose cased larvae crawled onto Hickin's clothing when he accidentally camped on its long-lost breeding grounds. There were elusive insects that lived inside trees such as the white-barred clearwing and the alder wood-wasp, or beautiful ones such as the pearl-bordered fritillaries that flutter like tawny guineas around the bugle flowers in May. Fortunately, these newspaper pieces have since been gathered together and published in book form [60]. We can also read Hickin's autobiography, *Forest Refreshed*, which records a full half-century's close acquaintance with Wyre and its secrets. One day, I am sure, a tourist board will dub these wooded hills and valleys on the banks of the Severn as Hickin Country.

In the century before Hickin, another Wyre naturalist, George Jorden of Bewdley, walked in the forest nearly every day between 1830 and 1870. And, through a paper he published at the end of that period, we can judge that the forest was then even richer [61]. There was, for example, a forest bog in which fragrant orchids were common. One of them, a stunted albino, was mistaken for a now-extinct orchid, the summer ladies-tresses, so that for many years the forest was listed as a supposed locality for that plant. The bog was later drained and its very site lost until the forest's warden, John Robinson, following clues in nineteenth-century journals, managed to locate it. The now disused forest railway line had cut through it, but the depression is still wet. Sedges and hemp agrimony abound and the rare sword-leaved helleborine grows nearby. An old bore-hole for coal is now a clear, deep pool full of stoneworts. Alas, the fragrant orchids have gone. Woodland ecologists have another reason to remember George Jorden. It was he who, on discovering small-leaved limes in hedges near the forest edge, correctly deduced that they were formerly part of the wood and that

'they truthfully record the arboreal history of our primitive forests'. It took scientists another hundred years to reach the same conclusion.

The Wyre Forest is one of the largest ancient and natural woods in lowland England. It was a late forest, undeclared until 1461 (the new king, Edward IV, owned land in the area), and was disafforested 200 years later. Why was it not then grubbed up for farmland or converted wholesale to timber plantation, like many other wooded forests? The most probable answer is that Wyre Forest was worth more as coppice. While it did provide standard oaks for ship- and house-building, the prices fetched by selling underwood as charcoal for iron-smelting and bark for tanning were higher. The great daleside ironworks of the early Industrial Revolution lay not far away, while the River Severn provided ready access by barge to the seaports. Some of the wood was used in the forest itself for fencing stakes and pit props for its coal mines. The Wyre Forest, then, was an important supplier of raw materials for industry which ensured that the forest did not succumb to the competing claims of other land users.

Coppicing created a varied structure that proved ideal for the many species of plants and animals for which the forest has become well known. Wyre is a transitional place: its hillsides are reminiscent of the oak coppices of Wales, while the clearly demarcated valley woods of ash, elm, lime and alder are much more typical of the West Midlands. There are also patches of ash-hazel woodland in which you could imagine yourself in East Anglia. Since the 1930s, however, its woods have become more monotonous and even-aged in appearance through lack of traditional management. Today, this trend is to be reversed within the Wyre Forest National Nature Reserve where an ambitious target of 4ha (10 acres) of restored coppice per year over the next thirty years has been set. At the time of writing, some 8ha (20 acres) of overgrown coppice has been cut for use as fencing stakes and firewood, and already a beneficial change in wildlife is noticeable. The future of Norman Hickin's forest looks brighter today than at any time since 1914.

Wyre is the last place in England (there are a few others in Wales) where the lost craft of bark-stripping is still practised. I have derived the following information from an article by L. M. C. Babb[62]. Oak bark is rich in tannic acid, which turns hides and skins into leather by preventing putrefaction and making them water-resistant while retaining their natural strength and pliability. Today, chemical methods are used to achieve the same purpose. But at the Wyre Forest a small company, Far Forest Works, operated by the Doolittle family, continues to harvest oak poles for barking.

Bewdley, the principal town near Wyre, was for a long time a major centre of the tanning industry. There was a ready source of bark from the nearby forest, a plentiful supply of soft running water from the Severn and access to the sea along the same river. Bark was obtained not from mature trunks but from oak coppice poles ('black poles') between 15 and 30 years old. Stripping or 'peeling' them was a difficult art and it took several seasons to become proficient at it. Poles could be peeled easily only in the spring when the sap is rising and the bark becomes supple and juicy. Really juicy bark flies up in splinters when the axe strikes it. After the pole is lopped, the peeler slips a spatula-shaped iron between bark and sapwood and, with a flick of the wrist and what one retired woodman remembers as 'a lovely scraunch', rips it away. The trick is to tear off as large a piece as possible without being spattered by sticky sap in the process. Dexterity was more important than strength, and patience was essential. A barker might take several hours to work a single large coppice stool.

At Wyre, the coppicing was often carried out by itinerant gangs and involved the whole family. The men were usually employed in the heavier work, felling, cutting and stacking, leaving the women in their large aprons and broad-brimmed sun hats to wield the barking irons. Bark dries out quickly and must be stripped as soon as possible after felling, so the women, in gangs of up to forty, would follow the men as they cut their way through the allotted coppice 'sale'. Following in turn came the children, picking up brushwood, tidying up, larking about and generally getting in the way. Visitors sometimes came to watch and listen to the thwacks and scraunches and to cheer them on; they were expected to tip the foreman half a crown, which the gangs spent on cider. At the close of the season some of the gangs moved on to the hop yards and peafields at Tenbury and Bromyard. Waggons transported the bark from the forest to the Bewdley tanyards where it was stored for up to a year in airy lofts before use. Wyre tanbark was of good quality and cost £3 5s per ton. These scenes were repeated each spring until the early 1930s, although the last of the Bewdley tanyards had closed in 1928. But in this corner of Worcestershire at least, the craft is still alive, ready to be handed down to a new generation.

HEREFORDSHIRE

Today Herefordshire is better wooded than Worcestershire. In the early Middle Ages, it was the other way round, despite the fact that Hereford was a wild border county, much devastated from raids by Normans and Welshmen. What horrors lie behind this laconic reference in the Domesday Book to Harewood: 'Edwy held it. 4 hides. The whole of this land has been turned back into woodland. It was waste and pays nothing'?

Most woods lie on poor soils, often on hilltops, or line steep slopes, and they are typically situated near the edge of the parish farthest from human settlement. The rich agricultural land of the Herefordshire lowlands is relatively poorly wooded. Characteristic Herefordshire woods are the ferny vales or 'dingles' and, in complete contrast, woods crowning ridges and hills, sometimes with a prehistoric camp on the summit. The combination of a mild climate and mineral-rich soils over so much of the county often produces lush, humid woods of great beauty and character. The woods lining the steep limestone gorge of the River Wye are considered to be among the finest of their kind in Western Europe.

In the Middle Ages four areas in the centre and west of the county were Royal Forest, and there were also a number of private chases. Most have shrunk or vanished, leaving little trace today. Haywood, the 'hays of Hereford', was privatised and enclosed by Queen Elizabeth's favourite, Christopher Hatton, at which time there was a total of 370ha (914 acres) of 'waste', of which about 100ha (247 acres) were considered good coppice, 206ha (508 acres) less good, and the rest bare land. Most of its woods were grubbed up after the land was privatised for a second time in 1650, leaving only 38ha (93 acres) of pollards and underwood [63]. Aconbury Forest, too, was parcelled out as farmland after disafforestation in Stuart times, though it remains a fairly well-wooded district today. Treville, around Abbey Dore, was disafforested early, perhaps because it had few large woods.

What preserved many of the woods in the Hereford forests and elsewhere was not so much their hunting as their value as a source of industrial fuel. From the sixteenth century onwards, many were enclosed as coppices and cut over regularly to supply wood and charcoal to iron forges. Woods situated near swift rivers, where water power could be harnessed to operate the bellows, were considered the best. Charcoal hearths can still be found in such woods, cut into the steep slopes by level-ling and embankment. The heyday of industrial coppicing was the eighteenth century, when it was considered one of the most profitable of all forms of land use. But well into our own century, Herefordshire coppices continued to be maintained in production for tanbark and a range of rustic products, especially hop poles. Hereford was second only to Kent as a hop-growing area, and the steady demand from the hop yards provided a ready local market, particularly for the farm woods of the central lowlands.

Another way in which ancient wooded landscapes were kept in being was as parks. Hereford is a county of parks, great and small, many of them dating back to the Middle Ages. Penyard Chase, for example, once a place of disportment for the bishops of Hereford (who did not hesitate to excommunicate poachers and unlicensed cutters), survives as the large Penyard Park and the enclosed coppice called Chase Wood. Many of the great trees of Penyard Park were felled around 1700 and here, as elsewhere, most of the present-day trees are planted. Eastnor Park, enclosed from Malvern Chase towards the end of the Middle Ages, has a red deer herd, some fine mature sessile oaks and one of the biggest wild service trees in England, complete with knots of mistletoe in its boughs. This is a large compartmented park with open 'groves' and enclosed coppices. Even more spectacular parks, full of vast, spreading, barrel-chested trees, lie near the western marches of the county. **Brampton Bryan Park** (165ha) [408 acres] near Kingston was emparked in 1309, and, remarkably, has remained in the same ownership ever since. The origin of **Moccas Park** (139ha) [343 acres] a few miles east of Hay-on-Wye is more mysterious, but it too probably dates from the early fourteenth century. There are few places which more perfectly preserve the physical setting, and here much of the detail, of a medieval park than these two with their glades and hillsides of bracken, fish-ponds, Norman mottes and herds of cattle and fallow deer grazing between the great trees. At Moccas there is even a traditional post-and-rail pale fence of oak and chestnut. There is a water colour of one of the greatest of the Moccas oaks hanging in Moccas Court, painted by Thomas Hearne about 1790. It depicts in detail the branchy hulk of the aged 'doddard'; men in tricorn hats stand beneath it marvelling, measuring its girth with outspread arms. This tree still stands. I have seen it from exactly the same angle as the remarkably accurate Hearne portrait. It has changed hardly a whisker or twig in two hundred years.

Ast Wood: wild daffodils and war-games

AREA: 18ha (45 acres)

ACCESS: Private but a public bridleway runs past the wood

TYPE: Calcareous ash-maple-hazel woodland

GRID REFERENCE: SO 673382

Ast Wood, ('ash' or possibly 'east' wood) is set in the agricultural red clay country of south-east Herefordshire, a rich land of hop yards and orchards, celebrated in the poetry of John Masefield and the Dymock poets, Rupert Brooke and Edward Thomas. Part of the wood is owned by the parents of my friend Charles Watkins, who wrote the second volume of this series, *Woodland Management and Conservation*. When he took me round it in 1989, I realised what had inspired Charles to devote his life to studying and conserving woodland. Ast Wood is a wonderful place, full of unusual and interesting trees, historic banks, a spring of pure water and a profusion of spring wild flowers. Until the early 1970s, it also retained intact its medieval shape, all sinuous corners and doglegs within a large boundary bank and ditch. A third of the wood was cleared in the 1970s to make way for a new field but the old boundary is still marked by a field bank and a line of big oaks and ashes. More recently some of the wood has been churned up and trampled by rally drivers and war-gamers. There was also a plan, thankfully averted, to carve golfing fairways through it.

Charles Watkins has unearthed nineteenth-century records showing that the wood was then coppiced at between twelve to fourteen years' growth and the poles sold for use in local hop yards and by a spokemaker in nearby Ledbury. The ten coppice compartments of the wood were known by the Herefordshire word 'fall'. In 1901, a clause in the standard purchaser's contract forbade the use of traction engines to remove the wood, presumably fearing that they would get stuck in the mud – a precaution that their modern successors have failed to observe. The wood was sold in 1916, when it was described in the sales particulars as 'an enclosure of thriving woodland and excellent game covert . . . a mixed coppice wood with a large number of well grown oak trees and poles'. Since then it has received comparatively little management apart from some small-scale coppicing and selective felling and a small plantation of Christmas trees.

The trees of Ast Wood include a rare standard small-leaved lime, a large number of service trees, including full-sized ones, some brookside alders standing as straight and twice as high as telegraph poles, and large stools of ash, sweet chestnut and wych elm. The elm stools are often bizarre objects. The largest are blackened decaying hulks, the cadavers of elm disease fellings in the 1970s, surrounded by a spritely circle of pole-sized springs – a good example of natural coppicing. Here they emerge from the ground several feet from the stump, as though shrinking from contact with the diseased member.

Springtime reveals the full beauty of the woodland flora. Ast Wood lies in the 'golden triangle' of wild daffodil country in Herefordshire. Here the daffodils grow not only in woods but in meadows and fields and in such abundance that the Great Western Railway company used to run special trains to Dymock, packed with daffodil enthusiasts. Daffodils and wood anemones are the first episode in Ast Wood's long spring. After them come splashes of bluebells, an unusual abundance of herb paris, wood-sorrels in the peaty clefts of decaying stumps, and kingcups and wild redcurrant along the brooks. In late spring, the wild

⇧ *Piles of coppice wood, cut into sections (cordwood) and stacked, can make excellent habitats for insects and molluscs after a year or two as here at Lea and Pagets Wood, Herefordshire. October*
(PETER WAKELY)

service trees along the edge of the wood burst into blossom.

I mentioned the growth-sport of war-gaming in the non-Watkinsian part of the wood. These games sound tremendous fun. The would-be soldiers build barricades and trenches and 'forts' and charge about shooting paint at one another. Woods provide the cover needed for this sport, which is particularly popular around London and in East Anglia, where a number of important ancient woods such as Ufford Thicks in Suffolk and Hook Wood in Hertfordshire have been among the battle grounds. Wet woods such as Ast Wood can soon become quagmires around the base camps and car parks and wherever the soldiers have got stuck in the mud. Logs and cast boughs are apt to become incorporated in the defences. Woodbanks are eroded, stumps and shrubs knocked over. One can imagine badgers bolting down to their underground bunkers and refugee beasts and birds fleeing along the lanes. And, of course, there are paint splashes everywhere. While there are places, like wind-thrown plantations and rhododendron thickets, that might benefit from a pitched battle or two, conservationists are not enthusiastic about war-games in ancient and natural woods, especially in Sites of Special Scientific Interest. There may be room for compromise in large dry woods by spreading the wear and tear and rotating the games through the wood, and fencing off any boggy bits. In wet woods, war-games are to be resisted. Unfortunately, they offer tempting financial inducements to some woodland owners: most alternative ways of making woodland profitable involve more effort on their part.

The Wye Valley

The most dramatic woods of Herefordshire are in the upland half of the county, among the hills and vales, dingles and gorges that melt into the Welsh and Shropshire hills. The gorge of the River Wye skirts round the Woolhope Dome, crowned by Haugh Wood, then passes in a series of great loops about the promontories of the Seven Sisters and Huntsham Hill. This is one of the most exciting wooded areas in all Britain. The Nature Conservancy Council's formal descriptions of wildlife sites, generally written in a deliberately downbeat style, in this instance unbends a little:

> The lower Wye valley is one of the key areas of ancient woodland in Britain. Taken as a whole these woods have more in common with the woods of central and southern France than with woods elsewhere in Britain. They rank with the New Forest, the native pinewoods of Scotland and the western oceanic oakwoods as one of the four most important woodland areas in the country. Semi-natural woodland is almost continuous on the steep sides of the gorge. An unparalleled mixture of woodland types are found, some rare like lime-sessile oak on limestone, and beech in a natural mixture of both oaks, wych elm and ash, and are believed to be similar in composition to the original woods of the valley. Rare trees like large-leaved lime and local whitebeams are prominent, as are some near the edge of their European range like beech and Midland hawthorn. With the woods are limestone bluffs, calcareous grassland and disused stone mines used by overwintering horseshoe bats . . .

Lords Wood (60ha) [148 acres] opposite Lady Park Wood on the steep valley sides near Symond's Yat is a beautiful wood of just this type, with the addition of miniature yew woods clinging hard to limestone cliffs. Rather more accessible, however, is the following wood, which I have chosen as an example of an ancient wood on the Hereford limestone.

Lea and Pagets Wood:
a Wye Valley wood

AREA: 28ha (70 acres)

STATUS: Nature reserve owned by Herefordshire Nature Trust

ACCESS: Nature trail

TYPE: Sessile oak-lime woodland with ash, wych elm, hazel and alder

GRID REFERENCE: SO 598343

On the older, harder rocks of Herefordshire most woods lie not on level clay but along steep valley sides, accompanied by crag and scree. At Lea and Pagets Wood we are not quite in crag country, but the scenery is nonetheless strongly geological. We are at the edge of Woolhope Dome, a great eroded mound of hard limestone with a soft centre of shale so that, from the air, the 'dome' looks more like a saucer. Lea and Pagets Wood is perched on the saucer's rim on either side of a valley. Lea Wood lies on one bank, Pagets on the other: they meet at a tiny brook in the middle without any intervening open space.

Some woods have one or two particular qualities that lift them above the common herd, an outstanding lichen flora, say, or an unusually well-documented past. Lea and Pagets Wood has no single outstanding features but contains almost everything that characterises ancient and natural woodland and is an ideal wood for educational purposes. On entering the wood the first impression is one of close-spaced sessile oaks. Closer inspection reveals huge spreading coppice stools of sweet chestnut and bushy, burry ones of wych elm. There are scattered stools and boundary stubs of both kinds of native lime, a grove of giant cherry trees, valley alders and occasional stands of wild service tree, holly or yew. In the middle of the wood, marking a now defunct ownership boundary, stands a fine oak pollard. As if to reinforce its significance as a boundary post, a wire fence grows *through* the bolling of this tree: the old and the new forms of boundary marks have physically fused.

The bottom of the valley is exceptionally wet, because the underlying shale is almost impervious to water. In May, lady's smock is so abundant that from a distance it forms a lilac haze, shot through with the yellow sunbursts of kingcups. The banks are lush in the way that only moist, ungrazed limestone banks can be – bright with woodruff, celandine, primroses, bluebells, anemones and archangel, spurts of colour against a leafy sheet of mercury. Sharp eyes will pick out less conspicuous flowers such as herb paris, twayblade and bird's-nest orchid. As usual, late spring is the best time for the woodland flora, but one special plant, meadow saffron, appears as leafless blooms along muddy pathsides in August and September. Lea and Pagets is also a bird-rich wood: there is sufficient mature timber for woodpeckers and nuthatch, and the pied flycatcher, the emblem of the Hereford Nature Trust, breeds in the nest boxes.

Signs of the wood's past are numerous. There is a limestone quarry cut into the bank of Lea Wood, and the large kiln that converted the quarried stone to quicklime still stands at the entrance to the wood, partly hidden behind an earth bank. Thus Lea Wood has contributed towards the fertility of the surrounding farmland by providing the fuel to bake the lime to spread on the fields. The Hereford Nature Trust has restored the wood to a coppice rotation by dividing it into six compartments and cutting one each year. The regrowth regenerates at different rates, with sweet chestnut leading the field at up to ten feet of growth within two years. Ash, hazel, oak, birch and maple grow more slowly, but still often double their height in a year. Neat stacks of cordwood mark the currently worked area, and the Trust recoups some of its expenses from sales of oak and chestnut cleft stakes. Bramble control is a major task, but fallow deer, though present, are not yet the scourge of tender growth that they have become farther east. The recently managed areas are generally the richest in flowers and butterflies. One encouraging sign is the recent return of the beautiful silver-washed fritillary butterfly to the coppiced glades.

The Hereford Uplands

The character of the larger upland woods has been heavily influenced by planting or selection in favour of oak, since Herefordshire was pronounced especially suitable for that tree in the late eighteenth century. From that time onwards, large woods have been progressively converted from coppice to high forest, although the underwood has often survived. Replanting with conifers gathered pace after the 1920s, and now nearly half the ancient woodland area, including nearly all the large woods, has been replaced by conifer plantations with a leavening of broadleaved trees. Woods such as Wigmore Rolls, Gatley Long Coppice, Haye Park Wood and Knill Wood would scarcely be recognised by those that named them: their identity has been all but lost.

There is a second limestone district in the north of the county in which is one of those strange, unexplained knots of ancient countryside where native lime trees are prominent. No fewer than eight types of limewoods were recorded by the NCC surveyors in 1984, of which the most widespread is lime coppice under oak and ash standards. The supreme example is **Downton Gorge** (48ha) [119 acres], a magnificent ravine on the River Teme which, in the complexity of its rocks and woodland, is rather like the Wye Gorge in miniature. This is one of the surviving woods of Bringewood Chase. Both small- and large-leaved limes are present, including some mighty pollard limes lining both banks near the base of the slope. These rare trees seem to indicate a wood-pasture phase between around 1600 to 1800. This is one of a handful of places, most of them in the West Country, where you can find not only coppice stools of both species of native lime but pollards and maiden trees too. The gorge and its tributary dingles are lush and ungrazed, and much of the lower slopes are covered in attractive natural gardens of yellow archangel, wood spurge, mercury and soft shield-fern.

Away from limestone districts, the character of upland Herefordshire woodland changes to one of poor soils, often on sandstone rocks, with heather on the crest of the hills and wood-rushes on the slopes. Many of these woods have been replanted, initially with shipbuilder's oak, and later with conifers. The two that are most intact are Dinmore Hill Woods and Wellington Wood, which lie only a few miles apart in the middle of the county. Both are hilltop sessile oak woods with mixed woodland on the flanks. **Wellington Wood** (146ha) [361 acres] on its hill of Devonian cornstones is one of the largest ancient and natural woods in the county and is in private ownership. It is well documented and its history has been traced back to 1189 when an agreement over tithes mentions 'the wood of *Walentunia*', a Saxon name which had been corrupted to Wellington by 1663. Most of the wood was coppiced and was described in sales particulars of 1855 as 'in good and regular course, and average a *fall* (ie, a felling) of about 12 acres a year'. By that time the wood also contained 'fine young thriving oak and other timber', probably planted, so that today the canopy is a mixture of multiple-stemmed coppice stools, some of them large, and standard trees.

There is little underwood on the summit of the hill but along the flanks coppiced ash and hazel become frequent, together with scattered stools of maple, small-leaved lime and wild cherry. Such associations of sessile oak, maple and lime are uncommon nationally. Most of the coppice has grown up to high forest, but other parts must have been cut as recently as the 1960s. Exceptionally, for a wood of this size, there are no plantations of exotic species. Perhaps the most remarkable feature of Wellington Wood is the deep gullets that cut through the reddish cornstone at the western end so that one has the unusual experience of walking through deep rocky corridors and peering upwards into the roots of the coppice stools.

Dinmore Hill Woods (153ha) [378 acres] are best known for a latterday accretion, Queenswood Country Park, at the top of the hill. This was rescued from probable felling by the then Council for the Preservation of Rural England in the 1920s, and was later handed over to the County Council 'for the enjoyment of the public for all time'. In 1953, a special Coronation Fund was launched to buy trees for a new arboretum, a collection of trees from all over the world, set in the heart of an ancient oak coppice. Today, the original coppice flora of anemones, bluebells and spotted orchids still thrives under a delightfully incongruous canopy of Japanese maples, Californian redwoods and the like. Farther down the slope there is some rather dull oak high forest singled from former coppice, with some spindly hazels and a lot of bracken and bramble. Recently, some attention has been diverted from the arboretum to the surrounding natural woods and, with revived coppicing by the Council's 'countryside rangers', their latent interest is likely to increase. The view from the hilltop 'toposcope' across to the Malverns to the east and the Black Mountains to the west is spectacular; indeed Herefordshire as a whole is a county of rewarding vistas from comparatively easy climbs. Much of Francis Kilvert's ability to describe scenery so evocatively stemmed from his good fortune in having so much of it.

So far, I have confined this brief survey of Herefordshire to ancient and natural woods. But because so many of the large ancient woods in the county have been changed dramatically by planting, let us pay a short visit to **Haugh** (pronounced 'hoff') **Wood**, a big wood (342ha) [845 acres] crowning Woolhope Dome and owned by the Forestry Commission. A pleasantly effortless stroll through Haugh Wood along well-made forestry tracks is quite a contrast with the mud-bespattered, bramble-flayed experience of many a natural wood. And what variety one meets in a short space! At one end there is some native vegetation: recently coppiced ash with a few big spreading yews. (Some say that the yews were spared so that the woodman had somewhere to shelter from the rain.) Nearby is one of four small Herefordshire Nature Trust reserves, a disused lime quarry harbouring rare hellebores. Then, in quick succession, we wander past a young plantation of Corsican pine, an oakwood with lakes of bluebells, a garlicky dell, some silver firs, a belt of limes with a large, possibly native, stool of large-leaved lime, a ferny dingle complete with gurgling brook, and a beech plantation in which some of the former underwood – service, elm and hazel – survives: all this in about half a mile (800m). Haugh Wood has been designated as a Site of Special Scientific Interest, despite its high proportion of replanted woodland, because of its exceptional importance for butterflies and moths. By no means all plantations are as interesting, but this one, on its well-lit hilltop with spacious views on all sides, has the appearance of a well-run tree farm in which much of the indigenous wildlife has adapted to, and even thrives in, the new conditions.

SHROPSHIRE
Shropshire is a moderately well-wooded county with about 25,000ha (61,750 acres) or 7.2 per cent of the land surface under trees. Roughly 9,300ha (23,000 acres) is considered to be woodland of ancient origin. This is a county of transition, divided by 'the great wildlife corridor of the River Severn' between the Midlands plain of the north and east and the hard, ancient rocks of the hilly west and south. The majority of Shropshire's ancient woods lie on steep hillsides and, except in limestone areas, the predominant type is western sessile oak coppice. There are dense concentrations of woodland at the Wyre Forest on the border with Worcestershire, Clun Forest on the marches with Wales, on Wenlock Edge and The Wrekin and along the sides of the Severn valley between Bridgnorth and Leighton. Much of the lowland plain in the north of the county is, by contrast, sparsely wooded. This is one of the counties where ancient woods have been replanted on a very substantial scale. The Shropshire Wildlife Trust estimate that 543ha (1,341 acres) in ninety-five woods have been lost or damaged since 1980. Virtually every large wood over 100ha (247 acres) has been substantially replanted and, in places such as Clun Forest, ancient and natural woodland has all but disappeared.

Telford's famous iron bridge spans the River Severn at Coalbrookdale in the midst of one of the most densely wooded landscapes in Shropshire. These woods played a major role in Shropshire's iron-smelting, coal mining and tanning industries, supplying charcoal, pit props and bark in large quantities over at least 300 years. Shropshire belongs in part to the Oakwood Province of western Britain, where sessile oak assumes a complete dominance in many ancient woods. Such woods generally lie on acid soils and usually on steep hillsides. Until the nineteenth century, most were cut over regularly as coppice, because local industry needed small-diameter poles and bark, not big oak planks and beams. The main centres of oak coppicing were the Severn valley, the Wyre and Clun Forests, and the Coal Measures in the southeast of the county. Most coppices were cut once every sixteen to eighteen years but, because oak grows relatively slowly, there were in some woods two ages of coppice, a long rotation for oak and a shorter one for other trees. At times of peak demand, Shropshire landowners learned to exercise considerable thrift with their valuable natural crop. Nothing was wasted: large oak stems were sold for pit props, small cordwood between 2.5 and 10cm (1-4in) in diameter was cut for charcoal, and irregular wood from the branches boiled and split to make oak swill baskets.

Helmeth Wood (24ha) [59 acres] is an oak coppice on a hummock at the foot of Caer Caradoc Hill near Church Stretton. It is bounded by an ancient holloway, Cwms Lane, and has the rounded boundary and raised banks of a medieval wood. Though lately used as a sheep shelter, this wood had been coppiced for centuries and includes some huge oak stools up to 2.74m (9ft) in diameter. There is no evidence that oak standards were grown here before the nineteenth century. Most of the present growth is young, dating back only to World War I when the whole wood was evidently clear-felled 'by two Russians and two land girls'. Though wide-spaced sessile oaks dominate the wood, there are a few big cherries and lime stools, some hazel underwood, and alders in the damper pockets. On the windy crest of the wood the oaks are stunted and twisted into fantastic shapes as they corkscrew slowly and tortuously from the broken stumps.

On the more base-rich soils, oak coppice gives way to mixed woodland in which ash, elm, hazel and sometimes lime are prominent. **Benthall Edge Wood** and its neighbour **Tick Wood** lie on west- and north-facing slopes overlooking the Severn valley at Ironbridge. Their rocks are a mixture of acid sandstones and calcareous shales, and the complex geology is reflected in the wood's composition which varies from oak-birch woodland on the poorer soils to ash-wych elm, ash-hazel and ash-lime woods on the richer. Past owners did not seem to discriminate between the different stand types: the whole wood was cut over as coppice. About twenty native trees and shrubs grow somewhere in Benthall Edge Wood and, in April, a sudden glorious blossoming reveals the presence of wild cherries. Cherry is a common woodland tree in Shropshire. One of Shropshire's most famous sons, A. E. Housman, celebrated it in a poem, beginning

> Loveliest of trees, the cherry now
>   Is hung with bloom along the bough,
> And stands about the woodland ride
>   Wearing white for Eastertide.
>
> (from Reveille)

Wenlock Edge is one of Shropshire's best-known landmarks, a 20km (12.4 miles) ridge of limestone with a wooded north face, celebrated in Housman's well-known lines from *A Shropshire Lad* and set to music by Ralph Vaughan-Williams:

> On Wenlock Edge the wood's in trouble;
>   His forest fleece the Wrekin heaves;
> The gale, it plies the saplings double,
>   And thick on Severn snow the leaves.

Trouble of a different kind has come to Wenlock Edge in the form of modern forestry, and far too much of it has been converted to conifer plantation. Where natural woodland survives, as at Blakeway Coppice, Wolverton Wood and Alcaston Coppice, it is very similar in composition to Benthall Edge Wood, with well-developed sessile oak and ash-wych elm woodland on poorly drained heavy soils, and attractive carpets of ramsons, sweet woodruff and sanicle. Such woods are confined to the Silurian limestones of the West Midlands. Much of the Wenlock Edge woodland is now in the care of the National Trust, which has a policy of removing conifers and encouraging native trees.

The history and character of Shropshire's ancient woods has much in common with Herefordshire, though the latter county has more oak high forest and less oak coppice. Shropshire has no equivalent of Hereford's medieval parks, but an interesting relic of former wood-pasture survives at **The Stiperstones**, about ten miles south-west of Shrewsbury, a wonderful heathery ridge scored by curving dingles with patches of bog and birch scrub on the hillside and splinters of bare quartzite projecting along the crest. The cottagers of this area were part miners and part crofters, a lost way of life described in Mary Webb's novel, *Gone to Earth*. Much of The Stiperstones was used as common grazing for the crofters' cattle and sheep, and boughs of trees were cut for winter browse whenever deep snow prevented grazing. Being winter green and palatable, holly is particularly useful for winter feed, and this was the purpose behind the magnificent groves of old pollard hollies at the northern end of The Stiperstones, one of our few remaining examples of ancient holly wood-pasture known as *hollins* [64]. Their great girth argues an age of at least 250 years, and the largest trees may be as much as 400 years old: perhaps the oldest stand of holly in Europe.

9

THE PENNINES

Strictly speaking, this chapter should be titled 'the southern Pennines and the lowlands to the east, west and south of it'. Here we look at woods in the counties of Derbyshire, Cheshire, Merseyside, Greater Manchester, Lancashire, and South, West and North Yorkshire. The title will just hold because each of them (except for Merseyside, which has few ancient woods anyway) contain bits of the hills of Carboniferous limestone and Millstone Grit that we lump together as the Pennines.

With the exception of the Vale of York and some of the broader valleys, most ancient woodland lies on the slopes of the valleys or in narrow dells known as cloughs that streams have scored in the hillside. Oak and birch are the main trees on the poorer soils of the gritstone and Coal Measures. On the richer soils irrigated by mineral-rich water or on more base-rich rock, ash, elm and hazel are frequent. In the limestone dales, ash replaces oak as the dominant tree, but elsewhere stands of ash and wych elm generally form zones of fertility and floristic diversity in an otherwise heath-like wood given over to grass, bracken and bluebells. Alderwoods often line the permanently wet soil at the bottom of a valley and were often coppiced regularly in the past to produce poles for turning and 'blocks' for clog making. Open stands of alder are generally the lushest parts of these northern woods, and are often full of tall flowers, bushes of wild currants and luxuriant masses of that exotic colonist, Himalayan balsam or 'policeman's helmet'.

To most eyes, the most beautiful Pennine woods are on the limestone, in the sweet dales of the 'White Peak' in Derbyshire (which is actually mellow pastureland and not at all 'peaky') and the more elemental countryside of scars, pavements and tarns in the Craven district of North Yorkshire. Where they have successfully evaded the sheep, such woods can be very rich in wild flowers, including many northern and upland species.

The history of these woods is still little known. In some areas, such as Lathkill Dale in Derbyshire and the Forge Valley in the Yorkshire Moors, the woods were at one time managed intensively for fuelwood, charcoal and pit props. In the upper dales of Yorkshire and Derbyshire, many woods were, and a few still are, commons, used by the whole of the local community. Much of the moorland was forest in the Middle Ages, forest in this sense meaning 'waste' rather than 'wood'. Some attempt was made to safeguard the greenery of the forest woods, but whether we owe any Pennine

Approximately one-third of Derbyshire's woods ⇨ are believed to be of ancient origin. Many woods in the Peak District are of recent origin and hence not shown. The larger ancient woods all lie in the lowlands, especially on the Coal Measures and in the Derwent Valley

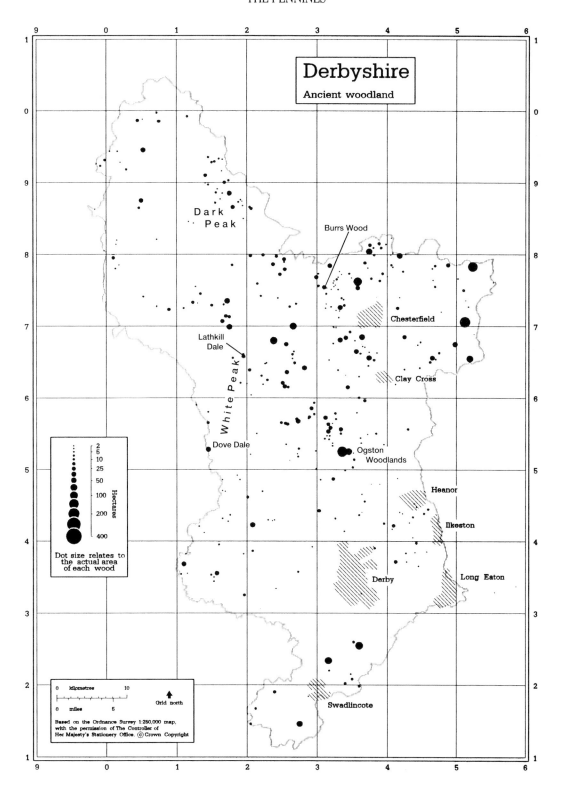

Derbyshire

Ancient woodland

Dark Peak

Burrs Wood

White Peak

Lathkill Dale

Chesterfield

Clay Cross

Dove Dale

Ogston Woodlands

Heanor

Ilkeston

Long Eaton

Derby

Swadlincote

Hectares

2
5
10
25
50
100
200
400

Dot size relates to
the actual area
of each wood

0   kilometres   10

0   miles   5

Grid north

Based on the Ordnance Survey 1:250,000 map,
with the permission of The Controller of
Her Majesty's Stationery Office. © Crown Copyright

woodland to Forest Law is doubtful. In this area, ancient woods survived by good fortune rather than by any effective conservation policy.

DERBYSHIRE

Derbyshire is best known for the beautiful ashwood dales of the White Peak. The sparser, more austere hillside and clough woods of the Dark Peak and the Coal Measures are less often admired, and in the rest of the county we are back in a poorly wooded Midlands landscape on the rolling fields of the Keuper Marl. Even here, however, there are local-ised concentrations of ancient woodland along the Derwent Valley, and in the narrow gorges known as 'grips' cut into the Magnesian limestone.

In the White Peak of Derbyshire, that well-loved landscape of sweet dales, pure trout streams, stone-walled fields and well-vegetated crags, ancient and more recent woodland merge almost impercepti-bly. Woodland is virtually confined to the valleys, and there are none of the high-altitude woods that one encounters in the North Pennines. Much of the plateau was permanently cleared in prehistory and the last remnant of it, in the parish of Peak Forest, had gone by the seventeenth century. The limestone dales, too steep and rocky to plough, were probably well-wooded in 1086, when the Domesday Book indicates that fully a quarter of Derbyshire was woodland.

The rights of commoners to graze livestock and take wood were not balanced however by any organised system of temporary enclosure to en-sure regeneration. The dales were treated as pas-tures, with wood as a bonus. Hence, over the years, woodland became restricted increasingly to steep rocky places which livestock could not reach. In the nick of time, eighteenth-century enclosures meant that woods could be managed as coppiced 'spring woods'.

From about 1770 onwards, the dales became an industrial landscape. Industry needed quantities of wood for fuel and ash 'puncheons' for props in the lead mines and coal pits. At the same time pasture improvement at the bottom of the dales lessened the grazing pressure on the woods, par-

Ancient woodland is confined to the steepest, least accessible slopes over much of the White Peak, as here in Monk's Dale. July
(PETER WAKELY)

ticularly because the new improved breeds of cattle and sheep were less agile than their pre-decessors and ill-adapted to craggy slopes. This combination of circumstances saved many old woods and led to the spread of woodland in the dales. The new woods were dominated by ash which, like sycamore and birch, is an effective coloniser of ungrazed land. The years of agricul-tural slump after 1815 led to a decline in the value of marginal pasture and accelerated the woodland recovery further. Thus the dales of the White Peak from the 1820s onwards were rather like the val-leys of the Alps in the 1990s: upland pastures turning into woodland. This process was accom-panied by tree planting, especially of beech and larch.

Large lime stools are a reliable indicator of ancient woodland in the White Peak. Dr Donald Pigott, who has published a fine study of Peak District limes [65], found enormous stools projecting from rocky bluffs whose age he estimates at more than a thousand years. They are invariably hollow and therefore impossible to date by annular ring counts, but Pigott developed an ingenious method of calculating the rate of erosion of soil from the roots to reach an approximate age. In some cases, so much soil has worn away that the roots have become exposed, producing 'coppice stools on stilts'. In the Peak District, limes rarely regenerate from seed and may be doomed to slow decline. It seems likely that these woods are another exam-ple of prehistoric limewoods which, through grazing and lime's inability to recolonise new sites, have turned into ashwoods.

Lathkill Dale near Bakewell is among the best-documented wooded dales in the Peak District. There are no limes here, probably because the dale had been grazed intensively by sheep from two Cistercian granges at Meadow Place and One Ash Grange. Walking in this peaceful place today,

it is difficult to imagine the scene between c 1770 and 1860 when there was a big lead mine at Mandale Deep Shaft, an aqueduct to channel water to a water wheel, which pumped water from the mine, an agent's house and paddocks for horses and ponies. All are now overgrown by woodland – a dense stand of sycamore marks the site of spoil pits. Lathkill Dale is orientated west to east and so one side receives much more sun than the other. The sunny south-facing slopes were grazed harder, and had become completely open by Tudor times. The long-established woodland is confined to the more shaded north-facing side of the valley, and it probably provided wood for pit props during the mining period. This woodland is believed to be ancient on the grounds of its mixed composition and rich flora: there are dogwood, rock whitebeam, bird cherry and hazel here among the ashes and wych elms and many of the special flowers of the area, like lily-of-the-valley, nodding melic and stone bramble. Upland ashwoods are justly celebrated for the beauty of their flora, not only in the spring but throughout the growing season, under the light, dappled shade of the main trees. There is even a winter-flowering shrub, the rare mezereon, once so prized by gardeners that it survives mainly in places remote from human settlement.

If the White Peak is in many ways like the Mendips, the Dark Peak is pure Pennines, a dour landscape of windswept moors and gritstone edges, kept bare by centuries of grazing and burning. Here and there, along stream cloughs and on rocky hillsides not worth cultivating, are what remains of the ancient woodland: woods of sessile oak and birch above grass and heather. The commonest type of woodland in the Dark Peak is old overgrown oak coppice, now used to shelter sheep. The highest is Ladybower Wood, a gritstone wood managed by the Derbyshire Wildlife Trust, which reaches about 350m (1,150ft). Lower down, near a village with the lyrical name of Unthank, is the Woodland Trust's **Burr's Wood** (12ha) [30 acres], a typical Pennine oak coppice last cut over about a century ago. It contains some moderately large oak coppice stools, some of them twisting from outcrops of shale, which suggest that coppicing lasted at least a couple of centuries at Burr's Wood. Similar woods supplied bark to the Sheffield and Manchester tanneries during the nineteenth century. Other trees were often weeded out, but here a few hazels, ashes and alders survive near the stream. Once sheep are excluded, oak sometimes regenerates well, but at Burr's Wood vigorously seeding sycamores are a problem. Recognising sycamore's competitive edge over most native trees, the Woodland Trust is doing its best to keep it in check.

Deer parks are an important feature of the Derbyshire scene, and some of them contain scattered old trees and small woods. Scarcliffe Park dates back to the Middle Ages, though most of its woods have been replanted. At Calke Park, Chatsworth Park and Keddleston Hall Park, wood-pasture management has preserved large old trees of considerable importance for invertebrates that live in dead wood and, to a smaller extent, for bark lichens.

Although it is easy to forget the fact, most of Derbyshire lies outside the Peak District and is much more like parts of Nottinghamshire and South Yorkshire. In the Derbyshire lowlands, ancient woods survive mainly on slopes too steep to farm, when they are often known as dumble woods, or on patches of sandy or ill-drained soil. As in neighbouring Yorkshire, Derbyshire coppices are called spring woods. Alas, few large ones survive, for most have been felled and restocked with conifers. The **Ogston Woodlands** (32ha) [79 acres], although much modified by planting, is still perhaps the best example of a largely natural mixture of oak, rowan and holly on shallow gritstone soils, with possible primary woodland in the valleys.

Perhaps the most distinctive lowland woods

are in the narrow 'grips' of the Magnesian limestone in the north-eastern corner of the county where streams have cut through the soft yellow rock to form narrow steep-sided valleys. These are like smaller-scale versions of the Durham denes, and the woodland is of much the same type, dominated by ash and wych elm with groves of yew clinging to the sides. Although this is limestone, birch and rowan are abundant, as they are in similar woods farther north and west. Here and there one finds those famous ancient woodland trees, large-leaved lime and wild service. In spring and summer, the floor of the typical grip is a flood of dog's mercury, but along the sides an ancient woodland flora stands almost side by side with limestone flowers and ferns otherwise confined to the rocks and slopes of the White Peak.

CHESHIRE

Cheshire is one of the most poorly wooded lowland counties: only 3 per cent of its land surface is under trees, and only 1 per cent is considered to be ancient woodland. The surviving ancient woods are nearly all small and confined to steep-sided river valleys, especially those of the Rivers Dane, Weaver and their tributaries, or areas of poor soil. It would be hard to recognise Cheshire nine centuries ago when, with woodland covering about a quarter of the land, it was among the most densely wooded English counties. Like Norfolk and Warwickshire, Cheshire later became a farmer's county where pasture was valued above woodland. There were no large-scale iron industries or hop yards to lease and protect the woods and, from the early Middle Ages onwards, the rolling Cheshire plain became increasingly a place of cows, grass and ponds. Large parts of the county were once under Forest Law, but not all of the forests were well wooded. Wirral, at least, was fertile farmland that apparently had been declared a forest in order to punish the inhabitants! Delamere and Mondrem were contiguous forests between the Rivers Gowy and Weaver, but little was left of their woods for the eighteenth-century mapmakers to record.

The present-day oaks of Delamere were planted

on heathland between 1812 and 1825, and have been partly replaced with conifers in our own time. The pattern here, as elsewhere on mid-Cheshire's infertile deposits of sand, was for ancient woodland to turn into heath through over-grazing, then subsequently revert to woodland either through natural regeneration, as at the Woodland Trust-owned Snidley Moor Wood, or by planting, as at Delamere. In either case, the original woodland flora has vanished. The same can be said for the fourth medieval forest, Lyme (later Macclesfield) which Cheshire shares with Staffordshire. This was an austere upland gritstone forest. Parts were certainly well wooded in the early Middle Ages (it was a noted place for breeding goshawks), but again surviving ancient woodland is now confined to steep cloughs, where the trees had some respite from grazing. Around Lyme Park, by the River Dane and the Shell Brook, are pollard trees that may indicate former wood-pasture.

Ancient woodland in Cheshire falls into two broad types. On the fertile but poorly drained Keuper Marl, the best preserved woods lie in narrow channels known as *cloughs*. These are not the oak cloughs of the Pennines, but rather mellow woods of ash, maple and hazel, sometimes with standard pedunculate oaks. Some contain wild service tree, crab apples, and small-leaved lime and are characterised by large patches of bluebells, wild garlic and wood anemone. Former coppices are often called *shaws* or *coppys*. **Warburtons Wood**, near Warrington (3ha) [7.4 acres] in its steep V-shaped clough, is a good example. Though small, it is well preserved and attractive, being noted for blossoming cherry trees, small-leaved lime and spring carpets of wood anemone, bluebell and stichwort.

A second type of ancient woodland is found on the comparatively infertile acid soils of the Pennine fringe, the mid-Cheshire Ridge and the Frodsham-Helsby scarp. Although many of these woods are of secondary origin, there are small areas of mature ancient woods characterised by a canopy of oak (both sessile and pedunculate) and

a species-poor ground flora in which bluebells and greater wood-rush are conspicuous. Woods on level, fertile ground are more likely to be planted as fox coverts in Cheshire. They often stand around old clay pits, and are generally dominated by trees that regenerate well from seed, notably oak, sycamore and ash.

GREATER MANCHESTER AND MERSEYSIDE

In Greater Manchester and Merseyside, the range of ancient and natural woodland is limited. Most are narrow 'clough woods' characteristic of northern England. **Cotteril Clough** (10ha) [25 acres], a largely natural wood by Manchester airport, occupies a deep ravine cut through Keuper Marl by the diminutive Cotteril Brook. It was well known to Victorian botanists, whose records appear in contemporary local floras. Cotteril Clough is a typical upland valley wood, grading from acid oak-birch at the top of the valley to ash-wych elm on the more fertile soils farther down and alder along the wet valley bottom. The depths of such woods are humid and heavily shaded; here the lower slopes are covered by a deep-green, smelly expanse of wild garlic. Recently the wood has suffered the death of most of its big elms and a veritable invasion of sycamore. The latter has left the Trust with little alternative but to try to fell and remove every seeding sycamore, though the use of heavy machinery in this steep ravine risks damage to the soils and surface vegetation.

Dibbinsdale (47ha) [116 acres] in the Wirral is more substantial, but is essentially Cotteril Clough scaled up. Ash-wych elm and valley alder fill the winding gash of the Dibbinsdale and Clatter Brooks, and in places planted pedunculate oak and sycamore outnumber the native trees. The great botanical spectacle of Dibbinsdale is its weird and wonderful understorey of redcurrant, blackcurrant and gooseberry bushes, more like an allotment than a wood, and accompanied by that rampant denizen of rich, moist soil, the Himalayan balsam.

Gale Clough and Shooterslee Wood (9ha) [22 acres] near Bolton is the best example of a clough wood on acidic upland soils. The upper slopes are

birch-oak woodland, which becomes more widespread on the Millstone grit and Coal Measures as
one travels north. Its valley bottom, by contrast, is
an alderwood, with flushes, marsh and areas of
open, wet grassland. Because of the varied topog-
raphy and soils of these deep narrow woods, the
number of plant species and communities quite
belies their size. They are by far the richest inland
wildlife sites left in this densely populated area
and deserve complete protection.

LANCASHIRE

Lancashire is a poorly wooded county and there is
no reason to suppose it was much better wooded
in the recorded past. Domesday Book records are
too few and vague to help us, but the surviving
records of the various medieval forests suggest
that most of them were hill pastures, not woods
(though the lowland Quernmore Forest was evidently well timbered). In Lancashire, the term
'forest' was used more loosely than usual, rather
like today when a 'forest' can mean a Forestry
Commission plantation, a treeless moor or, in the
case of Bowland, the bounds of a local authority. In
his excellent review of Lancashire woodland
Geoffrey Morries [66] suggests that 'it is conceivable
that the natural woodland was pushed back to
more or less its present-day limits over much of

the County as long ago as the 13th century'.

Today, ancient woods are concentrated in the
Silverdale-Arnside area in the north of the county,
and in the upland valleys of the Rivers Lune,
Hodder and Ribble. There is little woodland above

300m (984ft) and much of the former fenland in the west is virtually woodless. Silverdale apart, this is now a county of undermanaged ancient woods. Coppicing had virtually ceased by 1918, and wartime fellings had also stripped most woods of their timber. Traditional woodmanship continued longest north of the Ribble, where some woods continued to be managed as coppices to provide wood for making swill baskets, tool handles, chairs, cotton bobbins and other traditional products. Charcoal and tanbark were also sold, but not on the industrial scale of the High Furness in the Lake District. Perhaps the rural industry most associated with Lancashire was clog-sole making, using blocks of alder wood. However, the county's woods were not sufficient to supply the full needs of the clog-block cutters, who used to roam as far as the Welsh borders in search of suitable material.

Typical Lancashire woods are found in steep river valleys and folds in the hills. Looking down from the bare hills, most of them seem to be dominated by short, twisty oaks and birch pressed to the valley sides by the sharp coastal winds. There is often a sparse understorey of rowan and holly, a lot of grass, wet moss-covered boulders and wandering sheep doing their worst. Deeper in the valleys, however, where grazing animals cannot get at them, the better woods also have a much more developed woodland of wych elm, gean, sycamore, ash, hawthorn and other trees and a rich assortment of woodland flowers. The largest continuously wooded valley lies in a steep tight loop of the Ribble called Red Scar and extends along its tributary, the Tun Brook. **Red Scar and Tun Brook Woods** (64ha) [158 acres] lost most of their timber oaks in World War I, and since then has consisted of overgrown and largely natural underwood. This is one of the most varied natural woods, and reflects the succession of different rocks exposed in the ravine and the contrasting rich and poor soils along the gradient of the valley. The valley is a mixture of 'western valley ash-wych elm woodland' with valley alders, characteristic of well-preserved woods in the Ribble and Hodder valleys. Elsewhere in the Pennines, such woodland is normally confined to the base of the slope, but here on fertile soils derived from glacial drift it extends in places to the very top.

Silverdale, in the north-west, stands apart from the rest of the county. This is Carboniferous limestone country, a perfect paradise for the naturalist, with hanging woods on the sides of low craggy hills and around the brim of water-worn stone pavements. The predominant type of natural woodland on these shallow soils is one of our most floristically rich types, 'northern calcareous hazel-ash woodland', characterised by dense hazel scrub, a great deal of birch of both species, and the rare whitebeam *Sorbus lancastriensis*. **Gait Barrows** (69ha) [170 acres] is among the best examples in Britain of this rather rare type of woodland. Two other Silverdale woods are of comparable quality. **Cringlebarrow and Deepdale Woods** (50ha) [123 acres] lie on a west-facing limestone hillside. This is former coppice, promoted to high forest a century ago by singling the stools and planting oak among them. By contrast with otherwise similar woods in the Furness district of Cumbria, most Silverdale oaks were grown as standards, not as coppice. There is much yew scrub and regenerating beech and sycamore of recent origin. The outstanding feature of Cringlebarrow is its extensive area of another rare type of natural woodland, sessile oak-ash-lime woodland, which we last met in the Wye valley. These floristically very rich woods are closely related to those on dry and limestone soils in southern France. Despite the difference in climate, Cringlebarrow Wood would hardly seem out of place in the Dordogne of Gascony.

SOUTH YORKSHIRE

The county of South Yorkshire was carved out of the former West Riding after local government reorganisation in 1974. It includes the mining and manufacturing towns of Sheffield, Barnsley, Rotherham and Doncaster and the countryside around them. Although much of the county is still rural and is moderately well wooded, some of the best-preserved woods are suburban. Sheffield in particular has a fine collection of woods managed by the City's Recreation Department as public amenities. Most ancient woods in South Yorkshire are small or medium-sized. They fall into three main zones closely related to the underlying rocks. The western one, consisting of the gritstone moors and dales of the Pennines, is comparatively bare of trees. The few ancient woods are confined to the steep-sided valleys: small hanging woods of birch and sessile oak on acid soil gathered above the becks. Woodland cover is much more extensive on the Coal Measures between Barnsley and Sheffield. Here again they lie on almost wholly acidic soils. Many woods used to be managed as coppice and known as 'spring woods'. Farther east there is an abrupt change to the band of soft Magnesian limestone either side of Doncaster. Here are the county's richest woods, in which oak and birch give place to ash, wych elm, small-leaved lime and yew.

That South Yorkshire is better wooded than most of its neighbouring counties is probably because of industry, and especially the centuries-old iron industry. Records suggest that the main woodland products were charcoal, bark and wood, in that order, and that to obtain them in quantity woods were carefully preserved and managed as coppices. In the north of England, and especially in the West Riding of Yorkshire, these woods were called *springs*, an old word of Saxon origin that operates both as a noun and a verb, and refers to the new growth from the cut stump or *stoven*. The ironmasters required *cordwood* (wood of fixed length) of a certain diameter for charcoal, and so the spring was cut after a fixed period, which on one large estate was around eighteen years [67]. A few young oaks were generally left as standard trees. At the peak of production in the eighteenth century, colliers (charcoal burners) and pillers (bark peelers) used to work in close partnership, the latter moving ahead to strip the bark before the colliers cut the spring into regular lengths. In mining districts, woods also supplied larger bore wood for pit props. Coppicing had virtually ceased in this area by 1918, by which time owners had already begun to restock their woods with timber trees. In the local historian George Redmonds' words, 'many patches of small woodland which still survive doubtless owe their existence not to sentiment or aesthetics, but to earlier economic necessity' [67].

The woods in the care of the City of Sheffield are managed with the help and advice of amenity and conservation interests, and in many instances to a written plan. They have been reviewed in detail by Jones [68]. Small glades have been cut in several woods to 'increase habitat diversity' and to help absorb their heavy public use. The glades have become attractive play areas, children romping about playing cowboys and indians with surprisingly little damage to the sprouting stumps and resurgent bluebells. What discord there is is not so much between conservation and amenity, as between those with forestry training who persist in regarding woodland trees as 'the crop' and believing that they should be managed as such, and those who argue that premature felling and over-tidiness leads to dullness and sterility [69]. The argument is not confined to Sheffield.

The richest woods in the county are those that lie on the Magnesian limestone. In prehistory they were probably limewoods, but management has promoted ash at the expense of lime and, since the mid-nineteenth century, beech has been used for restocking woods. **King's Wood** (53ha) [131 acres], which belonged to Roche Abbey near Maltby, is one of the finest examples. Here are rare natural associations of sessile oak, ash, wych elm and small-leaved lime and a host of plants indicative of ancient woodland, such as yellow star-of-Bethlehem, green hellebore, lily-of-the-valley and hard shield-fern. The rare large-leaved lime is also quite frequent here in one of its few scattered strongholds in the north. **Anston Stones Wood** (34ha) [84 acres], a craggy wood four miles to the south, is also famous for its rich flora despite the rude intrusion of a colliery railway.

WEST YORKSHIRE

To most naturalists the name of West Yorkshire is likely to conjure up the wonderful limestone dales, hills and pavements of the Craven district. Unfortunately, the abandonment of the old West Riding in 1974 meant that the dales now form part of the sprawling new county of North Yorkshire. In post-1974 West Yorkshire, we are left with the industrial cities of Leeds, Bradford, Halifax and Huddersfield, and their surrounding moors and valleys. The range of ancient and natural woodland is limited. In the west, the majority of woods are of sessile oak on acid gritstones and shales and have a pronounced upland character. Some are gill woods, typical of the northern Pennines, where only ragged strips of woodland in deep valleys have escaped from the relentless burning and grazing on the surrounding hillside. More substantial woods lie on the sides of the Calder and its tributaries, and were valuable sources of bark, pit props and fuel from coppice between about 1760 and 1850. The favoured trees were oak and, to a lesser extent, alder for clogs and charcoal, and woodmen probably weeded out other trees. Oak was also planted to replace worn-out or dead coppice stools. One such 'spring wood' is **Hetchell Wood** (14ha) [35 acres] on the side of a gritstone scarp near Leeds, where sessile oaks and downy birches are rooted in heather, bilberry, bracken and softgrass. Farther downhill there is a contrasting stand of ash, wych elm and alder carr where the soil is enriched by springs and floodwater. Like many Yorkshire woods, Hetchell Wood has also been quarried for stone. An eighteenth-century excavation called 'Pompocali', now forms one of the few examples of lowland heath in the county. Once oak coppicing ceased to be profitable, many of these woods were planted with beech and sycamore whose self-sown descendants are now widespread.

South and east of Leeds the county is of softer character with arable farmland and country houses set in parkland, and coal bings and pylons on the horizon. The relatively few ancient and natural woods that survive show the influence of Magnesian limestone in their dense underwood of ash, wych elm, hazel, guelder rose and spindle above a green expanse of dog's mercury.

NORTH YORKSHIRE

The county of North Yorkshire, since 1974 the largest in England, includes the North York moors, the lowland Vales of York, Mowbray and Pickering, and three of the finest Pennine Dales, those of the Wharfe and its tributary the Skirfare (Littondale), the Ure (Wensleydale) and the Swale. It is best known as a spacious open landscape of heather

moors, limestone cliffs and pavements, walled fields full of buttercups and scattered stone barns and the romantic beauty of the ruined Cistercian abbeys. Of its woods, many will know Farndale with its beautiful displays of wild daffodils, and (at least by reputation) the strange ashwood at Colt's Park on its pedestal of bare limestone. Forge Valley, Rievaulx Abbey, Hackfall Wood and Bolton Abbey all have well-used woodland walks. In general, however, Yorkshire's woods are somewhat neglected and unsung by archaeologists and ecologists, and there are probably interesting places still awaiting discovery.

The majority of ancient woods in North Yorkshire are small: three-fifths of them measure only 10ha (25 acres) or less. Big woods are rare and Howardian Hills near Malton and the dales of the North York Moors are the only really densely wooded landscapes in the county.

The Vale of York

Most ancient woods in lowland Yorkshire are confined to steep banks (a bank is almost synonymous with a wood in northern English place-names) or to wet, uncultivable land such as Askham Bog near York. However Bishop Wood in Selby District, the largest single wood in the entire county is more or less flat. Once part of a large common, Bishop Wood was a supplier of coppice wood, as its nearby *hagg* place-names attest. Today, however, nearly all of it has been replanted. Its fate is typical of most of the more accessible woods in this area, which were stripped of their mature timber during the two world wars and thereafter replanted with conifers. The best ancient and natural wood left is **Birkham Wood** (28ha) [69 acres] near Knaresborough, which has come into prominence recently through the County Council's desire to build a bypass through it, a controversy that led in the 1980s to two public inquiries. This wood is of great interest both historically and scientifically. The whole of its rounded medieval perimeter has survived. Ancient woods in the Vale of York usually lack woodbanks, but Birkham has an impressive one running for 1km (0.62 miles) along one edge and crowned by old hazel stools. Much of the vegetation is now neglected underwood and, although some of the coppice was cleared between 1914 and 1918, large stools up to 7m (23ft) in girth testify to its previous use as a 'spring wood'. The northern end is on limestone with pockets of sandy drift, which respectively support ash-wych elm and oak-hazel woodland. Ancient woodland plants include small-leaved lime, spindle, herb paris, yellow archangel and toothwort, and the bird population is remarkably diverse for a small wood. Much of it seems destined to be lost.

The wooded banks and scars of the Rivers Went, Nidd and Ure and their tributary gills are more upland in character. Most of them are oakwoods, with varying amounts of rowan, holly, birch and alder, and sometimes damp, sheltered banks where ferns, mosses and lichens are prominent. Where the River Went cuts through the Magnesian limestone in Selby District, oak is largely replaced by ash and non-native sycamore, and the floor of hair-grass and bramble by dog's mercury. Some of these woods were landscaped and prettified by their owners a century or two ago, a process taken to extremes at Hackfall Wood by the Ure, which bristles with temples and follies built by William Aislabie during the 1800s.

The North York Moors

The largest heather moor in England is scored by streams running through deep valleys, some of which contain extensive ancient woods. Perhaps the finest example is the **Forge Valley Woods** (63ha) [156 acres] owned by Scarborough District Council and, in 1977, designated a National Nature Reserve. This is an old industrial wood and, from the Middle Ages until 1815, it supplied charcoal for the local forge, producing, among other things, nails for Scarborough's boat-builders. The ruins of the forge are close to the car park and the start of a guided woodland walk. Forge Valley Woods are typical of a large number of steep wooded valleys north and west of Scarborough, characterised by sopping wet glades of moor-grass and steep bouldery banks. Most of these woods are in vary-

ing states of neglect, or have been 'coniferised' with varying degrees of success, woods with a great deal of visible history in them, both crudely exploitive and benign. The best preserved present a gradation from bottomland alders, through ash-wych elm woodland on the richest soils to oaks and birches on the poorer soils farther up the hill. At Forge Valley, dead elms and rampant sycamore are being managed by group fellings.

Farndale, the valley of the River Dove, is a patchwork of unimproved countryside of small woods, rushy meadows and alder carrs, and is justly celebrated for its wonderful displays of wild daffodils. So long as they grow on moist ground near the river, however, the daffodils do not seem to mind whether they are under trees or not. Farndale's woods have *hagg* names and are former coppices, of oak, ash and hazel at the lower end and of oak alone farther up the dale. Farndale was one of the first and biggest Local Nature Reserves: 300ha (741 acres) of daffodil country of which 157ha [368 acres] is notified as a Site of Special Scientific Interest.

Beast Cliff (20ha) [49 acres], a coastal landslip a few miles north of Scarborough, has patches of apparently ancient and natural scrub kept from developing further into woodland by landslips and salt-pruning winds. It is of considerable ecological interest, for such undisturbed habitats are rare – in this case preserved by its dangerous location, accessible only to the most agile naturalist.

The Forest of Pickering

On the south side of the North York Moors lies a horseshoe of Jurassic limestone forming a series of hills and dales surrounding the Vale of Pickering. This is predominantly ancient countryside with extensive woods along the flanks of the Howardian Hills, in Ryedale and along the deep valleys that penetrate the moors north of Pickering. The present-day ancient woodland corresponds quite closely with that of 700 years ago. Place-names such as 'hagg wood' and 'spring wood' are frequent. **Duncombe Park** in Ryedale is one of the great wood-pastures of northern England, an array of old oak, elm, ash, beech and other trees on a bank above the looping river, with an exceptionally rich insect fauna.

In the Middle Ages, much of this wild area was common land and contained one of the larger medieval forests: the Forest of Pickering. The vivid records of this forest in use suggest that life in these northern fastnesses was far removed from the highly organised parks and game lodges of the south. Pickering was remote from the main centres of population. Kings rarely came that way, and their interests were represented by stewards behind the well-fortified walls of Pickering Castle. It is perhaps from places such as these that the Robin Hood legends took root, though the flouting of the law was not confined to outlaws. These untamed northlands had their own conventions and taboos, and local people tended to thumb their noses at authority imposed from outside. What other motive could there be behind the gesture of a band of local *gentry* who, during a rare royal visit in 1334, illegally killed forty-three harts and hinds, and stuck their antlered heads on stakes where the king was most likely to see them? Twenty years earlier, monks from Whitby Abbey had attempted to assassinate the king's forester, but succeeded only in wounding the forester's lad. They were outlawed by the forest court, and no doubt continued their poaching careers in the forest, a whole band of Friar Tucks [70].

The Forest of Pickering was owned by the royal Duchy of Lancaster from 1267, but it was not vested in the Crown until 1485. The abbeys of Whitby and St Mary's in York had their own forests nearby, and the Whitby monks were notorious poachers at Pickering. Upland northern forests were not usually well wooded: the Yorkshire forests of Langstrothdale and Arkengarthdale, for example, were treeless moors. Even at Pickering, woodland was probably confined to the dales. Medieval records speak mostly of oak, though that may reflect oak's financial value and not necessarily its ecological importance. Other references are to 'thorn', hazel, alder ('aller'), holly and 'other brushwood'. Ash seems to have been much less common then than now. Some of the forest was managed as wood-pasture, providing holly, ivy and oak for fodder during bad weather.

From the seventeenth century onwards, and perhaps earlier, Pickering woods were enclosed as coppices or 'haggs', with some 'dottards' or 'dotterells' retained for firewood. The commoners of Pickering owned grazing rights in all the king's woods except for the two hunting enclosures or 'hays'. They could also take green wood for house repair under supervision, and as much dry wood as they could carry. The haggs were meant to be fenced for seven years after cutting, but it is clear that tenants resented the loss of pasture and that fences were often pushed over or allowed to fall down. Some of the coppice wood was sold as charcoal, but a major use of Pickering wood, reflecting its proximity to North Sea ports, was for kippering herrings and making fish barrels.

Pickering's fame owed less to its woods than to its wild game. This was one of the last strongholds of boars and wolves in England. Boars evidently flourished under the Normans and early Plantagenets but failed to outlast them. One of the last reliable records is Henry III's dispatch in 1231 to the royal huntsmen to procure thirty boars and fifty hinds from Pickering and the nearby Forest of Galtres for the king's dinner table. Wolves seem to have outlived wild boars by at least another century and a half. Thirteen wolf hides, presumably native ones, were tanned there in 1394, at a cost of one shilling and ninepence.

By Tudor times, however, the wolf was only a memory and even the once thriving deer herds and rabbit warrens of Pickering had become much depleted. Unavailing attempts were made to ban hunting to allow stocks to recover. By the early 1600s, the area had ceased to be a hunting forest in any real sense; in the place of deer there were now vast flocks of sheep. Much of the land had been enclosed and to some extent tamed by then, producing a patchwork of woods, moors and fields that is still present today. The remaining common waste of Pickering was finally enclosed by Act of Parliament in 1785.

The Yorkshire Dales

Many woods of great conservation importance are surprisingly small. Nowhere is this more true than in the Yorkshire Dales, where two high-level ashwoods of no more than a few hectares each are National Nature Reserves, and a pair of modest ravines at Ingleton and a small wood lining a waterfall at Kisdon Force in Swaledale are listed in the NCC's *Nature Conservation Review* as nationally important woodland sites. The wonderful limestone scenery of the Ingleborough area, where three of the aforementioned woods lie, has long held a particular attraction for naturalists. **Ling Gill** (5ha) [12 acres] and **Colt Park Wood** (6.5ha) [16 acres] among the headwaters of the River Ribble are the classic examples of high-level ashwoods. In areas overrun by sheep, unfenced ashwoods can survive only in places that sheep cannot reach, conditions met at Ling Gill by a steep ravine and at Colt Park by a stone wall. Under the light shade of ash, these have become wonderfully flower-rich woods, natural rock gardens full of colourful plants of northern pastures and meadows such as baneberry, globeflower, mountain pansy and mossy saxifrage, amid more widespread woodland flowers such as wood anemone, primrose and early purple orchids.

The delights of Colt Park Wood are not apparent on the approach to the wood, for the dwarf ashes and their understorey of hazel, hawthorn and bird cherry seem to be rooted in a ledge of bare rock halfway up the grassy slope. It is only when one clambers into the wood (not a safe activity in wet weather, and one which needs permission at all times) that one finds that the rock has been worn by water along the joints to produce deep soil-filled fissures ranging from a few centimetres to a metre or more in width. Most limestone pavements are bare of trees, but Colt Park Wood may preserve their original wooded appearance.

Lower down the Dales, in Wharfedale, Wensleydale and Lower Swaledale, there are larger 'scar woods' of ash and hazel. Some have been preserved from enclosure and subsequent clearance by ancient common rights, either of pasture or wood gathering *(estover)*. **Bastow Wood** (52ha) [128 acres] overlooking the sweet pastures of Wharfedale near Grassington was originally not so much a wood as a field with scattered trees, and was for centuries heavily grazed by commoners' sheep and goats. Its name implies the former presence of lime, whose fibre or *bast* used to be stripped from the tree to make cheap matting. Perhaps grazing has turned Bastow Wood from a limewood to an ashwood. Another wood-pasture survives at **Oxenber Wood** (69ha) [160 acres] near Austwick where 'gait holders' still hold stock-grazing rights and the parishioners can, if they wish, gather sticks and stones from the wood.

Other woods were managed for wood production only, and instead of a grassy floor have carpets of woodland flowers and a dense underwood. **Freeholder's Wood**, where the commoners of Caperby gathered dry wood for fuel, is a rare example in the dales of a simple hazel coppice, once again in beneficial use through the good offices of the Yorkshire Dales National Park. **Grass Wood** (77ha) [190 acres] too is a coppice, and a complete contrast to its neighbour, Bastow Wood. It is perhaps the archetypal ancient wood of the limestone dales, containing a variety of limestone 'scars', scree and pavement, neglected coppice of ash, wych elm, and hazel, and a wonderfully lush ancient flora in which northern plants such as lady's mantles and nodding melic are prominent.

Parts of Grass Wood and Bastow Wood are ancient secondary woods overlying Celtic settlements and fields, and are also pockmarked by old mineshafts. Attempts to improve their timber quality began in the nineteenth century when part of Grass Wood was interplanted with beech and sycamore. These now blend with the native trees, but in the 1960s an attempt was made to replace part of the wood with plantations of beech and larch. Fortunately, these were not 'cleaned' subsequently so the result is a jumble of planted saplings and regenerating underwood. The Yorkshire Wildlife Trust, who now own the wood, have a major task in restoring the plantation areas to a more natural broadleaved woodland.

10

NORTHERN ENGLAND

Ancient woodland does not change character at the Scottish border. Rose arbours do not suddenly become thistle thickets. If a north-south divide exists at all, it lies elsewhere, or rather in two places. One is along the Highland boundary fault. The other would link southern Cumbria with the Humber. The latter line marks the approximate northern limit of native small-leaved lime, maple, yew, wild service tree, spindle, privet and buckthorn. As a result, north of that line woodland trees and shrubs suddenly become much fewer, a deficit only partly made good by northern shrubs such as bird cherry, juniper and one or two subalpine willows. However, woods do not become gradually poorer in trees, shrubs and flowers as one travels north. The ancient woods on the Morecambe Bay limestone are much richer than those on the gritstones of Lancashire (for that matter, Morrone Birkwood on the mountainside at Braemar has more species of flowers than an average oakwood in Cornwall). The subtleties of rock, soil, water and climate rarely operate in straight lines.

The Furness area of the Lake District is the most richly wooded part of northern England. There is more managed coppice and coppice-with-standards woodland here than in any other area north of the Midlands. There is greater variety too, from hanging yew-woods and oakwoods to ancient wood-pasture and mixed woods with sessile oakwoods on hillsides, with alders at the bottom and ash-hazel woods on the neighbouring ridge of limestone. Furness contains some of the most attractive English woods in a wonderful setting of mountains and lakes, with a great deal of woodland history visible on the ground in the banks and lanes, charcoal hearths, ruined forges and bobbin mills. In the middle lies perhaps England's most interesting plantation, Grizedale.

The charms of Northumberland and Durham are more muted, but their wooded dales and coastal denes can seem alive with birds and they are often interesting and unpredictable. It is an odd experience in parts of Tynedale and Upper Teesdale to search for rare orchids and other choice plants on the toxic debris from old lead mines. In Allendale I once found more specimens of the appropriately named death cap toadstool than in all my other woodland rambles put together. And despite their reputation as industrial heartlands, parts of Durham and most of Northumberland are wild, remote and, compared with the Lakes, virtually unvisited. The ancient woodlander is still an explorer in this part of England.

CUMBRIA

To the traveller, Cumbria looks better wooded than in fact it is, because much of the native woodland lies on valley sides above the settlements and roads. A large proportion of the county's ancient woodland lies within the Lake District

National Park. Here, much of the ancient woodland remains unplanted because of an agreement between the Forestry Commission and the Council for the Protection of Rural England made in 1936 to end state afforestation in the central Lake District.

The commonest kind of ancient woodland in Cumbria is upland birch-sessile oak woodland on acid soils, which has little underwood and a grassy or heath-like floor. Some woods contain base-rich enclaves at the base of a slope or where water runs over the surface, and these can support a sometimes sharply contrasted type of woodland with ash, wych elm and hazel. Outcrops of limestone are often marked by groves of yew. Most Cumbrian woods are former coppices, worked hard for 200 years but almost completely neglected in our own time apart from the depredations of two world wars and some underplanting with conifers, sycamore and beech. Many have become open through long overgrazing, where scattered thorns and inedible trees such as alder stand on bare hillsides marked on old maps as woodland.

The effects of geology are everywhere evident, in woods no less than the bare hills. The most densely wooded land is in the south of the county, on the gritstones of High Furness or the Carboniferous limestones at the head of Morecambe Bay. This concentration owes little to geography and nearly everything to history for the Furness woods were carefully managed as coppices at a time when the rest of the fells were being given over to sheep. Cumbria's important iron and tanning industries depended on them. Elsewhere Cumbrian woods occupy land too steep to be farmed, hanging onto valley sides above the stone-walled outbye land or bunched beneath rocky bluffs. Tiny strips of woodland penetrate bare hill areas in steep-sided valleys, known as clough or gill woods. Their importance belies their size for some of them are unaffected by planting or grazing and may well be primary woodland. A gill wood is a true moorland oasis, an island of fertility full of beautiful tall herbs such as globeflower and wood cranesbill, delicate ferns such as the misnamed beech and oak ferns (who has ever found beech fern under beech?), and sometimes even mountain plants such as yellow mountain saxifrage and alpine sorrel.

The early history of Cumbrian woods has been reviewed in print by J. E. Satchell [71]. Here, we shall confine our exploration to the three most important areas of ancient woodland.

The Furness Woods

It is said of the woods in the southern Lake District that a squirrel (which here are still red) could leap from Low Furness to Langdale without touching the ground. While that would require some mighty jumping today, it is still more or less true of the Furness Fells between Coniston Water and Windermere, for here native woodland covers the hilltops as well as the valley sides. This is the foundry land of the Industrial Revolution, the place that supplied charcoal for iron-smelting, bark for tanning and wood for a score of local industries. The Furness woods had three great advantages for the ironmasters: they were close at hand, they were on poor land not worth cultivating and they contained a great deal of the desired tree: oak. The use of oak charcoal for smelting dates back to the Middle Ages and, probably, to the Romans. Furness Abbey cut 'lytell short okes' for smelting iron and tenants had the right in some woods to make charcoal and smelt iron for their own use, so long as they confined themselves to the 'shreadings, tops, lops, crops and underwood', leaving the timber, where it existed at all, untouched [71]. Potash from wood was used to make soap. To this day common surnames in Furness include Woodburn and Ashburner.

The high prices paid for charcoal in the mid-eighteenth century, and also, later, for oak tanbark, preserved this well-wooded area from the sheep: to their owners, wood was worth more than mutton. The story of charcoal production in the Furness woods is too well known to repeat here. Readers of Arthur Ransome will be particularly well-versed in local woodland lore. What is perhaps worth emphasising is that these woods were not geared to charcoal production only. On the

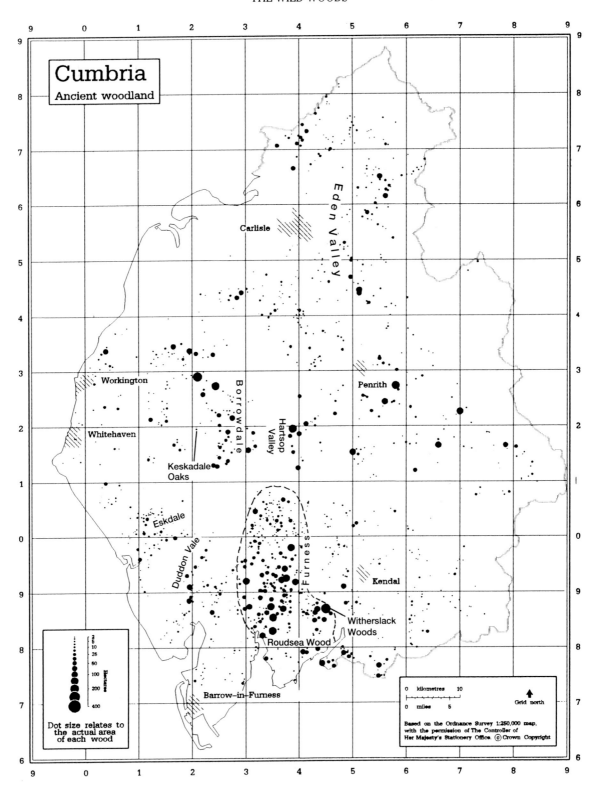

Cumbria
Ancient woodland

⇠Cumbria's ancient woodland is concentrated in the Furness District between Kendal and the River Duddon, and in Borrowdale and the Hartsop valley farther north. Outside the Lake District, the Eden valley and the valleys east of Carlisle bear a scatter of small woods. The plain of the Solway and the high Pennines in the east have very few woods

whole, their natural mixed composition was preserved because craftsmen found uses for trees other than oak. Satchell reproduces a wood merchant's list of sales from Town Head Wood near Finsthwaite for 1815-17 which, in addition to the big sales of bark, charcoal and hoops (in that order), records spokes, poles, 'smarts' (oak laths), rods, wood for pit props and swill baskets, powder wood and brush sticks, which used not only oak but alder, ash, birch and hazel, and probably also minor trees such as juniper and sallow [71]. Furness parishes were major centres for woodland crafts. According to Jones [72] a single parish in 1786 provided enough income for six charcoal burners, five chairmakers, four carpenters, four coopers, two candle-box makers, a turner, a clogger, a basketmaker and one, just one, wood-cutter! Elsewhere, large numbers of craftsmen must have been employed on making the 4,000 barrels needed annually by the gunpowder mill at Gatebeck near Kendal, or the quantities of woven hazel coal-baskets known as *corves*, used by the mining industry.

Coppicing in the Lake District began to decline from the 1850s onwards, and increasingly the stools were singled and the woods stored as high forest or replaced by plantations. Some small wood was still being cut on a commercial scale in the first few decades of this century, notably for dockyard use as packing crates and bundles of poles used for ships' fenders, while birch, a humble wood, continued to be used in vast quantities by the water-powered bobbin mills to supply Lancashire's cotton industry (though the more favoured wood was sycamore, often planted for the purpose). In our own times, by far the greatest use of native wood has been the original one: firewood, though some traditional crafts, such as charcoal burning and peg-making, are returning.

The limestone woods

Some of the loveliest woods in Cumbria lie near the head of Morecambe Bay. Here the principal rock is Carboniferous limestone, which supports a remarkably rich type of woodland on shallow soils similar to that of Silverdale in Lancashire. Ash, hazel and, locally, yew are the main trees, with scattered wych elm and small-leaved lime. On the steep slopes and crags, the woods become open and scrubby and possibly not very different from the natural woodland that colonised this area 10,000 years ago. The crags are one of the isolated places in western Britain where one finds rare whitebeams, including the local speciality *Sorbus lancastriensis*, a small tree with toothed oval leaves and crimson berries. But limestone alternates with a softer rock, Silurian slate, which weathers to produce deep, acid soils on which tall sessile oak replace ash as the dominant tree, with pockets of birch and alder in the wet hollows. In places one could almost lay a tape between the two different types of woodlands.

Two of the largest and best preserved of the Morecambe Bay woods are **Roudsea Wood** (69ha) [160 acres] and **Witherslack Wood**. Both names are Old Norse and no doubt date from the time when the Cumbrian coastlands were under Viking domination. Witherslack is *vidar slakki*, a wooded valley; Roudsea is Roud's *ea* or island, which suggests that the present bogs that surround it were once tidal marshes. So inhospitable was this coastal plain that as late as the nineteenth century travellers preferred to pick their way across the sandflats of the bay at low tide. The inaccessibility of these woods seems to have preserved them from intensive exploitation. Nevertheless, Roudsea was cut over from time to time to provide smelt-wood or charcoal, and its birches supplied Lancashire bobbin-mills. Witherslack, too, has hazel coppice, and parts of it have been commercially replanted. But the composition, if not the structure, of these woods is close to what one would expect in a

⇧ *The rainiest valley in England:*
Borrowdale in Cumbria looking towards
Seathwaite from Seatoller Wood. Bird cherry
(Prunus avium) *flowering in foreground. May*
(PETER WAKELY)

The trunks of these striking ash pollards at ⇧
Seatoller Wood are host to a large number of
mosses, liverworts and lichens confined to stands
of 'old forest'
(PETER WAKELY)

purely natural wood, a point to which I must
return.

At Roudsea and Witherslack we say farewell to
maple, dogwood, spindle, privet, wild service tree
and buckthorn (and to a familiar beast – the dormouse). This is also close to the northern climatic
limit of small-leaved lime. Indeed, it is only the
great age that lime can attain that preserves it so
far north for, as Donald Pigott has shown, the
present Cumbrian summers are too short and too
cool for this tree to ripen seed [73]. Cumbrian limes
are nearly all big coppice stools often shading a
pool of that other ancient woodland plant, the lily-

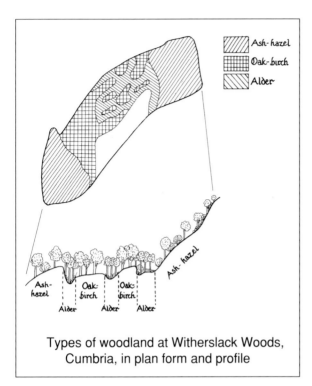

Ash-hazel
Oak-birch
Alder

Types of woodland at Witherslack Woods,
Cumbria, in plan form and profile

present today in roughly similar proportions. Birks concluded that Roudsea Wood is descended directly from the wildwood, an indication of the remarkable long-term stability of woodland. It is extremely unlikely that all of these trees would recolonise bare ground: lime certainly cannot. So, although the wood has been cut over often, as its large oak, lime and alder coppice stools prove, there seems never to have been selection in favour of particular species and so the natural composition has been maintained. Thus, we have at Roudsea a phenomenon barely appreciated twenty years ago: a wood that is nearly natural, *despite* the use that was made of it by generations of woodmen. The character of Roudsea Wood suggests that the wildwoods of these northern limestones were very different from the ash-dominated woods of today's limestone dales, and that in ancient woodland on lime-rich soils no single kind of tree is able to achieve mastery over its fellows.

Borrowdale

As you walk or drive along this beautiful wooded valley from Derwent Water to the head of the pass at Seathwaite you pass through successively rainier landscapes to the wettest inhabited place in England: poor Seathwaite, which receives 330cm (130in) of rain annually – at least five times as much as London and twice that even of Keswick only 12km (7.5 miles) away. In such conditions, intensive agriculture is of course impossible: this is cattle and sheep country, whose traditional life is described in the *Herries Chronicles* of its resident literary man, Hugh Walpole. Borrowdale was valued for wood production as well as grazings, and its largest woods, Great Wood, Johnny Wood, Frith Wood and High and Low Stile Woods, are enclosed by old stone walls. Until the Reformation, these were monastic woods, owned on the eastern side of the valley by Fountains Abbey and on the western by Furness Abbey. They were evidently managed as simple coppice, because a survey made in Tudor times mentions as timber only 'dotered' (that is, pollarded) and 'scrude' oak among a mixed underwood of birch, hazel, holly,

of-the-valley. The other special plant of Roudsea Wood is the large yellow sedge *Carex flava*, which is confined to a narrow zone where thin peat overlies the edge of the limestone. Perhaps these peculiar conditions have preserved the sedge from hybridisation with its nearest relatives, a fate that seems to have overtaken it in its few other British localities.

Apart from its natural beauty and wealth of flowers and trees, Roudsea Wood has another unusual quality. Because it is surrounded on three sides by bog, a record of its past is preserved in form of pollen grains deep inside the layer of peat. Dr H. J. B. Birks has investigated the pollen record in layers approximately 5,000 to 7,000 years old, the period of the 'forest climax' in Britain [74]. His results suggest a wood remarkably similar in composition to that of today: a mixture of oak, birch, elm, small-leaved lime, ash, alder and hazel with no overall dominant tree, and smaller quantities of pollen from maple, spindle, buckthorn, wild service and dogwood. All these trees and shrubs are

ash, hawthorn and blackthorn. Later, some oak timber was promoted from coppice stools for pit props, but much of the underwood continued to be cut over by charcoal burners, whose rounded hearths or pitsteads, made on level stone revetments, can still be seen. But after the Jacobite Lord Derwentwater lost his head in 1715, his successors increasingly took to planting and felling, especially at the lower end of the valley. Fortunately, the Borrowdale woods were among the early properties acquired by the National Trust. Ironically one of the reasons for the Trust's establishment was to prevent the felling of a commercial plantation by the shores of Derwent Water.

The Borrowdale Woods are hanging woods, craggy above, and, as one might expect, well watered by rocky streams. They are rather open with boulder screes, grassy clearings and patches of bracken. Most of the older oaks are overgrown coppice, last cut in about 1890, but there has been some regeneration since. Pockets of richer soil have hazel and ash, and, at Borrowdale Yews, the eponymous yew. Great Wood, at the relatively dry end of the valley overlooking Keswick, has some fine mature wych elms. King's How Wood, Stonethwaite Wood and Seatoller Wood are wood-pastures with some magnificent hammer-headed oak and ash pollards. These have long been used as sheep shelters and there is little but grass beneath the trees. It is in the enclosed woods, and on broken ground and rock ledges, that one finds a profusion of bilberry and ferns and the rare flowering plants of the area, which include alpine and intermediate enchanter's nightshades and wood fescue. In damp stream valleys you can find that exotic lakeland speciality, touch-me-not balsam, so named from the ripe fruit capsules that burst open violently when prodded. There is a pretty little moth, the netted carpet, that feeds exclusively on this plant.

The outstanding aspect of the Borrowdale woods is their flora of mosses, liverworts and lichens. The richest site for mosses and liverworts in all England is the Lodore Cascade below Shep-herd's Crag at the southern end of Derwent Water, where delicate liverworts, sensitive to the slightest drying, are kept moist in the perpetual spray. Away from waterfalls, the best woods, unsurprisingly, are the wettest. **Johnny Wood** (35ha) [86 acres] below a bluff near the head of the valley is full of moss-covered boulders, and has a particularly fine number of mosses and liverworts of extreme western or 'Atlantic' distribution. Good numbers of these plants are regarded as a sign of relatively undisturbed, primary woodland, especially when, as here, they occupy a south-facing slope where only tree cover preserves them from drought.

Borrowdale's equally precious flora of lichens is centred on old, well-lit trees. The ash pollards of Seatoller and the soaring oaks and elms of the Great Wood (43ha) [106 acres] boast some of the finest examples in Europe of the *Lobarion*, a spectacular community dominated by three species of large 'lungwort' lichens that often cover the trunks in angular lobes and frilly-edged plasters. These species are thought to be relics of ancient forest and, except in high rainfall areas, are characteristic of very old trees. With them on living trunks and branches grow lichens of western or Atlantic distribution. **Seatoller Wood** (85ha) [209 acres] contains 182 species of lichens, and a single tree might have more than 30. Their identification is, in general, a specialist undertaking, though the Lobarias and other large species are easy enough, but the unusual wealth and variety of these small plants should indicate why naturalists and scientists are excited by woods such as these in Borrowdale. Those on holiday in the Lakes may have cause to bemoan the fickle weather, but the dark skies and frequent downpours do at least allow some of Europe's richest plant communities to flourish there.

Before leaving Borrowdale, we should pay our respects to the nearby Newlands valley where the two highest oakwoods in England cling to the steep fellsides. These are **Birkrigg** (3ha) [7.4 acres] and **Keskadale Oaks** (6ha) [15 acres], 'discovered' by W. Leach, whose scientific paper about them [75]

209

↑*Keskadale Oaks in Cumbria: weatherbeaten mountain oaks whose dwarf size and contorted limbs recall those of Wistman's Wood on Dartmoor. May*
(PETER WAKELY)

has been one of the cornerstones of all subsequent botanical works about the Lake District. These are dwarf woods of wind-pruned, rain-drenched sessile oaks on shallow stony ground, reminiscent of Wistman's Wood on Dartmoor. Mosses cover the rocks, but most of the rare Atlantic species of Borrowdale are missing. Keskadale Oaks was cut over repeatedly in the past, apparently for tanbark, but Leach demonstrated that *natural* coppicing can also occur after the destruction of the old shoots by fire, fungal attack or even from rolling boulders. The NCC's *Nature Conservation Review* rates these

woods highly, commenting that 'these woodlands represent relict fragments of high-level sessile oakwood and may be near the altitudinal limit for oak woodland in western Britain'.

DURHAM
The great majority of ancient and natural woods in Durham and its metropolitan neighbours lie on steep slopes unsuitable for agriculture and difficult for forestry. Some line major river valleys, especially the upper Tees and the Derwent; others line the banks of upland streams, where they are known as gill woods. Still others fill the great coastal limestone ravines or denes. Three woods stand out for their rich wildlife and magnificent setting: **Castle Eden Dene** (described below), **Horsleyhope Ravine** in a mighty chasm in the Derwent Valley (including the tangle of gill woods known collectively as Pontburn Woods) and

Shipley and Great Woods (63ha) [165 acres] in Teesdale. This latter is believed to be near-natural woodland with a wide range of trees of different ages. Its formerly superb flora of old forest lichens has unfortunately been diminished by Dutch elm disease, which has stricken most of the best trees.

Some exquisite limestone woods can be found along the banks of the Tees and its tributary becks, especially either side of Barnard Castle. These are northern ash-wych elm woods with an abundance of that ubiquitous Durham weed, the sycamore. In the open glades and flushes, a rich and colourful flora is reminiscent of the Yorkshire and Derbyshire Dales, with large grazing-sensitive plants such as greater bellflower, wood cranesbill, globeflower, melancholy thistle, marsh hawk's-

beard and wood forget-me-not. That sweet little lily, the yellow star-of-Bethlehem, is quite frequent locally in the early spring, keeping company with flowers such as moschatel and toothwort. The tiny woods of Upper Teesdale, set in an elemental scene of rock and water at around 305m (1,000ft) in altitude, seem to be near-natural fragments of

Durham contains about 4,120ha (9,965 acres)⇓
of ancient woodland, of which three-quarters is
still natural. Woods trace the course of the Rivers
Tees and Wear. The only large woods are
Castle Eden Dene near Peterlee and Horsleyhope
Ravine below Consett

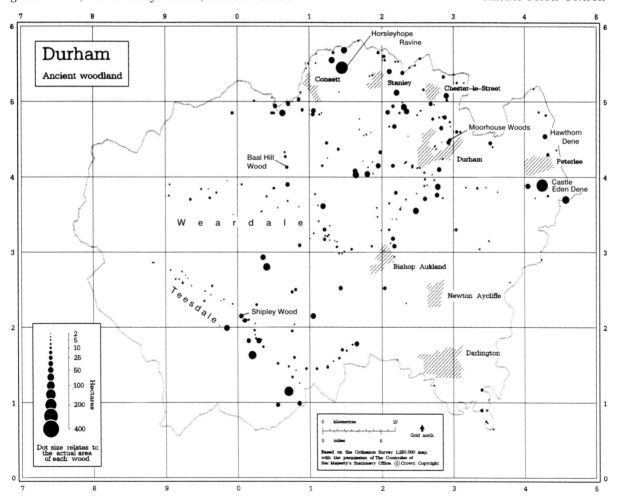

earlier times although they differ interestingly from one another. **Brocker's Gill** is an ashwood, **Millbeck Wood** a birch-hazel gill, formerly cut over as coppice and grading at the upper end into juniper scrub, **Park End Wood** is a wet birch and alder wood, and **Sun Wood** a simple northern birchwood. To these we should add the juniper wood near High Force waterfall which may be one of the most ancient woods in the land, for pollen evidence proves that junipers were growing here in the late Ice Age landscape, 10,000 years ago.

Weardale is much less wooded than Teesdale despite its Royal Forest status in the Middle Ages. Today, this landscape of grouse muir, sheep-walk and industrial ruins has only scraps of native woodland along the gills and in enclosures on the valley sides. It appears that Weardale was almost treeless even when the Bishop of Durham's hounds were pursuing roe deer and wolves over the fells. Contemporary accounts, which have been pieced together by Drury [76] to produce a portrait of Weardale in the high Middle Ages, are about grazing, mining and hunting rights, not wood-cutting. The Weardale deerhounds were greyhounds, accustomed to hunting by sight, not smell, and hence useful only in open country. The bishop probably imported much of his building timber, because although he owned a number of enclosed parks in the County Palatinate, only Wolsingham Park seems to have been well stocked with big oaks. Very little medieval wood-pasture has survived in Durham. The trees of Raby Park, for example, are almost entirely of planted origin. **Baal** (pronounced 'Bale') **Hill Wood** and **Backstone Bank**, on the steep west-facing bank of Waskerley Beck overlooking Tunstall Reservoir, is perhaps the most complete surviving example of Weardale woodland. This is a bluebell wood. Its history has been traced back to Tudor times, when much of it was managed as oak coppice. The wood lies on acid Millstone grit with runnels of lime-rich water. It is full of roe deer, and hence without much underwood, and the more palatable plants, which include a few unexpected small-leaved lime stools high up by Spring Gill, are restricted to stream channels.

The woods that line the majestic sweep of the Derwent gorge near Crooked Oak are among the most remarkable in northern England. Some of the banks are virtually inaccessible, and the very rich lichen flora of the mature trees, apparently little affected by the fumes and dust of Consett steelworks, suggests that they may be natural high forest, not much modified from its original state (though, as usual in Durham, sycamore has made itself at home). The Woodland Trust's **Pontburn Woods** (24ha) [59 acres] is a meeting of wooded gorges 'like a three-pronged wishbone' with Hamsterley Viaduct towering above it. Some replanting with conifers has taken place, but these again are woods of largely natural character, humid and shady with an underworld of primitive plants – ferns, liverworts and mosses. This is one of the red squirrel strongholds in the north-east.

The lowland woods of Durham need not detain us long. Much of the Coal Measures is poorly wooded, while planting for amenity and forestry has altered the character of most of the larger ancient woods. One natural wood of considerable historical interest is **Moor House Wood** (24ha) [59 acres] on either side of the A1 motorway near Durham City. This is in fact three contiguous ancient woods which appear in almost their present form on a map of 1570 and lie partly on the site of the Durham Priory's deer park (whose bank runs through Raintonpark Wood). This is evidently an old coppice, partly clear-felled and replanted in Georgian times and cut over again during World War II, since when it has regenerated naturally. Despite its erratic past, the wood remains a typically ancient mix of acid and basic and wet and dry soils. Some of the small-leaved lime stools were probably alive when the 1570 map was made. There are also large hornbeam and beech stools on the banks of the River Wear, well outside their native range and so presumably planted, but later cut over indiscriminately as coppice along with the other trees. This wood is not rich in flowers except along the gills, but, so the National Trust's literature informs us, it is noted for 'very local flies, a local Harvestman and Bug'.

Castle Eden Dene

AREA: 193ha (477 acres)

STATUS: National Nature Reserve

ACCESS: Open to the public

TYPE: Northern calcareous ash-wych elm and oak-hazel woodland

GRID REFERENCE: NZ 434396

It is hard to envisage a place which more perfectly captures the vision of picturesque beauty in a wild natural setting that so enraptured nineteenth-century tourists than this magnificent wooded ravine. Castle Eden Dene was well known to the select few from the 1820s onwards, but its real heyday began in 1850 when its owner, the Reverend John Burdon, laid out carriageways and bridges through the ravine and opened it to the public. In Victorian times, a genuine admiration of wild, elemental scenery went hand-in-hand with a desire to take some of it home to adorn rock gardens and cabinets. Engravings of the era show carriages of top-hatted and parasoled visitors, sweeping past grottos and cascades and hanging woods, pausing now and again to pack flowers and ferns into their hampers or trying out their yodelling skills among the echoing rocks. At the end of their journey, they could find a tea of new baked bread, butter and eggs at one of the cottages then standing at Denemouth, or a tankard of Nimmo's beer, brewed from Dene water piped uphill to the brewhouse above the crags [77].

The rocks of Castle Eden Dene are of yellow Magnesian limestone capped by boulder clay, soft enough to be cleft by streams and sculpted by the elements into fissured cliffs, hollows and caves. The visitor, walking in the footsteps of the Victorian naturalists, passes rock formations with names such as White Rock, Bruce's Ladder, Black Bull's Hole, The Seven Chambers and Pegjellima's Cave. One can watch geology in action as the burn continues to slice through limestone into clay,

causing spectacular slippages, mud slides and rock falls. One particular pile of broken rocks is supposed to have slipped from the Devil's apron strings as he conveyed a load of stone to Durham to sabotage the building of the cathedral. Nearby is Gunner's Pool, a 'deep blue pellucid pool in a bason of the rock' which drowned an unfortunate Mr Gunner many years ago. Those who brave the Dene on the coldest days in winter will be rewarded by icescapes of frozen water, crystalline chandeliers and organ-pipes hanging from frosted yellow rock.

The Dene was famous for rare plants and insects. A small brown butterfly dubbed the Castle Eden Argus was once thought to occur nowhere else in the world, though it has since been found elsewhere in northern England and is now believed to be a race rather than an individual species. A regular entomological visitor of the 1820s and 1830s, one Captain Blomer, discovered two moths then new to science: the barred carpet and his very own Blomer's rivulet. Fifty-six species of birds have bred here and migratory species regularly use the Dene as a convenient shelter after landfall. Botanists can still admire a splendid range of flowers and ferns of woodland, marsh and limestone rocks, although some of the once well-known orchids of Castle Eden – fly, sword-leaved helleborine and lady's slipper – are now either rare or extinct.

Much of the woodland, especially the steep 'hangers' lining the ravine, is ancient and natural and has probably never been wholly cleared. Some of it seems to be natural scrub of ash, hazel and yew, prevented from maturing into woodland by the perpetual instability of the underlying boulder clay. Ash is the dominant tree at Castle Eden, with wych elm as a principal partner. The latter remained disease-free until the 1980s and, although most of the trees have since succumbed, the roots remain healthy and the elm has a future as managed coppice. There are small stands of hitherto healthy hazel – though its enemy, the grey squirrel, has lately arrived in numbers – spring-line alders and a scattering of shipbuilders' pedunculate

⇧The interplay of rock, water and woodland of the Durham denes form one of the most attractive woodland scenes. Here the Castle Eden Burn has cut through boulder clay and soft Magnesian limestone, producing a shady defile dominated by wych elm. May
(KEITH KIRBY)

oak. Sycamore is too common but, under the present-day policy of encouraging oak and hazel by thinning and planting, it is kept in check. Above all, perhaps, the Dene is a place of wild yews, whose tufted dark green masses make a delightful contrast to the ash trees in new leaf. The yew groves of Castle Eden are among the most extensive in the country.

The apparent wildness of Castle Eden Dene is an illusion. In the eighteenth century, small-bore wood was cut in quantity to make bobbins and weaving rollers for a nearby sailcloth factory, or as fuel for limekilns. Much of the oak timber was felled in the last century, bound for the nearby shipyards of Hartlepool. The twentieth century saw the general shift from woodmanship to silviculture, which meant that the natural woods became neglected, except as an occasional source of timber, while some of the native woodland on better soils and less steep inclines was replaced by blocks of larch and beech. Meanwhile, the Dene's popularity as a tourist attraction waned. The seaward end, for long the main entrance, was blocked by a road embankment in 1926 and the rock pools and clean sand of an earlier era became part of Durham's infamous black beach of colliery waste. Even the Castle Eden Burn, with its crystal clear whirlpools, natural limestone pavings and pebblebeds, became a conduit for coal dust from the inland Shotton Colliery.

The last twenty years have witnessed a gradual improvement in its fortunes. A new town, Peterlee, grew up around the head of the Dene, transforming it from a rustic retreat to a kind of wild back garden for the town. Recognising the attendant dangers, the Peterlee Development Corporation, which inherited the Dene in 1951, designated it a Local Nature Reserve. Little was done to improve access, however, until 1969, when an advisory committee was set up to conduct a scientific survey and begin to repair the old Victorian paths and terraces. A visitor centre with information about the Dene and its wildlife was built in 1981. When the day came for the corporation to be wound up in 1985, the custodianship of the Dene passed to the Nature Conservancy Council, which is carrying on the latterday good work with the help of a special government fund and an energetic wardening team.

TYNE AND WEAR

In this industrial county, extensive ancient woodland is restricted to the rural south-west, with smaller woods to the south-east of Gateshead and along the river valleys of the Team and the Wear. There is very little remaining woodland north of the Tyne. Woods near Newcastle have long provided timber for shipbuilding and coppiced wood for pit props, charcoal and tanbark. A traditional use for hazel was for making coal baskets. Tyneside industry goes back a long way. Lands Wood in Blaydon is pockmarked with medieval bell-pits, the collapsed remains of small mines, some of which have become deep ponds. The larger woods have all been replanted to varying degrees, first with ship oak and, increasingly after 1850, with conifers. **Chopwell Wood**, much the largest ancient wood in the county, supplied timber for a line of mighty ships of war, including the seventeenth-century *Royal Sovereign*. Most of the wood is now a conifer plantation, though gnarled old oaks and yews still twist from Chopwell Crags.

Amenity is an important use of woods in this area, and several are owned by borough councils and managed as country parks. **Thornley Wood** (14.8ha) [36.5 acres] near Gateshead is a particularly well-preserved Coal Measures wood of sessile oak with a great deal of birch, hazel and holly on the upper slopes and alder, wych elm and ash farther down near Thornley Beck. Despite its proximity to a large conurbation, it supports many woodland animals and birds including red squirrels, woodcock, nuthatch, redstart and badgers.

CLEVELAND

The awesome petrochemical plants of Teesmouth are but a few miles away from wild moorland country, the great north-facing rampart of the North Yorkshire moors. It is by the fast-running moorland becks, spreading out below in fenny vales, that most of Cleveland's ancient woods occur. At the end of the Ice Age these streams, made swollen and powerful by glacial meltwater, cut through the surface boulder clay and into the underlying shales and sandstones. The woodland that subsequently colonised these gills used to be cut over as coppice, probably mostly for firewood. With the advent of domestic coal they fell into neglect and a new generation of self-sown trees has sprung up among the old stools.

Thorpe Wood (25ha) [62 acres], a typical gill

wood gathered around a small beck, is a nature reserve owned by Cleveland County Council. It was present in 1719 when it was managed as coppice. Clear-felled in World War I and then neglected until 1960, when some conifers and sycamore were planted, it is now a wood of young, largely natural, growth, of oaks, ash, wych elm and hazel which are developing into high forest. Like other woods in the area, it has ferny nooks and banks of golden saxifrage, and a number of uncommon plants such as wood vetch, great bitter-cress and Dutch rush.

NORTHUMBERLAND

Northumberland is a county of huge upland plantations, covering hill and dale indifferently, and tiny ancient woods, virtually confined to the main river valleys. Nowhere else in England are ancient woods so subordinate to plantations: here they amount to only 1 per cent of the total land under trees. Nor are they so insignificant: nearly three-quarters of them measure only 10ha (25 acres) or less. No ancient woods exceed 100ha (247 acres) and only a dozen or so are between 50 and 100ha (123-247 acres). Two-fifths of the ancient woodland has been replanted, mostly since 1945. In some instances, such as at Holystone in the Harbottle Moors, afforestation has taken place between isolated ancient woods, leaving the latter as islands of native vegetation within a much larger plantation. Woodland clearance is insignificant; twenty-seven woods have experienced some clearance, mostly for agriculture but in a few cases also for quarrying and urban development.

Northumberland woods occasionally have names such as 'hagg' and 'spring', which suggest former intensive management as coppice, but more often their names are simply taken from a nearby farm and they were probably used mainly by the local farmer as a source of wood. Streams (here, Scottish burns, not Yorkshire becks) and woods often share the same name. Thus Dipton Burn Wood is named after the stream of that name, which is in turn named after a tiny settlement called Dipton. The northern strain is present in the

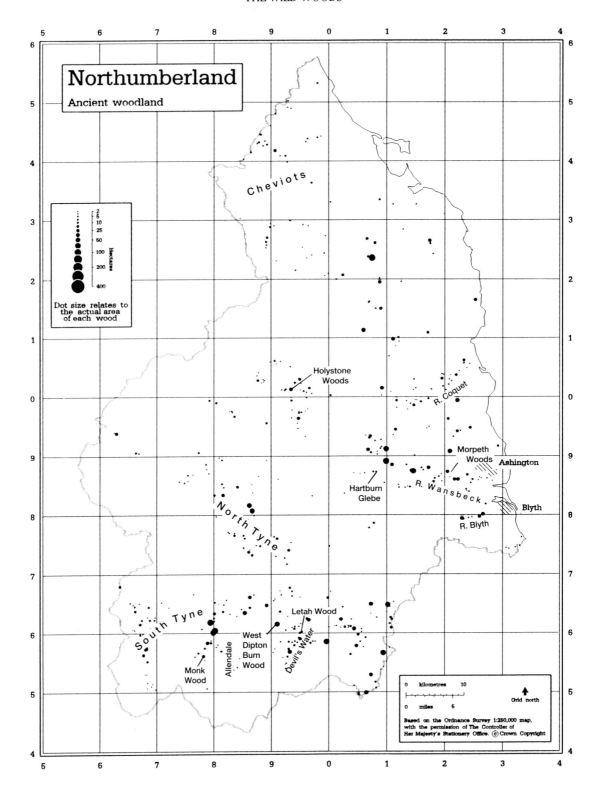

Northumberland

Ancient woodland

Hectares

2
5
10
25
50
100
200
400

Dot size relates to
the actual area
of each wood

Cheviots

Holystone
Woods

R. Coquet

Morpeth
Woods

Ashington

Hartburn
Glebe

R. Wansbeck

Blyth

North Tyne

R. Blyth

South Tyne

Letah Wood

West
Dipton
Burn
Wood

Devil's Water

Allendale

Monk
Wood

0   kilometres   10

0   miles   5

Grid north

Based on the Ordnance Survey 1:250,000 map,
with the permission of The Controller of
Her Majesty's Stationery Office. © Crown Copyright

⇦ Most of Northumberland's ancient woods are situated along steep river valleys. From south to north these are the Rivers South Tyne (including Allendale), the North Tyne, the Blyth, the Wansbeck and the Coquet. No ancient woods exceed 100ha (247 acres), and the great majority are smaller than 10ha (24.7 acres)

names of banks – *scars* or *haughs* (pronounced 'huffs'), of narrow ravines called gills or *linns*, or in narrow belts of trees called *shaws*.

The history of Northumberland's woods has not been studied in any detail, and there are no Domesday records for this county. In all likelihood, the county lost most of its woods in prehistory, and those that survive show few signs of systematic management. Ancient woodbanks, boundary pollards and even old coppice stools are scarce. Some woods were cut over to provide small round-wood for firewood and other purposes, but there seems to have been little discrimination between trees: timber trees such as oak were coppiced along with the rest. Because there was little apparent attempt to nurture the more useful trees, ancient Northumbrian woods have generally remained as mixed woods, usually dominated by oak or ash, with abundant sycamore and stands of alder on wet ground. 'Typical' Northumbrian woods are narrow and steep, lining a steep bank above a fast-flowing burn. The underwood is usually rather sparse. A few woods are descended from enclosed medieval parks, notably Hesleyside Park in Tynedale – although its magnificent beeches were planted in the eighteenth century. **Monk Wood** in Allendale was part of Whitfield Park and consists of open-grown ash, wych elm, sycamore and huge 250-300-year-old sessile oaks towering above a recently acquired thicket of rhododendron. Its exceptionally rich lichen flora, including abundant lungwort, suggests that this is a primary wood relatively little modified from its natural state.

The predominantly Carboniferous rocks of this county are a mixture of limestone and lime-rich shales, and acid gritstones and Coal Measures. In wooded gorges, many different rock types may be present, producing a range of natural woodland from dense stands of ash-wych elm in base-rich places to sparser sessile oak, hazel and holly on the poorer soils. **Broomhaugh Wood**, for example, lies on the border between acid Millstone Grits and calcareous sandstones. The latter supports what is technically wet ash-wych elm woodland, though the elm component has been decimated by disease, and alderwood. On more acid soils, there are sessile oak standards with abundant sycamore and a scatter of straggly hazels. Much of the wood is ungrazed and wet, but the lack of recent coppicing or thinning has produced a shade flora dominated by green leaf carpets of dog's mercury, wild garlic, non-flowering brambles and buckler-ferns. Riverside banks of greater wood-rush are a characteristic feature of these northern woods. Mosses are prominent, but less so than in the much rainier Lake District. Northumbrian woods are generally rich in birdlife and the larger ones, such as Broomhaugh, are still graced by the native red squirrel.

Most woods are variants on these basic themes. One of the largest stretches of ancient woodland in the county lies along the conjoined River Allen shortly before it reaches the South Tyne. Here the National Trust's **Morralee Wood** faces the Trust's nature reserve of **Briarwood Banks**. Although these woods are much-modified by replanting with beech and conifers, and stricken by elm disease, the steeper slopes and parts of the valley floor still have extensive native oak and ash woodland, and contain rare lichens, beetles and slugs confined to old forest. The woods are interspersed with bracken glades, limestone bluffs and old meadows on terraced banks, while at the centre of Morralee Wood is a large artificial tarn.

West Dipton Burn Wood, just south of Hexham, is more gorge-like in character. Ash, alder and hazel occupy the richer soils near the burn, but this is otherwise a sessile oakwood which is partly high forest of close-set maiden trees and partly former coppice, without any obvious internal compartmentalisation. West Dipton has a good collection of the more characteristic plants of Northumbrian ancient woodland, most of which occur on permanently moist soil near the burn and include wood fescue, wood vetch, alternate-leaved golden saxifrage, wood stitchwort, mountain melic and large bitter-cress. Not far away is the small but delightful **Letah and Nunsbrough Woods** (30ha) [74 acres], composed of oak, ash and dead elm clothing the steep Devil's Water (not Old Nick but a Norman family named D'Eivell). The winding river carves steep 'scars' in the hillside while depositing sediment on the flat 'haughs', some of which were cultivated for potatoes during World War II, though they have now scrubbed over again. Letah Wood, probably named after its millrace or leat, is Northumberland's only wild daffodil wood: a fluttering and dancing bank of them graces a particularly tight circuit of the river. These woods have seen much violence in their time. On a haugh known as The Linnels was fought the battle of Hexham, one of the armoured clashes of the Wars of the Roses, while just to the south is the place where the Saxon King Penda defeated and killed the 'last of the Britons', King Cadwalladr, at the battle of Heavenfield in AD 634. Nunsbrough itself was probably some sort of castle – 'brough' means a fortified place.

Pennine birch-sessile oakwoods of decidedly upland character occur on the poorer grits and sandstones. **Holystone Oaks** is the outstanding site, though it is not one wood but three – plus a large grove of junipers as a bonus – in the heart of the 'blacklands' of Harbottle Moors. They are almost pure oak; two are evidently open grown and were probably former wood-pasture, but the third is full of multi-stemmed and twisty trees, suggesting former coppice. There is no underwood at all.

The trees are rooted in bilberry, bracken and grass, brightened in June by the white starry flowers of chickweed wintergreen.

There is room to mention just two more small but interesting Northumbrian woods. **Cotting Wood**, Castle Morpeth, is a valley wood with a broad sedgy bottom brimming with a miniature 'coal forest' of giant horsetails. Its main claim to fame is its association with the Tudor naturalist and herbalist William Turner, who in 1548 wrote of 'a wodde besyde Morpeth called Cottingwod' where one could gather a strange herb he named the One Berry or 'Libardsbayne', which we know today as herb paris. 'It hath foure leaves lyke unto great plantaine, and in the overmost top a litle blacke bery lyke a blacke morberry, but blacker and greater.' It is pleasant to be able to report that the libardsbayne still grows at Cottingwod, possibly in much the the same place.

Our second example is **Hartburn Glebe Wood**, 'glebe' indicating its former ownership by the Church of England. This is a romantic wood, crossed by the 'Devil's Causeway', the Roman military road to Hadrian's Wall, known here as Harpeth Loaning. Two hundred years ago, the vicar of Hartburn, Dr Sharpe, created walkways along the Hart Burn, including a fine stone footbridge. He also adapted a tall cave in the cliffs as a changing room for bathers, connected to the water's edge by a tunnel. Coy, fig-leaved statues of Adam and Eve once stood in recesses in the cave walls. There is also an allegedly bottomless pool and, until 1958, when the church chopped them down, two silver firs called the 'King and Queen of Northumberland', which were said to be the tallest trees in the county. This wood is being restored by its new owner, the Woodland Trust.

11

WALES

The ancient woods of Wales are dominated by oak and line the steep sides of river valleys. In South Wales they are most extensive in the upper reaches, but in the north, the valleys of Teifi and Rheidol, the Afon Artro and the Vales of Maentwrog and Conwy are well-wooded along much of their length. This chapter looks briefly at each Welsh county in turn before taking a closer look at three kinds of woodland that are particularly characteristic of Wales: the Snowdonian oakwoods, with their 'Atlantic' flora of mosses and liverworts, the montane beechwoods of Abergavenny and the limestone ashwoods of the Brecon Beacons and elsewhere.

The history of ancient woods in Wales has been related in a fine book by Dr William Linnard [78]. In late Saxon times, parts of Wales were much better wooded than today. Welsh laws written down in the late twelfth or early thirteenth centuries indicate that Welsh woodmanship could be quite sophisticated, and that woods were valuable properties. Coppicing and lopping techniques are mentioned, while Gruffydd ap Cynan, King of Gwynedd, is said to have 'planted old woods' and orchards, and created woodland gardens. In 1351, the first recorded forestry experiment in Britain was undertaken to determine the ideal height to cut coppice. Despite such early evidence of woodmanship, however, the story of Welsh woodland is one of gradual decline, attributed by the Tudor traveller Leland to uncontrolled felling, browse damage by livestock and deliberate clearance. It would seem that the Welsh made less distinction between woodland and wood-pasture than the English, and that overgrazing has been a widespread problem for many centuries, gradually denuding the hills of their tree cover by preventing regeneration.

Many Welsh woods were preserved by industry. Lead-smelters and ironmasters have been blamed for destroying woodland, but the record suggests that they often understood how woods work and took good care to conserve them. Industrial woods were managed on a coppice rotation to supply charcoal and bark and, later, pit wood. Sheep were kept out by well-maintained stone walls. The industrial valleys of Glamorgan remained well-wooded with native trees so long as coppice wood was needed. It was only when the system fell into disuse in the late nineteenth century, that the woods of the Rhondda, Ebbw Vale and other valleys began to share the fate of the woods of rural Powys and became increasingly open, park-like, bracken-infested, sheep shelters. World War I stripped many Welsh woods of their timber, even immature oaks being felled in large quantities to provide pit props and cogwood for the South Wales coalfields. The war left large areas of woodland devastated and many were later replanted with fast-growing conifers.

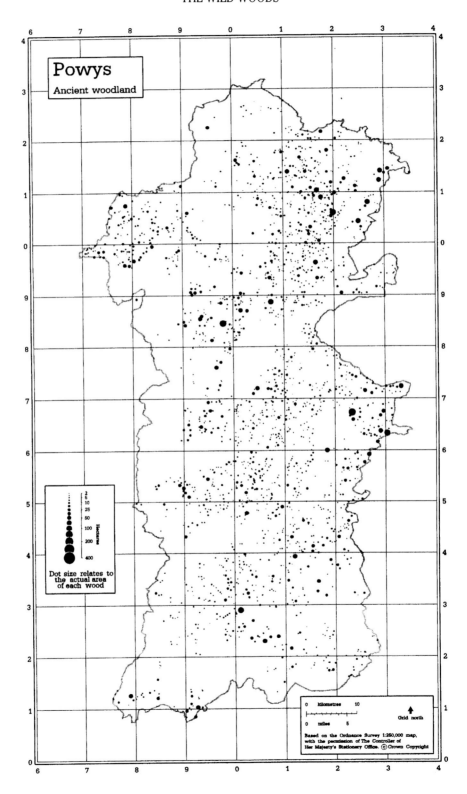

Powys

Ancient woodland

2
5
10
25
50
100
200
400

Hectares

Dot size relates to
the actual area
of each wood

0   kilometres   10

0   miles   5

Grid north

Based on the Ordnance Survey 1:250,000 map,
with the permission of The Controller of
Her Majesty's Stationery Office. © Crown Copyright

A TOUR OF THE WELSH COUNTIES

The predominant ancient woodland of 'wild Wales' is of sessile oak with birch and rowan. Despite their rugged character, most woods are close to roads, villages and farmhouses and were cut over frequently in the past, often supplying fuel or charcoal to nearby mills and smithies or bark for tanneries. In recent times, heavy grazing has severely limited their natural regeneration, though an increasing proportion is now being fenced against stock by conservation bodies.

I reserve the woods of Gwynedd, where many of the finest oakwoods occur, for separate mention below. The sessile oakwoods of Dyfed rival those of Gwynedd in their rugged beauty and rich communities of Atlantic mosses, liverworts and lichens. Among the most exciting are the hanging woods of the steep Rheidol valley; Ty Canol Wood in Pembroke, a Tolkeinesque place of contorted mossed oaks and deep chasms; Pengelli Forest, also in Pembroke, a fantasy of natural oak sculpturing from ancient coppice stools; and Penderi with its extraordinary man-high cliff oaks whose growth follows the contours of the rock face. There are also fine, mellow woods along the vale of Teifi, ivy-festooned wooded bluffs above tidal creeks in the old counties of Carmarthen and Pembroke, and some extraordinary wind-pruned dwarf woods clinging to the sea-cliffs of Cribach Bay. Dynefor Park is one of the great ancient wood-pastures, with deer and, until recently, wild white cattle grazing beneath mighty ancient oaks and beeches.

Powys is mostly sparsely inhabited hill country whose woods are also predominantly of oak and more often than not used to shelter stock. Many ancient woods were formerly coppiced to pro-

⟨▭Powys is mainly sparsely inhabited hill land. Woodland has become extremely fragmented: small ancient woods abound, but very few exceed 100ha (247 acres). Montgomery in the north is the most densely wooded district, but nearly half of its woods have been replanted or have failed to regenerate since 1930. Shelter for sheep is the main use of woodland throughout the county

duce charcoal and (especially in Radnor) bark for the tanneries. As elsewhere in Wales, Powys woods tend to be small and confined to steep valley sides. In the east, there are steep sandstone stream valleys or dingles, and hilltop woods similar to those across the border in Herefordshire. Many woods were virtually stripped of their timber during World War I, and the losses were increasingly made good thereafter by plantations of conifers. Losses to agriculture were also considerable: no other part of Wales so eagerly took up the challenge of successive governments after 1945 to produce more food. Generous grants to reclaim agricultural land were taken up avidly and they led to widespread woodland clearance. Neither steep slopes nor sodden ground saved the woods; with astounding virtuosity hillsides as steep as a house roof were put to the plough and woods too wet to walk through were successfully drained.

In Montgomery, the wildlife interest of woods has also suffered severely at the hands of enthusiastic foresters. Every fashion in forestry can be traced in these heavily managed woods. Natural diversity remains in the dank woodland gorges of the far north-west with mosses, liverworts and lichens enough to rival the best in Gwynedd. Fine spacious, park-like woods survive at Gregynog near Newtown and in the extensive oakwoods and parkland of Powys Castle in the east near Welshpool.

South of the Brecon Beacons, the upper valleys of the Rivers Nedd and Mellte support one of the most magnificent gorge woodlands in Britain. Mostly owned by the Forestry Commission, these spectacular waterfalls and cliff woods of oak, ash and small-leaved lime can be visited on a series of challenging paths. In the north of Brecknock the ancient oakwoods near Elan Village were purchased recently by the Royal Society for the Protection of Birds (RSPB). There is nowhere better to see the contrast between large mature oaks and the regrowth from fellings made during two world wars.

The old county of Glamorgan (now the separate counties of Mid-, West- and South Glamorgan) is the most industrialised in Wales, and its ancient

221

THE WILD WOODS

⇩*Coedydd Maentwrog, Gwynedd in October.
Decades of grazing by sheep and goats has
removed the understorey and reduced the
ground flora to little more than bracken, moss and
hair-grass.* (PETER WAKELY)

woods have been correspondingly hard-worked. Oak, in particular, was in constant demand for charcoal to smelt iron and lead ore, pit props for the mining industry and bark for tanning leather. This led in the Vale of Glamorgan to a greater degree of organisation than usual in Welsh woods, with woodbanks, ditches and compartments comparable to those in English woods. Old estate maps suggest local idiosyncrasies however. 'Woods with grazing' may be synonymous with wood-pasture, but 'woods with arable' sounds like an old continental practice known in Germany as *hackwald,* which was once widespread in remote, hilly countryside where agriculture was difficult without the aid of forestry. Field crops, usually rye but also wheat, oats and potatoes, were sown in autumn in woodland glades after the ground had first been fertilised by the ashes from 'cut-and-slash' coppice wood. The method is very labour intensive, requiring a great deal of hand hoeing, sowing and reaping. In Germany, former *hackwald* is often marked by stands of broom. It would be interesting to determine whether this is also the case in South Wales.

Gwent stands apart from the rest of Wales for its magnificent mixed broadleaved woods in the Wye Valley and the lowlands west of Chepstow, and for the unique montane beechwoods at the heads of the valleys. Its ancient woods share much in common with neighbouring Gloucestershire, and together with the county of Glamorgan, Gwent's woods show a greater degree of past systematic management than most Welsh woods. On the other hand, Gwent shares fully the twin problems of most uplands in Britain of excessive grazing and the remorseless stripping of native timber during the wartime emergencies, which has resulted in the neglect of small woods and restocking with conifers in the larger ones.

The county of Clwyd consists of the old counties of Flint and most of Denbighshire, plus a small part of Merioneth. Much of Clwyd is upland, rising on the Berwyn to over 800m (2,624ft). There are considerable areas of improved and unimproved grassland, heather moor and blanket bog, as well

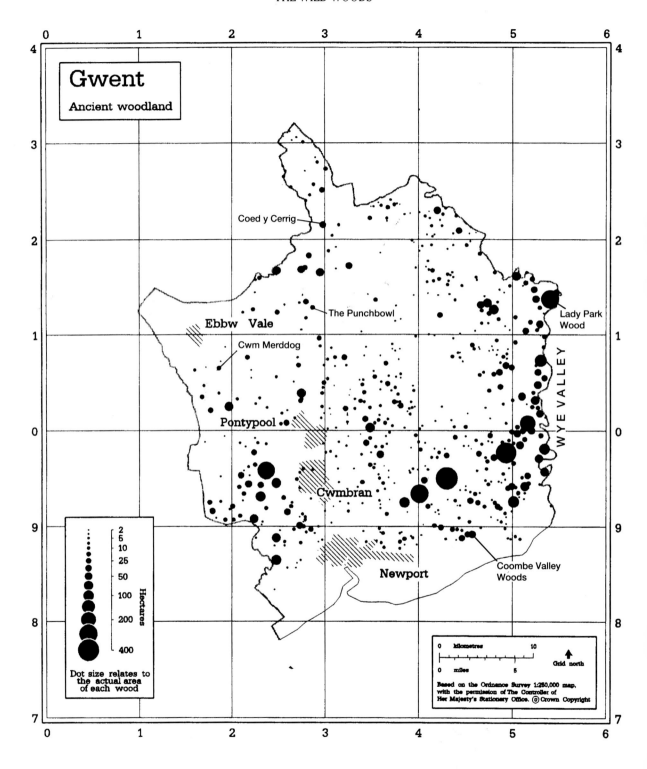

Gwent

Ancient woodland

Coed y Cerrig

The Punchbowl

Ebbw Vale

Cwm Merddog

Lady Park Wood

WYE VALLEY

Pontypool

Cwmbran

Coombe Valley Woods

Newport

2
5
10
25
50
100
200
400

Hectares

Dot size relates to
the actual area
of each wood

0   kilometres   10

0   miles   5

Grid north

Based on the Ordnance Survey 1:250,000 map,
with the permission of The Controller of
Her Majesty's Stationery Office. © Crown Copyright

Gwent is among the most densely wooded Welsh counties, and contains some of the largest ancient woods. It is also exceptional in that many natural woods are dominated by beech. The Wye Valley and its coastal hinterland is the most important area, but the valleys of the Rivers Usk and Ebbw are also well-wooded

as conifer plantations. The inland valleys of the Dee and the Vale of Clwyd form an agricultural landscape of fields and hedges, and ancient woods are confined mainly as small strips along the steeper river valleys. The majority of Clwyd woods are of sessile oak on hard acidic rocks and these are most prevalent in the west of the county. There are also woods of ash, wych elm and pedunculate oak on the heavy clays of the Wrexham district and the Vale of Clwyd, with occasional maples, spindle trees and dogwoods, which become rarer as one travels west. Ashwoods occur on the limestone with very occasional small-leaved limes and wild service trees, often on crags. Tree-planting for timber and amenity has been widespread on Clwyd estates since the late eighteenth century, as in Hereford and Shropshire, but most of the replanting of ancient woods is believed to have taken place since 1945.

Woodland place-names in Wales

Welsh wood-names often look and sound as strange and beautiful (to a non-Welsh-speaker) as the places they describe [79]. The commonest name is *coed*, which means, simply, a wood, the equivalent of the Gaelic *coille*. *Coedydd* (pronounced coydeeth) means two or more *coeds* joined together, a plurality of woods. *Allt*, with its variation *gallt*, indicates a hillside or wood, generally with a stream flowing beneath, while *hennallt* means a 'white' – possibly an *old* – wooded hillside. Other common names are *cwm*, a valley (not necessarily a mountain valley though *cwm* also means a cirque or corrie); *celli*, which indicates a hazel grove; and *garth*, which can mean a hill or ridge or, less often, a small plot or garden area where it may be an indication of secondary woodland. Welsh wood-

names are often merely borrowed from the nearest farm and therefore have little to tell us about the wood. Sometimes tree names are used and could refer either to the trees themselves or the place where they grow. Thus *derw* and its variants *dderw*, *deri* and *derwen* (anglicised into derwent) mean oak, *bedw* or *fedw* mean birch, *onnen* means ash and *wern* or *gwern* means alder. Because a wood is named after a particular tree, this does not necessarily mean that the tree is present now. *Gwern* names are common on the wet hillsides of upland Wales, but alderwoods are now very scarce; many have turned into oak-birch woods.

In general, a Welsh wood-name is regarded as an indication of ancient origin, an anglicised name of more recent origin. A name to be treated with particular caution, however, is *bryn*; although this usually means a hill, which implies planting, it might in some cases be an ancient wood used as a tree nursery. *Planhigfa* is a plantation – but there may be ancient plantations because the Welsh were planting trees long before the seventeenth century. Equal caution is needed with the word *newydd* (new). Coed Deri-Newydd in West Glamorgan is 'New Oak Wood', but large stools in that wood indicate that the oaks, and hence the wood, are far from new. Very likely it was not the wood that was new but the farm of that name, and the wood was then renamed after the farm.

A minority of names are of greater historical interest. Coed Cadw, in the Nevern valley in Pembroke means 'preserved woodland', perhaps for pannage (outpasturing pigs) or the regulated harvesting of wood products. The term is used in Welsh laws, written down in the 1300s but in use much earlier. The place-name is presumably ancient. Coed y Moch, 'wood of the pigs', also indicates woods formerly used for pannage. Other names indicate the widespread use of Welsh woods as sources of fuel for smelting ore. Coed Cwm-y-gof is 'the wood of the valley of the smithy'; Coed yr Odyn is 'the wood of the kiln'; and Coed Bryn-yr-efail is 'the hill of the smithy wood'. Some names seem to be pure poetry: Coed Bedd-y-coedwr is 'the wood of the grave of the woodman'.

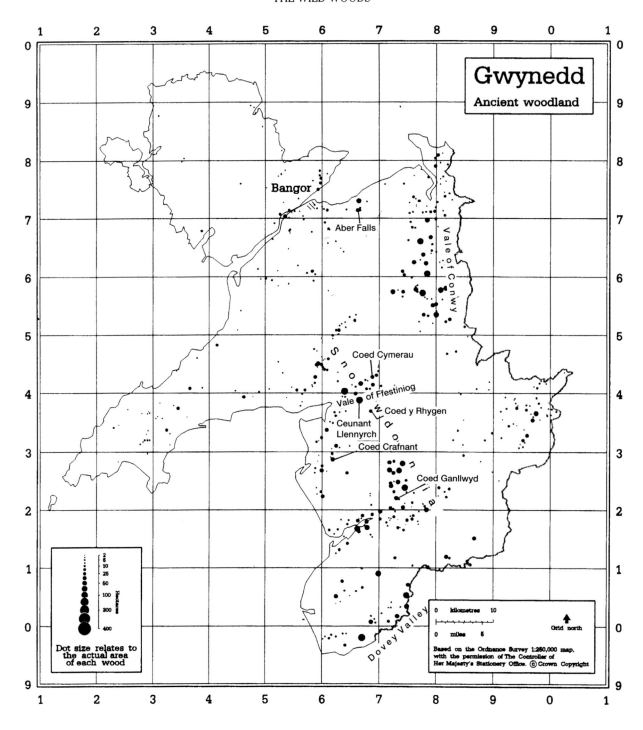

Gwynedd
Ancient woodland

Bangor

Aber Falls

Vale of Conwy

Coed Cymerau

Vale of Ffestiniog

Coed y Rhygen

Ceunant Llennyrch

Coed Crafnant

Coed Ganllwyd

Dovey Valley

Hectares
2
5
10
25
50
100
200
400

Dot size relates to
the actual area
of each wood

kilometres
0   10

miles
0   5

Grid north

Based on the Ordnance Survey 1:250,000 map,
with the permission of The Controller of
Her Majesty's Stationery Office. © Crown Copyright

The Gwynedd oakwoods

Giraldus, the celebrated twelfth-century traveller, described 'Merionyth' as 'the rudest and least cultivated region, and the least accessible', in all Wales. It was also, by the same token, the best wooded. By the time Leland toured the Principality, 350 years later, much of upland Wales had become treeless moorland, but its north-western corner still 'hath (a) meatley good plenty of wood'. The flocks of the Cistercian monks and their secular successors had evidently not penetrated the mountain fastnesses of Snowdonia and Merioneth. The Vales of Ffestiniog and Maentwrog in Snowdonia and Dyffryn Artro (the Artro valley) below the craggy Rhinog hills near Harlech, remain magnificently wooded to this day, partly because of the efforts of enlightened landowners such as the Vaughans of Nannau and the Oakeleys of the vale of Ffestiniog who, valuing oak timber for its investment potential, took care to ensure its regeneration. Like everywhere else in Wales, these woods have seen their share of mass fellings and conifer plantations, but in the steeper and less accessible parts, there are ancient hanging oakwoods, wonderful places of twisty lichenous oaks and moss-laden boulders in which the sound of running, sometimes roaring, water is ever present.

These woods have attracted naturalists, fern collectors and lovers of romantic scenery for at least 200 years. Travellers were always complaining about fellings. The view at the Rhaiadr Ddu waterfalls, for example, was supposed to have

↩ *Gwynedd is an upland county of old, hard rocks where ancient woods are small and confined to the sheltered river valleys. On our map, you can trace the course of the Dovey in the south, of the Afon Artro and the Vale of Ffestiniog farther north, and of the Vale of Conwy in the east. By contrast, the 'pointing hand' of the Lleyn Peninsula and Anglesey have few ancient woods*

been 'completely spoiled' by extensive fellings about 1850, but the trees have grown up again in the way trees always do, provided they are not overshaded or eaten. Of greater wisdom was the ancient Owl of Cwm Cawlwyd in the early Arthurian tale, *Culhwch and Olwen*, whose long life granted it a sense of perspective:

> When I first came hither, the great valley you see was a wooded glen, and a race of men came thereto and it was laid waste. And the second wood grew up therein; and this wood is the third. [80]

Studies by Mary Edwards [81] of the layers of pollen preserved in the boggy woods of Snowdonia suggest just such a chequered past for the apparently wild Snowdonia woods, with some coppicing here, a mass felling there, and intervals of heavy grazing in which little or no regeneration was possible. The pollen history of **Coed Ganllwyd** in the Coed-y-Brenin Forest shows two major declines of oak, each of which was followed by a slow recovery. For perhaps a century, it seems to have been managed as a coppice, but once the demand for coppice wood declined, every tree the woodman could reach was felled. The trees there today are rather even-aged and may have been planted or have grown up since from the stumps, or as maiden trees from seed.

The shaggy, rock-girt wood of **Coed-y-Rhygen**, by contrast, has spreading open-growth mossed oaks estimated at up to 350 years old, which suggests that this wood was once fairly open wood-pasture. Perhaps it was too remote for the removal of timber and underwood. The remains of old walls within the wood suggest use as a sheep shelter. In part of the wood the local farmer occasionally cut oak and hazel for fodder in hard winters, probably an ancient practice in Snowdonia. One area on steep rocky ground was coppiced about forty years ago, and there has been a profuse regeneration recently of oak and birch.

Yet another wood, at **Ceunant Llennyrch** in the Vale of Ffestiniog, appears today as more or less pure oak high forest of 50 to 100-year-old trees derived from coppice. The 'Atlantic' flora of mosses and liverworts is much less rich than those of Coed-y-Rhygen and Coed Ganllwyd, which might indicate a greater degree of past disturbance. The pollen record shows that Ceunant Llennyrch has been transformed over the past three hundred years from an open, grassy, probably sheep-ridden wood to an organised coppice and thence allowed to grow up to form a dense closed canopy wood.

The 'disturbance history' of these woods therefore determines to some extent their appearance today; none is a virgin wood. On the other hand, many of the oakwoods of Snowdonia are certainly ancient, and some are probably primary woods in the sense that trees have always been present along deep stream channels and gorges and wherever else their removal was difficult. Pollen evidence indicates that there has been a slow change from relatively mixed woods to ones dominated by just one or two species. This is an area of acid rocks and very high rainfall, in which the natural progression is to ever greater soil acidity. This has meant that acid-tolerant trees such as oak and birch have stood their ground or increased, while lime, alder and hazel have declined. But the natural process has been hastened by human activity, by cutting, burning, and above all by man's main wood-depressing agent, sheep. Each activity removes nutrients from the ecosystem and 'pushes' the soil farther on the path from rich woodland earth to peat. Other things being equal, less disturbed woods should therefore contain more species than those with a history of sudden reversals and over-exploitation. Coed Ganllwyd, for example, still contains a rich flora of ferns, lichens, mosses and liverworts, and some wych elm, cherry, ash, alder, hazel and alder buckthorn are scattered among the oaks. Ceunant Llennyrch, by contrast, has lost a much greater proportion of its original flora. Alder and lime had both disappeared by about 1700, probably through over-exploitation, and the wood has become a relatively dull place of young growth except in the deep gorge of the Ceunant Llennyrch.

The advent of nature conservation and the purchase of the finest of the Merioneth oakwoods as nature reserves by the NCC, the North Wales Wildlife Trust, the RSPB, the Woodland Trust and others, came in the nick of time to save woods that were struggling to recover from wartime fellings. A small fortune was spent on fences to keep out sheep and, in the case of the Artro valley, the marauding herds of goats that descend from the Rhinogs to browse the saplings and gnaw the bark of young trees. **Coed Dolybebin** (29ha) [72 acres], battered by timber extraction and heavy grazing, now has a chance to regenerate behind its high fence. Some of the goats have been caught and sentenced to transportation. During the past few years, natural regeneration has been copious with scattered young hollies and oaks amid thickets of birch and rowan. An attempt to assist this growth by planting nursery oaks was, on the other hand, a complete waste of time. The respite from grazing is already changing the floor of fenced woods from grass and bracken with little regeneration, to a shadier, more humid environment with carpets of wood-rush, bilberry and ferns.

We have yet to consider the most celebrated aspect of these woods, and the one which brings to the best of them an international distinction. The rainfall of Snowdonia is among the heaviest in Europe. As anyone who has spent a holiday here will know, low cloud, sea mists and endless rain are the lot of these wild valleys. There are many sheltered places in the woodland ravines, streamsides and rock crevices that are wet and humid all year round. It is in such places that one must seek the most weather-sensitive group of all wild plants: the Atlantic mosses and liverworts.

'The Atlantics'

I have used this term as a nickname for those mosses, liverworts and filmy-ferns that demand permanently wet, frost-free 'oceanic' conditions. Britain is one of the world's most important refuges for such plants, though as a group they can be found in soggy nooks and crannies all along the Atlantic seaboard from Norway to the Azores.

Although the precise needs and tolerances of the different species vary, the best habitat for the group as a whole is in certain ancient woods that combine relative freedom from disturbance with an abundance of wet rocks, stream gorges and waterfalls. Like human beings, the 'Atlantics' prefer romantic scenery. A humid ravine with a waterfall or two, a rainbow playing in the spray, half-rotten timbers fallen askew against moss-laden rocks, and a stream course tumbling and gurgling on its way to the sea, is ideal Atlantic country. This is an unusually stable environment where the difference between summer and winter is minimal. In Britain, such conditions are found mainly in areas of old, hard rocks, notably the schists of Lochaber and Argyll, the volcanic rocks of the Lake District and, here, the Cambrian grits and shales of Merioneth. Many individual species can be found elsewhere – the driest wood in England might shelter one or two of them in rotten stumps – but in these three areas, plus the Killarney district of Ireland, one finds the largest number at their peak of health and vigour.

The wooded gorges of Ffestiniog, Ganllwyd, Mawddach and the Artro valley, as well as the Vale of Conwy farther east, contain many of the best Welsh sites for Atlantic mosses and liverworts. At first sight, the most spectacular displays are found on the banks of gritstone boulders, which are often mantled and draped by a thick fold of moss. But these are composed almost entirely of robust common species, drought-resistant feather mosses, 'bottle-brush' mosses and the like. Because these act as water-retaining sponges, they can also harbour some of the more delicate species, such as the big liverwort *Bazzania trilobata*, and the creeping stems of *Lepidozia pearsonii*. But the really demanding species must be sought in more reliably damp places, usually near running water or dripping rocks. Searching for them is something of an art. Because they are too small to find until a few inches from your nose, the bryologist usually heads straight for the likeliest looking place before going down on hands and knees and unhooking his hand lens. This habit risks a circu-larity of argument: because the bryologist spends most of his time among rocks and banks near running water, it is hardly surprising that that is where these rare species are usually found. Proof that stream gorges are indeed vitally important was furnished recently by Mary Edwards [81], who systematically recorded every patch she could find of the leafy liverwort *Adelanthus decipiens* at Coed Ganllwyd, and discovered that in virtually every case the plant grew in places close to, but not in, streams, and in seepages.

Now *Adelanthus* is fairly robust by liverwort standards and it is reasonable to suppose that other, more delicate species are even more local-ised. Plants such as *Jubula hutchinsiae*, a glistening dark-green blob, nine-tenths of it water, can hardly be called a terrestrial plant at all for it grows only in dripping caves or the bottom of ravines. Not much to look at at first sight, *Jubula* reveals under a ×10 hand lens its beautiful 'prickly' leaves, rather like sprays of holly. The only impressive thing about *Drepanolejeuna hamatifolia* is its name, un-til magnification reveals an intricately branched little plant whose tiny leaves resemble a line of teacups on hooks in a dresser. Growing with it in deeply shaded ravines are the various species of *Radula*, named after their likeness to the horny strips of teeth owned by snails. *Radula voluta*, which forms tight yellow-green patches with a character-istic bluish tinge, is the choosiest, preferring the spray zone of waterfalls above all else. Slightly more tolerant to temporary drying are liverworts such as *Lepidozia cupressina*, which forms com-pact cream tufts on wet rocks and can thus tighten up to reduce evaporation in dry weather. Other species, such as lurid purple *Nowellia curvifolia* and dark-green, sometimes reddish-tinged *Jamesoniella autumnalis*, prefer rotting logs.

In Wales, some of these plants are virtually confined to ancient woods. Places such as Coed Ganllwyd and Coed-y-Rhygen, that are particu-larly rich in Atlantic bryophytes, invariably pos-sess a wet microclimate, helped by waterfalls with plenty of nearby rocks, mature tree stumps and fallen dead wood. The presence of a rich flora of

Atlantics is a good indication that a wood is a direct descendant of the original Welsh Wildwood. But we must be cautious. By their ecological choosiness and poor powers of colonisation (many are infertile in Britain), Atlantic mosses and liverworts make good habitat indicators, but it is stable moist conditions that they are indicating, not necessarily woodland. Mary Edwards' investigations of the history and age of woods in Merioneth indicate that even the richest of them were cut over or even clear-felled in the past, and that must have produced temporary periods of drought. What is vital for the survival of these species, in her view, is not so much the trees themselves as an availability of coarse-grained rocks to provide permanent moisture and shelter. The interstices of the rocks form safe havens to tide the mosses and liverworts through the unfavourable period until the trees grow up again. As a result, woods on softer, smoother rocks such as shales and slates are rarely as rich as those on hard grits, because in the former there was no escape from the drying sunshine and wind after the trees were cut down.

The 'Atlantics' are well worth getting to know because it is their presence that helps to distinguish the really special woods from the ordinary

⇐ *The banks of the waterfall at Coed Ganllwyd, Gwynedd, have one of Britain's richest floras of Atlantic mosses and liverworts. October*
(PETER WAKELY)

⇓ *Welsh woodland at its wildest: the rocky, moss-smothered wood of Coed-y-Rhygen, Gwynedd in October*
(PETER WAKELY)

ones. Those to look out for in Wales are *Adelanthus decipiens, Leptoscyphus cuneifolius, Lepidozia cupressina, Plagiochila punctata, P. exigua (= P.corniculata), P. atlantica* and *Radula voluta* among the liverworts; and among the usually more robust mosses *Isothecium holtii* and *Dicranum scottianum.* Two ferns, Tunbridge filmy-fern and hay-scented buckler-fern, show similar preferences. At their best, these specialised communities of tiny plants must be seen to be believed. The eastern botanist is used to finding leafy liverworts as rather scrappy patches and flakes hiding in seepages and rotting logs. In some of the Coeds and Coedydds of Merioneth, the same plants grow in luxuriant masses, rather resembling miniature tender-green bushes of sycamore or horse chestnut.

Humid ravines are among our most stable, least disturbed natural habitats. The coastal ones may also be our oldest habitats. Warm ocean currents probably maintained ice-free enclaves in these sheltered western valleys throughout the coldest periods, and it is possible therefore that their flora of mosses, liverworts and ferns may, like the equatorial rain forests, have evolved over millions of years, and not merely during the last ten thousand. Although the Atlantic mosses and liverworts are not as sensitive to acid rain as the lichens, some species have been affected by pollutants dispersed from the tall chimney stacks of distant industrial areas. It would be a sad irony if our Atlantic mosses and liverworts were to be destroyed by the same mist and rain that sustains their life.

The Abergavenny beechwoods

What is your most surprising woodland experience? Among the woods I did not know existed were a grove of miniature Scots pines standing on top of an otherwise bare mountain called Creag Ghiubhais ('hill of the firs'); the remains of an ancient limewood virtually on my doorstep in what I thought was a quarry; and a dwarf alpine wood composed wholly of rare willows high up in an Angus corrie.

High on any list of the most surprising woods in

Britain must be the mountain beechwoods of south-east Wales. Surprising because, although we have become used to seeing beechwoods on dry limestone hillsides, notably in the Cotswolds and the Chilterns, here are woods of well-grown, sometimes giant, trees perched high on the rainy hillsides that hem the South Wales coalfield. Here one finds ancient beech in its full variety of form and function, beeches that were lopped as pollards, or cut over as coppice or grown as standards; stately beeches 1.8m (6ft) or more in girth, gnarled beeches high up above the valley sides or beneath precipitous cliffs; and multi-stemmed beeches arching over steep banks to form shady green tunnels.

Though it is widely planted in Wales, beech is native only east of a line running from Cardiff to Merthyr Tydfil. In the lowland woods of Glamorgan and Gwent, it is usually one constituent tree among many, but at the heads of valleys along the edge of the coalfield beech and sessile oak reign supreme. The greatest density of Welsh beechwoods can be found near the towns of Blaenavon and Abergavenny in Gwent. From Tudor times onwards, this was an iron-making district that used charcoal from coppiced woods to smelt the ore until local coal took over in the 1840s. Oak would have been the preferred species, but the occasional remains of charcoal hearths among old beech coppice stools suggests that beech, too, was used on occasion. Probably, as in the Chilterns, the main use of beech was for domestic fuel, though hill farmers may also have lopped boughs for fodder.

These beechwoods were at one time valuable properties and were divided into coppices and common wood-pasture. On the northern slopes of that great sandstone whaleback, the Blorenge, is one of the largest beech coppices in Gwent, Coed-y-Person. This wood is full of historical meaning, with lines of beech stools and stubbs along a woodbank, and high cut stools of oak and beech, as well as some old pollard elms. On the steep slope above are what appear to be oak standards over the scattered remains of a hazel, beech, oak and wych elm underwood that had been coppiced up to about 1910. Glebe Wood at the lower end is a simple coppice of beech with some oak. Like many ancient woods in South Wales, Coed-y-Person was heavily exploited by industry. There are charcoal hearths inside the wood, disused mines on the plateau above, and an old rackway with the iron rails still in place.

On the eastern slope of the Blorenge, less than a mile away, is a very different scene. Here the scene is dominated by the **Punchbowl**, a spectacular swirl of wooded hillside with an artificial lake in the middle. This was probably once a wood-pasture common, and is now a place of mature ash and great pollard beeches, two or three hundred years old. Farther upslope, where the increasingly stunted beech and ash finally peter out, is the open moor of the former Forest of Blorenge. As at Exmoor, physical woodland useful to commoners had been excluded from the upland area declared by some Marcher Lord to be his hunting forest. The highest of the mountain beechwoods is **Coed tyn-y-Gelli** (5ha) [12 acres] near Ebbw Vale, which reaches 451m (1,482ft) with individual trees as high as 493m (1,618ft). As at Coed-y-Person, it lies next door to a common and, since the 1940s, has become a sheep shelter. Fortunately, the local authority is now ring-fencing the wood to make it stockproof and is rearing beech saplings from local mast to plant into the wood.

Being shady, acidic and, too often, over-run with sheep, Welsh beechwoods are not places in which one would expect to find a rich flora. The beechgroves near Blaenavon are typical of most: floors of wavy hair-grass, bracken and moss, strewn about with fallen boughs (many woods were battered by the 1990 gale). In the lowlands, particularly in Gwent, there are also woods on limestone soils that possess a small-scale mosaic of different tree communities. The **Coombe Valley Woods** between Caerwent and Shirenewton, for example, have patches of rare beech-lime coppice, with giant stools of both species, among younger stands of ash-hazel, maple-hazel and wych elm-hazel woodland. The original flora has become impoverished from too much shade and grazing, and has

been reduced mostly to sheets of dog's mercury, scrambling ivy and patches of bramble, bluebell and bracken. Resumed coppicing at the NCC's **Penhow Woodlands** has produced a vigorous regeneration and bursts of spring flowers, including the rare upright or Tintern spurge, and shown that it is possible still to restore these woods to their former glory.

The limestone ashwoods

Hard, white Carboniferous limestone outcrops puncture the prevailing acid rocks and impoverished soils of Wales from the Great Orme at Llandudno to the Gower Peninsula, to produce botanically rich oases. The limestone crags jut above steep stony slopes that are impossible to cultivate, and, as a result, are often covered with woodland and scrub. Such woods are usually small, but are often of a richness, including rare species, that belies their size. Ancient woods associated with Welsh limestone vary from sessile oak on the poorer soils to flower-rich ash-hazel woods with wych elm, maple, spindle, dogwood and, occasionally, lime. Yew is not uncommon on the thinnest soils.

Certain isolated upland ashwoods in Brecknockshire and the Glamorgans are refuges for rare whitebeams. **Coed Penmoelallt** in the Afon Taf Fawr gorge in Glamorgan is a Forest Nature Reserve designed to protect one of the world's rarest plants, the whitebeam *Sorbus leyana*, of which there are no more than a few dozen trees clinging to rock faces. **Craig y Cilau** in Brecknock has no fewer than four kinds of rare whitebeams on the narrow ledges and fissures in vertical rock faces. Growing with them is another rare tree, the large-leaved lime. Dr C. D. Pigott has drawn attention to records of pollen from this tree preserved in a bog beneath the cliff. Most of the lime pollen belonged to layers datable from 4000-2000 BC, but there is also a scatter of grains in later layers right up to the present surface which suggests that the tree has been present throughout that time. Pollen of its commoner relative, the small-leaved lime, was also found. Evidently lime was commoner on

Welsh limestone in the past than in the present, and survives today mainly in these steep places where the sheep cannot reach it.

Limestone woods are vulnerable because the stone beneath them is worth more than the trees. An application to quarry stone at **Carmel Woods** near Llandeilo in Dyfed is still very much a bone of contention. This is a beautiful ashwood on a ridge of hard limestone at the northern edge of the coalfields. It is also, like many woods in Wales, a mystical place. King Arthur's knights are said to sleep among the hibernating horseshoe bats in caves at Craig Derwyddon (Druid's Crag). The legend probably originates in the use of the caves for burial, because twelve human skeletons were found in one of them in 1813. On a more prosaic level, the flora of the wood is one of the richest in Wales, and includes mezereon, herb paris, lily-of-the-valley, yellow bird's-nest and wild columbine. The fauna includes a very rare harvestman that lurks in deep shade among dead leaves and moss. Unfortunately, in their desire to win stone from the wood, the quarry company proposes to revive an old Interim Development Order, which has lain dormant, like King Arthur's knights, for more than forty years.

◁A wet day at Cwm Merddog, Gwent, one of the remarkable mountain beechwoods of south-east Wales. In the foreground is part of the large medieval bank that enclosed this wood. May (PETER WAKELY)

Coed Cymru

Saving the scattered remnants of the Welsh 'wildwoods' is perhaps the most daunting prospect in British woodland conservation. Nearly every wood has a different owner, sometimes several owners. About four out of five woods are in poor heart, either neglected or misused as shelters for hill sheep, which promptly nip off the top of any sapling that appears. And there are so many such woods, most of them no more than a dozen or so hectares, that as one travels through the country passing woods full of sheep and bracken all the way, it is hard to know where to start.

Realising, nevertheless, that the problem had to be tackled soon if Wales was not to become a country of bare moors and conifers, twenty Welsh voluntary and statutory bodies grouped together to launch, in 1985, the Welsh Wildwood Campaign, Coed Cymru. The project's purpose is simply to 'encourage the protection, use and enhancement' of Welsh native woods. The project also offers training, free help and advice on small wood management and marketing. The approach is similar to that of Project Sylvanus in Devon, Woodland Care in Suffolk and other regional 'small wood' enterprises; the difference is in the scale of the task. In its first two years, Coed Cymru helped Welsh farmers to bring some 1,574ha (3,889 acres) of native broadleaved woodland into sympathetic management by such measures as fencing out livestock, creating glades to encourage natural regeneration, and, where all else fails, by planting trees indigenous to the area. The area thus salvaged had increased to 2,600ha (6,425 acres) or 10 per cent of all Welsh native woods by 1990: a notable achievement.

Coed Cymru has helped to invigorate a renewed interest in native woods by the farming community and by potential users of hardwoods, exemplified by the growing craft industry in Wales and the increasing use of Welsh oak instead of chemically treated softwoods in country parks. With the technological advances of the past ten years it is becoming possible to market low-grade hardwood formerly considered worthless. Hence, more and more woods on Welsh hill farms are becoming valued as wood producers for the owner and the local community, and merely not as barns with leaves. David Jenkins, Coed Cymru's coordinator, is optimistic that the majority of Welsh farm woods will be in some form of beneficial production by the year 2000.

12

SCOTLAND

INTRODUCTION

The story of native woodland in Scotland is focussed on three trees: oak, Scots pine and birch. Until the transformation of Scotland's roads and farming system in the eighteenth century, most woods probably served only their local community. Scotland had less need of wood for fuel and timber than southern England because adequate supplies of peat and stone were generally available. Woods were more valuable as pasture and shelter for cattle and sheep. The scarcity of pollard trees, compared with Scandinavia, suggests that the continental system of lopping trees for winter feed was not much practised in Scotland. From the seventeenth century onwards, some woods in the central and western Highlands were coppiced, and in some places the practice was probably introduced much earlier (see below). But, on the whole, the Celts and the Gaels were breeders of cattle, not harvesters of trees.

Scottish woodland history is bedevilled by a lack of reliable sources. Anderson [82] compiled a great mass of information, but no clear picture emerges from it apart from a negative one in the lack of evidence of woodmanship. Until Messrs G. Hammersley and J. M. Lindsay proved otherwise[83], it was widely believed that commercial exploitation was responsible for the destruction of the Highland woods. In practice, the development of markets for timber, wood, bark and charcoal seems to have led rather to the first effective *conservation* of woods through stock fencing and careful management. The hard-worked coppices of Rannoch, Menteith, Loch Lomond and Argyll, which supplied the charcoal to fuel the ironmasters' forges, still survive. It was in places where meat production had priority over timber that woods failed to regenerate and eventually became treeless moors. In parts of the Highlands, this continues to happen before our very eyes.

Another widely held myth is that, because Royal Forests and deer parks were plentiful in medieval Scotland, the land must therefore have been well-wooded. It is impossible to determine how much ancient woodland was lost in Scotland during the Middle Ages, but the broad thrust of the evidence is one of steady decline to a state, in the lowlands at least, of near woodlessness by about AD 1500. But Scotland probably lost most of its primary woodland in prehistory. At Ettrick Forest, there was evidently enough woodland for William Wallace to hide in, in 1303, because contemporary accounts refer to 'fellers of trees' and 'branches and timber in the Forest', but the rise of monastic sheep farming in the Borders destroyed all the remaining woods on open hillsides, reducing tree cover to stream gullies and inaccessible crags. My colleague Chris Badenoch draws attention to the strange lack of any documentary evidence for local bark-peeling in this area – yet bark for tanning was undoubtedly needed in plenty by the *souters* (shoemakers) of Selkirk and for curing the innumerable sheep and goat skins. The planting in 1658 of native trees, including birch and rowan, in neighbouring Tweed-dale, suggests a chronic shortage of natural woods. In 1715, Alexander Pennecuick could claim that there was 'not one wood worth naming in all this open and windie Country'. It was much the same story throughout eastern Scotland from Berwick to Buchan. Samuel Johnson claimed that he travelled from Lothian to Aberdeen without seeing so much as a tree.

The picture is not one of continuous decline, however. Some natural woods have expanded under favourable management and continue to do so today. In Deeside, dense young birchwoods crowd slopes and abandoned grouse muirs that were bare in Queen Victoria's day. The native pinewoods are widely believed to be shrunken remnants of a once continuous Caledonian Forest. This may be true of the woods of the Western Highlands and the Cairngorm Glens, but not of the great woods of Abernethy in Speyside and Glen Tanar in Deeside, which have, if anything, *expanded* during the past two hundred years. Unlike lowland woods, highland woods change their ground over the years, and any assessment of rates of decline has to take this into account.

Space forbids a regional treatment of Scottish ancient and long-established woods in the way I have attempted for England. In view of the scarcity of reliable historical information it would be, in my opinion, premature to do so. This chapter focusses instead on aspects of ancient woodland history and wildlife that have received attention recently.

Scottish wood-names

In general, long-established woods in the Highlands have Gaelic names, and those in the lowlands have English names. Some woods in the Western Highlands also incorporate Viking words. The majority of English names are borrowed from a nearby settlement or from physical features such as hills and streams. A common Scottish usage is 'the wood of . . .' such as the Wood of Cree

in Galloway and the Old Wood of Drum in Deeside. In a few cases, such names have been traced back to medieval documents. Mugdock Wood, for example, is mentioned in a charter of 1253 conferring 'the castle, park, wood and loch of Mugdock' on the Grahams. At Ettrick and Lauderdale in the Borders there are numerous *shaw* names of ancient Celtic origin, such as Headshaw, Langshaw and Shawburn.

The most misleading woodland name in Scotland is 'forest'. As in England and Wales, the Royal Forests, of which there were many, were places of deer, not necessarily trees. The name has been taken over by Highland estates whose deer forests are invariably moorland, and by the Forestry Commission, whose planted forests have nothing to do with the medieval hunting forests, though they sometimes occupy the same piece of ground. Nevertheless, past writers have tended to assume that medieval forests were full of trees, and invented melodramatic tales to account for their removal. One still reads stories of great conflagrations started by Viking marauders, or by General MacKay in 1689. It is much more likely that the medieval forests were sparsely wooded from the outset.

Gaelic names can be used as a historical clue to ancient woodland. Craigendarroch (crag of the oaks) near Ballater in Deeside is a Gaelic place-name in an area where English had already begun to replace Gaelic by the sixteenth century. The name properly belongs to the hill rather than the wood at its foot, but it underlines the probability that oaks were growing here at the time when the local inhabitants still had Gaelic as their first language. A short way up the valley from Craigendarroch is Creag Ghiubhais, crag of the pines, which is still crowned by a small, probably native, pinewood. The commonest names of actual woods are *coille*, the equivalent of the Welsh *coed*, and *doire*, a grove or thicket. Both names are common in western Scotland.

The largest Scottish woods, curiously enough, have no ancient names at all. Native pinewood names such as Ballochbuie and the Black Wood at Rannoch are the exception rather than the rule.

↑ *Cragbank Wood in the Scottish Borders, a well-preserved ancient wood of ash, wych elm, sessile oak and silver birch. This became the 200th National Nature Reserve in Britain, when it was 'unveiled' in June 1985*
(PETER WAKELY)

Glen Tanar in Deeside is full of Gaelic names that hint at past land usage. Thus, in the heart of the wood are *bad na muic*, 'the place of the pigs', *rin na geroch*, 'hill of the sheep', and, intriguingly, *bad na ban*, 'place of the women', as well as hills, passes and crags with names such as Fungle, Strone and Drum. But the wonderful pinewood that stretches for miles over hill and dale bore no name at all; it was simply part of the scenery. In these wooded landscapes, it was the clearings and shielings within the wood that were named, not the wood itself.

SCOTTISH OAKWOODS

For a period of less than two hundred years – between about 1680 and 1880 – Scottish oak was managed intensively for commercial use. The peak period of profitable oak management, from about 1750 to 1820, spanned only a single human lifetime, and less than a quarter of the life of a healthy oak. Scottish oaks commonly have corkscrew limbs and crabbed crowns, like a stag's antlers, and only the very best (usually planted) trees are of timber value. The main markets for oak were provided by ironmasters, who needed oak charcoal to smelt the ore, and tanners who required enormous quantities of oak bark. To produce such wood in quantity, oakwoods had first to be made stockproof and then cut over every twenty years or so. In their productive heyday, therefore, Scottish oakwoods were rather open woods of short, scrubby oaks, in varying states of regrowth from coppice stools.

Coppicing was not confined to the short period of high prices and commercial management however. There are large oak coppice stools in woods in central Scotland that must be several hundred years old. A stool more than 1.8m (6ft) across near the edge of Mugdock Wood in Central Region[84] was probably flourishing well before Union of the Crowns in 1603. Living evidence of medieval coppicing survives in the strangely shaped ancient oaks in the deer park of **Dalkeith Palace**. These appear to be the remains of a coppiced oakwood last felled about four hundred years ago when the site became a park. Some of the stool bases are older still, however, and take us back to Robert the Bruce. Thus these awesome trees are living evidence that the Scots were managing woods as coppice in the Middle Ages[85].

Until the late seventeenth century, Scottish oakwoods seem to have been managed in a fairly haphazard way, with small-scale fellings to provide wood for local use and for small iron-smelters or 'bloomeries'. The earliest successful attempt to put natural woods to work on a large scale was that of the Graham Marquesses of Montrose, who owned enormous estates along the edge of the Highlands at Menteith and Atholl. The well-known oakwoods on the east bank of **Loch Lomond** formed part of the Graham lands, and their history has been worked out by Ruth Tittensor[86]. Some timber was grown locally to sell to the Clydeside sawmills and shipyards, and to furnish beams and rafters for the Grahams' ambitious building projects. But most of the natural woods were organised as coppice. There was a belief that coppiced oaks should be cut every twenty-four years (though in practice, coppice rotations seem to have varied considerably, depending on how successful had been the regrowth).

A wood was divided into 'haggs', equal in number to the years of cutting, so that a regular income could be obtained from it. For that reason, big woods of 40ha (100 acres) or more were the most profitable. Haggs were often marked by march stones or by turf dikes topped with brushwood. To maximise wood production, stone walls or fences

had to be built and maintained, boggy woods drained to warm the soil, and 'barren timber', which in Scotland could mean almost anything that was not healthy oak, weeded out. At Loch Lomond, birch, hazel, ash and alder were also put to local use, while on the island of Inchcailloch, coppiced alder was cut as blockwood for clog making. The general opinion was that planted pedunculate oak was preferable to the native sessile oak, so oak planting became widespread in woods, especially from 1770 onwards. Partly for that reason, Scottish oaks today are difficult to separate out as pedunculate or sessile, for they generally have characteristics of both. We should be content to call them simply oak.

Along the Highland fringe, especially in Perthshire, native woods were increasingly brought into commercial use for two main products: bark for curing hides into leather and small-bore wood for making spokes. Spokewood was needed in unprecedented quantities because road improvements in the eighteenth century had revolutionised Scotland's communications and internal trade. Still more commercially valuable was oak bark, which trebled in price during the Napoleonic Wars, partly because of the enormous demand from Wellington's leather-shod and leather-draped army. Originally, Scotland imported most of its leather from England, but price rises made it increasingly profitable for estate owners to tan their own hides using bark obtained from their oakwoods. The transformation was aided by political factors. The Act of Union increased cross-border traffic and many Scots landowners, who had backed the wrong horse in the Jacobite struggle and found themselves in exile, spent their spare time studying improvement techniques, returning in the fullness of time to their estates, their heads full of Sassenach ideas for making money.

The great advantage of the Loch Lomond woods compared with most Highland woods was that transport costs for produce were low. The timber logs and sacks of weathered bark could be hauled out of the wood and loaded onto low barges or 'scows', themselves built of local oak, before being transported across the loch and down the River Leven to the factories of Clydeside. When the demand for tanbark slumped after 1815, a new use lay ready for Lomondside oak coppice at the 'Pyroligneous Acid Factory' at Balmaha, a distillation works that produced vinegar, tar, creosote and printing dyes from wood products. Other consumers of wood at Balmaha included lime-kilns and a sawmill. As a result, throughout most of the nineteenth century some coppiced oakwoods remained in production as the barges passed to and fro between Lomondside and the factory.

The extensive oakwoods around the sheltered inlets and bays of Argyll and Lochaber led in 1753 to the establishment of a charcoal-fuelled blast furnace at Bonawe in Lorn. Until its closure in 1876, this furnace produced around 700 tonnes of iron a year, requiring 3,500 tonnes of wood – the equivalent of 30ha (74 acres) of well-stocked coppice – every year. To guarantee a regular supply of wood, the Lorn Furnace Company made contractual agreements with woodland owners. In some cases, as at the parish of Muckairn by Loch Etive, the local woods passed under a long lease into the company's direct control. J. M. Lindsay has demonstrated that, far from destroying these woods as is sometimes claimed, the ironmasters were extremely efficient woodland managers [83]. At Muckairn, the area of woodland actually doubled during the period in their care. **Glen Nant**, close to the present-day ruins of the Bonawe Furnace and one of its principal suppliers of wood, is now a woodland nature reserve. After the closure of the furnace, the woodland was left to develop naturally and it has become a delightful place of lichen-smothered trunks and branches. As the reserve booklet points out, 'To the untrained eye, there is hardly any indication at Glen Nant of the impact of the industry on the visible landscape, showing nature's ability to recover from sensible exploitation.' If more oakwoods had been subjected to such 'sensible expoitation' there would be more of them surviving today.

Even at the peak of oak production, foresters often complained about the poor quality of man-

Ancient woodland in the District of Argyll and ⊏⟩ Bute. In this, the most densely wooded part of Scotland, the older woods are confined to the shelter of sea-lochs and glens. The mild, humid climate of the west coast gives some of these woods a lush, sub-tropical, character. Many, however, have been felled and converted to plantations in the past fifty years

agement in many Scottish woods. Livestock tended to be let in while the regrowth was still tender. Cutting was sometimes haphazard and poorly conducted, so that rainwater collected on the stools and rotted them. Scottish landowners also tended to include too many standard trees in coppice woods in the expectation of being able to sell them as high-grade timber. What happened, rather, was that a mass of poor-quality crabbed oaks grew up, overshaded the more valuable oak underwood and resulted in a disastrous decline in bark production. After 1850, most people lost interest in oak altogether, except as an amenity tree to adorn their policies and parks. Coppice management in oakwoods had all but ceased by the late nineteenth century and, as the boundary walls fell down, sheep and goats moved in. Oak grows slowly and regenerates poorly in most of Scotland, and oakwoods are therefore vulnerable to overgrazing. Almost every other change over the past century and a half has also been detrimental to oak. Rhododendron, originally planted by gamekeepers, quickly becomes rampant in woods on damp, acid soils. Wartime lumbermen took their pick of the best oak timber. Too many fine oakwoods have since been cleared and replanted with conifers. Since the 1950s, foresters have tended to see oak as an expensive luxury, and much can go wrong in the full century that Scottish oak takes to mature.

Oakwood wildlife
Mugdock Wood (206ha) [509 acres], a large wood beneath the Campsie Fells, is a good example of a 'typical' lowland oakwood. It is composed of a mixture of old coppice stools and trees that were

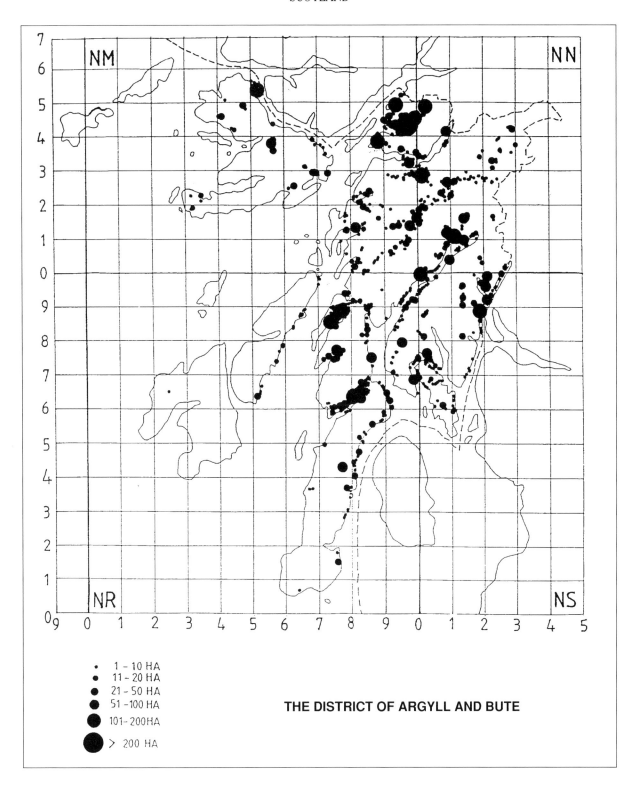

1 – 10 HA
11 – 20 HA
21 – 50 HA
51 –100 HA
101– 200HA
> 200 HA

THE DISTRICT OF ARGYLL AND BUTE

↑ *The banks and islets of Loch Lomond as seen from Conic Hill (the islets mark the line of the Highland boundary fault). The oak-covered islet nearest to land is Inchcailloch, with Torrinch and Inchmurrin farther out. June*
(PETER MARREN)

either grown as standards or have sprung up as maiden trees since coppicing was abandoned about sixty years ago. The unequal size range of the oaks suggests that management at Mugdock Wood followed the Scottish custom of leaving standards of a mixture of ages. The biggest trees are perhaps two hundred years old, and were lucky to escape the wartime lumbermen. Regeneration is presently confined mainly to birch, sycamore and ash. Alder is the dominant tree on wet level ground by the Allander Water. Except for the latter area, the ground flora is one of free-draining acid soils with a long history of grazing, resulting in bracken, mosses, hair-grass and patches of heather. There are similar oakwoods on the margins of cultivation from the Borders to the Moray Firth, mostly on steep slopes or in ravines. Evidence for their past use as coppice is most pronounced in Perthshire and Central. At Mugdock the oldest tree is an oak, but at **Methven Wood** at Almondbank the biggest coppice stools are an ash and a wych elm, suggesting that this wood may have had a more mixed composition before management began to select in favour of oak in the eighteenth century. The few oakwoods in Aberdeenshire tend to be even-aged and, in some cases, consist almost entirely of oaks planted in the first half of the nineteenth century, though age has lent them a mellow natural character. **Paradise Wood**, by the River Don, contains a magnificent eighteenth-century arboretum and landscaped garden that has since turned into an oakwood, an unusual number of 'garden escapes' having survived the change.

Perhaps the most dramatic, and also among the most floristically rich, ancient Scottish oakwoods lie on the lower slopes of glens along the ragged western coastline between Loch Fyne and Ardnamurchan. **Taynish Wood** in Knapdale covers a humpbacked promontory of schist between warm tidal inlets full of sponges and brittle stars. Between Strontian and Salen along Loch Sunart, lie Britain's most westerly oakwoods, including **Ariundle** (70ha) [173 acres] on the steep south-facing bank of Strontian Glen. The mild humid climate of the west coast is well suited to oak, and in prehistoric times dense oak woodland probably covered south-facing glens throughout the area, with the hardier, more frost-resistant birch and Scots pine occupying north-facing slopes or at a higher zone above the oaks. Places such as Taynish and Ariundle have probably been wooded continuously since the end of the Ice Age.

The rain-laden westerly winds and the winter-warming current of the Gulf Stream produce in these sheltered glens an almost Mediterranean climate that explains the miraculous garden of Inverewe in the wilds of Sutherland. A regular drenching in mist and rain, assisted by the spray from cascading burns, allows drought-sensitive mosses to blanket the boulders and banks, and large, lobed lichens to plaster the bark and hang

⇩ *The River Dee runs between stands of mature Scots pines near old Invercauld Bridge at one of the few places where Caledonian pine forest abuts a major public road*
(PETER WAKELY)

from the boughs like seaweed. Ariundle alone harbours 250 species of mosses, liverworts and lichens, many of them 'Atlantic' species which depend on a mild oceanic climate and an unpolluted atmosphere. Such woods have an air of deep antiquity, yet virtually all of them were managed quite intensively for a time, providing oak charcoal to the Bonawe Furnace and pitwood for local lead mines. Today, Taynish Wood, Ariundle and Mealdarroch on the sheltered coast south of Tarbert are National Nature Reserves, in which the dwindling woods have at last been given some respite from sheep, cattle and deer. A walk in the gentle spring rain through the mossy, flower-spangled woods of Ardnamurchan or Knapdale, surrounded by land and water, is an experience not easily forgotten.

THE NATIVE PINEWOODS

There can be no more evocative sight in Britain than a wood of grand old Scots pines against a backdrop of river, moor and snowy mountaintops. Memorable views of Old Scotland that decorate countless calendars and shortbread tins include the great arena of Ballochbuie from Invercauld Bridge, the wonderful view of Loch Maree and Slioch from the pinewood shelter at Beinn Eighe, or the ruined castle on the island of Loch an Eilein in Speyside. Naturalists visit native pinewoods in hopes of seeing crested tit, capercaillie, Scottish crossbills and tree-nesting golden eagles. In undisturbed parts, the pinewood floor can be a beautiful mixture of textures and hues from the intermingling heather, blaeberry and cowberry, junipers fluted into columns or spread out in masses like cumulus clouds, and cushions and carpets of golden-green moss. Flowers such as chickweed wintergreen, twinflower, creeping lady's-tresses and lesser twayblade are associated with pinewoods. Less well known are rare mosses and lichens and a remarkable array of fungi, including many species found nowhere else in Britain.

The native pinewoods of Scotland are popularly referred to as the Caledonian woods, in the belief that they represent fragments of a former vast 'Forest of Caledonia', a name used by the Roman historian Tacitus. Thirty-five pinewoods were described by Steven and Carlisle in their *The Native Pinewoods of Scotland*[87] as places 'where the trees had descended from one generation to another by natural means' and hence were probably descendants of the great forest. Their book has since been brought up to date in a review by Clifton Bain for the RSPB[88].

There are about 12,000ha (29,562 acres) of native pine woodland altogether. Nearly half of it is concentrated in four very large woods: Abernethy (1,885ha) [4,658 acres] and Rothiemurchus (1,539ha) [3,803 acres] in Speyside, Glen Affric (1,341ha) [3,558 acres] in Inverness and Glen Tanar (1,038ha) [2,565 acres] in Deeside. The other large pinewoods are Ballochbuie (529ha) [1,307 acres], the Cairngorm Glens in Mar (720ha) [1,779 acres], Inshriach and Invereshie in the western Cairngorms (459ha) [1,134 acres], Glen Strathfarrar (770ha) [1,903 acres] in Inverness and Beinn Eighe/Loch Maree (340ha) [840 acres] in Ross. Bain identifies a further fifty woods in Highland, Grampian and Strathclyde Regions which contain mature Scots pine considered to be native, amounting to an additional 500ha (1,236 acres). He calculates that about a third (3,887ha) [9,605 acres] of the total has been lost between 1957 and 1987, mostly through forestry operations[88]. In 1978 the Forestry Commission started a special scheme, open to twenty privately owned pinewoods chosen from Steven and Carlisle's book, which offered enhanced planting grants in an attempt to combine timber production and nature conservation objectives. The take-up of the Native Pinewood Grants Scheme was poor, however, and most conservationists believe that it overemphasised timber production and failed to address properly the problems of excessive deer grazing. The scheme contrived to protect the genetic strains of native pine without protecting the native pinewood *character*.

A common historical thread runs through the larger native pinewoods. The history of **Abernethy** in Speyside, worked out recently by O'Sullivan[89], reveals a surprisingly high degree of exploitation over three centuries. Until the early seventeenth-century, the forest contained only two saw-mills, which served only local needs. The first recorded commercial felling was in 1631, when Commissioners of the Scottish Navy paid the Grants of Abernethy £20,000 Scots for a forty-one-year lease, introduced water power to improve the efficiency of the mills and used the River Spey to transport the pinelogs to the sea. Nearly a century later, commercial exploitation began in earnest when in 1728 the York Building Company paid £7,000 sterling to the Grants to extract 60,000 trees over seven years. Two years later, four furnaces for smelting iron ore were built at nearby Nethybridge. The company soon went broke, but extraction continued. In 1769, the Grants sold 100,000 choice trees from Abernethy and Dulnain, and similar large sales followed in 1798, 1803 and 1808. In the 1850s, a nursery was established to restock the devastated forest and much of the lower ground was replanted.

So long as it was not overgrazed, Abernethy was large enough to absorb even this rate of felling, though its appearance probably changed in the process from an age-old wood of mature pines to one more resembling a plantation with single-aged stands of young, close-spaced trees. Such a transformation certainly happened at **Glen Tanar** in Deeside which experienced a comparable level of disturbance over the same period [90]. In the second half of the nineteenth century, however, deer stalking became a fashionable pursuit for the wealthy and, in a sudden reversal which ended crofting and lumbering at both forests, deer replaced people. The trees were thus given a forty-five-year respite from cutting, which resumed again only during World War I. Memories of the earlier exploitation faded and people started once again to call them 'natural woods'. So they are, but only in the same sense as ancient and natural woods elsewhere in Britain, that is, woods that retain many of their natural characteristics despite having been exploited for timber and underwood for centuries. O'Sullivan estimated that even at Aber-nethy, the largest single expanse of ancient woodland in the British Isles, almost every part has been felled at least once.

The last two phases of Abernethy's chequered past bring us to modern times. Between 1969 and 1984 about 200ha (494 acres) of native pinewood was felled in what O'Sullivan described as a selective felling of the finest pines on a scale probably unequalled since the Napoleonic Wars. It was accompanied by ploughing and planting with a mixture of Scots pine and non-native lodgepole pine. This is unlikely to be repeated, for much of the pine forest is now part of a National Nature Reserve (1,921ha) [4,747 acres] or an RSPB nature reserve (8,400ha) [20,757 acres]. The latter is one of the largest nature reserves owned by a charitable trust in Western Europe.

Scots pine is unique among native woodland trees in that it burns when green. Birch trees occasionally catch fire in hot dry weather, but it is only in pinewoods that fire is an important part of the natural ecology of the forest, as it is in Mediterranean woodland. Fire of itself rarely destroys a forest. Mature pines have thick waxy bark that is fire resistant. A great fire that burned 400ha (988 acres) of Glen Cannich in living memory failed to kill many mature trees. What does burn is the layer of leggy old heather bushes and surface peat that inhibits pine regeneration. Far from being a disaster, therefore, fire supplies an important function in pinewoods by removing the sterile surface of peat and, by exposing the gravelly soil beneath, thus creating a suitable seed-bed for young pine. Glen Tanar has experienced at least nine large-scale fires since 1688 [90]. A great fire at Abernethy in 1746 destroyed an estimated two and a half million trees, but the forest seems to have recovered fully from the blaze a few decades later. Unfortunately, pinewoods are rarely given the chance to recover naturally from fire (nor, for that matter, from fellings). The usual practice is to shallow plough the burned area and plant it with seedlings from a nursery. Natural regeneration is further impeded today by the very large numbers of red deer and sheep that live in native pinewoods.

⇧*Mature Caledonian pine forest in Glen Derry,*
part of the Mar Lodge estate in the
eastern Cairngorms. July
(PETER WAKELY)

WOODS AT THE LIMITS

Shetland, contrary to appearances, is not completely treeless. There are stunted, twisted trees of hazel, birch, aspen, rowan and willow in some thirty places on steep rocky bluffs and loch islands, direct descendants perhaps of the prehistoric hazelnuts and bits of natural wood that occasionally appear in peat diggings on the islands. Woodland probably never covered much of Shetland, but some Hebridean islands, now bare, once had an extensive covering of wind-pruned scrub of this type. On the island of Eigg some wonderful mixed scrub of hazel, willow, hawthorn and blackthorn has survived, pressed by the wind into bank-like layers against the basalt cliffs of Beinn Bhuidhe. Though its canopy is no more than a few feet high, this dwarf wood provides shelter for oceanic mosses and numerous woodland flowers, including a scatter of bluebells. Another Hebridean wood that may well be descended from the prehistoric woodland of the isles is **Allt Volagir** on South Uist, a bouldery defile with scattered stunted birch, hazel, alder, grey sallow, rowan and aspen, and sheltering sixty species of flowering plants and ferns. On Jura, Mull, Bute and Colonsay you can find miniature oakwoods, pruned to head height by the salty west winds, and have the pleasure of watching the wildlife of the treetops without any need for a ladder. The oaks, hazels and ashes of **Coille Mhor** on Colonsay are festooned in large lobed lichens, like crinkly lettuce leaves.

On the islands of Jura, Lismore, Mull, Eigg and Raasay are pockets of deeper, more base-rich soil that support more developed woodland of ash, wych elm and hazel. In places where sheep cannot get at them, a flora of red campion, sanicle, dog's mercury and false brome, familiar to a Cambridgeshire botanist, grows root by branch with an oceanic one of mosses and lungwort lichens and northern flowers such as globeflower and melancholy thistle. At **Coille Thocabhaig** (also known as Ord Wood or anglicised as 'Tokavaig Wood') on Skye, ash woodland on Durness limestone with elm in the ravines stands next to oak woodland on the poorer soils of the Torridonian sandstone.

These are all 'hiding place woods' which, through their inaccessible location, have survived centuries of assault from moor burning, grazing and tree cutting. Where, if anywhere in Scotland, are the equivalents of Wistman's Wood and Coed-y-Rhygen, woods of crazily contorted trees on the open hillside, which seem to dare the elements to do their worst? Candidates might include Rassal Wood, an oasis of mossed and lichenous ashes and hazels on an outcrop of Durness limestone in Wester Ross surrounded by bleak open moors; or Achanalt, also in Ross, a sinking island of stunted pines in an ocean of peat. Perhaps the best example of woodland at the limits, however, is **Carn a' Mhadaidh**, near Kyle of Tongue in Sutherland, a remarkable little wood of contorted birches rooted among massive boulders up to the size of a house. There are grassy heaths and bogs among the heather and blaeberry, bluebells on sandstone ledges and a scatter of plants such as the creeping lady's-tresses orchid and the 'ostrich feather moss' *(Ptilium crista-castrensis)* which normally grow under pines. Not far away, is another fine block-scree wood, **Coille na Cuile**, a place of dwarf birches and rowans on the western slopes of Ben Loyal. Farther uphill, are bogs with miniature birch groves composed of the rare hybrid between downy birch and the exquisite little dwarf birch, *Betula nana*. There are similar woods close to the Arctic Circle in Norway.

From the summit ridge of Ben Loyal we gaze east across an endless rolling plain of peat moss and pools, the 'flow country' of Sutherland and Caithness. We have reached the farthest limit of ancient woodland in Britain. Preserved inside those flows are the remains of oak, hazel and other trees that grew here thousands of years ago. But the climate was warmer and drier then. Today this is our largest naturally treeless landscape. During the past decade, much of it has been turned into the most sterile kind of modern forest with the aid of heavy machinery, inorganic fertilisers and financial investment. The new plantations consist of only one or two kinds of trees and have no woodland flora at all. Will they, after the passage of numberless generations, one day come to look like Coille na Cuile or Abernethy or Methven Wood? We cannot know, but it is unlikely. The original forest of the flow country seems to have perished in a single generation, the victim of a volcanic explosion on Iceland that unleashed a holocaust of acid rain and tipped the environmental scales firmly and for ever against farmers and trees. Today each car, aeroplane and industrial chimney behaves like a miniature volcano, polluting the atmosphere with long-term consequences that cannot be foreseen. We cannot create ancient woods. We cannot plan on a millennial scale. We probably cannot avoid causing damage to those woods that remain. But, unlike the hay meadows, natural marshes and lowland heaths that are nine-tenths gone, and despite the worst excesses of two world wars and a postwar afforestation policy, we still have plenty of ancient woods. We already know quite a lot about them. We are learning to cherish them. One day we may understand them.

REFERENCES

1. Published accounts of the NCC's ancient woodland inventories: Kirby K.J., Peterken, G.F., Spencer, J.W. and Walker, G.W. *Inventories of ancient semi-natural woodland.* (Nature Conservancy Council, 1989); Walker, G.J. and Kirby, K.J. *Inventories of ancient, long-established and semi-natural woodland for Scotland.* (Nature Conservancy Council, 1989); Spencer, J.W. (forthcoming). An inventory of ancient woodland for England and Wales: methodology and results. To be published in *Biological Conservation.*

2. Woodland classifications: Peterken, G.F. *Woodland Conservation and Management* (Chapman and Hall, 1981); Rodwell, J. *British Plant Communities* (Cambridge University Press, 1990).

3. Peterken, G.F. and Harding, P.T. 'Recent changes in the conservation value of woodlands in Rockingham Forest'. *Forestry.* (*47*, 1974) 109-28.

4. Following details based on Pettit, P.A.J. *The Royal Forests of Northamptonshire. A study in their economy 1558-1714* (Gateshead, 1968) and Steane, J.M. *The Northamptonshire Landscape* (Hodder and Stoughton, 1974).

5. Bellamy, B. *Geddington Chase. The history of a wood.* (Privately printed, 1986).

6. Best, J.A. *Kings Wood, Corby. Description, history, explanation of habitats and wildlife.* 3 vols. (Nene College, Northampton, 1983).

7. Peterken, G.F. and Welch, R.C. (ed) *Bedford Purlieus: its history, ecology and management.* (Natural Environment Research Council, 1975).

8. Mendel, H. and Owen, J.A. '*Limoniscus violaceus* (Müller) (Col: Elateridae), the violet click beetle in Britain'. *The Entomologist* (*109*, 1990) 43-6.

9. Details based on Perrins, C.M. 'Classic sites: Wytham Wood'. *Biologist* (*36*, 1989) 5-9.

10. Kirby, K.J. and Wright, F.J. (ed) *Woodland conservation and research in the clay vale of Oxfordshire and Buckinghamshire* (Nature Conservancy Council, 1988).

11. Details based on Thomas, R.C. *The historical ecology of Bernwood Forest.* Unpublished PhD thesis, Dept of Biology, Oxford Polytechnic.

12. Preece, P. 'Abbey Wood or College Wood: Chilterns coppice over the centuries'. *Oxfordshire Local History* (*22*, 1986) 150-60. For an historical overview, see Roden D. 'Woodland and its management in the medieval Chilterns'. *Forestry.* (*41*, 1968) 59-71.

13. Williamson, L. 'The lost tent-peggers who made millions'. *The Countryman* (*90*, 1985) 33-8.

14. Abbot, M. 'Forestry and the modern chair bodger'. *Quarterly Journal of Forestry* (*84*, 1990) 81-93.

15. Smith, C.J. *Ecology of the English chalk.* (Academic Press, 1980) p.58.

16. Hornby, R. 'Nature conservation in Chiltern woodlands - a Nature Conservancy Council view'. *Quarterly Journal of Forestry* (*31*, 1987) 116-21.

17. Mitchell, P. 'Repollarding large neglected pol-

lards: a review of current practice and results'. *Arboricultural Journal* (*13*, 1989) 125-42.

18. For a proprietor's history of Savernake, see Earl of Cardigan, *The Wardens of Savernake Forest* (London, 1949).

19. Grose, D. 'A botanical survey of Colerne Park,' in Stearn, L.F. (ed.) *Supplement to the Flora of Wiltshire* (Wiltshire Archaeological Society, 1975) 83-90.

20. Cited in the Victoria County History for Hampshire and the Isle of Wight (*2*, 1912) p. 228.

21. Hooke, D. *The Anglo-Saxon landscape: the Kingdom of the Hwicca* (Manchester, 1985).

22. Colebourne, P. *Ancient Woodland* (Hampshire County Council, 1983); Brough, P., Gibbons, B. and Pope, C. *The Nature of Hampshire and the Isle of Wight* (Barracuda Books, 1986); Tubbs, C.R. *The New Forest* (Collins, 1986).

23. Rackham, O. *The History of the Countryside* (Dent, 1986) p. 78.

24. The clearance of the Weald is discussed at length in Brandon, P. and Short, B. *A Regional History of England. The South East from AD 1000* (Longman, 1990) pp. 49-56.

25. Peterken, G.F. and Hubbard, J.C.E. 'The shingle vegetation of southern England: the holly wood on Holmstone Beach, Dungeness'. *Journal of Ecology* (*60*, 1972) 547-72.

26. Warren, M.S. 'The status of the heath fritillary butterfly *Mellicta athalia* Rott. in relation to changing woodland management in the Blean Woods, Kent'. *Quarterly Journal of Forestry* (*79*, 1985) 175-82.

27. Edlin, H.L. *Woodland Crafts in Britain* (Batsford, 1949) pp. 47-51.

28. Tittensor, R.M. 'A history of the Mens: a Sussex woodland common'. *Sussex Archaeological Collections* (*116*, 1978) 347-74.

29. Watt, A.S. 'Yew communities of the South Downs'. *Journal of Ecology* (*14*, 1926) 282-316.

30. Tittensor, R.M. *A sideways look at nature conservation in Britain.* University College London, Discussion Papers in Conservation (*29*, 1981); see also Williamson, R. *The Great Yew Forest. The natural history of Kingley Vale* (Macmillan, 1978).

31. Pigott, C.D. 'The status, ecology and conservation of *Tilia platyphyllos* in Britain'. In Synge, H. (ed) *The Biological Aspects of Rare Plant Conservation* (Wiley, 1981).

32. Staples, M.J.C. 'A history of box in the British Isles'. *Boxwood Bulletin* (*10*, 1970) 18-23, 34-7, 55-60.

33. London Ecology Unit. *Ecology Handbooks* (*1-13*, 1985-89).

34. Corke, D. (ed) 'Epping Forest: the natural aspect?' *Essex Naturalist* (*2*, 1978), 16-75; Baker, C.A., Moxey, P. and Oxford, P.M. 'Woodland continuity and change in Epping Forest'. *Field Studies* (4, 1978) 645-69.

35. Salisbury, E.J. 'The oak-hornbeam woods of Hertfordshire'. Parts I and II. *Journal of Ecology* (*4*, 1916) 83-117; Salisbury, E.J. 'The oak-hornbeam woods of Hertfordshire'. Parts III and IV. *Journal of Ecology* (*6*, 1918)14-52.

36. *Wildlife Matters.* Hertfordshire and Middlesex Wildlife Trust(*81*, 1990) p. 4.

37. Sage, B.L. (ed) *Northaw Great Wood. Its history and natural history* (Hertfordshire County Council, 1966).

38. Rackham, O. (forthcoming) *Ancient woodland of England: the woods of the Helford River, Cornwall.* I have read a draft dated 1987.

39. Christy, R.M. and Worth, R.H. 'The ancient dwarfed oak woods of Dartmoor'. *Transactions of the Devon Association for Science, Literature and Art* (*54*, 1923) 291-342.

40. Proctor, M.C.F., Spooner, G.M. and Spooner, M.F. 'Changes in Wistman's Wood, Dartmoor: photographic and other evidence'. *Reports and Transactions of the Devonshire Association for the Advancement of Science* (*112*, 1980) 43-79.

41. Hallam, O. 'Vegetation and land-use on Exmoor'. *Somerset Archaeological and Natural History* (*122*, 1978) 37-51; Teverson, R. *An historical approach to the management of ancient woodlands for conservation: the case of Horner Wood.* University College London, Discussion Papers in Conservation, 1981.

42. Penistan, M.J. 'Woodland nature reserves' in Dennis, E. *Everyman's Nature Reserve. Ideas for*

REFERENCES

action. (David & Charles, 1972) 60-70.

43. Hendry, G., Bannister, N. and Toms, J. 'The earthworks of an ancient woodland'. *Bristol and Avon Archaeology 93*, 1984) 47-53.

44. Tasker, A. (ed) *The Nature of Warwickshire* (Barracuda Books, 1990).

45. Peterken, G.F. *Woodland Conservation and Management* (Chapman and Hall, 1981) pp. 218-24.

46. For Nottinghamshire woods in general, see Bee, L., Gilbert, E. and Myhill, N. 'Woodland - ancient and modern' in Marquiss R. (ed) *The Nature of Nottinghamshire* (Barracuda Books, 1987) and Watkins, C. 'An historical introduction to the woodlands of Nottinghamshire' in Watkins, C. and Wheeler, P.T. (ed) *The Study and Use of British Woodlands* (University of Nottingham, 1981)1-24.

47. Holt, J.C. *Robin Hood* (Thames and Hudson, 1983).

48. For the flora of old woods in Lincolnshire see Peterken, G.F. 'A method for assessing woodland flora for conservation using indicator species'. *Biological Conservation, 6*, 239-45; Peterken, G.F. and Game, M. 'Historical factors affecting the distribution of *Mercurialis perennis* in central Lincolnshire'. *Journal of Ecology (69*, 1981) 781-96; 'Historical factors affecting the number and distribution of vascular plant species in the woodlands of central Lincolnshire'. *Journal of Ecology (72*,1984) 155-82.

49. Boatman, D.J. 'Burton Bushes: an ecological view'. *Hull Natural History Society Bulletin (3*, 1971), 8-14.

50. Rackham, O. *Trees and Woodland in the British Landscape* (Revised edn., Dent, 1990) pp. 138-40.

51. Rackham; pp. 136-138.

52. Rackham; pp. 116-118.

53. Druce, G.C. *Flora of Buckinghamshire*. Arbroath.

54. Rackham, O. 'The ancient woods of Norfolk'. *Transactions of Norfolk and Norwich Naturalists Society (27*, 1986) 161-77.

55. Rackham, O. *The last Forest: the story of Hatfield Forest* (Dent, London, 1989).

56. Parrott, S. and Doe, J. *Gloucestershire Commons. Their history, wildlife and future.* (Gloucestershire Trust for Nature Conservation, 1989).

57. Holland, S.C. (ed) *Supplement to the Flora of Gloucestershire* (Bristol, 1986) 134-36.

58. Peterken, G.F. and Jones, E.W. 'Forty years of change in Lady Park Wood: the old growth stands'. *Journal of Ecology (75*, 1987) 477-512; Peterken, G.F. and Jones, E.W. 'Forty years of change in Lady Park Wood: the young growth stands'. *Journal of Ecology (77*, 1989) 401-29.

59. Kingsbury, J.G. 'Nunnery and Perry Woods, Worcester: Historical ecology and land-use changes'. *Transactions of the Worcestershire Archaeological Society (9*, 1984), 67-85.

60. Hickin, N. *The Natural History of an English Forest* (Arrow Books, 1971).

61. Jorden, G. Records in Amphlett, J. and Rea, C. *The Botany of Worcestershire* (Birmingham, 1909).

62. Babb, L.M.C. 'Bark peeling and tanning in the Forest of Wyre'. *Folklife (18*, 1980) 49-53.

63. Robinson, S. 'The forests and woodlands of Herefordshire'. *Transactions of the Woolhope Naturalists Field Club*(1925) 193-220.

64. For details on the use of holly as a fodder crop see Radley, J. 'Holly as a winter feed'. *The Agricultural History Review (9*, 1961) 89-92.

65. Pigott, C.D. 'The status of *Tilia cordata* and *T. platyphyllos* on the Derbyshire limestone'. *Journal of Ecology (57*, 1969) 491-504.

66. Morries, G. *Lancashire's Woodland Heritage* (Lancashire County Council, 1986).

67. Redmonds, G. 'Spring Woods 1500-1800'. *Old West Riding (3*, 1983) 4-9.

68. Jones, M. *Sheffield's Ancient Woods* (Sheffield Polytechnic, 1986).

69. Gilbert, O.L. 'The management of urban woodland in Sheffield'. *Ecos (3*, 1982) 31-4.

70. Wightman, W.R. 'The pattern of vegetation in the Vale of Pickering area c. 1300 AD'. *Transactions of the Institute of British Geography (45*, 1968).

71. Satchell, J.E. 'The history of woodlands in Cumbria'. In *Cumbrian Woodlands - past, present and future* (HMSO, 1989) 2-11.

72. Jones, G.P. 'A short history of the manor and parish of Witherslack to 1850'. *Cumberland and Westmorland Antiquarian and Archaeological Society* tract series (*18*, 1971).

73. Pigott, C.D. and Huntley, J.P. 'Factors controlling the distribution of *Tilia cordata* Mill. at the northern limits of its geographical range. III. Nature and causes of seed sterility'. *New Phytologist* (*87*, 1981) 817-39.

74. Birks, H.J.B. 'Mid-Flandrian forest history of Roudsea Wood National Nature Reserve, Cumbria'. *New Phytologist* (*90*, 1982)339-54.

75. Leach, W. 'Two relict upland oakwoods in Cumberland'.*Journal of Ecology* (*13*, 1925) 289-300.

76. Drury, L. 'Durham Palatinale Forest Law and administration, especially in Weardale up to 1440'. *Archaeologia Aeliana* (*5*, 1978) 87-105.

77. Monck, B. *Castle Eden Dene. An illustrated guide* (Peterlee Development Corporation, 1980) pp. 34-5.

78. Linnard, W. *Welsh woods and forests: history and utilisation* (Cardiff, 1982).

79. The following details are based on notes in the NCC's unpublished ancient woodland inventories for Welsh counties.

80. Linnard, W. op. cit. p.13.

81. Edwards, M.E. 'Disturbance histories of four Snowdonian woodlands and their relation to Atlantic bryophyte distributions'. *Biological Conservation* (*37*, 1986) 301-20.

82. Anderson, M.L. *A history of Scottish forestry*. 2 vols. (Nelson, London, 1967).

83. Hammersley, G. 'The charcoal industry and its fuel'. *Economic History Review* (26, 1973) 593-613;

Lindsay, J.M. 'Charcoal iron smelting and its fuel supply: the example of the Lorn furnace, Argyllshire, 1753-1876'. *Journal of Historical Geography* (*1*, 1975) 283-98.

84. Stevenson, J.F. 'How ancient is the woodland of Mugdock?' *Scottish Forestry* (*44*, 1990) 161-72.

85. Rackham, O. *Trees and Woodlands in the British Landscape* (Dent, 1990) p. 142. See also Fairbairn, W.A. 'Dalkeith Old Wood'. *Scottish Forestry* (*26*, 1972) 5-28.

86. Tittensor, R.M. 'History of the Loch Lomond oakwoods'. *Scottish Forestry* (*24*, 1970) 100-18. For an account of oak coppicing in Menteith, Lorn and elsewhere, see Lindsay, J.M. 'The history of oak coppice in Scotland'. *Scottish Forestry* (*29*, 1975) 87-93; and for Knapdale, Rymer, L. 'The exploitation of woodlands in the parish of North Knapdale, Argyllshire'. *Scottish Forestry* (*31*, 1977) 244-50.

87. Steven, H.M. and Carlisle, A.*The Native Pinewoods of Scotland* (Oliver and Boyd, Edinburgh, 1959).

88. Bain, C. *Native Pinewoods in Scotland: A Review* 1957-1987 (RSPB, 1987).

89. O'Sullivan, P.E. 'Land-use changes in the Forest of Abernethy, Inverness-shire (1750-1900 AD)' *Scottish Geographical Magazine* (*89*, 1973) 95-106.

90. Marren, P.R. 'Human history in Glen Tanar'. In Cameron, E. (ed). *Glen Tanar. Its human and natural history*. (Nature Conservancy Council, 1986) 1-13.

INDEX

Numbers in **bold** indicate illustrations